MW00817997

General Nathanael Greene

and the American Revolution in the South

General Nathanael Greene

and the American Revolution in the South

—∞∞∞—

Edited by Gregory D. Massey and Jim Piecuch

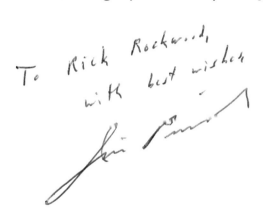

*To Rick Rockwood,
with best wishes*

Jim Piecuch

The University of South Carolina Press

© 2012 University of South Carolina

Published by the University of South Carolina Press
Columbia, South Carolina 29208

www.sc.edu/uscpress

Manufactured in the United States of America

21 20 19 18 17 16 15 14 13 12   10 9 8 7 6 5 4 3 2 1

LIBRARY OF CONGRESS CATALOGING-IN-PUBLICATION DATA

General Nathanael Greene and the American Revolution in the South /
    edited by Gregory D. Massey and Jim Piecuch.
        pages cm
    Includes bibliographical references and index.
    ISBN 978-1-61117-069-6 (cloth : alk. paper)
        1. Greene, Nathanael, 1742–1786. 2. Southern States—History—Revolution,
    1775–1783. 3. South Carolina—History—Revolution, 1775–1783. 4. United
    States—History—Revolution, 1775–1783—Biography. 5. Generals—United
    States—Biography. 6. United States. Continental Army—Biography. I. Massey,
    Gregory D. II. Piecuch, Jim.
    E207.G9G46 2012
    973.33092 — DC23
    [B]   2011050008

This book was printed on a recycled paper with 30 percent postconsumer waste content.

Contents

Illustrations

Acknowledgments

Although the essays collected here were commissioned specifically for this book, the original idea for this volume was conceived at a 2006 symposium on Nathanael Greene held at Camden, South Carolina. The editors wish to thank the organizers of the symposium, Joanna Craig, executive director of Historic Camden Revolutionary War Site; event coordinator Charles B. Baxley, publisher of *Southern Campaigns of the American Revolution*; his assistant, David P. Reuwer; and Dr. John Maass, program coordinator.

Also deserving thanks are Alexander Moore of the University of South Carolina Press for his guidance and patience as we worked through the long process of editing the essays in this book and Beth Bilderback of the South Caroliniana Library at the University of South Carolina in Columbia for working with us to provide maps and illustrations. Finally we wish to thank the contributors, who labored diligently to prepare their essays for this volume.

Introduction

GREGORY D. MASSEY AND JIM PIECUCH

*F*or nearly two centuries, Major General Nathanael Greene languished in near obscurity. Although he contributed more to American military success in the war for independence than any other leader save George Washington, few historians in the decades following publication of William Johnson's *Sketches of the Life and Correspondence of Nathanael Greene* in 1822 devoted much attention to the Rhode Island officer. Two of Greene's descendants, George Washington Greene and Francis Vinton Greene, published biographies of the general in the nineteenth century, as did novelist William Gilmore Simms; yet Nathanael Greene remained overshadowed by his Revolutionary contemporaries. That is not surprising. Greene won no major battles, and his most important service came in the South, a theater of the war that was almost as neglected by historians as Greene himself.[1]

The approach of the bicentennial of the United States revived interest in the country's war of independence. Between 1960 and 1972, five new studies of Greene appeared. In general these works attracted little attention, but the biography written by Theodore Thayer remains among the best scholarly studies of Greene.[2] At the same time historians' interest in the Revolutionary War, the southern campaign, and Nathanael Greene increased because of federal government support for historical documentary editing. Historian Richard Showman and a team of editors at the Rhode Island Historical Society began collecting, editing, and publishing Greene's correspondence. Between 1976 and 2005, Showman, Dennis Conrad, and Roger Parks supervised the publication of the thirteen volumes of *The Papers of General Nathanael Greene*. As these volumes made Greene's correspondence widely accessible to scholars, both Greene and the southern campaign began to receive long overdue attention. Recent biographies of Greene by Gerald M. Carbone, Terry Golway, Spencer C. Tucker, and others have acquainted thousands of readers with Greene's life and military service.[3]

Despite the relatively large number of recent biographies, many aspects of Greene's career have not been fully explored. Yet an understanding of Greene's character and military leadership, not easily covered in a standard biography, is crucial to a more complete portrait of Nathanael Greene as a person and an officer. The editors of this book asked several historians of the American Revolution to contribute essays on various aspects of Greene's life and leadership. These essays have been assembled in this volume with the goals of increasing knowledge of Nathanael Greene and the war for independence and of sparking further research and deeper exploration of Greene's role in the southern campaign and the American Revolution.

In the first essay Dennis Conrad, a former editor of *The Papers of General Nathanael Greene*, reassesses Greene's military career and his reputation as the premier strategist of the Revolution. Conrad argues that Greene was not a strategist in the conventional sense, in which strategy is defined as the execution of a preconceived plan. Conrad explains that Greene's strategic success in the southern campaign was instead the result of his resourcefulness and ability to adjust his plans rapidly to the fluid military situation in the South. Conrad supports his arguments by examining key decisions Greene made during the course of his campaign, which contributed to the Americans' ultimate success.

Curtis Morgan assesses how Greene's experiences in the North from 1775 to 1780 influenced the general's later performance as commander of the Continental army in the South. Greene filled a variety of roles in that five-year span, including field command under George Washington in many engagements. Greene's most controversial action during this time was his decision to defend Fort Washington on the Hudson River, resulting in the disastrous loss of the post in November 1776. Washington had acceded to Greene despite misgivings. In March 1778 Greene became quartermaster general of the Continental army, a post he accepted reluctantly at Washington's insistence. While effective in his new role, Greene later became embroiled in controversies with Congress and resigned. Nevertheless, Morgan demonstrates, the experience Greene gained on the battlefields of the North and with logistics and supply issues as quartermaster general made him a more effective leader in the South.

One of the problems Greene faced in the South was dealing with state officials, who were far more assertive than their northern counterparts. As David Wilson notes, "southern provincialism"—the tendency to put local concerns ahead of the common interest of the thirteen states—had posed serious difficulties for Greene's predecessors in the southern command. Generals Charles Lee, Robert Howe, Benjamin Lincoln, and Horatio Gates all had to deal with recalcitrant southern governors, legislatures, and militia officers. These civil and military officials challenged the authority of Continental commanders to varying degrees, often refusing to allow their states' militia to submit to Continental authority and even pressing their own questionable military plans upon the generals. Wilson explains how Greene managed to navigate these treacherous shoals through a combination of an open commitment to the importance of civil government and an adroit handling of politicians, among them Virginia governor Thomas Jefferson and South Carolina governor John Rutledge and militia leaders such as Thomas Sumter.

Greene also had to deal with his own Continental subordinates, and these officers could prove to be every bit as irascible as Rutledge and Sumter. Greg Brooking examines this aspect of Greene's leadership, discussing the important influence of Greene's relationship with George Washington in shaping Greene's interactions with his subordinates. Brooking then analyzes Greene's relations with several of his officers, including prickly Brigadier General Daniel Morgan, stolid Maryland colonel Otho Holland Williams, and flamboyant Lieutenant Colonel Henry Lee. Brooking also covers the tensions between Greene and Colonel John Gunby of the Maryland Line, whom Greene blamed for the American defeat at Hobkirk's Hill, South Carolina, in April 1781. Although Greene usually went to great lengths to placate his subordinates, Gunby's case serves as a notable exception to that policy.

John Buchanan focuses on another aspect of Greene's command: his dealings with South Carolina's partisan leaders. Recognizing that partisan operations were essential to American victory in the South, but also understanding the limitations of guerrilla warfare, Greene strove to coordinate the activities of the partisans with those of the main Continental army. The task proved difficult. Buchanan discusses how Greene adopted an individualized approach to each of the three major partisan leaders to achieve cooperation. Andrew Pickens proved steadily reliable; Francis Marion showed great skill and, though sensitive to criticism, was generally willing to follow Greene's directions; Thomas Sumter, egotistical and often insubordinate, frequently defied Greene's efforts to operate in tandem. Nevertheless, Buchanan demonstrates, Greene generally succeeded in establishing a sufficient degree of coordination between Continentals and partisans, leading to the ouster of the British army from the South.

Some of the issues raised by Buchanan and Wilson also figure heavily in the two essays that follow theirs. John Moseley and Robert Calhoon focus particular attention on Greene's decision to return to South Carolina in April 1781 rather than follow British general Charles, Earl Cornwallis, to Virginia. Moseley and Calhoon argue that a commitment to republican ethics guided Greene's generalship and decision making in the South. Greene's recognition of the importance of restoring functioning civil governments, as well as his respect for public opinion, support for moderate, conciliatory policies, and frequent consultation of his subordinate officers, all reflected a commitment to republican ethics. This commitment, the authors state, was ultimately crucial to Greene's success.

James Mc Intyre studies Nathanael Greene's activities in South Carolina, pointing out that, when Greene led his Continentals back into that state following the March 1781 Battle of Guilford Courthouse, he found himself operating in a political vacuum. The South Carolina state government existed in name only, and the British had not established a functioning government in the reconquered colony. Thus Greene bore the burden of maintaining some semblance of state authority while simultaneously campaigning against the British. Mc Intyre asserts that Greene took a three-pronged approach to the problem: he cooperated with the remnants of the state's civil authorities to give them legitimacy, struggled to restrain the violence between Whigs and Loyalists that threatened to plunge the state into chaos, and used the Whig militia whenever possible both to fight his opponent and to maintain domestic order where none would otherwise exist.

John Maass examines how Greene encouraged state leaders to pursue reconciliation over retribution in their policy toward Loyalists. Maass shifts the focus to North Carolina, a state where Greene's Continental forces spent a relatively brief time. Without the presence of regular American forces, the military situation there rapidly degenerated into a bloody civil war between Whig militia and Loyalists backed by a small British garrison at Wilmington. Many state leaders advocated a harsh policy of violent suppression and vengeance against North Carolina's Loyalists. Greene, however, recognized that such measures would only inspire Loyalist retribution and fuel a cycle of increasing violence that would devastate the state. He therefore struggled to reduce plundering and killing by the Whig militia in hopes of promoting eventual conciliation with the Loyalists and sparing North Carolina from unnecessary destruction. Maass notes that, in spite of opposition from many state officials, Greene did achieve some success.

Jim Piecuch deals with Greene's abilities as a military tactician. Because Greene was defeated in all four of his battles with British forces in the South, most historians believe that, despite his strategic abilities, Greene did a rather poor job of directing his troops in combat. Piecuch reviews Greene's performance at Guilford Courthouse, Hobkirk's Hill, and Ninety Six to demonstrate that Greene displayed a considerable level of tactical skill. Piecuch then shifts his focus to a detailed examination of the September 1781 Battle of Eutaw Springs in South Carolina. There Greene ably managed the opening phases of the battle, nearly routing the British army before its commanders, Lieutenant Colonels Alexander Stewart and John Harris Cruger, rallied their troops and forced Greene to withdraw. Piecuch attributes the American failure not to

Greene's lack of tactical skill but to his inability to rein in independent-minded subordinates Henry Lee and William Washington, as well as to Greene's failure to grasp the nature of the obstacles he faced after driving most of the British army from the field.

Gregory Massey examines the issue of slavery, which complicated affairs for both sides in the South. While the British made some attempts to use slaves to support their forces, southern state governments resisted every effort by the Continental Congress and Continental commanders to persuade them to arm slaves in defense of their independence. Massey assesses Greene's role in this dispute and the postwar change in the general's attitude toward slavery. Although he came from a slaveholding family, Greene saw the need to arm slaves to strengthen the Continental army and repeatedly urged officials in South Carolina and Georgia to take such a step. Congress had offered to compensate slave owners for those slaves who enlisted, as they would be freed at the conclusion of their term of service. Greene's own efforts made little headway. Massey observes that, after the failed attempt to enlist slaves, Greene's attitude toward slavery underwent a profound change. In financial distress Greene decided to recoup his fortunes by resettling his family in the South and becoming a rice planter. Having been granted plantations in Georgia and South Carolina by the two grateful state governments, Greene transformed himself from a general advocating that slaves be armed to a slave owner dependent on slave labor for his economic success.

Together the essays in this volume shed new light on the multiple roles Greene filled as Continental commander in the South. As a military officer, he had to be simultaneously a strategist, tactician, logistician, and manager of his Continental and militia subordinates. Greene also had to maintain and demonstrate his commitment to his republican ideals and to uphold those principles in his political role, promoting the restoration of civil authority while dealing with state officials who often challenged his policies. At the same time he had to grapple with the divisive issue of slavery. While providing a detailed and nuanced examination of several facets of Greene's life, character, and leadership, these essays by no means exhaust the study of Nathanael Greene, and the editors hope that this collection will inspire further exploration of this complex individual who contributed so much to the winning of American independence.

NOTES

1. William Johnson, *Sketches of the Life and Correspondence of Nathanael Greene, Major General of the Armies of the United States, in the War of the Revolution*, 2 vols. (Charleston, S.C.: A. E. Miller, 1822); William Gilmore Simms, *The Life of Nathanael Greene, Major-General in the Army of the Revolution* (New York: Cooledge, 1849); George Washington Greene, *The Life of Nathanael Greene, Major-General in the Armies of the Revolution*, vol. 1

(New York: Putnam, 1867); vols. 2 and 3 (New York: Hurd & Houghton, 1871); Francis Vinton Greene, *General Greene* (New York: Appleton, 1893).

2. The first twentieth-century works on Greene were Theodore Thayer, *Nathanael Greene: Strategist of the American Revolution* (New York: Twayne, 1960); M. F. Treacy, *Prelude to Yorktown: The Southern Campaign of Nathanael Greene, 1780–1781* (Chapel Hill: University of North Carolina Press, 1963); Clifford L. Alderman, *Retreat to Victory: The Life of Nathanael Greene* (Philadelphia: Chilton, 1967); Ralph Edgar Bailey, *Guns over the Carolinas: The Story of Nathanael Greene* (New York: Morrow, 1967); Elswyth Thane, *The Fighting Quaker: Nathanael Greene* (New York: Hawthorn, 1972).

3. *The Papers of General Nathanael Greene*, edited by Richard K. Showman, Dennis R. Conrad, and Roger N. Parks, 13 vols. (Chapel Hill: University of North Carolina Press, 1976–2005). The many recent biographies of Greene include Lee Patrick Anderson, *Forgotten Patriot: The Life and Times of Major-General Nathanael Greene* (N.p.: Universal Publishers, 2002); Gerald M. Carbone, *Nathanael Greene: A Biography of the American Revolution* (New York: Palgrave Macmillan, 2008); Terry Golway, *Washington's General: Nathanael Greene and the Triumph of the American Revolution* (New York: Holt, 2005); Steven E. Siry, *Greene: Revolutionary General* (Washington, D.C.: Potomac Books, 2007); Spencer C. Tucker, *Rise and Fight Again: The Life of Nathanael Greene* (Wilmington, Del.: Intercollegiate Studies Institute, 2009).

General Nathanael Greene

An Appraisal

DENNIS M. CONRAD

*T*here are two sobriquets applied to Nathanael Greene that have resonated with the general public. The first is "Fighting Quaker," and the second is "Strategist of the American Revolution." Both designations are colorful, memorable, and in a sense exaggerations.

Nathanael Greene was certainly raised as a member of the Society of Friends. It was not, however, a happy experience for him. In a letter to a young friend in 1772, Greene wrote: "I lament the want of a liberal Education. I feel the mist [of] Ignorance to surround me, for my own part I was Educated a Quaker, and amongst the most Supersticious sort, and that of its self is a sufficient Obstacle to cramp the best of Geniuses, much more mine. This constrained manner of Educating their Youth, has prov'd a fine Nursery of Ignorance and Supersticon, instead of piety; and has laid a foundation for Form instead of Worship."[1] After the death of his father, who was a devout member of the Society of Friends and one of the "Supersticious" sorts Greene wrote of, Nathanael Greene Jr. only infrequently attended the Friends meeting.[2] By then, thanks to the influence of his friend and fellow resident of East Greenwich, Rhode Island, James Mitchell Varnum, Greene had been exposed to the ideas of some of the more liberal theologians in the area, most notably John Murray, the founder of Universalism.[3]

Although Greene did not formally sever his connection with the East Greenwich Society of Friends until April 1777, it was not his military activities that led to the break, as some writers have contended. Instead Greene rejected his Quaker upbringing and became, like many of his contemporaries in Revolutionary America, a deist.[4] The only mention of Quakerism that has been found in Greene's later writings is in a letter written after the Battle of Guilford Courthouse in March 1781, when he wrote the members of the New Garden, North

Carolina, Monthly Meeting, addressing British attempts at "exciting" their "apprehensions respecting religious liberty" and soliciting their help in tending for the wounded of that battle. In this letter Greene wrote: "I know of no order of men more remarkable for the exercise of humanity and benevolence. . . . I was born and educated in the professions and principles of your Society; and I am perfectly acquainted with your religious sentiments and general good conduct as citizens. . . . I respect you as a people, and shall always be ready to protect you from every violence and oppression which the confusion of the times afford but too many instances of."[5] As can be seen from this letter, authors make a mistake when they try to define Greene's military career by his having been brought up in the Society of Friends or by his decision to become a military leader in contravention to the pacifism that the sect preached.[6]

It is also something of a misnomer to call Greene the "Strategist of the Revolution." To today's nonspecialists, such a designation conveys the idea that Greene at some point early in his command in the South conceived of a plan to fight the war in that region and then put it into execution. When today's laypeople think of strategy, they think of grand plans executed by great armies, such as the Germans' Schlieffen plan in World War I, their Blitzkrieg in World War II, the American "island hopping" in the Pacific in World War II, the American "shock and awe" campaigns in the two Iraq wars, or maybe even the so-called southern strategy practiced by the British in the American South during the Revolution.[7] While Greene did have some "principles" that he adhered to throughout his campaigns in the South, his real genius as a general was his ability to adapt to changing situations and to extract the greatest strategic advantage from a fluid situation. By examining three of the pivotal decisions that have come to define his campaigns in the South, we can see that he did not follow a prearranged plan but was in fact forced to alter his plans dramatically, adapt them to new and changing conditions, and devise and even improvise what proved to be brilliant responses. As Thomas Jefferson wrote of him in 1822, Greene was "second to no one in enterprise, in resource, in sound judgment, promptitude of decision, and every other military talent," but he was not a strategist as we have come to define one in the twenty-first century.[8]

The sobriquet "Strategist of the Revolution" was used as the title of the best modern biography of Nathanael Greene,[9] whose author, Theodore Thayer, was determined to give General Greene his due as a military genius, which is harder than one would think. While Greene is the best general who fought in the American Revolution, George Washington, who served as Greene's mentor, is considered to be its best military leader—and Greene has the problem of never having won a battle. Although Congress recognized him as the victor at the Battle of Eutaw Springs, fought in September 1781 in South Carolina, most historians consider that battle to have been a draw. How does one acknowledge greatness for a general who never achieved the usual benchmark for military greatness—winning battles? Thayer overcame this dilemma by calling Greene the "Strategist of the Revolution."

In a moment of self-pity, Greene wrote to his friend and fellow general Henry Knox, Washington's artillery commander, just before the British surrender at Yorktown, Virginia, in 1781: "We have been beating the bush and the General [Washington] has come to catch the bird. . . . The General is a most fortunate Man, and may success and laurels attend him. We have fought frequently and bled freely, and little glory comes to our share. Our force has been so small that nothing capital could be effected, and our operations have been conducted under every disadvantage that could embarrass either a General or an Army. We have done all we could, and if the public and our friends are not satisfied we cannot help it."[10] On another occasion Greene characterized his campaigns by saying: "We fight get beat rise and fight again."[11]

While Greene never won a battle, it has been almost universally acknowledged that Greene's defeats always cost his British antagonists more than it cost Greene's army, so with every defeat the American situation improved, and the British lost ground.[12] In Greene's colorful words: "Our army has been frequently beaten and like a Stock Fish grows the better for it. Lord Cornwallis who is the modern Hannibal, has rambled through great part of the Southern States, and his Tour has sacrificed a great number of Men without reaping any solid Advantages from it, except that of distressing the poor Inhabitants."[13]

It is also acknowledged that, when Greene accepted battle, which he did willingly and often enough, he did so in such a way as to allow him to withdraw the Southern Army intact afterward. This is an example of one of the principles by which Greene operated during his command in the South. Greene believed that it was important to keep the regular army intact and not to jeopardize it for the sake of tactical advantage. This principle is one explanation of why Greene never won a battle. He was unwilling to gamble his army's existence in an attempt to defeat the enemy in combat. Rather than force the issue, Greene would break off and withdraw. At the battles of Guilford Courthouse, Hobkirk's Hill, and Eutaw Springs, Greene may well have won had he ordered one more attack and chanced victory or total defeat. He did not. The army survived to "fight again," and British control over the lower South became yet more tenuous.

One reason that Greene's army could break off a battle and successfully retreat is because the Southern Army through much of Greene's tenure of command enjoyed superiority in mounted troops. In stark contrast to his predecessor, Major General Horatio Gates, Greene understood that the open fields of the southern theater put a premium on cavalry. As he explained to Washington: "To the northward, cavalry is nothing . . . but to the Southward a disorder, by a superior cavalry may be improved into a deficit, and a defeat into a rout. The cavalry [are] . . . the security of an army and the safety of a country."[14] To Governor Thomas Jefferson of Virginia, Greene wrote: "Nothing but light Horse can enable us, with the little Army we have, to appear in the field; and nothing but a superiority in Cavalry can prevent the Enemy from cutting to pieces every detachment coming to join the Army or employed in collecting supplies. From the open State of this Country their services are particularly necessary, and unless we can keep up the Corps of Cavalry and constantly support superiority it will be out of our power to act or to prevent the Enemy from overrunning the Country, and commanding all its resources."[15] Elsewhere Greene posited that the Southern Army—at least during the first days of his command—should be a "flying Army to consist of about eight hundred horse and one thousand Infantry."[16] As a result Greene put a great deal of emphasis on having and equipping his mounted troops.

One of the first actions Greene took as southern commander was to obtain the transfer to the Southern Army of Henry "Light-Horse Harry" Lee's Legion.[17] This elite unit became a bedrock of Greene's army and its most effective operational tool. When acting as either the vanguard or the rear guard of the army, Lee's Legion gave Greene's army a superior mobility that he utilized well. Greene also understood how important a superior mounted force was to getting effective service from the militia or partisans. "Had we a superiority in horse the Militia would be useful," he wrote, "but for want of which the Militia dare not go within Miles of the Enemy."[18]

Another principle that Greene emphasized during his command, at least until he moved his army in late 1781 to the South Carolina lowcountry near Charleston, was mobility. The resources of the country were so "straightened," wrote Greene, that it was impossible to support a large army or numbers of infantry. A small, mobile army could be both supplied and effective.[19] Therefore a mobile army was a requirement both to advance and to retreat. As Greene rather sardonically put it. "I had a Letter some time since from Mr John Trumbull wherein he Asserts that with all my Talents for Warr, I am deficient in the great Art of making a timely retreat. I hope I have convinced the World to the contrary, for there are few Generals that has run oftner, or more lustily than I have done, But I have taken care not to run too farr; and commonly have run as fast forward as backward, to convince our Enemy that we were like a Crab, that could run either way."[20] Mobility was another general principle that Greene valued and emphasized in his generalship.

Finally, as a military commander, Greene demonstrated a willingness to work well with militia and politicians. While Greene may have privately felt disdain for some militia officers and political leaders, he was careful to treat both publicly with respect.[21] As a result Greene had the ability to make good use of partisan militia and, at least until the end of his time in the South, worked well with politicians. Moreover Greene understood the importance of the political dimension of the struggle for American independence and did what he could to assist states in reestablishing or securing their political foundations. For example Greene was responsible for sending Nathan Brownson to be governor of Georgia and for assigning Joseph Clay the task of reestablishing the government there.[22] Greene also moved his army into a precarious position close to Charleston so as to cover the meeting of the reconstituted South Carolina legislature, which convened at Jacksonborough in January 1782. Finally Greene gave all the support he could to Thomas Burke, the activist governor of North Carolina, who attempted, before his capture by Loyalist raiders, to reinvigorate the war effort in that state. Greene the general understood that the southern states had to have a political existence in case of a negotiated peace, and he worked to establish and create functioning state governments. While never asserting a superior position vis-à-vis the civilian authorities in the South, Greene's role in the reestablishment of government in the Deep South was such that he, rather than South Carolina governor John Rutledge, could have easily been called the "dictator" of the South.[23]

Having established some of Greene's general principles as southern commander, let us examine some of the key military decisions he made during his campaigns, exploring how and why he made the decisions that he did and what they say about his generalship. Greene made several key decisions shortly after he took command of the Southern Army at Charlotte on December 3, 1780. The first involved his reorganization of the supply situation in the South. As a former quartermaster general, Greene recognized the importance of the supply departments to the functioning of an army. In contrast with Horatio Gates, who abdicated any responsibility for matters of supply when he was southern commander, Greene took time to establish the supply departments as best he could given the South's lack of manufacturing capability and its loss of its store of military supplies in the destruction of two American armies in less than a year.[24]

One important decision he made was choosing the location of his magazines. Perhaps Greene's most notable innovation while quartermaster general was to establish grain depots to supply forage to George Washington's forces wherever they might be. Washington, like Greene in the South, was fighting a reactive war governing his movements by those of the British and often shifting his forces to counter an enemy threat—a war of movement. Greene's innovation of establishing several small magazines along a "line of communications" running from the Hudson River to Head of Elk, Maryland, afforded the Continental army maximum flexibility. By limiting the size of these depots so they would not become targets for British operations and by placing them high upstream on rivers to protect them from waterborne British raiders, Greene maximized the depots' benefit and minimized the risk. With these depots as well as his energetic acquisition of teams, wagons, and boats, he transformed Washington's army into a mobile fighting force.[25]

Greene could not entirely replicate this system in the South because of the lack of large towns, the dispersal of food supplies, the shortage of transport, and the rivers that mostly ran west to east, hindering rather than abetting the collection and transportation of supplies. After a careful study of the North Carolina topography, Greene did establish two main magazines at Salisbury and Oliphant's Mill on the Catawba River and "several small ones upon the North side of the Pedee as high up towards the narrows as possible that the position of this army may cover them."[26] Although it was months before these magazines were established and—because of foot-dragging by local officials and military operations within North Carolina—they never operated as planned, Greene's study in anticipation of their establishment gave him a knowledge of the supply possibilities in North Carolina and of the topography and river system of that state and upper South Carolina.[27] This knowledge served Greene well during the so-called race to the Dan between his army and the British army under General Charles, Lord Cornwallis. As the armies basically marched from grain mill to grain mill, the river system influenced their movements.[28]

Greene's ability to master such information is legendary. Joseph Graham, a North Carolina militia officer, recalled William Lee Davidson, commander of the Salisbury, North Carolina, militia district, saying that, "though General Greene had never seen the Catawba before, he appeared to know more about it than those who were raised on it."[29] Greene's subordinate and adviser Henry Lee later wrote of Greene: "No man was more familiarized to dispassionate and minute research than was General Greene. He was patient in hearing everything offered, never interrupted or slighting what was said; and having possessed himself of the subject fully, he would enter into a critical comparison of the opposite arguments, convincing his hearers, as he progressed, with the propriety of the decision he was about to pronounce."[30] Greene's ability to retain and use information concerning topography and supply issues was a hallmark of his generalship. While many officers in the era of the Revolution did not trouble themselves with such information, particularly concerning supply matters, Greene's willingness and ability to do so explains in part the success he enjoyed.

Another matter Greene addressed in the first days of his command was the role of the partisan militia in his operations. As the American regular army had been pushed out of South Carolina and Georgia, resistance to British rule in those states had fallen to small, semiautonomous groups of partisans led in many cases by charismatic leaders such as Francis Marion, Thomas Sumter, Andrew Pickens, and Elijah Clarke. The North Carolina Board of War—the arm of the state government charged with conduct of the war—pushed Greene to fight a partisan war using militia.[31] Greene, however, was not willing to sacrifice his regulars or the development of a regular Continental army to support the operations of militia or partisans. As he wrote Thomas Sumter on January 8, 1781:

> The salvation of this Country don't depend upon little strokes; nor should this great business of establishing a permanent army be neglected to pursue them. Partizan strokes in war are like the garnish of a table, they give splendor to the Army and reputation to the Officers, but they afford no substantial national security. They are matters which should not be neglected, & yet they should not be pursued to the prejudice of more important concerns. You may strike a hundred strokes, and reap little benefit from them, unless you have a good Army to take advantage of your success. The enemy will never relinquish their plan, nor the people be firm in our favor until they behold a better barrier in the field than a Volunteer Militia who are one day out and the next at home.
>
> There is no mortal more fond of enterprise than myself, but this is not the basis on which the fate of this country depends. It is not a war of posts but a contest for States dependent upon opinion. If we can introduce into the field a greater army than the Enemy, all their posts will fall of themselves; and without this they will reestablish them though we should take them twenty times. Nevertheless I would always hazard an attack when the misfortune cannot be so great to us as it may be to the enemy.[32]

Greene's statement demonstrates two important elements of his strategy—at least in the first days of his command in the South. The first was the primacy of the regular Continental army. Throughout his time as commander, Greene hoped to create a strong regular army. His many letters to the executives and legislatures in the states of the Southern Department attest to that fact.[33] There is even evidence that Greene was not above subterfuge to achieve what he considered such a vital outcome. His focusing on the bad performance of the North Carolina militia at the Battle of Guilford Courthouse in after-action reports—while failing to mention that the Second Maryland Continental regiment broke and ran at an equally critical moment of the battle—was probably an attempt on Greene's part to convince North Carolina state authorities that their reliance on militia instead of raising regulars was a flawed policy.[34] In fact the North Carolina legislature did thereafter mandate that the militiamen who ran during the battle were liable to being drafted and serving one year in the Continental service.[35] Equally suggestive are Greene's attempts later in the war to convince the legislatures of South Carolina and Georgia to raise their quota of

Continental troops by drafting African American slaves who would be rewarded
with their freedom at war's end in return for good and faithful service—a plan
that prompted some of its opponents to characterize Greene as a closet aboli-
tionist.[36]

Yet Greene made good use of partisans and militia in battle, sometimes as
adjuncts to the regular army and in other operations as forces operating independently. Because of the tendency of partisan and militia forces to plunder and
despoil, however, Greene was reluctant to allow them to fight without Continental involvement. Finally he used them as a home guard to suppress Loyalist activity and maintain order. Historian Don Higginbotham believes that
Greene's "finesse in dealing with partisans and politicians" was key to his success in the South.[37]

Another important element of strategy demonstrated in Greene's statement
to Sumter was Greene's desire to achieve victory by battle and not by a "war of
posts." By "war of posts" he meant a systematic attack on and capture of small
outposts that protected British supply and communication lines. It is a tribute
to Greene's willingness and ability to adapt that just a short time after writing
this letter he did initiate a successful "war of posts" in South Carolina and Georgia by waging a coordinated partisan-regular campaign against British posts. In
the end, largely through the success of that campaign, he forced the British to
retreat by successive stages. By the end of 1781, a year after Greene had assumed
command in the South, the British hold on the two states consisted of little but
the immediate environs of Charleston and Savannah.

The final and most-famous strategic determination Greene made in his first
days of command—the one that Thayer and others believe has come to define
Greene's legacy—was his decision to split his army and send a small but sizable
force of some of the best troops in the army under the command of Brigadier
General Daniel Morgan to western South Carolina while Greene and the remainder of the army moved to a "camp of repose" in the Cheraws area of South
Carolina on the upper reaches of the Pee Dee River.

To an unidentified correspondent—often said to be George Washington—
in a letter written about this time, Greene discussed why he had split his army:
"It makes the most of my inferior force, for it compels my adversary to divide
his, and holds him in doubt as to his own line of conduct. He cannot leave Morgan behind him to come at me, or his posts of Ninety-Six and Augusta would
be exposed. And he cannot chase Morgan far, or prosecute his views upon Virginia, while I am here with the whole country open before me. I am as near to
Charleston, as he is, and as near to Hillsborough [the seat of government of
North Carolina] as I was at Charlotte; so I am in no danger of being cut off
from my reinforcements; while an uncertainty as to my future designs has made

it necessary to leave a large detachment of the enemy's late reinforcements in Charleston."[38]

Historians have made much of this explanation in arguing that, although Greene violated a prime military dictum by dividing his force in the face of a numerically superior enemy, he was able to seize the initiative and effectively put the British on the defensive. John Morgan Dederer, who sees in these tactics and strategy a precursor to the guerrilla strategy of Mao Zedong and Vo Nguyen Giap, argues that Greene, "fighting a non-linear war, effectively encircled Cornwallis. . . . An unknowing British bull stood encircled by snapping American terriers; Greene had turned the tables on Cornwallis without the British General's knowledge."[39]

That would have been the case if Greene had really believed that he or Morgan could assume the offensive. That, however, was not the case. Morgan did not have any artillery, and it seems unreasonable to believe that he could have threatened either fortified Ninety Six or Augusta. Six months later Greene's main force was unable to capture Ninety Six even with artillery and a twenty-nine-day siege. Greene indicated as much to Morgan in a letter of January 8, 1781, when Morgan solicited permission to move his force into Georgia. Greene replied, "Should you go into Georgia and the enemy push this way your whole force will be useless. The Enemy having no object there but what is secure in their fortifications, will take no notice of your movement, but . . . oblige you to return by making a forward movement themselves, and you will be so far in the rear that you can do them no injury."[40] It is also unreasonable to expect that Greene could seriously believe he might threaten Charleston with only part of his force.

It is most telling that, when Greene got the scenario laid out in the supposed statement of strategy, he did not react as he indicated he would. After the Battle of Cowpens a weakened Cornwallis went in pursuit of Morgan. The road to Charleston lay open for Greene and his army. He did not, however, invade the South Carolina lowcountry but instead immediately set his army in motion to join Morgan in central North Carolina.

Then why did Greene split his army, and what does it say about his generalship? The answer is to be found in his discussion of that decision in a letter he wrote to Samuel Huntington, president of the Continental Congress, on December 28, 1780:

> Soon after my arrival I was fully convinced that the Army could not be subsisted for any length of time at Charlotte; the whole country being in a great degree laid waste. No position afforded me the least prospect of support in the impoverished condition of the Country except this [the Cheraws].

. . . Our prospects are mended but I am afraid we shall not be able to form any considerable Magazines until a more perfect arrangement can be made of the Commissary's department of N. Carolina. The probability of the Enemy's taking post here and at Cross-creek [modern-day Fayetteville, North Carolina] was another reason which determined my choice of this position as the possession of those two places would have given them command of all the provisions of the lower Country, which is much less exhausted by the enemy and Militia than the upper country.

Previous to my marching from Charlotte I made a detachment from the Army to operate on the West side of the Catawba under the command of General Morgan consisting of between 3 and 400 choosen [*sic*] Infantry and Lt Colonel [William] Washington's regiment of Dragoons; which I expect will be joined by 300 Militia horse under the command of Genl [William L.] Davidson and near 400 Militia that were lately with General [Thomas] Sumter and Colonel [Elijah] Clarke. His instructions are to act upon the offensive or defensive as occasion my warrant. But to take every precaution to guard against a surprise. The object of the detachment is to straighten the Enemy's limits upon that quarter, keep up the spirits of the people, give protection to the well affected and collect the provision and form it into magazeines. The detachment is organized so as to move with great celerity; most of the Militia being on horse back and in great measure unencumbered with baggage or stores.[41]

One drawback to the position in the Cheraws was that the Southern Army was farther from the British force at Winnsboro, South Carolina, than it had been at Charlotte. It was also far to the east of the route that Cornwallis would likely have taken had he moved forward into North Carolina. Greene, who had a feel for public perception and the political situation, realized that any appearance of retreat in the face of a threatened British advance would bolster the enemy and dishearten the patriots. He needed to encourage the Whigs without creating the danger of a general engagement. To this end he sent Morgan westward. Morgan was to "straighten the Enemy's limits upon that quarter, keep up the spirits of the people, give protection to the well affected and collect the provision and form it into magazeines," or, as Greene wrote to General Robert Howe, former commander in the South, Morgan was to act as a "Partizan."[42] Morgan's troops, then, were to conduct "safe" offensive operations using superior mobility to avoid danger.[43]

Greene would have been distressed had he known that Morgan had allowed Lieutenant Colonel Banastre Tarleton's British detachment to steal a march on him and forced him to fight the Battle of Cowpens on January 17, 1781. Tarleton's force was small and designed for speed, so the opposing forces at Cowpens were nearly equal in firepower, and Morgan's detachment actually outnumbered Tarleton's. Given these conditions and Morgan's superior tactics, the Americans won the day.[44]

To return to the reason that Morgan was dispatched and what it says of Greene's generalship is to emphasize that Greene was a leader who was attuned to public opinion and morale. The British armies in the South, including that of Cornwallis, had a habit of marching into an area, calling for Loyalist support, rallying that support to their banners, and then marching away leaving those same Loyalists behind to suffer the revenge of their patriot neighbors. While circumstances often forced Greene to allow the British to operate freely in Whig strongholds, he did what he could to limit British activity. Such was the case when he returned immediately to North Carolina after the race to the Dan River or when his army reentered South Carolina after the Battle of Guilford Courthouse, or when he diverted to Virginia reinforcements sent or raised to support his operations in order to limit the movements and depredations of Cornwallis's army after it moved into North Carolina in April 1781. A hallmark of Greene's generalship was his recognition of the importance of public perception and opinion when the contest was for the loyalty of the citizenry, as it was in the South in 1781.

Greene's next key "strategic" decision in the campaign occurred after the Battle of Cowpens, when he chose to retreat with his army across the breadth of North Carolina in the face of a dogged pursuit by Cornwallis's force of trained veterans. Cornwallis had even destroyed his army's supply train in order to increase the pace of its march and overtake the retreating Americans. Some historians contend that Greene's decision was made a few days after the Battle of Cowpens, when he learned that Cornwallis had moved into North Carolina in pursuit of Morgan. In their view Greene decided to wage a "mobile war" and conduct a "strategic retreat," trading space for time with the intention of drawing Cornwallis farther and farther from his base of supplies while moving the Americans closer toward their own "base" in Virginia, which was the most populous and strongly patriot southern state.[45]

While that is what happened, it was not Greene's intention when he left the Southern Army's "camp of repose" at Hick's Creek, South Carolina, on January 28, or even when he overtook Morgan's detachment at Sherrald's Ford on the Catawba River in North Carolina on January 30.[46] First at the fords of the Yadkin River near Salisbury, North Carolina, and then at Guilford Courthouse, where the two detachments of the American army united, Greene attempted to organize a defense and engage the British with a view to stopping their advance.[47]

Greene's wish to engage Cornwallis's army was not merely wishful thinking on Greene's part but the result of an astute reading of his opponent. As he wrote

Detail showing the routes Cornwallis took in South and North Carolina, 1781. All images courtesy of South Caroliniana Library, University of South Carolina, Columbia.

to his second in command, General Isaac Huger, who was then moving to join Greene with the major part of the army: "It is not improbable from Lord Cornwallises pushing disposition, and the contempt he has for our Army, we may precipitate him into some capital misfortune. I wish to be prepared, either for attacking, or for receiving one."[48] The timidity of the local militia and the rapidity of Cornwallis's movements frustrated Greene's intentions.[49] However, it was not because Greene did not want to stop and fight. In fact at Guilford on February 9, Greene convened a council of war of his senior officers—something he rarely did—to ratify a course of action that he found obviously distasteful and for which he only reluctantly opted.[50]

Almost immediately after Greene resolved to retire, he began to plan how he might exploit a successful "strategic retreat" and turn it into a counteroffensive. Four days after he crossed into Virginia, Greene was writing to North Carolina militia leaders urging them to gather and organize their men and promising them that "I am not without hopes of giving Lord Cornwallis a run in turn. . . . I think we shall be able to attack the Enemy with a prospect of success."[51]

But before Greene could counterattack, he had to survive the retreat, the so-called race to the Dan, a river that forms a natural barrier on the border between North Carolina and Virginia. In a grueling four-day, seventy-mile race, the last leg of a marathon that had begun after the Battle of Cowpens, the Americans won the race by mere hours.

This retreat was a stunning achievement, more impressive because Greene's army lost virtually no men to desertion and was able to save its meager cache of supplies, even though the army's transport service was barely functioning.[52] Moreover the action highlights key elements of Greene's style of generalship: his knowledge of the southern terrain, his ability to make and revise plans quickly, his foresight, and probably most important his knowledge of his senior subordinates, which allowed him to assign to them tasks for which they were well suited.

On at least two occasions, the rapid rise of North Carolina rivers gave Morgan's detachment precious time to distance itself from the pursuing British. From the knowledge of North Carolina he had gleaned from earlier surveying expeditions he had ordered, Greene was able to foresee the "miracle" of the rising water. Therefore, when it rained on February 1, Greene was most anxious to have Morgan cross the Yadkin River by February 3.[53] When Morgan arrived at the Yadkin, the river was already too deep for his men to cross, but the second element of Greene's generalship came into play, and Morgan's men were able to cross the river in boats that Greene had the foresight to order collected.[54]

At the Dan River crossing, a similar scenario played out. Cornwallis, having intelligence that the lower crossings of the Dan were not fordable and that too few boats were available to ferry Greene's army across the swollen river, inclined his march initially toward the upper fords. Thanks to the survey of the rivers that his quartermaster, Edward Carrington, had supervised during the first days of Greene's command, Greene, however, knew that there were five boats available for a crossing at Boyd's Ferry (at present-day Danville, Virginia), so he inclined his march in that direction and in the end won the race.[55]

Just as important was Greene's creation of a light-infantry command, which joined with Lee's Legion to act as the army's rear guard and was charged with the task of convincing the British in the first days of the "race" that the Southern Army was indeed planning to use the upper fords of the Dan River. After Morgan declined the appointment because of ill-health and returned to his home in Virginia, Greene assigned Colonel Otho Holland Williams to command the light-infantry force. Together Williams and Lee did a masterful job of decoying and then slowing the British advance, buying time for the slower, main portion of Greene's army to traverse the miles to the Dan. As with Morgan, Greene knew his subordinates well enough that he could assign the right man to the job. Greene demonstrated this talent repeatedly during his time in the South. In selecting Williams, Greene bypassed his second in command, General Isaac Huger. Huger was not known for independent initiative, and Greene was correct to use Williams and before him Morgan as commander of the light infantry. Later, in the "war of posts" in South Carolina, Greene showed an uncanny knack for pairing Continental and militia/partisan officers for operations. As a result the brilliant yet volatile Henry Lee was paired with steady, capable partisan officers such as Francis Marion and Andrew Pickens and was never allowed to serve with the equally volatile and infinitely more irascible Thomas Sumter. This ability to understand his subordinates' capabilities and make the most of them was a key ingredient in Greene's success as a general.

Once the Southern Army crossed the Dan River it was safe from further pursuit. The average general might have set up a bivouac, rested his troops, and awaited reinforcements before again entering North Carolina. That, however, was not the genius of Nathanael Greene. As he explained to Governor Thomas Jefferson of Virginia in a letter written just days before the Battle of Guilford Courthouse:

> My force has never been during any stage of the Campaign equal to any decicive efforts. When the Enemy first took their departure from the Dan they had every prospect of great reinforcements from the Tories of Carolina, and I reflected that if they were permitted to roam at large in the State that it would indubitably impress the Idea of Conquest upon the Minds of

the disaffected and perhaps occasion those who were wavering in their sentiments to take an active and decicive part against us. I instantly determined as the most effectual Measure to prevent it to advance into the State without waiting for those reinforcements which the Spirit of the Virginians at that time seemed to promise me. It was necessary to convince the Carolinians that they were not conquered, and by affording immediate protection to their property engage the continuance of their confidence and friendship. I trust the Efforts that have been made have in a great measure had that effect.

. . . Hitherto I have been obliged to practice that by finesse which I dare not attempt by force. I know the People have been in anxious suspence waiting the event of an Action, but let the consequence of Censure be what it may, nothing shall hurry me into a Measure that is not Suggested by prudence or connects with it the interest of the department in which I have the honor to command.[56]

Another element of Greene's generalship is evident in this interim period between the crossing of the Dan River and the Battle of Guilford Courthouse almost three weeks later. Greene as commander in the South is known for his attempts to lessen the chaos caused by the internecine warfare that characterized the Revolution in the South by advocating reconciliation with Loyalists.[57] To give just one of many possible examples, Greene wrote Griffith Rutherford, a North Carolina militia leader with a reputation for harsh treatment of Loyalists, asserting that "it has ever been my wish to avoid cruelty and the dignity of our cause requires it should be marked with humanity, justice and moderation."[58] On February 25, 1781, there occurred an atrocity that Greene not only did not condemn but celebrated. This atrocity was the so-called Pyle's Massacre, which occurred when a party of Loyalist militia were slaughtered after "Light-Horse Harry" Lee's dragoons, pretending to be a detachment of Banastre Tarleton's British Legion, launched an attack with sabers while the Tories' arms were slung, making them defenseless. In this one-sided engagement Pyle's command suffered an estimated three hundred killed and wounded while the Americans lost one horse.[59] Greene's only reaction was to note "Lt. Col. Lees falling in with the Tories upon the Haw [River] almost put a total stop to their recruiting service."[60] While Greene's impulse was to foster a spirit of conciliation, he was pragmatic or hypocritical enough to accept that ideals must sometimes be set aside in the name of expediency. He did so again when he gave his imprimatur, albeit reluctantly, to Thomas Sumter's plan to pay newly raised ten-month men with slaves expropriated from Loyalists in South Carolina, the so-called Sumter's Law.[61] This hardheaded pragmatism also typified Greene's generalship.

The Battle of Guilford Courthouse itself demonstrates another element of Greene's leadership. When Greene believed that his army had been sufficiently reinforced with militia from Virginia and North Carolina, he moved to Guilford Courthouse, the place where he had earlier contemplated offering battle to Cornwallis. When arranging his forces for the battle, Greene borrowed the tactical disposition used by Daniel Morgan at Cowpens.[62] In doing so he demonstrated a lack of ego and a willingness to adopt proven ideas that were not his own.[63] Morgan's disposition also coincided nicely with Greene's principle of preserving the regular army; it placed the regulars in a third line well removed from where the battle began and also maximized their opportunity to withdraw successfully should things go badly. On a later tour of the battlefield, George Washington, however, criticized Greene's arrangement of his regulars in the third of his three lines, asserting that he would have put the Continentals in the first line and used the militia in support.[64] For Greene it was more important to keep an "army in being" than to win the battle. Morgan's tactics presented that opportunity, so Greene used them. As historian Russell Weigley contended in his landmark study *The American Way of War*, if Washington and Greene were fighting a war of attrition, Greene at least was willing to fight only to the last militiaman.[65]

In the aftermath of that battle came the third strategic decision that Thayer believes made Greene deserving of the title "Strategist of the Revolution." Although Cornwallis's army prevailed at the Battle of Guilford Courthouse, it was a Pyrrhic victory. While Cornwallis acknowledged losing almost one-quarter of his army in killed, wounded, and missing, his subordinate Brigadier General Charles O'Hara wrote to his patron Augustus Henry Fitzroy, Duke of Grafton, a month after the battle: "I wish it [the battle] had produced one substantial benefit to Great Britain, on the contrary, we feel at this moment, the sad and fatal effect of our loss on that Day, nearly one half of our best Officers and Soldiers, were either Killed or Wounded, and what remains are so completely worn out . . . [that] entre nous, the Spirit of our little Army has evaporated a good deal."[66]

Immediately after the battle, Cornwallis began to march his army to British-held Wilmington on the North Carolina coast, where the troops could be protected and resupplied by the Royal Navy without American interference. As soon as he learned of the British retreat, Greene marched in pursuit of Cornwallis, but it soon became evident that the Southern Army would be unable to overtake the British force. At Ramsey's Mill, some forty-five miles northwest of Cross Creek, Greene decided to break off pursuit of Cornwallis's army and move into South Carolina. Two factors contributed to his determination. The army was having difficulty obtaining adequate provisions in North Carolina, and the term of service of the Virginia militia, which then composed the bulk of the army, was about to expire, and its members were unwilling to extend their tour of duty.[67]

Nonetheless it was a risky move. Greene was violating established military principles by leaving an enemy army virtually unchallenged in his rear. He acknowledged the unorthodox nature of his decision when he wrote James Emmet, a North Carolina militia officer, on April 3: "Don't be surprisd if my movements don't correspond with your Ideas of military propriety. War is an intricate business, and people are often savd by ways and means they least look for or expect."[68] In his memoir Henry Lee asserted that the plan to break off pursuit had originated with someone other than Greene and implied that Lee himself had been the author.[69] Although some historians have accepted Lee's claim, the chronology of when the decision was made clearly establishes that Greene was the plan's author.[70] On March 29, eight days before Lee said Greene heard a spirited debate among his senior officers concerning the plan and then chose to abandon pursuit of Cornwallis and move into South Carolina, Greene explained his decision to Washington and added: "All things considered I think the movement is warranted by the soundest reasons both political and military."[71] He provided an even fuller explanation in a letter to Baron Friedrich von Steuben of April 3:

> From a persuasion that the Enemy wish to get full possession of this State [North Carolina], and are making every effort to effect it; and as their advance northward secures their possessions Southward I think it will be our true plan of policy to move into South Carolina, notwithstanding the risque and difficulty attending the manoeuvre. This will oblige the Enemy to follow us or give up their posts there. If they follow us, it will releive us in this state. That whether they go or stay an advantage must result from the measure. Besides this advantage, it will keep the Enemys force divided and enable us to employ a greater body of Militia against them, and also to fight them to more advantage, as the force of the Militia don't encrease with the regular troops in the same proportion as their numbers encrease; on the contrary the militia constantly losses their comparative force as their numbers are augmented.
>
> From these considerations I am determined to march immediately into South Carolina, being persuaded that if I continue in this State the Enemy will hold their ground in the southern States; and this also. Another advantage may result from it, which is we shall live upon the resources which the Enemy have at command; and the boldness of the manoeuvre will make them think I have secret reasons which they cannot

comprehend. If I can get supplies and secure a retreat I fear no bad consequences.[72]

Despite what he wrote to Steuben, Greene expected Cornwallis to follow him into South Carolina and was surprised when the British general did not.[73] The decision to abandon pursuit of Cornwallis's army and move into South Carolina is seen by some commentators as the beginning of the "war of posts." This concerted attack on small British posts guarding their lines of communication and supply quickly broke British power in South Carolina and Georgia.

The "war of posts" came later, however, and was not the reason that Greene moved into South Carolina. Greene's initial movement was to put his army in a position to confront the main British force in the state, an army under Lieutenant Colonel Francis, Lord Rawdon, occupying Camden. With the idea of overwhelming and destroying the major British force in South Carolina, Greene hoped to force Rawdon to fight him. Greene was not interested in defeating the British piecemeal but in overwhelming them completely in one blow. While it is true that Lee's Legion, reinforced by a company of Maryland Continentals and Marion's partisans, opened a siege of Fort Watson, a post of communication on the Santee River, and successfully concluded it before the Battle of Hobkirk's Hill, when Greene's and Rawdon's army met, the primary mission of Lee and Marion was to prevent British reinforcements from reaching Rawdon from Georgetown.[74] Only after the battle of Hobkirk's Hill—another tactical defeat for the Americans—when the battle's victor found that winning had not measurably improved his situation and so was forced to abandon the post at Camden, did Greene begin the "war of posts" in earnest. In a matter of weeks, that brilliantly "improvised" strategy reduced British power and forced them to abandon much of the interior of South Carolina and Georgia. Again Greene altered his intended strategy to fit developing circumstances, brilliantly maximizing his assets and exploiting British weaknesses.

It is a disservice to characterize Greene as merely a strategist in the modern sense of that term. From the three strategic decisions that most defined his campaigns in the South, it is clear that Greene began with one plan and then seamlessly, quickly, and effectively changed it to best exploit the evolving situation. While Greene adhered to certain principles throughout his campaigns, including preserving his Continentals, using militia and partisans regularly and effectively, emphasizing mounted troops, and stressing and utilizing the mobility of his army, his genius was in his ability to adapt to circumstances and find a way to succeed. As former professional football coach Oail Andrew "Bum" Phillips is reputed to have said of a rival coach: "He can take his'n and beat yourn, and then can take yourn and beat his'n."[75] Such could be said of Greene as well, except in battle.

NOTES

1. Greene to Samuel Ward Jr., October 9, 1772, *The Papers of General Nathanael Greene*, edited by Richard K. Showman, Dennis R. Conrad, and Roger N. Parks, 13 vols. (Chapel Hill: University of North Carolina Press, 1976–2005), 1:47.

2. Ibid., 1:62n.

3. Ibid., 1:14n.

4. Greene to his brother Jacob Greene, June 4, 1777, ibid., 2:104, 104n; see also ibid., 1:70n.

5. Greene to the members of the New Garden Monthly Meeting, near Guilford Courthouse, March 26, 1781, ibid., 7:469–70.

6. See for example Elswyth Thane, *The Fighting Quaker: Nathanael Greene* (New York: Hawthorn, 1972).

7. For a detailed discussion and analysis of Great Britain's southern strategy, see Paul H. Smith, *Loyalists and Redcoats: A Study in British Revolutionary Policy* (Chapel Hill: University of North Carolina Press, 1964), and David K. Wilson, *The Southern Strategy: Britain's Conquest of South Carolina and Georgia, 1775–1780* (Columbia: University of South Carolina Press, 2005).

8. *The Works of Thomas Jefferson*, edited by Paul Leicester Ford, 12 vols. (New York & London: Putnam, 1905), 12:246.

9. Theodore Thayer, *Nathanael Greene: Strategist of the American Revolution* (New York: Twayne, 1960).

10. Greene to Henry Knox, September 20, 1781, *The Papers of General Nathanael Greene*, 9:411–12.

11. Greene to Anne-César, Chevalier de La Luzerne, April 28, 1781, *The Papers of General Nathanael Greene*, 8:168

12. See for example Dave Richard Palmer, *The Way of the Fox: American Strategy in the War for America, 1775–1783* (Westport, Conn.: Greenwood Press, 1975), 172; Don Higginbotham, *The War of American Independence: Military Attitudes, Policies, and Practice, 1763–1789* (New York: Macmillan, 1971), 374.

13. Greene to Jeremiah Wadsworth, July 18, 1781, *The Papers of General Nathanael Greene*, 9:41.

14. Greene to George Washington, June 22, 1781, ibid., 8:441.

15. Greene to Thomas Jefferson, April 28, 1781, ibid., 8:166.

16. Greene to George Washington, October 31, 1780, ibid., 6:448.

17. Greene to Joseph Reed, September 8, 1780, Greene to George Washington, September 12, 1780, ibid., 6:272, 279.

18. Greene to Isaac Huger, February 1, 1781, ibid., 7:231.

19. Greene to Ezekiel Cornell, December 29, 1780, ibid., 7:21.

20. Greene to Jeremiah Wadsworth, July 18, 1781, ibid., 9:41.

21. For a statement of how Greene intended to treat politicians, even those he did not respect, see his letter to General Robert Howe, December 29, 1780, ibid., 7:17.

22. On Greene's role in the reestablishment of state government in Georgia, see Greene to Joseph Clay, July 24, 1781, and Governor Nathan Brownson to Greene, December 17, 1781, ibid., 9:70–71, 10:70–71.

23. Robert W. Barnwell Jr., "Rutledge, 'The Dictator,'" *Journal of Southern History* 7 (May 1941): 215–24.

24. On Gates's command see Paul David Nelson, *General Horatio Gates: A Biography* (Baton Rouge: Louisiana State University Press, 1976), 220–28. For a summary of Greene's steps concerning supply matters during the first days of his command in the South, see Thayer, *Nathanael Greene*, 293–94.

25. Edward Payson, "Nathanael Greene and the Supply of the Continental Army" *Quartermaster Review*, May–June 1950, http://www.qmfound.com/greene.htm (accessed March 8, 2006).

26. Greene to George Washington, December 7, 1780; Greene to North Carolina Board of War, December 7, 1780, *The Papers of General Nathanael Greene*, 6:543–44, 548.

27. On the problems of establishing and operating these magazines, particularly that at Oliphant's Mills, see William Johnson, *Sketches of the Life and Correspondence of Nathanael Greene*, 2 vols. (Charleston, S.C.: A. E. Miller, 1822), 1:343.

28. On armies in the South and mills, see Lawrence E. Babits, "Military Documents and Archaeological Sites: Methodological Contributions to Historical Archaeology," Ph.D. diss., Brown University, 1981.

29. William A. Graham, *General Joseph Graham and His Papers on North Carolina Revolutionary History* (Raleigh: Edwards & Broughton, 1904), 290.

30. Quoted in Johnson, *Life and Correspondence of Greene*, 2:159.

31. See Alexander Martin to Greene, January 3, 1781, *The Papers of General Nathanael Greene*, 7:45.

32. Greene to Thomas Sumter, January 8, 1781, ibid., 7:74–75. As seen in the source note to that document, the signed letter that Sumter received from Greene is torn, and portions of the text are missing, so the editors used a later transcript of the letter to supply that text. Those portions taken from the transcript appear in angle brackets; ibid., 7:75n. To another advocate of militia, the North Carolina legislature, Greene wrote on February 17: "The Militia can fight the enemy to advantage in detachments but not in general actions"; ibid., 7:304.

33. See for example Greene to delegate to Congress Ezekiel Cornell, December 29, 1780, ibid., 7:20–21.

34. See Greene to Joseph Reed, March 18, 1781, and Greene to Governor Abner Nash, April 3, 1781, ibid., 7:450, 8:436–37.

35. Governor Abner Nash to Greene, April 3, 1781, ibid., 8:42.

36. Greene to Governor John Rutledge, January 21, 1782, ibid., 10:228–30; South Carolina representative Aedanus Burke made the charge that Greene's real goal in proposing the plan was to abolish slavery; Burke to Arthur Middleton, January 25–February 5, 1782, "Correspondence of the Honorable Arthur Middleton, Signer of the Declaration of Independence [Part One]," edited by Joseph W. Barnwell, *South Carolina Historical and Genealogical Magazine* 26 (October 1925): 194.

37. Higginbotham, *The War of American Independence*, 374.

38. Greene to unidentified correspondent, between December 26, 1780, and January 23, 1781, *The Papers of General Nathanael Greene*, 7:175.

39. John Morgan Dederer, *Making Bricks without Straw: Nathanael Greene's Southern Campaign and Mao Tse-Tung's Mobile War* (Manhattan, Kans.: Sunflower University Press, 1983), 43.

40. Greene to Daniel Morgan, January 8, 1781, *The Papers of General Nathanael Greene*, 7:73.

41. Greene to Samuel Huntington, December 28, 1780, ibid., 7:7–8.

42. Greene to General Robert Howe, December 29, 1780, ibid., 7:18.

43. See Greene to Daniel Morgan, January 3, 1781, January 8, 1781, January 19, 1781, ibid., 7:41–42, 72–73, 146–47.

44. For an excellent analysis of the Battle of Cowpens, see Lawrence E. Babits, *A Devil of a Whipping: The Battle of Cowpens* (Chapel Hill: University of North Carolina Press, 1998).

45. See for example Dederer, *Making Bricks without Straw*, 50–51.

46. William Johnson, Greene's first biographer, called Greene's decision to travel more than one hundred miles to join Morgan's detachment, accompanied only by a party of five, to be "the most imprudent action of his life." Johnson, *Life and Correspondence*, 1:394.

47. See Greene to General Isaac Huger, February 5, 1781; Greene to the "Officer Commanding the Militia in the Rear of the Enemy," February 6, 1781; Greene to General John Butler of the North Carolina Militia, February 8, 1781; Greene to Governor Abner Nash of North Carolina, February 9, 1781; *The Papers of General Nathanael Greene*, 7:251, 253–54, 256, 263–65. The combination of the wings of the American force at Guilford Courthouse is hailed as a triumph of Greene's foresight and planning. See also, Dederer, *Making Bricks without Straw*, 50.

48. Greene to General Isaac Huger, February 5, 1781, *The Papers of General Nathanael Greene*, 7:252,

49. Greene to Governor Abner Nash of North Carolina, February 9, 1781, ibid., 7:263–65.

50. Proceedings of a council of war, February 9, 1781, ibid., 7:261–62.

51. Greene to Richard Caswell, February 18, 1781, ibid., 7:309.

52. See Greene to General Thomas Sumter, February 21, 1781, ibid., 7:328.

53. Johnson, *Life and Correspondence*, 1:418.

54. On the basis of intelligence he had received, Cornwallis anticipated that no boats would be available and that the Americans would be trapped against the swollen river. Franklin Wickwire and Mary Wickwire, *Cornwallis, the American Adventure* (Boston: Houghton Mifflin, 1970), 282–83.

55. Henry Lee, *The Campaign of 1781 in the Carolinas; with Remarks Historical and Critical on Johnson's Life of Greene* (1824; reprint, Spartanburg, S.C.: Reprint Co., 1975), 116–17.

56. Greene to Governor Thomas Jefferson, March 10, 1781, *The Papers of General Nathanael Greene*, 7:419–20.

57. See John Maass's essay in this volume.

58. Greene to General Griffith Rutherford, January 29, 1782, *The Papers of General Nathanael Greene*, 10:277.

59. While Lee later took great pains to deny that a massacre had occurred, British sources charged that the dragoons had continued to slaughter the Loyalists even after they had called out for quarter. Henry Lee, *Memoirs of the War in the Southern Department of the United States*, 2 vols. (Philadelphia: Bradford & Inskeep, 1812), 1:312. Charles Stedman, *The History of the Origin, Progress, and Termination of the American War*, 2 vols. (London, 1794), 2:233–34.

60. Greene to Joseph Reed, March 18, 1781, *The Papers of General Nathanael Greene*, 7:449.

61. On the plan and a sampling of historians' views of it, see General Thomas Sumter to Greene, April 7, 1781, and the editors' notes following that document, ibid., 8:65–67 and 67n.

62. In fact Morgan sent Greene advice on how to arrange his lines. See General Daniel Morgan to Greene, February 20, 1781, ibid., 7:324.

63. Greene later did the same at the siege of Ninety Six, when he borrowed the idea of the "Maham tower," a variation on a medieval siege machine conceived by South Carolina partisan officer Hezekiah Maham and used to capture Fort Watson in April 1781.

64. Historian John Buchanan sees this criticism as evidence that Washington was limited in his abilities as a tactician. See John Buchanan, *The Road to Valley Forge: How Washington Built the Army That Won the Revolution* (Hoboken, N.J.: Wiley, 2004), 314–15.

65. Russell F. Weigley, *The American Way of War* (New York: Macmillan, 1973); see also Weigley's response to Brian McAllister Linn in *Journal of Military History* 66 (April 2002): 531–32.

66. General Charles O'Hara to Augustus Henry Fitzroy, Duke of Grafton, April 20, 1781, "Letters of Charles O'Hara to the Duke of Grafton," edited by George C. Rogers Jr., *South Carolina Historical Magazine* 65 (July 1964): 177.

67. Greene to General Thomas Sumter, March 30, 1781, *The Papers of General Nathanael Greene*, 8:12–13.

68. Greene to Colonel James Emmet, April 3, 1781, ibid., 8:33.

69. Lee, *Memoirs*, 2:31–40.

70. See for example Edward McCrady, *The History of South Carolina in the Revolution, 1780–1783* (New York: Macmillan, 1902), 159–61. For a discussion of how the chronology of the decision-making process demonstrates that Greene was the author of the plan, see *The Papers of General Nathanael Greene*, 7:482n. Another hallmark of Greene's style of leadership was that, through consultation and discussion, his subordinates came to feel "ownership" for the plans of their commander.

71. Greene to General George Washington, March 29, 1781, *The Papers of General Nathanael Greene*, 7:481.

72. Greene to Baron Friedrich von Steuben, April 2, 1781, ibid., 8:24.

73. See Greene to Marie Joseph Gilbert du Motier, Marquis de Lafayette, April 3, 1781, ibid., 8:34.

74. Colonel Henry Lee to Greene, April 23, 1781, ibid., 8:138; on the siege of Fort Watson, see General Francis Marion to Greene, April 23, 1781, ibid., 8:139–41 and 141n.

75. Roscoe Nace, "Brown Finds the Road Home, *USA Today*, November 1, 2005, http://www.usatoday.com/educate/college/careers/CEOs/11-1-05.htm (accessed March 2, 2007).

"A merchandise of small Wares"

Nathanael Greene's Northern Apprenticeship, 1775–1780

Curtis F. Morgan Jr.

*M*ajor General Nathanael Greene was the most successful military commander of the American Revolution. In just two years between December 1780 and December 1782, he effectively expelled all British forces from North Carolina, South Carolina, and Georgia. The British abandoned Savannah and Charleston, the premier port cities of the South, because they were no longer able to feed themselves from country districts under patriot control. In the space of seven months Greene fought three major battles (Guilford Courthouse, Hobkirk's Hill, and Eutaw Springs) and besieged the British backcountry strongpoint at Ninety Six, South Carolina. On each occasion, although he was unsuccessful in driving British forces from the field of battle, he inflicted such grievous casualties on them that they withdrew from Greene's vicinity to refit and regroup. In each instance Greene was in possession of the original battlefield soon after and permanently.

Like almost all America's battlefield commanders, Greene was self-taught in the art of war. Military works found in Greene's library included Caesar's *Commentaries on the Gallic War*, Sharpe's *Military Guide*, the *Reveries* of Marshal Maurice de Saxe, and Frederick the Great's *Instructions to His Generals*. Greene was a voracious reader who used the written word to guide his own thinking.[1] But nothing instructs like experience; and he was not bereft of human teachers. He quickly became a disciple of General George Washington, whose military skills Greene surpassed by the war's end. This essay will examine the lessons Greene learned at Washington's side from the war's beginning in the summer of 1775 to Greene's appointment to command the disintegrated Southern Army in the fall of 1780. Over five years Greene was a student in America's first "war

MAJOR GENERAL NATHANIEL GREENE

Major General Nathanael Greene. Engraving by Putnam after a portrait by Charles Willson Peale.

college," and in the South he applied the lessons he had learned in several crucial "classes": preserving the army as opposed to defending places; conducting operations with a "home-made" force against a more-experienced, better-led, and better-equipped enemy; maintaining civilian political support; and finally using logistics defensively and offensively.

George Washington was named commander in chief of the Continental forces in June 1775. Nathanael Greene became the youngest and lowest-ranked of eight brigadier generals.[2] He soon reported, "His Excellency General Washington has arrivd and is universally admird. The excellent Charactor he bears, and the promising Genius he possesses gives great spirit to the Troops, and I make no doubt his conduct will manifest the Wisdom and prudence of the Continental Choice." What Washington thought of Greene at this time is unclear, but Greene was less circumspect: "His Excellency is a great and good man. I feel the highest degree of respect for him."[3] A partnership of vital importance to the fortunes of America had begun.

Following the successful siege of Boston, Greene was briefly military governor of the liberated port city. Washington correctly guessed that the British would return and attempt to capture the premier American port of New York. At the beginning of August 1776, Greene was kept busy on Long Island trying to anticipate where the British were most likely to land. His daily correspondence and the burden of "clerical Employments" drove him to distraction. "The time devoted to this employment is not the only injury that I feel," he wrote Washington, "but it confines my thoughts as well as engrosses my time. It is like a merchandise of small Wares." Greene's troops nevertheless seemed ready to defend Long Island. At this critical moment, however, Greene himself was "confined to my Bed with a raging Fever." Washington relieved him from command, replacing him with General John Sullivan.[4] This turn of events was unfortunate. Greene knew the ground over which the American forces were about to fight; Sullivan did not. The troops were familiar with Greene; Sullivan was new to them and thus did not inspire their confidence.[5]

Confusion in command, ignorance of the terrain, poor placement of the troops, Washington's inexperience and indecision, the poor quality of most of the American troops, the lack of cavalry to scout and screen, and the complete opposite of these circumstances on the British part, all contributed to the defeat and near dissolution of the American forces on Long Island. Washington managed to retrieve the situation by a quiet overnight withdrawal across the Hudson to Manhattan, aided by a providential fog and a rainstorm that prevented the British from approaching New York by sea, and by General Sir William Howe's unwillingness to press the pursuit. Playing an overlooked role was the state of the defensive works Greene had erected, which helped to buy time and cover the withdrawal of the American forces.[6]

Recuperating in New York City, Greene reacted to the news of Long Island with a mixture of "survivor guilt" and envy. If only he had been there! He poured out his feelings to his brother Jacob:

> Providence took me out of the way. I have been very sick for near three weeks; for several days there was a hard struggle between nature and the disorder. I am now a little better, though scarcely able to sit up an hour at a time. I have no strength or appetite, and my disorder, from its operation, appears to threaten me with long confinement. Gracious God! to be confined at such a time. And the misfortune is doubly great as there was no general officer who had made himself acquainted with the ground as perfectly as I had. I have not the vanity to think the event would have been otherwise had I been there; yet I think I could have given the commanding general a good deal of necessary information. Great events sometimes depend upon very little causes.[7]

Greene was nevertheless in a good position to learn from the manner of Washington's skillful withdrawal across a river in the face of a superior enemy, keeping the army intact and living to fight another day. He later participated more fully in several such withdrawals under Washington and used such "redeployments" to advantage in his Carolinas campaigns several years later.

One such retreat occurred in mid-September, after the Americans had reluctantly decided to evacuate New York City. (Greene was one who had urged abandoning the city to save the army.) The retreat was underway not a moment too soon; early on the morning of September 15, 1776, Howe launched an amphibious operation at Kip's Bay on the eastern coast of Manhattan Island. The American troops stationed there, mostly militia in hastily erected field works, panicked and fled. Greene reported that "Fellows and Parsons whole Brigade run away from about fifty men and left [Washington] on the Ground within Eighty Yards of the Enimy, so vext at the infamous conduct of the Troops that he sought Death rather than life" and had to be led away from certain capture or death, swearing at his fleeing men and brandishing his sword. Under the circumstances Greene's characterization of the army's movement north as "disgraceful," a "miserable, disorderly retreat" is an understatement.[8]

Once again the Americans' knack for light-footed "redeployment" combined with Howe's caution to snatch rout from the jaws of annihilation. Few of Washington's men actually headed for home and safety; somewhat sheepishly (doubtless under the contumely of Greene and others) they filed into hastily prepared positions on the brow of Harlem Heights overlooking the road north to Kingsbridge. Here Washington was ready to make a stand. He was confident of his position (wooded high ground overlooking a flat, open "Hollow Way") but not of his troops. Kip's Bay had shaken him badly, and he feared another such collapse of morale would be the end. He did what he could to improve his odds. In position closest to the likely British avenue of approach, he placed the division commanded by Nathanael Greene, who had not yet seen combat. Greene later recalled: "The Enemy next day at Harlem Heights, flushed with the Successes of the day before, approached and attacked our lines, where I had the Honor to Command." When the Americans prudently (and in surprisingly good order) withdrew, Washington heard British officers taunting the Americans with fox-hunt bugling and decided to strike back. He drew up a plan to lure part of Howe's advance guard into the "Hollow Way" by a feigned retreat and then to send a flanking force to swing around behind and cut them off. The envelopment nearly worked, but overeager Americans fired prematurely, warning the British; they hastily withdrew with the Americans in surprised pursuit. The British were driven up and over the opposite slope, and it was all Washington could do to call off a chase that could have become as disastrous as the retreat at Kip's Bay had been. It was vital to keep the army intact and under control, even in a minor victory. Greene later faced a similar situation at Eutaw Springs in 1781 and called off a pursuit that threatened to disrupt the integrity of his force. Nevertheless the effect of action at Harlem Heights on morale was electrifying. "Our people beat the enemy off the ground," Greene wrote. The Americans had seen the "lobster backs" run for the first time. Greene was every where, riding back and forth to "animate the Troops." Six years later, Greene told Colonel Henry Lee "I fought hard at Harlem."[9]

Reflecting on his experiences, Greene wrote: "The enemy never could have driven us from Long Island and New York if our rear had been secured. We must have an army to meet the enemy everywhere; to act offensively as well as defensively. Our soldiers are as good as ever were, and were the officers half as good as the men they would beat any army on the globe of equal numbers."[10] Greene wrote these words from Fort Constitution (soon to be rechristened "Fort Lee"), one of a pair of riverside forts (the other "Mount" or Fort Washington) guarding the Hudson River, with sunken hulks and other would-be obstructions between them. On September 17 he had been given command of all American forces on the New Jersey side of the Hudson, a force of some 3,521 men, including one regiment of militia, all at Fort Lee. It was his first detached command since taking charge of liberated Boston. He commanded a division, one of seven in the recently reorganized army. Once he took command, "There was immediately a great change with respect to the discipline of the troops which before that was very lax," Private John Adlum recalled. "The first thing that was done after General Greene arrived was to review our brigade, when he observed our officers were generally so deficient in their movements that he ordered them to be drilled first in the manual exercise, and also to be taught how to take their places in the regiment which they were obliged to submit to for about three hours after breakfast. In the afternoon they were exercised with their companies and sometimes by regiments."[11]

Meanwhile the main army under Washington, some 14,500 strong, fell back to the north, taking position at White Plains, New York, by October 21. In executing this maneuver, Washington left the troops at Fort Washington exposed. The British could "mask" the fort with superior numbers, denying to Washington the use of the fort's 1,400 troops under Colonel Robert Magaw. Although Greene was later blamed for the decision to try to hold the fort against British attack, it was the decision by the council of war on October 16 to leave the garrison in place there that effectively doomed the fort—and Greene was not present at the council that day.[12]

Greene was busy at Fort Lee with logistical matters. He wrote directly to the president of Congress, John Hancock, for an immediate shipment of cartridges from Philadelphia, pointing out that Washington's supply line to Connecticut "may be shortly cut off." Congress ordered 200,000 cartridges "to be instantly forwarded to you." Greene informed Washington that cartridges were en route, that provisions would be ferried over to Fort Washington, and that he had ordered three month's provisions for twenty thousand men to be placed "upon the Back Road to Philadelphia. . . . The principal Magazine will be at Equacanack [Aquacknock]. I shall Fortify it as soon as possible and secure that Post and the pass at the Bridge which is now repair'd and fit for an Army to pass over with the Baggage and Artillery." He wrote to expect a shipment of 119,000 musket cartridges. "I have been to view the roads again," he reported, and had selected Aquacknock, Springfield, Boundbrook, Princeton, and Trenton as magazine sites. "They are all inland Posts and I hope the Stores will be secure," he wrote. He followed up on October 29 with a detailed breakdown of provisions needed at each place, including five months provisions for two thousand men at Fort Lee and provisions for twenty thousand men for a week's march to Philadelphia. His chain of depots was well placed, lying west of the main road between New York City and Philadelphia. Greene did not know, but perhaps guessed, that this supply line would be vital to cover Washington's retreat to the Delaware River, should he choose that route. Greene's actions here, made without prior guidance from Washington, saved the army and the Revolution in December. Washington still had a force with which to strike at Trenton because provisions were available along the route to the Delaware. Few took notice of this in the confusion that reigned at the end of the year, but Washington clearly did. Four years later, Greene was careful to line his route of retreat in Virginia and North Carolina in a similar manner.[13]

On October 28, after a vicious firefight with General Howe, Washington withdrew from White Plains. Fort Washington was all but doomed, as Washington now realized. When Howe unexpectedly turned south, Washington informed President John Hancock that "I expect the Enemy will bend their force against Fort Washington and invest It immediately. From some advices it is an Object that will attract their earliest attention." It already had. The day before the Battle of White Plains, two British frigates attempted to run past the forts on the Hudson but were repulsed under heavy fire from American batteries. A small landing party was also driven off. The result raised morale, with unfortunate effect. It apparently convinced the garrison's commander, Colonel Magaw, and his men, as well as Greene, that Fort Washington was impregnable.[14]

It was not. In fact it was barely a fort at all. It was a pentagonal set of earthworks and bastions with no buildings except "a wooden magazine and some offices," no out works except "an incipient one at the north ["Fort Independence"], nor any of those exterior, multiplied obstacles and defences, that . . . could entitle it to the name of fortress, in any degree capable of withstanding a siege," according to British captain Alexander Graydon. Fort Washington did not even have an interior water source. Its only purpose was (together with Fort Lee across the river) to prevent British ships passing up the Hudson to threaten the American rear. But the forts had already been bypassed in early October, and Washington's "Grand Army" now withdrew to fortified lines near North Castle, New York. Fort Washington was designed to protect about a thousand men; yet more than twice that many occupied it and various outlying positions. By the end of October, "Fort Independence," near Kingsbridge, was abandoned as Howe's forces approached. Greene saw to getting "every thing of Value away" and destroying the bridges over the Harlem River.[15]

On October 31 Greene wrote to Washington for instructions, beginning an exchange that reveals the two men's mutual confusion and indecision, aggravated by a rare and disastrous breakdown of communications between them. "I should be glad to know your Excellency's mind about holding all the ground from Kings Bridge to the lower lines." Greene wrote. "If we attempt to hold the ground the Garrison must still be reinforced, but if the Garrison is to draw into Mount Washington and only keep that, the number of Troops on the Island is too large." He then told Washington he was reinforcing the fort with Colonel Moses Rawlings's regiment. Washington replied through his secretary, Colonel Robert Harrison, "that the holding or not holding the Grounds between King's bridge and the lower lines depends upon so many circumstances, that it is impossible for him to determine the points. He submits it intirely to your discretion and such Judgment as you will be enabld to form from the Enemy's movements and the whole complexion of things." The purpose of the two forts, he reminded Greene, was "that the Enemy should be prevented from having a passage up and down the River for their ships."[16]

On November 7, Washington seemed to awaken to the danger facing Fort Washington, one month after British warships had run the forts on the Hudson. The forts were clearly untenable now, and "it is so plain a proof of the inefficacy of all the obstructions we have thrown into [the Hudson] that I cannot but think it will fully justify a change in the dispositions which has been made." He went on, "If we cannot prevent vessels passing up, and the enemy are possessed of the surrounding country what valuable purpose can it answer to attempt to hold a post from which the expected benefit cannot be had?" He strongly suggested that Greene evacuate Fort Washington: "I am therefore inclined to think it will not be prudent to hazard the Men and Stores at Mount Washington, but as you are on the Spot, leave it to you to give such Orders as to evacuating Mount Washington as you judge best, and so far revoking the order given Colo Magaw to defend it to the last." He then urged Greene to remove unnecessary stores from Fort Lee and surrounding districts.[17]

Greene then did something rare. He argued with his commander in chief—though, to be fair, Washington had left a huge opening to do just that by saying "leave it to you to give such Orders . . . as you think best." Washington's command style encouraged his subordinates to debate all proposed moves freely, and Greene had grown comfortable with speaking his mind. If Washington was indecisive at this time, Greene was not. He had seen American troops stand up to British and Hessian troops at Harlem Heights and had heard of their good performance at White Plains; he had convinced himself that American troops, if properly supplied and led, could "bid defiance to the world." He also felt he had good strategic reasons to hold Fort Washington. He made his case to Washington on November 9:

> The passing of the Ships up the River is, to be sure, full proof of the insufficiency of the Obstructions in the River to stop the Ships from going up but that Garrison [at Ft. Washington] employs double the number of men to Invest it, that we have to Occupy it. They [the British] must keep troops at Kings Bridge to prevent a communication with the Country, and they dare not leave a very small number for fear our people should attack them. Upon the whole I cannot help thinking the Garrison is of advantage, and I cannot conceive the Garrison to be in any great danger. The men can be brought off at any time, but the stores may not be so easily removd. . . . Our giving it up will open a free communication with the Country by way of Kings bridge, that must be a great advantage to them and injury to us.[18]

Greene was arguing that Fort Washington was tying down thousands of British and Hessian troops who would otherwise be available to invade New Jersey. He warned that another retreat would be devastating to morale—a strange statement, since he was otherwise insistent that the garrison's morale was excellent. He reported to Hancock a few days later that "I expect General How will attempt to possess himself of Mount Washington but very much doubt whether he'll succeed in the attempt. Our Troops are much fatigued with the Amazeing duty, but are generally in good Spirits." Greene's weary commander, fearful of the risks but tired of running and itching for another fight— in which American troops would face the enemy from prepared positions— acquiesced. It is another indication of how much Washington trusted Greene.[19]

Uncertain of the direction of Howe's next move, Washington divided his "Grand Army" into four parts. The largest portion, seven thousand troops, would remain under General Charles Lee east of the Hudson to protect against a move into New England. General William Heath would take three thousand and guard the Hudson highlands near Peekskill. Washington, with the smallest portion (two thousand or so) would cross the Hudson into New Jersey to meet expected reinforcements from there and Pennsylvania. Greene commanded the fourth division, which was partitioned by the Hudson: some men with Greene at Fort Lee and the garrison under Magaw at Fort Washington, by then reinforced to more than two thousand. By November 13 Washington had joined Greene at Fort Lee, and two days of consultations followed. Greene, supported by Magaw, was insistent that the fort could be held and at the same time that evacuating the troops across the Hudson was feasible. As a result Washington convinced himself that Howe would be tied down by dealing with the fort. Still uneasy, however, Washington left Fort Lee on November 15 for Hackensack, New Jersey, to check on the awaited reinforcements. The same day British forces closed the ring around Fort Washington and then demanded the fort's surrender. Magaw notified Greene: "We are determined to defend the post or die." Greene informed his chief that he had ordered Magaw "to defend the place until he hears from me" and concluded by declaring he was heading "to the Island" for a look.[20]

This news brought Washington hurrying back to Fort Lee. Was there any chance that the garrison could be evacuated? He got into a boat and began to cross the Hudson, only to encounter another boat returning from New York with Greene and General Israel Putnam, "who were just returning from thence, and informed me that the Troops were in high Spirits and would make a good Defence." It was too late at night to do anything more; the party returned to New Jersey. The following morning, November 16, they set out again across the Hudson to confer with Magaw. Greene described to Henry Knox what happened next:

Just at the moment we stept on board the Boat the Enemy made their appearance on the Hill where the Monday action was, and began a severe Cannonade with several field pieces. Our Guards soon fled, the Enemy advanced up to the second lines. This was done while we were crossing the River and geting upon the Hill. The Enemy made several marches to the right and to the left, I suppose to reconnoiter the fortifications and lines.

There we all stood in a very awkward situation; as the disposition was made and the Enemy advancing we durst not attempt to make any new disposition—indeed we saw nothing amiss. We all urged his Excellency to come off. I offerd to stay. General Putnam did the same and so did General Mercer, but his Excellency thought it best for us all to come off together, which we did about half an hour before the Enemy surrounded the fort.[21]

This is a truly amazing scene: a party of American generals (including two major generals and the commander in chief) crossing and recrossing the Hudson without molestation by the British Navy and then observing from a short distance the beginning of the end of Fort Washington. Even then the leadership of the American forces could not see the predicament into which their indecision had placed a fort and 2,900 men. The British swept the Americans from their outworks into the overcrowded fort. Greene continued: "After the Troops retreated in the fort very few Guns was fird. The Enemy approacht within small arm fire of the lines and sent in a flagg, and the Garrison capitulated in an hour." A bit disingenuously, Greene told Knox he had been "afraid of the fort," something he had apparently neglected to tell Washington. "The Redout you and I advised to was not done, or little or nothing done to it. Had that been compleat I think the Garrison might have defended themselves a long while or been brought off," Greene wrote. He spoke the truth, however, when he told his friend Knox: "I feel mad, vext, sick and sorry. . . . This is a most terrible Event. Its consequences are justly to be dreaded." The American forces lost 2,870 men captured at Fort Washington; 54 had died defending it.[22]

Washington was, if anything, even more "vext" than Greene; nevertheless his after-action report to Hancock was calm and evenhanded, carefully pointing out that Greene had decided to reinforce the fort after Washington had "directed him to govern himself by Circumstances" and to defend or evacuate it "as he should think best." He ended his letter almost languidly, "The Loss of such a Number of Officers and Men . . . will I fear be severely felt." But the loss of "Arms and Accoutrements" (including 146 precious cannon) was even worse. More troops were needed and soon. The drastic and disastrous turn of events shattered Washington, but he had the presence of mind to order the immediate abandonment of the now useless Fort Lee. As his troops began the epic retreat through New Jersey, Washington tried to explain what had gone wrong to his brother Augustine: "I did not care to give an absolute Order for withdrawing the Garrison till I could get round and see the Situation of things and then it became too late as the Fort was Invested. I had given it, upon the passing of the last Ships, as my opinion to Genl. Greene under whose care it was, that it would be best to evacuate the place; but, as the order was discretionary, and his opinion differed from mine, it unhappyly was delayd too long, to my great grief."[23]

Washington's error had been to defer to the judgment of a loyal subordinate who was not in a position to know the facts on the ground; Greene's error had been identical, yielding to the misplaced zeal of a young officer, Magaw, who could not see the strategic forest for the tactical trees and did not understand that the risk of battle or siege defending an isolated outpost with the Hudson River at his back (a river open to enemy vessels) outweighed any short-term advantage that might be gained from defending it. This lays bare the fatal flaw of the American command structure: there really was not one. Ultimately no one was responsible for the debacle at Fort Washington because everyone was. Washington felt constrained to exercise a collective leadership over his generals, deferring to their wishes by majority vote. Washington clearly disagreed with the decision to hold the fort, but he felt that he could not overrule his generals. Greene also hesitated to overrule Magaw (and ignored Putnam, Magaw's actual superior).

In the end this affair revealed to Washington and Greene that a clear chain of command was vital. Both men learned from their errors. It might be said that American egalitarianism (at least among the officer corps) died on the ramparts of Fort Washington. From then on, both Washington and Greene strove for the creation of a European-style professional army with established and understood ranks and clear lines of authority. It is no accident that within a month Greene was pressing Congress to grant Washington near-dictatorial powers. These powers were intended not merely to free Washington to direct the overall war effort and acquire needed supplies; they would also signal to Washington's junior officers that his orders were to be carried out. He would *consult* his generals; the final *decision* would rest with him. All did not go smoothly; Washington faced insubordination from Charles Lee, and in South Carolina Greene was later frustrated by General Thomas Sumter's independence; but in the future neither man allowed subordinates to make decisions for them.

Chastened by the Fort Washington disaster, Greene wasted little time getting on with the job at hand. He personally oversaw the evacuation of Fort Lee on November 20, even as General Charles, Lord Cornwallis, landed five thousand troops a mere five miles north of the fort, at the one place Greene had neglected to post guards. As the British struggled up to the palisades, Greene sent for Washington, who was in Hackensack six miles away. They conferred on evacuating Fort Lee, and this time Greene was careful to defer to his superior's

wishes. After receiving Washington's orders to evacuate the fort, Greene supervised the removal of what stores the men could carry on their backs. They
headed toward New Bridge over the Hackensack River, Washington in the lead.
The race to the Delaware River had begun.[24]

The Americans were still disposed in three divisions: Washington with
about 5,400, including Greene's men withdrawing from Fort Lee; Heath at
Peekskill with another 3,200 effectives; Lee at North Castle with about 5,500.
With the divisions widely scattered, no one division was in position to help the
others. The army had lost most of its tents and supplies with the fall of the
Hudson forts. Winter was far advanced at the end of November, and the men
lacked clothing. It is no surprise that desertions soared, to a rate averaging
20–25 percent. Greene observed that by the time Washington's force reached
New Brunswick on November 29, "we had not 3000 men, a very pitiful army to
trust the Liberties of America upon." Greene described the breakneck pace of
the retreat in a letter to Governor Nicholas Cooke of Rhode Island, written
from Trenton on December 4: "We retreated to Hakensack; from Hakensack
to Equacanock [Aquacknock]; from Equacanock to Newark; from Newark to
Brunswick; from Brunswick to this place. Here we are endeavoring to collect an
efficient force to give the Enemy battle or at least to stop their progress." Nevertheless Greene was "in hopes the General will give orders to advance upon the
Enemy tomorrow." Perhaps this was just bravado, and perhaps this was one of
the reasons Washington liked having the Rhode Island bantam around. Greene
had lost Fort Washington because of overconfidence more than anything else;
but at a time like this, any confidence was a rare commodity.[25]

On December 21, 1776, after the army had crossed the Delaware to take
refuge in Pennsylvania, Greene wrote to Congress of the army's dire straits.
"Altho I am far from thinking the American Cause desperate, yet I conceive it
to be in a critical situation." He recited the same doleful litany as his chief: the
British in possession of New Jersey and threatening Philadelphia; 1776 enlistments expiring within days with "very few enlisted upon the New Establishment"; the public rapidly losing faith in the cause and withholding desperately
needed supplies from the ragtag army, refusing in most cases to accept the
worthless Continental paper money. Many officers were unhappy with their
rank and pay. Greene proposed a solution to these troubles forthrightly because
what he asked was not for himself but for his commander, his cause, and his
country:

> Effectually to remedy those Evils and oppose the Enemy, to put the Recruit-
> ing Service in a favorable Train, to establish the Artillery and [munitions
> factory] upon a proper footing, to check the disaffected, and call out Assis-
> tance, to give a Currency to the Continental Money and form the necessary

Magazines, greater powers must be lodged in the Hands of the General [Washington] than he has ever yet exercised. It is impossible in his present Situation and the short Time he has to prepare for the ensuing Campaign for him to be in Readiness so early as General Howe will take the Field unless you delegate to him full Power to take such Measures as he may find necessary to promote the Establishment of the New Army. Time will not admit nor Circumstance allow of a Reference to Congress.

Greene anticipated objections by pointing out that Congress could confirm or overrule any of the commander in chief's actions after the fact. Washington should be permitted to appoint any officers he saw fit to serve "at large," that is without reference to state ties. "This is no Time to be particular about Proportions or attentive to Oeconomy; the Measure of our Force should be the Extent of our Funds." Confronted by the finest military machine on earth, the American political establishment must temporarily yield to the needs of the military called forth to defend it. "I am no advocate for the Extension of Military Power, neither would I advise it at present but from the fullest Conviction of its being absolutely necessary." Congress need not fear the advent of a new Caesar or Cromwell: "I can assure you that the General will not exceed his Powers altho' he may sacrifice the Cause. There never was a man that might be more safely trusted nor a Time when there was a louder Call."[26]

Receiving this letter on December 26, Congress resolved: "That General Washington shall be, and he is hereby, vested with full, ample, and complete powers" for six months to raise troops, to promote and appoint officers, to establish magazines, and "to take, wherever he may be, whatever he may want for the use of the army, if the inhabitants will not sell it, allowing a reasonable price for the same; to arrest and confine persons who refuse to take the continental currency, or are otherwise disaffected to the American cause; and return to the states of which they are citizens, their names, and the nature of their offences, together with the witnesses to prove them." Congress had used Greene's letter to enumerate Washington's new powers. For the only time in its history, the government of the United States established a temporary military dictatorship; Nathanael Greene had convinced it to do so.[27]

The same day that Congress granted Washington his unique authority, American forces, having recrossed the icy Delaware River, attacked a Hessian outpost at Trenton, New Jersey. As with Harlem Heights, Greene's role in the Battle of Trenton must be surmised from the writings of others. The only account he left was in a letter to his wife a few days after the action: "Before this reaches you doubtless you will hear of the Attack upon this place [Trenton]. We crost the River Delaware at McKonkees Ferry Eight miles above this place on the 25 of this instant and attackt the Town by Storm in the morning. It raind, haild and snowd and was a violent Storm. The Storm of nature and the Storm of the Town exhibited a Scene that fild the mind during the action with passions easier conceivd than describd. The Action lasted about three quarters of an hour. We kild, wounded and took Prisoners of the Enimy between Eleven and twelve hundred. Our Troops behavd with great Spirit. General Sullivan commanded the right Wing of the army and I the left."[28]

Greene further proved himself at Princeton in January 1777 and played an important role in the redeployment to winter quarters at Morristown, New Jersey. But more tests awaited him. In the meantime his "northern apprenticeship" had taught him several valuable lessons.

First he saw in operation the logistical maxims of Frederick the Great that he had read about for several years. The army survived the race across New Jersey in 1776 thanks to food and fodder that he placed along the route beforehand. Without those stores the American army would probably have disintegrated before it reached the Delaware. This same supply line proved useful again when the army invaded New Jersey at the end of the year. The march for Princeton in the first days of 1777 was not just a tactical stroke; it was also a strategic change of front, a shift of supply line from Philadelphia to Morristown, New Jersey, that foreshadowed the similar moves of General U. S. Grant around Vicksburg more than eighty years later. The tables had been turned. In autumn 1776 Howe threatened Washington's line of communications to Philadelphia. A few weeks later, Washington threatened Howe's line of communications to New York. Greene had perceived that control of the supply route through northern New Jersey was key, and he had acted on it. Washington noticed Greene's work here and saw to it that Greene was named army quartermaster general just over a year later. Greene went on to position himself in a similar manner in 1780–81; Daniel Morgan's victory at Cowpens threatened Cornwallis's supply line through Camden to Charleston; Guilford Courthouse forced Cornwallis to abandon this supply line for one in Virginia based on Yorktown, leaving South Carolina wide open for Greene to isolate British garrisons left behind.

Second Greene observed firsthand in New Jersey the utility of a well-conducted withdrawal. The American withdrawal across New Jersey in 1776 prevented the destruction of the patriot forces and preserved a remnant to fight at Trenton and Princeton.[29] Washington was determined to avoid sacrificing the army to protect high-value political assets such as New York and Philadelphia. The American strategy for the remainder of the war was established: withdraw before superior British forces, look for opportunities to strike the enemy, and above all never forget that the American army *was* the Revolution. Although useful as supply centers, cities and towns were also traps. They tied armies down and seduced commanders into ceding the initiative to a more mobile enemy. The following year Washington abandoned Philadelphia, the patriot "capital," for Valley Forge, Pennsylvania, a rural strongpoint that protected the army but was easy to leave when circumstances permitted. Conversely the British captured Philadelphia in September 1777 and barely moved until evacuating it the following year, only to hunker down in New York once more. Greene learned that an army's greatest asset was not firepower but mobility. A commander must keep his army ready to move at short notice, both to attack and to withdraw. Outnumbered and outgunned, the Americans had to approach war as if it were fencing, not wrestling. Greene put this axiom to use in the Carolinas, refusing to defend any strongpoint or urban center and abandoning the siege of Ninety Six when a relief force approached it; capturing the fort would be of little value if he lost his army (or part of it) in the process.

Third Greene learned that a competently led militia was a valuable asset. Greene was no fan of militia and shared Washington's low opinion of their reliability. But here is how Greene described the Philadelphia Associators, a militia regiment raised by John Cadwalader: "Great credit is due to the Philadelphia militia; their behaviour at Trenton in the cannonade, and at Princeton was brave, firm and manly; they were broken at first in the action at Princeton, but soon formed in the face of grapeshot, and pushed on with a spirit that would do honor to veterans, besides which they have borne a winter's campaign with a soldier like patience. General Cadwalader is a brave and gallant officer."[30] Greene saw that, with patience and understanding, most of all with appreciation of what such adjunct troops could be asked to do (were willing to do), under an officer who knew and understood them (a man such as Cadwalader, Daniel Morgan, or Francis Marion), militiamen were a valuable weapon in the American arsenal. They later proved themselves at Cowpens, performed adequately at Guilford Courthouse, and harassed the British supply lines in both Carolinas.

That summer and fall, Howe launched his long-awaited Philadelphia campaign, sailing into Chesapeake Bay and landing an expeditionary force at Head of Elk, Maryland. Washington maneuvered swiftly to meet him along the Schuylkill River west of Philadelphia. The first clash came at Brandywine Creek on September 11, 1777. Across this field Cornwallis and Greene, later the two antagonists of the southern campaign of 1780–81, met in battle for the first time. Greene was posted at Chadd's Ford, along the direct route from Wilmington, Delaware, to Chester and Philadelphia, at the left wing of the American position. Howe successfully turned the American right flank and Washington took Greene with him to orchestrate an orderly withdrawal from potential disaster. Almost a year later, Greene described what he had experienced and nonchalantly declared that "I think both the general [Washington] and the public were as much indebted to me for saving the army from ruin as they have ever been to any one officer in the course of the war; but I was never mentioned upon the occasion."[31]

The British were able to slip into Philadelphia, but Washington soon saw a golden opportunity to retrieve the situation. Howe had encamped outside Philadelphia at Germantown without entrenching; obviously he considered an American attack so soon after their drubbing at Brandywine to be highly unlikely. Washington used the early morning fog to hide his army's movement. Unfortunately Germantown was a favorable defensive position, and the fog worked as much against the Americans as for them. Washington's carefully timed operation began to come apart almost immediately. The four columns set out at dusk on October 3, but it was well past dawn the following morning before they reached their jumping-off points. After a furious assault, the attack ultimately failed, and Greene prudently ordered a retreat. From Washington down to many of the troops, the battle was perceived as a near win. Greene himself assured the men that "the Enemy suffer'd very severely." It may have seemed that way, but in fact the Americans came off worse: 152 killed, 521 wounded, and some 400 captured or missing, while British losses totaled about half that: 537 killed and wounded, 14 captured.[32]

Another casualty was the military reputations of both Washington and Greene. Placed beside the recent triumph of Horatio Gates and Benedict Arnold at Saratoga, New York, the twin failures at Brandywine and Germantown made Washington and Greene appear especially inept. Greene began to hear criticism that he had "shewed a want of activity in carrying the troops on to action, a want of judgment in the disposition, or a want of spirit in the action or retreat." Four years later the talk about him still rankled: "At Germantown, I was evidently degraced, altho I think if ever I merited anything it was for my exertions on that day. . . . But I never murmured or complained, notwithstanding I was held in indignation for faults and misfortunes I had no direction of."[33] Washington would have agreed, and the two men seemed to draw even closer together as the army withdrew into its winter camp at Valley Forge that December. The bond of mutual trust deepened over the coming months as Washington pressed Congress to appoint Greene quartermaster general.

Midway through his two and a half year tour of duty as quartermaster general of Washington's army, Greene wrote to his chief: "No body ever heard of a quarter Master in History as such or in relateing any brilliant Action." A later commander, Erwin Rommel, took a different view. He wrote: "The first essential condition for an Army to be able to stand the strain of battle [is an] adequate stock of weapons, petrol, ammunition. In fact, the battle is fought and decided by the quartermasters."[34] Why was Greene named quartermaster general? Because by 1778 Greene had become Washington's most trusted subordinate; the army's supply situation was catastrophic, revealed by the destitution of the troops in their camps at Valley Forge; and finally Greene was no stranger to logistics.

By the time the army encamped at Valley Forge in the winter of 1777–78, the supply arrangements had all but broken down. Blame began to settle on Quartermaster General Thomas Mifflin, who (except for a brief period in late 1776) had been in this post since the beginning of the war, and even more so on Commissary General Jonathan Trumbull. According to the most authoritative study of the Quartermaster Department, "The best [Trumbull] could do was to attempt to provide the soldiers with sufficient cooked rations to maintain 4 days' supply on hand." Washington would have noted that Greene had done more than this the year before, while preparing to defend Fort Washington. On December 23, 1777, Washington wrote to Congress, requesting that two or three members of the Board of War visit the camp to see the situation for themselves and formulate "the most perfect plan that can be devised for correcting all abuses." Within a month Francis Dana, Joseph Reed, and Nathanael Folsom arrived and began to investigate the logistics nightmare.[35]

By the end of January 1778, the committee informed Congress that "the Appointment of a Q[uarte]r Master Gen[era]l is a Matter of great Importance and immediate Necessity." Noting in another letter to Congress that the quartermaster general was the "great Wheel in the Machine," a person who had to be scrupulously honest and competent, they reported that a "Character has presented itself, which in a great Degree meets our Judgment and Wishes; we have opened the Subject to him, and it is now under his Consideration." The "Character" was Nathanael Greene. But Greene was reluctant; he had had a small business before the war and felt that "this large field of Business" was beyond his capability. But he also feared being shifted from the line to a staff position. He liked being a combat general and did not wish to relinquish his position fighting at Washington's right hand. If he accepted the appointment, he would be "taken out of the line of splendor." Only when it was agreed that he would retain his line commission, that he would have the aid of two men he respected, Charles Pettit and John Cox, as assistant quartermasters general, and that they would share a one percent commission on all army purchases, did Greene relent. In the end, however, it was not position, personnel, or pay that persuaded Greene to accept the post but his dedication to the patriot cause, his belief that the army had to survive, and Washington's insistence that Greene was the only man who could do the job. The committee reported to Congress: "Nothing but a thorough Conviction of the absolute necessity of straining every Nerve in the Service, could have brought these Gentlemen into Office upon any Terms." Congress appointed Greene quartermaster general on March 2, 1778. It was a wise choice. According to the most renowned student of this topic, of the four quartermasters general (Mifflin, Stephen Moylan, Greene, and Timothy Pickering), "Greene was the most effective."[36]

Greene assumed his new duties on March 23, 1778. The previous May, Mifflin had reorganized the Quartermaster Department with separate wagon and forage departments reporting to the quartermaster general. By the time Greene took over, these posts were filled capably by James Thompson and Colonel Clement Biddle. Procuring wagons and forage constituted the greatest challenges Greene and the army faced during the Revolutionary War; the editors of Greene's papers state that "there was a never-ending shortage of all the components of land transport: carts, wagons, sleighs, sledges, oxen, horses, harness, packsaddles, wagoners, carters, and forage." The situation was so dire that the Camp Committee wrote to inform Congress on February 12 that "almost every species of camp transportation is now performed by men, who without a murmur, patiently yoke themselves to little carriages of their own making, or load their wood and provisions on their backs."[37]

Greene threw himself vigorously at the problem. Supplies had to be brought to the camp at Valley Forge. Spring was coming and with it another campaign season. Indications were that the British were preparing to leave Philadelphia; if they left by land, Washington wanted to pursue. He urged Greene to "strain every nerve" to assemble the necessary supplies and transport. Greene wrote Washington that he had "given extensive Orders, almost without Limitation, for the Purchase" of horses and tents. He wrote to Henry Laurens, president of Congress, requesting money to hire more wagoners, who were "not to be got under Ten Pounds per Month. This is a most extravagant Demand, but Necessity will oblige us to comply with it; for that appears to be the current Price given for private Business." The price was well worth it, Greene insisted: "Good Waggoners will be a valuable Acquisition." He asked Washington's help in engaging wagoners from Virginia, telling him "time is so short." He ordered his deputy quartermaster at Head of Elk, Maryland, to hire, purchase, or impress wagons to carry supplies from there to Valley Forge; he requested that Pennsylvania exempt from militia fines any person employed by the army as a wagoner; he drew up new procedures for hiring wagons and teams; and he arranged for supplies to travel on the Schuylkill River to reduce the need for animals to draw them. He urged Washington to enlist wagoners for the duration of the war. So successful were Greene's efforts that Washington reported to Congress that summer that "by his conduct and industry [the Quartermaster Department] has undergone a very happy change, and such as enabled us, with great facility, to make a sudden move with the whole Army and baggage from Valley Forge in pursuit of the Enemy [to Monmouth, New Jersey] and to perform a march to this place [White Plains, New York]." Greene participated in the Battle of Monmouth, which was a draw, but again American troops acquitted themselves well.[38]

"Forage was to the revolutionary army what oil is to the twentieth-century army," wrote the editors of Greene's papers. Army historian Erna Risch agreed, declaring that "the heart of the transportation problem was forage supply." Greene was fortunate in having Clement Biddle as commissary general of forage. Biddle developed a general plan for a chain of forage depots along the army's line of operations from the Hudson highlands through New Jersey to Head of Elk on the Chesapeake. He submitted this plan to Greene, who immediately approved and augmented it, calling for two hundred thousand bushels of grain "and as much Hay as can be bought" at each of three magazines, on the Delaware, the Schuylkill and at Head of Elk; one hundred thousand bushels each on lines from the Susquehanna to the Schuylkill and from the Delaware to the Hudson River; and forty thousand bushels at Trenton. Washington quickly approved this setup, and Biddle got to work. It was an improvised forage-supply system, but it was vastly superior to having no system at all.[39]

Food, supplies, horses, wagons, and forage—the army needed them all quickly, however and wherever they could be found. Greene was forced to rely on hired purchasing agents of dubious reliability: "Gentlemen skilled in mercantile Business to make Purchases to whom I have not offered a Deputation in the Quarter Masters Line." They also worked on commissions, percentages of the purchase price of the commodities they bought. The declining value of the Continental dollar, the increasing resort to credit, the resulting inflation, and the skyrocketing prices of goods in short supply and high demand, all contributed to the explosion of expenditure in the Quartermaster and Commissary Departments. Supply had cost the United States some $5.4 million in 1776; it had nearly doubled the following year to more than $9.2 million; by 1778 it had quadrupled to more than $37 million. Congress grew increasingly alarmed and, goaded by Mifflin and other critics, blamed Greene, suspecting him and his aides of inflating purchases to turn a profit. Stung by these insinuations, Greene fumed to Washington that "I am more and more convinced there is measures taken to render the business of the quarter masters Department odious in the Eyes of the people, and if I have not some satisfaction from the Committee of Congress respecting the matter, I shall beg leave to quit the Department. I think I shall leave it upon as good a footing as is possible to put it under the present difficulties."[40]

Greene soldiered on, but he was still troubled by Congress's refusal to protect him and his department from lawsuits stemming from debts contracted by purchasing agents. Shocked by a report that 1779 supply expenses would exceed $200 million, Congress resolved that the states launch investigations into the financial dealings of everyone in the Quartermaster's and Commissary's Departments. Greene reacted by writing to his trusted deputy Charles Pettit: "It is my full determination to resign as soon as I can get out of the business without exposing myself to ruin or disgrace."[41]

In September Congress ordered that no new bills of credit be issued for any reason, hoping to halt the hyperinflation of Continental currency and gain some control of the budget. The result was chaos. Without money, no forage, transport, or food could be purchased, even on credit. Congress suggested the army ask the states for relief; the states refused. Forage officers were sued. Impressment was forbidden by state authorities, and the army's animals starved. Greene wrote to another deputy, John Cox, "What to do or which way to turn I know not. . . . We can no more support the army without cash, than the Israelites could make bricks without straw. The impolicy of Pharoh brought death upon the first born in Egypt, and this of the Congress will have the same effect upon themselves." Despairing, Greene wrote to Congress what the editors of his papers call a "conditional resignation":

> It has been my wish, for a long time, to relinquish the office of Quarter Master General. . . . I am desirous of returning to the line of the Army. . . . [T]he principal source of all our difficulties, is the state of our Money: the depreciation of which locks up almost every species of supplies, deprives us of the opportunities of making contracts, or of gaining credit, and obliges us to employ innumerable Agents to collect from the People, what they would be glad to furnish, was the representative of property upon a more stable footing. . . .
>
> In this distressing situation, without Money, and without credit— necessity obliges me to give Congress this information, and to ask their advice, what are we to do?[42]

Congress ignored him and continued to stall. The delegates seem to have been equally stymied by the whole situation. That winter of 1779–80 at Morristown was the worst of the war. As the summer of 1780 arrived, Washington intended to launch an attack against British-occupied New York City, and Greene had still heard no reply to his repeated requests to resign. Instead Congress sent a committee to headquarters to investigate the Quartermaster Department; they soon perceived Greene's difficulties and wrote him a gratifying letter that concluded: "In Justice to you Sir we Embrace this Occasion to declare that after having Examined your arrangement of the Quarter Master Generals department, we are Convinced the measures you have adopted and the principles on which those measures were founded, were well calculated to promote *service* whilst they fully evinced your attention to the public interest."

This persuaded Greene that a "cabal" at Congress was determined to blame him for the supply problems.[43]

Greene's last straw was a congressional plan to reorganize the Quartermaster Department, passed on July 15, 1780. It proposed a drastic reduction of personnel and other measures designed to trim costs and increase accountability. Among other things, commissions for deputy quartermasters were to be replaced by salaries. Greene feared he would lose Cox and Pettit, his trusted assistants. In a letter to the president of Congress, Samuel Huntington, Greene again protested Congress's interference with his administration of the department, its lack of confidence in him, and above all its refusal to provide the money needed to supply the army. "Systems without Agents are useless things, and the probability of getting one should be taken into consideration in framing the other," he wrote. "Administration seem to think it far less important to the public Interest to have this department well filled and properly arranged than it really is, and as they will find by future experience." The delegates bristled at being called "Administration," a term customarily reserved for the king's ministers. Congress had had enough of Greene and accepted his resignation with some anger. But this mood soon dissipated as news arrived that General Gates had been badly defeated at Camden, South Carolina, and Washington urged that Greene be appointed commander of the Southern Department. Greene's two-and-a-half-year ordeal as quartermaster general was over.[44]

Greene was relieved to be returning to the "line of splendor," and he was correct in saying that quartermasters were never remembered for glorious actions. Though Greene would perhaps not have perceived it, however, as quartermaster general he had kept Washington's army in the field despite great difficulties and made the winning of American independence possible. Most gratifying to Greene was the appraisal of George Washington, who wrote: "When you were prevailed on to undertake the Office in March 1778 it was in great disorder and confusion and by extraordinary exertions You so arranged it, as to enable the Army to take the Field the moment it was necessary, and to move with rapidity after the Enemy when they left Philadelphia. From that period to the present time, your exertions have been equally great, have appeared to me to be the result of system and to have been well calculated to promote the interest and honor of your Country. And in fine I cannot but add, that the States have had in you, in my opinion, an able, upright and diligent Servant."[45]

Greene's "northern apprenticeship" equipped him well to conduct the decisive American campaign of the war: the operations in the Carolinas and Georgia in 1780–82. The key to that triumph was how Greene kept his army fed and cavalry foraged while denying provisions to his British opponents. He gathered every boat in central North Carolina to assist his army's river-hopping withdrawal to the Dan, denied them to Cornwallis, and had them on hand to facilitate his army's advance to Guilford Courthouse. With Virginia at his back, his men were well-provisioned; Cornwallis's men were on reduced rations and exhausted.

Greene also successfully managed and employed a colorful cast of prickly personalities and expansive egos—such as "Mad Anthony" Wayne, Thomas Sumter, Francis Marion, Daniel Morgan, and "Light-Horse Harry" Lee—in a manner that would have made Dwight D. Eisenhower proud. Greene corresponded with, informed, wheedled, cajoled, and won the support of successive governors and legislatures of North Carolina, South Carolina, and Georgia. He kept Washington and Congress informed of his movements, plans, and actions. He was thus a politically savvy general, as well as an effective administrator (evoking yet another Second World War figure, George C. Marshall).

One could debate whether Nathanael Greene was a great (or even good) battlefield commander, but what is undeniable is that no other American commander worked so hard to create the preconditions for battlefield victory (or at least survival, which in the American context was just as good): food, clothing, forage, arms, ammunition, horses, transport, and political support (as well as the pay this made possible). In this he succeeded brilliantly and saved the American Revolution. He might have dismissed these logistical tasks as a "merchandise of small Wares," but in the end the business proved profitable indeed.

NOTES

1. Greene's library contained more than two hundred books, including works on law, history, philosophy, and religion as well as military history and theory. See Theodore Thayer, "Revolutionary War Strategist," in *George Washington's Generals and Opponents: Their Exploits and Leadership*, edited by George A. Billias (New York: Da Capo, 1994), 110, 121. This essay draws heavily on the documents published in *The Papers of General Nathanael Greene*, edited by Richard K. Showman, Dennis R. Conrad, and Roger N. Parks, 13 vols. (Chapel Hill: University of North Carolina Press, 1976–2005).

2. Worthington C. Ford et al., eds., *Journals of the Continental Congress*, 34 vols. (Washington, D.C.: U.S. Government Printing Office, 1904–37), 2:91 (cited hereafter as *JCC*). For Greene's June 22 appointment as brigadier general of the Continental army, see 2:103. In order of seniority the other seven brigadier generals were Seth Pomeroy, Richard Montgomery, David Wooster, William Heath, Joseph Spencer, John Thomas, and John Sullivan. Congress selected four major generals to serve as senior commanders under Washington: Artemas Ward, Charles Lee, Philip Schuyler, and Israel Putnam. Horatio Gates was appointed adjutant general. Robert K. Wright Jr., *The Continental Army* (Washington, D.C.: U.S. Army Center for Military History, 1989), 25–28.

3. Greene, quoted in George Washington Greene, *The Life of Nathanael Greene, Major-General in the Army of the Revolution*, 3 vols.: vol. 1 (New York: Putnam, 1867); vols. 2 and 3 (New York: Hurd & Houghton, 1871), 1:101, 126.

4. Greene to George Washington, July 25, 1776, George Washington general orders, July 26, 1776; Greene to Washington, July 26, 1776, and August 15, 1776; *The Papers of General Nathanael Greene*, 1:263, 270, 271, 287–88; Major William Livingston to Washington, August 17, 1776; Lieutenant William Blodget to Washington, August 18, 1776; Washington general orders, August 20, 1776; Washington to John Hancock, August 23, 1776, in *The Papers of George Washington: Revolutionary War Series*, edited by Philander D. Chase et al., 20 vols. (Charlottesville: University Press of Virginia, 1985–2010), 6:54, 59, 89, 111 (cited hereafter as *PGW*).

5. Henry Knox to John Adams, September 25, 1776, quoted in Theodore Thayer, *Nathanael Greene: Strategist of the Revolution* (New York: Twayne, 1960), 103. Christopher Ward calls Greene's replacement "unfortunate" as he was "a much abler general officer" than Sullivan. Matters were made worse by placing Israel Putnam over Sullivan. Putnam also was ignorant of the terrain and "was for other reasons totally unfit" to command. See Christopher Ward, *The War of the Revolution*, edited by John Richard Alden, vol. 1 (New York: Macmillan, 1952), 213. Colonel Daniel Morgan of Virginia had Greene moved to New York and "watched over him with the strictest attention" until he recovered. See *The Papers of General Nathanael Greene*, 1:292n.

6. *The Papers of General Nathanael Greene*, 1:292–93n. See also Greene's comment in his letter to Nicholas Cooke, September 17, 1776, ibid., 1:300.

7. Greene to Jacob Greene, August 30, 1776, ibid., 1:291, and accompanying notes, 292–93.

8. Greene to Nicholas Cooke, September 17, 1776, ibid., 1:300–301. For details on Kip's Bay, see Ward, *The War of the Revolution*, 1:238–45.

9. On Harlem Heights, see Ward, *The War of the Revolution*, 1:246–51, and *The Papers of General Nathanael Greene*, 1:301–2n2; Greene to Nicholas Cooke, September 17, 1776, Greene to William Ellery(?), October 4, 1776, ibid., 1:300, 307; Greene to Colonel Henry Lee, February 18, 1782, ibid., 10:379. See also George Washington Greene, *Life of Nathanael Greene*, 1:216–17.

10. Greene to Jacob Greene(?), September 28, October 3, 1776, *The Papers of General Nathanael Greene*, 1:303–5. Greene repeated his high opinion of American troops in the letter to William Ellery (?) cited above, stating that well-led and disciplined and trained "America[n troops] might bid Defiance to the whole World." Greene to William Ellery (?), October 4, 1776, ibid., 1:307.

11. The other divisions were commanded by Charles Lee (returned from a successful defense of Charleston), Heath, Sullivan (exchanged for a British general), Putnam, Spencer, and Lincoln. Ward, *The War of the Revolution*, 1:256, 260; George Washington Greene, *Life of Nathanael Greene*, 1:217–18; John Adlum, *Memoirs of the Life of John Adlum in the Revolutionary War*, edited by Howard H. Peckham, quoted in *The Papers of General Nathanael Greene*, 1:304–5n. For a breakdown of the troops Greene commanded at Fort Lee, see "A Return of the Forces Encamped on the Jersey Shore, under the command of Major General Greene," in Peter Force, ed., *American Archives*, 5th ser., 2:1250, http://dig.lib.niu.edu/amarch/ (accessed October 19, 2011), which gives a total rank and file (excluding militia) of 2,944. See also Greene to George Washington, October 31, 1776, *The Papers of General Nathanael Greene*, 1:329.

12. Council of war, October 16, 1776, *PGW,* 6:576; Magaw's force numbered in Lieutenant Colonel Robert Hanson Harrison (George Washington aide) to John Hancock, October 25, 1776, *PGW,* 7:27; Greene to Rhode Island governor Nicholas Cooke, October 11, 1776, *The Papers of General Nathanael Greene,* 1:314, 315–16n; Ward, *The War of the Revolution,* 1:256. Washington wrote to an unnamed officer on October 21: "Inform Col. Magaw that I shall depend upon his holding the Post at Mt Washington as long as a good Officer ought to do. . . . Magaw must take care to have a Sufficient Stock of Provisions & Water laid in for the Men he has for the Garrison, and a vigilant watch must be kept. If Colo. Magaw & Genl Green can devise any Plan to get the Boards remov'd to the Jerseys it woud be doing a good thing." *PGW,* 7:3.

13. Greene to John Hancock, October 20, 1776; Board of War to Greene, October 22, 1776; Greene to George Washington, October 24, 1776; Greene to [Quartermaster General Thomas Mifflin], October 27, 1776 (actually a letter to Washington; see note at *PGW,* 7:39); Greene to Washington, October 29, 1776; *The Papers of General Nathanael Greene,* 1:318–23, 326–27, 328n1. Unfortunately the British knew of these arrangements as soon as Washington did; see 328n2. Washington approved Greene's arrangements. Colonel Robert H. Harrison to Greene, November 3, 1776, *The Papers of General Nathanael Greene,* 1:330–31. See also editor's note, ibid., 1:331.

14. Greene to John Adams, March 3, 1777, *The Papers of General Nathanael Greene,* 2:29; George Washington to John Hancock, November 6, 1776, *PGW,* 7:96–97.

15. On the condition of Fort Washington and Graydon's description, see Ward, *The War of the Revolution,* 268–69; Greene to George Washington, October 31, 1776, *The Papers of General Nathanael Greene,* 1:328.

16. Greene to George Washington, October 31, 1776, *The Papers of General Nathanael Greene,* 1:328–29, 355–56. See also Edward F. De Lancey, *The Capture of Mount Washington, November 16th, 1776, the Result of Treason* (New York, 1877), 6–9, http://www.archive.org/details/capturemtwashoodelarich (accessed August 23, 2011); Colonel Robert H. Harrison to Greene, November 5, 1776, *The Papers of General Nathanael Greene,* 1:333.

17. Minutes of council of war, November 6, 1776, Force, ed., *American Archives,* 5th ser., 3:543–44; George Washington to Greene, November 7, 1776, and November 8, 1776, *The Papers of General Nathanael Greene,* 1:339, 342–43.

18. Greene to George Washington, November 9, 1776, *The Papers of General Nathanael Greene,* 1:344.

19. Greene to John Hancock, November 12, 1776, ibid., 1:349. Henry Lee wrote that Greene was "a very highly trusted councellor of the Commander in Chief, respected for his sincerity, prized for his disinterestedness, and valued for his wisdom." Quoted in George F. Scheer and Hugh F. Rankin, *Rebels and Redcoats: The American Revolution through the Eyes of Those Who Fought and Lived It* (Cleveland: Da Capo, 1957), 486–87. Washington's secretary, Tench Tilghman, wrote to Congressman William Duer on October 14 that Greene "is beyond doubt, a first-rate military genius and one in whose opinions the General places the utmost confidence." Quoted in Thayer, *Nathanael Greene,* 111–12.

20. George Washington to John Hancock, November 16, 1776, *PGW,* 7:163; Washington to President Joseph Reed, August 22, 1779; in *The Writings of George Washington,*

from the Original Manuscript Sources, 1745–1799, edited by John C. Fitzpatrick, 39 vols. (Washington, D.C.: U.S. Government Printing Office, 1931–44), 16:150–52 (cited hereafter as *WGW*); Colonel Robert Magaw to Greene and Greene to Washington, November 15, 1776, *The Papers of General Nathanael Greene,* 1:350–51.

21. Douglas Southall Freeman, *George Washington: A Biography.* vol. 4 (New York: Scribners, 1951), 249–52; George Washington to John Hancock, November 16, 1776, *PGW,* 7:163, 165; Greene to Colonel Henry Knox, November 17 1776, *The Papers of General Nathanael Greene,* 1:351–52.

22. De Lancey, *The Capture of Mount Washington,* 20–22. For a cogent analysis of the Fort Washington affair, its aftermath, and the extent of Greene's responsibility for it (as opposed to others), see *The Papers of General Nathanael Greene,* 1:352–59n2. See also *PGW,* 7:165–69nn4–9. Ward dismisses De Lancey's thesis that treachery contributed to the fall of the fort; see Ward, *The War of the Revolution,* appendix E, 2:940. For a British officer's impression of the defenders of the fort, see comments by Lieutenant Mackenzie reprinted in Scheer and Rankin, *Rebels and Redcoats,* 227.

23. George Washington to Hancock, November 16, 1776, *PGW,* 7:162–65; Greene to Governor Nicholas Cooke, December 4, 1776, *The Papers of General Nathanael Greene,* 1:361–62; Washington to Augustine Washington, November 19, 1776, *PGW,* 7:103–4. According to Howe's report, in addition to cannon the Americans lost eight thousand cannon shot, four thousand cannon shells, twenty-eight hundred muskets, four hundred thousand cartridges, wheelbarrows, and five hundred entrenching tools. *The Papers of General Nathanael Greene,* 1:363–64n2.

24. Greene to Governor Nicholas Cooke, December 4, 1776, *The Papers of General Nathanael Greene,* 1:361–63, and 363, 64n2. See also Ward, *The War of the Revolution,* 1:276–77.

25. Ward, *The War of the Revolution,* 1:275–76. For desertion rates see Don Higginbotham, "Military Leadership in the American Revolution," *Leadership in the American Revolution: Third Symposium on the American Revolution* (Washington, D.C.: Library of Congress, 1974), 104. Washington listed his strength as 5,410 in a letter to John Hancock, November 23, 1776, *PGW,* 7:196–97; Greene to Governor Nicholas Cooke, December 4, 1776, *The Papers of General Nathanael Greene,* 1:362; Washington to Hancock, November 30, 1776, *PGW,* 7:232–33.

26. Greene to John Hancock, December 21, 1776, *The Papers of General Nathanael Greene,* 1:372–74.

27. Congressional resolution, December 26, 1776, *JCC,* 6:1043–46. See also *The Papers of General Nathanael Greene,* 1:374n.

28. Greene to Catherine Greene, December 30, 1776, *The Papers of General Nathanael Greene,* 1:377.

29. On placing and operating magazines, see Frederick the Great's instructions to his generals, edited and translated by Brigadier General Thomas R. Phillips, in *Roots of Strategy: The 5 Greatest Military Classics of All Time* (New York: MJF Books, 2006), 324–25.

30. Greene to Thomas Paine, January 9, 1777, *The Papers of General Nathanael Greene,* 2:3. Greene repeated his praise in a letter to Governor Cooke (while saying the New Jersey militia did well, too), January 10, 1777, ibid., 2:5.

31. Greene to Henry Marchant, July [25?], 1778, ibid., 2:471.

32. This account draws on John Buchanan, *The Road to Valley Forge: How Washington Built the Army that Won the Revolution* (New York: Barnes & Noble, 2007), 270–84; Ward, *The War of the Revolution*, 1:362–71. See also editorial notes in *PGW*, 11:376–79, 395–401, and especially *The Papers of General Nathanael Greene*, 2:171–77. General Greene's orders, October 7, 1777, ibid., 2:171. See also editorial note, 176–77.

33. Greene to General Alexander McDougall, January 25, 1778, *The Papers of General Nathanael Greene*, 2:261. McDougall replied that he had seen no such sluggishness or inactivity on Greene's part that day; McDougall to Greene, February 14, 1778, ibid., 2:284; Greene to Henry Lee, February 18, 1782, ibid., 10:379. George W. Greene related a story about a conversation after Brandywine between Greene and Adjutant General Timothy Pickering in which Pickering said: "Before I came to the Army, I entertained an exalted opinion of General Washington's military talents, but I have since seen nothing to enhance it." Greene reportedly replied, somewhat equivocally, "Why, the General does want decision; for my part, I decide in a moment." George Washington Greene, *Life of Nathanael Greene*, 1:468.

34. Greene to George Washington, April 24, 1779, *The Papers of General Nathanael Greene*, 3:427. Field Marshal Erwin Rommel, North Africa, August 1942, quoted in Matthew Crilly, "El Alamein Train Station: Logistics," http://www.iwm.org.uk/upload/package/21/creteegypt/standegypt11.htm (accessed August 23, 2011).

35. Erna Risch, *Quartermaster Support of the Army: A History of the Corps, 1775–1939*, Special Studies Series, Center of Military History (Washington, D.C.: U.S. Army, 1989), 6–8, 11; *The Papers of General Nathanael Greene*, 2:262n7.

36. This account relies on the helpful summary found in *The Papers of General Nathanael Greene*, 2:308–10n2. For Greene's account of his appointment, see relevant correspondence: Greene to Henry Knox, February 26, 1778; to William Greene, March 7, 1778; to General George Weedon, March 7, 1778; to Joseph Reed, March 9, 1778; *The Papers of General Nathanael Greene*, 2:294, 303, 304–5, 307. For the text of the appointment, see *JCC*, 10:210. Erna Risch, *Supplying Washington's Army*, Special Studies Series, Center of Military History (Washington, D.C.: U.S. Army, 1981), 30.

37. On Mifflin and Quartermaster Department reorganization, see editor's note, *The Papers of General Nathanael Greene*, 2:312–13; Risch, *Quartermaster Support of the Army*, 41, 44, 45; Risch, *Supplying Washington's Army*, 43–45, 77–78. Greene to Colonel Clement Biddle, March 23, 1778, *The Papers of General Nathanael Greene*, 2:319–20 and 319–20n1. Camp committee letter to Congress, quoted in Risch, *Supplying Washington's Army*, 72, and Risch, *Quartermaster Support of the Army*, 45.

38. Greene to George Washington, May 3, 1778, and Washington to Greene, May 17, 1778, *The Papers of General Nathanael Greene*, 2:372, 372n1, 373, 394–95; Greene to Henry Laurens, March 26, 1778, and Greene to Washington, March 26, 1778, ibid., 2:322, 323. See also James A. Huston, *The Sinews of War: Army Logistics 1775–1953*, Army Historical Series (Washington, D.C.: U.S. Army, 1966), 62; Washington to Laurens, August 3, 1778, *WGW*, 12:277.

39. Editor's note, *The Papers of General Nathanael Greene*, 2:319; Risch, *Supplying Washington's Army*, 97 and 107 (forage depots); Risch, *Quartermaster Support of the Army*,

46; Greene to Colonel Clement Biddle, March 30, 1778, and George Washington to Greene, March 31, 1778, *The Papers of General Nathanael Greene*, 2:327, 329.

40. Greene to president of the Board of War, May 27, 1778, *The Papers of General Nathanael Greene*, 2:414. On supply costs see Risch, *Quartermaster Support of the Army*, 54–55. Greene to George Washington, April 22, 1779, *The Papers of General Nathanael Greene*, 3:423. Risch, *Supplying Washington's Army*, 47.

41. Risch, *Quartermaster Support of the Army*, 54, 56; resolution of July 9, 1779, *JCC*, 14:812–15; Greene to Colonel Charles Pettit, August 18, 1779, *The Papers of General Nathanael Greene*, 4:327–28. Risch, *Supplying Washington's Army*, 49–50.

42. Greene to Colonel John Cox, November 28, 1779, *The Papers of General Nathanael Greene*, 5:122–23. The biblical quotation is from 1 Peter 4:18. Greene to Samuel Huntington, December 12, 1779, *The Papers of General Nathanael Greene*, 5:164–67 and accompanying notes.

43. On the winter of 1779–80 at Morristown, New Jersey, see Risch, *Quartermaster Support of the Army*, 56–58. Greene's request for a reply to his resignation is found at Greene to Huntington, January, 13, 1780, *The Papers of General Nathanael Greene*, 5:265; see also Greene to Huntington, February 16, 1780, ibid., 5:391–93; committee at headquarters to Greene, July 16, 1780, ibid., 6:113–14. The editors of Greene's papers declared that Greene "could not have wished for a more favorable appraisal of his own role in the department—an affirmation he had fruitlessly sought from Congress." ibid., 6:114. See also Risch, *Supplying Washington's Army*, 52–53.

44. Greene to Samuel Huntington, July 26, 1780, *The Papers of General Nathanael Greene*, 6:155–57. For Greene's resignation, see "Headnote on NG's Resignation," ibid., 6:150–55. See also Thomas L. Wells, "An Inquiry into the Resignation of Nathanael Greene in 1780," *Rhode Island History* 24, no. 2 (1965): 41–48. For the text of Congress's reorganization plan, see resolution of July 15, 1780, *JCC*, 17:615–35. See also Risch, *Supplying Washington's Army*, 57–58.

45. George Washington to Greene, August 15, 1780, *The Papers of General Nathanael Greene*, 6:217.

"Against the tide of misfortune"

Civil-Military Relations, Provincialism, and the Southern Command in the Revolution

David K. Wilson

"*I* am appointed to the command of the Southern Army; and am now just setting forward on the journey. It is a most difficult command, and hitherto has proved a disgraceful one to all that has gone that way. I wish it may not be my lot."[1] So wrote Major General Nathanael Greene shortly after he had been chosen to command the Southern Department of the Continental army in October 1780. Greene's predecessors as commanders of the Southern Army included Major Generals Charles Lee, Robert Howe, Benjamin Lincoln, and Horatio Gates. Contrary to Greene's lament, Charles Lee had managed to escape from the southern theater with his character intact. Nevertheless Greene's point is valid. The southern theater had proved a graveyard for the reputations of most of the generals who had commanded there.

Each American commander in the southern theater had to face a variety of political, military, and logistical problems during his tenure. Two of the most difficult were the related issues of civil-military relations and southern provincialism. The Continental army commander in the South had to be a diplomat as well as a soldier if he were to get the resources he needed from the civil authorities that controlled them. Southern state governments jealously guarded their sovereignty, and state militia officers treasured their independence. On his arrival in the South, Greene observed that in that region "there is no such thing as national character or national sentiment."[2] Overcoming this provincialism in order to achieve common strategic goals—without inflaming delicate southern sensibilities—was a difficult task for all the southern theater commanders.

During the early phases of America's war for independence in the spring and summer of 1775, the attention of the Continental Congress was focused on military events in New England and Canada. Starting in the fall of 1775, however, various reports convinced Congress that the British were "preparing to make attacks upon Charleston, in South Carolina, and several places in Virginia, and probably in North Carolina."[3]

To bolster southern security, Congress passed a resolution on February 27, 1776, that created the Southern Department of the Continental army. The military district consisted of the colonies of Virginia, North Carolina, South Carolina, and Georgia. Recognizing the conflict was widening beyond New England, Congress simultaneously divided the remainder of the colonies into Northern, Middle, and Canadian military departments. Each department was to be an independent command with a major general at its head, reporting directly to Congress rather than to General George Washington, the commander in chief of the Continental army. Congress believed this hierarchy would help the government be more responsive to each region's military needs. Also the independence of the military departments was consistent with the Whig philosophy of keeping an abundance of military power out of the hands of one man.[4]

Major General Charles Lee was the overwhelming choice by the southern delegates to Congress for command of the Southern Department. Reputed to be the most capable officer in the American military, Lee had extensive military experience in both American and European theaters during the French and Indian War (known as the Seven Years' War in Europe). He received the appointment on March 1, 1776, and was soon on his way to Virginia, where he planned to set his headquarters at the colonial capital of Williamsburg.[5]

Virginia's security had been under threat for some time by the colony's last royal governor, John Murray, Earl of Dunmore. Lord Dunmore, as he was known, had been attempting to use the Loyalists of Virginia, emancipated slaves, and regular troops as the foundation of an army to retake the colony. He suffered a serious reverse at the Battle of Great Bridge in December 1775, which forced his army to abandon the land and seek safety aboard British ships offshore. An even more devastating setback followed on New Year's Day 1776, when the Loyalist stronghold of Norfolk was destroyed during a British bombardment of American forces occupying the city. Driven from the mainland, Dunmore nevertheless continued to menace both Virginia and Maryland with his small army operating from his fleet in the Chesapeake Bay.[6]

While Lord Dunmore was the most immediate threat to Virginia's security, Lee was alerted to a greater danger when he first arrived in the colony. A Tory merchant had been caught smuggling official dispatches from Dunmore to the royal governor of Maryland, Robert Eden. One of the confiscated letters was from Lord George Germain, the British secretary of state for the American colonies. It revealed plans for a military expedition to the southern colonies "consisting of seven regiments, with a fleet of frigates and small ships." This armament was to land first in North Carolina and then proceed to Virginia or

South Carolina, "as circumstances of greater or less advantage shall point out." Based on the timetable revealed in the captured letter, the enemy fleet could be expected to arrive at any time.[7]

Lee wanted to be ready to move into North Carolina to meet the anticipated British attack, but he needed to prepare Virginia's defenses before he left. Perceiving the possible conjunction of Loyalists, slaves, and British regulars to be the greatest threat to the colony, Lee took several measures to suppress and control the region's Tories and slaves. First he ordered the arrest of Maryland's royal governor on the charge he was the recipient of the "treacherous correspondence" from Lord Germain that had revealed the British plans—and thus a conspirator against American liberty. Lee next pressed to have all slaves and white Loyalists in Princess Anne and Norfolk Counties forcibly relocated to "an interior part of this, or some other colony" so they could no longer supply, reinforce, or provide shelter to Dunmore's marauding forces—or any future British force that may invade. Finally Lee ordered most of Virginia's military to concentrate around the colonial capital at Williamsburg, which he considered the most strategic location "in a country abounding with slaves."[8]

Surprisingly the Virginia Council of Safety approved with little debate Lee's dramatic suggestion to relocate the Loyalists of lower Virginia. Though some arrests were made, homes burned, and families displaced, whole populations were not relocated as Lee proposed. The program was apparently abandoned after Dunmore was permanently driven from the colony in the summer of 1776. The relocation effort spearheaded by Lee does, however, show the extent to which he was ready to go to suppress the Tory population.[9]

Interestingly it was the arrest warrant issued for Maryland's governor that proved the most controversial of Lee's actions. "Seize the person of Governor Eden," Lee wrote to a Maryland official, "the sin and blame be upon my head." And so it was. Maryland's Council of Safety countermanded the order, noting that the colony was not in the Southern Department and therefore outside of Lee's jurisdiction.[10]

In a hearing on the matter, the council censured the official whom Lee had sent to arrest the governor, finding him guilty of "the high and dangerous offense of assuming the supreme executive power in this province." Since the official was an ally of Lee's, the censure was an indirect—and not-so-thinly veiled—criticism of the general. Lee sent an apology to the council for the incident, insisting that he never intended to "extend the military authority, or trespass on the civil." Congress supported Lee in the matter, agreeing that Eden was a threat and should be arrested. But the Maryland Council of Safety saw things differently and chose to allow the governor to depart peaceably back to Britain.[11]

On May 3, 1776, a large British fleet began to gather off Cape Fear, North Carolina, and in mid-May, Lee transferred his headquarters to Halifax. Because North Carolina's Loyalists had been defeated at Moore's Creek Bridge in February, however, the British plan to invade the colony was stillborn. After a few raids on the coast, the fleet departed, leaving Lee to guess its destination. The intercepted letter from Lord Germain indicated that, after the British invasion force left North Carolina, it would head either to Virginia or South Carolina. Lee thought if Virginia were the object, the lack of a large urban center there would make their operations merely "piratical," something Virginia's military could handle on its own. On the other hand, if South Carolina were their objective, then the city of Charleston would almost certainly be their target. This would cause their operations to be "more regular," and thus his professional experience would be more useful to the defenders. Lee chose to go to Charleston, which was fortunate, as that was indeed the British objective.[12]

On his arrival in Charleston on June 8, Lee found that none of the South Carolina regiments had been transferred into the Continental army as Congress had authorized, and none of South Carolina's officers had accepted commissions in the Continental army. The reasons given by the South Carolinians for their failure to transfer their military forces to Continental control seemed trivial, mostly having to do with disagreements on articles of discipline for soldiers and officers and issues of pay and terms of service. These matters, however, were merely a veneer for the real reason that South Carolina had failed to transfer its regiments over to the Continental army. The colony wanted to maintain control over its military.[13]

To negotiate a legal basis for his authority to command the colony's troops, Lee immediately met with President John Rutledge, South Carolina's chief executive. Given that there was a fleet of British warships hovering just off the bar of Charleston's harbor, Rutledge had to compromise if he wanted Lee's help and the reinforcements he brought with him. Therefore Rutledge issued an order on June 8, 1776, stating that "the command of all regular forces and militia of this colony . . . being invested in Major-General Lee, orders issued by him are to be obeyed."[14]

In assessing the city's defenses, Lee thought the South Carolinians put too much reliance on an incomplete fort on Sullivan's Island at the mouth of Charleston Harbor. Lee told President Rutledge and his council that the fort should be abandoned as untenable, but he was rebuffed. Rutledge had in fact sent secret instructions to the fort's commander, Colonel William Moultrie, telling him not to abandon Sullivan's Island without Rutledge's own explicit order. Rutledge then added, "I will cut off my right hand sooner than write it."[15]

Lee was certain it was a mistake to occupy Fort Sullivan, but he also knew it was politically infeasible to order it to be abandoned as the South Carolinians who garrisoned the place would likely disobey the command. Faced with this reality, he could just issue a series of orders to try to improve the fort's defenses. Colonel Moultrie quickly obeyed most of the general's instructions but one: the building of a bridge of retreat. Moultrie said he could complete the bridge if he were sent a sufficient number of boats to build a pontoon bridge, only to have Lee respond that, "if I had boats, I should send them according to your request, but they are not to be had."[16]

Moultrie thought if a retreat were necessary, it could be done in boats. (He had enough boats to ferry his troops but not enough to build a bridge.) Yet Lee refused this sensible solution and insisted on the bridge. William Drayton, a prominent South Carolina statesman and chief justice of the South Carolina Supreme Court, summed up his opinion of Lee's stubbornness: "Lee is very clever—and very positive. . . . Every idea of his must be right, and, of course, every contrary idea in every other person must be wrong . . . even in cases as plain as my hand." Lee thought Moultrie's reasons for not completing the bridge were mere excuses or procrastination. His frustration with the South Carolina colonel grew until he considered relieving Moultrie of his command and putting a North Carolina officer in charge of Moultrie's troops. It is doubtful, however, that President Rutledge would have allowed this change had Lee actually put the matter to a test.[17]

Before the situation between Lee and Moultrie could come to a head, the British fleet attacked Fort Sullivan on June 28, 1776. In a battle that lasted from the morning until after dark, Colonel Moultrie and the American garrison put up a stalwart defense that wrecked the attacking warships and forced them to give up their attempt to take the fort. The British fleet soon departed southern waters and headed for the North, where it and the troops it carried joined in preparations for an upcoming attack on New York. Despite all earlier misgivings about Moultrie's leadership, Major General Lee was effusive in his praise of the colonel. While the country as a whole gave Lee much of the credit for the victory at Charleston, not all South Carolinians saw it that way. Chief among Lee's detractors was William Drayton, who "like many South Carolinians, gloried because Moultrie's fort had been successfully defended in spite of Lee's opinion that it would fall easy prey to the British."[18]

Word that Congress had declared independence on July 4, 1776, filtered down to Charleston by the end of the month.[19] As South Carolina and Georgia busied themselves with revising their constitutions to reflect their new status as autonomous states, Major General Lee turned his attention to a new threat to southern security. Southern Loyalists taking refuge in East Florida had formed themselves into partisan or paramilitary outfits and were raiding the border region of Georgia. The government of that state thought the conquest of East Florida was the logical solution to this problem, and Lee concurred in this view. Georgia lacked sufficient troops to mount the expedition alone, so Lee needed the aid of South Carolina's military in the venture.[20]

This did not appear to be an issue because on June 18, 1776, Congress passed a resolution placing most of South Carolina's forces "on the continental establishment." (Word of the resolution's passage did not reach the state until after the Battle of Sullivan's Island.) This placed Major General Lee officially in command of the state's regular regiments. The resolution, however, also said the Southern Department commander could not move "more than one-third of the effective men . . . without the express order of Congress or the consent of the president of that colony." This last clause meant that President Rutledge had an effective veto on military plans involving a majority of the state's troops.[21]

In obedience to the congressional resolution, Lee petitioned Rutledge for a regiment to use in an attack on East Florida. Rutledge, however, was not initially inclined to cooperate with any plan that involved stripping troops away from his state's defense, so he refused the request. The frustrated Lee protested that his request was for less than a third of South Carolina's troops, which the congressional resolution of June 18 gave him "plain, explicit, and positive" authority to move. "If there is any meaning in [the] language" of the resolution, Lee complained, "this is the meaning."[22]

Rutledge disagreed, insisting that "no such power" was invested in the Southern Department commander. Lee argued that Rutledge's position effectively made South Carolina's troops a "half continental, half provincial" hybrid unlike any other state's—a circumstance he thought would surely lead to "anarchy, perplexity, and confusion." Eventually Rutledge compromised by agreeing to have some South Carolina troops act to support Lee's operations, though not the specific ones Lee had requested. Lee agreed to the arrangement out of political expediency; yet he insisted on asserting his right "to move one-third of these troops out of the province from my own authority." In a conciliatory gesture he added, "although I have fortunately no occasion to exert this right at present."[23]

When Lee departed South Carolina for the North on orders from Congress on September 9, 1776, the invasion of British East Florida had failed to materialize, nor had the question of command supremacy in South Carolina been resolved. In an attempt to deal with the command issue, on September 19, 1776, the South Carolina legislature passed a resolution that said they "do acquiesce in the resolution of the Continental Congress of the 18th of June" placing the state's regiments "upon the Continental establishment."[24] The apparent definitiveness of the statement belied the difficulty future commanders of the Southern Department experienced in exerting control over South Carolina's Continental regiments.

On Lee's departure Brigadier General Robert Howe of North Carolina assumed command in South Carolina and Georgia. He even issued letters to the presidents of South Carolina and Georgia stating that command of the two states had "devolved" upon him. Howe's ascent to command, however, was complicated because of his rank as brigadier. Brigadier General John Armstrong, for example, had seniority over Howe, but he did not want command and so deferred to Howe. Armstrong shortly left for duty in the North, solving the issue, if there was any. Brigadier General James Moore, also Howe's senior, was in and out of South Carolina and Georgia from September 1776 to February 1777. While Moore was present, he was in command. After his departure for the North in February, however, no one questioned that Howe was theater commander.[25]

No one, that is, except Brigadier General Christopher Gadsden. The South Carolina native was a prominent statesman, soldier, and inveterate rebel. He was also the designer of the celebrated "Gadsden flag." Emblazoned with the words "Don't Tread on Me" underneath a coiled rattlesnake on a yellow field, it was—and is still today—one of the most recognizable American flags. In the spring of 1777, it seemed that Gadsden had intended the words on that flag to apply to Robert Howe as much as the British, for at that time he began challenging Howe's right to command in South Carolina. It was not a question of rank or seniority. Howe had received his brigadier's commission in March 1776, while Gadsden had not been promoted to the same rank until September. Gadsden was the junior officer, and he knew it. Instead Gadsden contended that Howe did not have written orders from Major General Lee authorizing him to leave Georgia in the fall of 1776. Without such orders Gadsden would have been in command in South Carolina while Howe's command would have been restricted to Georgia. Howe said he had verbal orders from Lee to take command in South Carolina and Georgia, but this claim failed to satisfy Gadsden.[26]

On receiving Gadsden's complaint, Congress expressed "surprise" that Howe's command in the southern theater gave "offence to anyone." Attempting to solve the problems related to Howe's rank, Congress promoted him to major general in October 1777. The promotion would seem to have rendered Gadsden's arguments immaterial. As one South Carolinian put it, "it seems a plain case [Howe] is a senior officer." Gadsden, however, was not satisfied, and he put his perceived grievance before the South Carolina legislature, asking for an investigation. When that body declined to pursue the issue, the designer of the rattlesnake flag angrily resigned his commission.[27]

Even out of uniform Gadsden did not give up his fight against the major general who had piqued him so. In the summer of 1778, he wrote a lengthy missive to Congress accusing Howe of, among other things, "mere subterfuge" and "downright low cunning, jockeying and sharping" to gain command. Howe believed that Gadsden's comments had now crossed the line into personal attacks, and he demanded satisfaction on the field of honor.[28]

Gadsden accepted the challenge, and the two southern patricians dueled on August 30, 1778. Both duelists missed their targets, with Gadsden firing his pistol across his shoulder to make sure of it. Honor being served, a second shot was declined by both participants. Gadsden, though never withdrawing his grievance, did not pursue it actively again. Nevertheless, while Howe had managed to avoid killing a prominent South Carolina statesman, he clearly did not understand that he needed to be a diplomat as well as a soldier if he were to succeed in his role as executive commander in the South. Gadsden's political allies in South Carolina became Howe's enemies in the legislature.[29]

Howe's political problems were unfortunately not limited to South Carolina. In the spring of 1777, another attempt to attack East Florida was proposed by Georgia's president, Button Gwinnett. He and other Georgians had been pressing to eliminate the threat posed by Loyalist raiders and British regulars based in East Florida. A lack of resources and support from the South Carolina government, however, prompted Howe to delay. In addition Gwinnett and the civilian leadership of Georgia operated under the notion that the president was in charge of all military forces in the state, including the Continentals. Howe did not want to cooperate with the attack on East Florida under these circumstances and, according to Gwinnett, seemed to "obstruct the attempt." Howe then withdrew most of the South Carolina Continentals from the state, leaving Gwinnett to grouse, "He came, he saw, and he left us in our low estate."[30]

The government of Georgia then attempted to organize its own attack on East Florida by enlisting the support of the state's senior Continental officer, Brigadier General Lachlan McIntosh. Because Gwinnett and McIntosh had been fighting a political feud for months, it was not surprising that the two found it difficult to cooperate. Both of them issued direct orders to the Georgia Continentals involved in the operation, and the confused "invasion" of East Florida amounted to little more than a desultory border raid before it was forced to turn back.[31]

When the expedition failed, Gwinnett (who had just lost his bid for reelection) got into a heated argument with McIntosh over who was responsible for the fiasco. The situation quickly escalated, and the two fought a duel just outside of Savannah on May 16, 1777. Both men were wounded, and Gwinnett died a few days later. George Walton, a Georgia politician, militia officer, and signer of the Declaration of Independence, said the duel had disturbed "the harmony & vigour of the Civil & military authorities." At his suggestion McIntosh was transferred out of the theater to preserve the peace.[32]

Duels were not the only source of civil-military tension in the South during Major General Howe's term as commander. Georgia's civilian officials were becoming increasingly irritated by Howe's inability or lack of desire to organize an invasion of East Florida. In addition Howe had earlier written a series of letters to the legislature suggesting measures to be taken to improve the state's defenses. The letters were strongly worded and seemed to imply neglect on the part of the elected officials. Samuel Elbert, a Continental officer from Georgia, observed that the letters caused "offense" to the civilian government "in consequence . . . of [Howe's] attempting to dictate to them."[33]

In March 1778 John Houstoun, who was governor of Georgia at that time, complained to Congress that Howe was disrespectful to Georgia's civilian government and asked for a resolution confirming the "subordinate relation in which the military stand to the civil." Congress instead ruled that Howe had not been "wanting in that attention and respect to the authority of Georgia." It also affirmed the right of "the general or commanding officer" to make decisions regarding "military operations."[34]

While affirming Howe's right to command, Congress nevertheless directed the general to find a way to placate the civilian government. Howe therefore began planning a new invasion of East Florida for the summer of 1778. Governor Houstoun committed his state's militia to the expedition, and South Carolina pledged a force of militia under Colonel Andrew Williamson to the venture. In theory the new Florida expedition would have upward of two thousand men plus naval support in the form of row galleys under the command of Commodore Oliver Bowen of the Continental Navy.[35]

Howe had hoped that Congress's resolution confirming his right to command "military operations" would put to rest all issues of who had command supremacy. After the expedition got underway, however, the situation quickly became chaotic. "We now find," wrote a South Carolina officer, "that we are to have as many independent commanders as corps." Again refusing to submit to Howe's orders, Governor Houstoun suggested that he should have overall command of the expedition. Colonel Williamson also did not acknowledge General Howe's right to command the South Carolina militia, and Commodore Bowen likewise said he had sole authority over the naval component. The expedition eventually had to be abandoned because of illness among the troops as well as the squabbling among the commanders. Howe later wrote, "If I am ever again to depend upon operations I have no right to guide and men I have no right to command, I shall deem it then, as now I do, one of the most unfortunate accidents of my life."[36]

On his return from the ill-fated East Florida expedition, Howe became involved in a controversial love affair in South Carolina. Few details of the romance have survived, but there is no doubt it was scandalous. The tryst soon became a matter for debate in Congress. Citing the affair, the delegates from South Carolina and Georgia demanded Howe's removal from theater command. The commotion may have had something to do with his murky marital status. Few sought divorce in that age, but he had legally separated from his wife in 1772. Howe was still technically married, and his biographers have suspected that philandering was the cause of his separation. His womanizing was no secret. One North Carolina woman described Howe as "a sort of woman-eater that devours everything that comes in his way, and that no woman can resist him."[37]

While loath to get involved in the "private amours of their generals," Congress felt it had no choice but to recall Howe. Perhaps with a new assignment, North Carolina delegate Cornelius Harnett wrote, Howe would have an opportunity to display his abilities on "the field of Mars as well as of Venus." There was never an official reason given for Howe's removal from command, and it is likely that his affair in Charleston was merely a convenient excuse for the South Carolina and Georgia delegates to rid themselves of an unpopular general. But whether it was because of his philandering or his more martial failings, Congress resolved to replace the seemingly forlorn commander with Major General Benjamin Lincoln in September 1778. Howe received word of his dismissal by dispatch the following month.[38]

It took Lincoln many weeks to make his way southward, however, and the interval between receiving word of his dismissal and the arrival of his replacement was an awkward time for Howe. Until Lincoln arrived Howe was still theater commander, and this happened to be when the British decided to renew their efforts at making the South a major theater of the war. A seaborne expedition had been dispatched from New York to invade Georgia, and the state's frontier was more active than ever with raids from British East Florida. Howe was therefore busy in Georgia when Major General Lincoln arrived in Charleston in mid-December. Lincoln immediately began reorganizing the Southern Department's military infrastructure in preparation for the expected British invasion from New York.[39]

The British attacked Savannah on December 29, 1778, with more than 3,000 troops supported by a fleet of naval vessels. To defend the city Howe cobbled together a force of 850 troops, of which only a little more than 200 were Georgia militia. The state's total militia force was estimated at 3,000 men. Their poor response to Howe's call to arms was owed to a variety of causes, but one had to be the broad dissatisfaction with his command in the state. The highly disciplined British forces quickly overwhelmed the outnumbered Americans, whose losses numbered in the hundreds. Howe was forced to withdraw into South Carolina, where he handed over what remained of his army to Major General Lincoln before going northward for a new assignment.[40]

Georgians blamed Howe for his defeat at Savannah and for his rapid withdrawal, which left "the state at the mercy of the enemy." So deep was their dislike of the general from North Carolina that, as the war drew to a close in late 1781, Georgia's government pressed for his court-martial. Howe was charged with sacrificing "the capital and troops of the state" in the 1778 battle, this being the "first cause of the distresses and consequences which ensued." He was nevertheless exonerated on all counts by the court, which concluded in January 1782.[41]

While Howe was getting the last of his reputation wringed out at Savannah, Major General Benjamin Lincoln had been feverishly assembling an army in South Carolina. He was successful but a few days too late to save Howe. A native of Massachusetts, Lincoln found the Continental army in the South differently organized from what he was used to in the North. When the American Southern Army (as the army of the Southern Department was commonly called) requisitioned medicine, foodstuffs, munitions, or other supplies, it was the "civil authority" of South Carolina that "granted them, or not, as their own judgments dictated." Lincoln thought that this process "created dissensions between the civil and military." Indeed Lincoln found the army had such an "abject dependency" on South Carolina's government that he could not even march his troops "without the consent of the President of this State, however urgent the necessity."[42]

Lincoln's strategic priority in early 1779 was to contain the British in southeastern Georgia. A column of British troops had occupied Augusta at the end of January, and Lincoln wanted to retake the town. To accomplish this goal, he had to rely on militia while he rebuilt his shattered Continental troops. Lincoln had proved capable of working with strong-willed local militia leaders such as John Stark in the 1777 Saratoga campaign. Congress hoped Lincoln could mend relations with the southern leaders, which had been so estranged by Howe. Referring to the civil-military strife that had preceded his arrival, Lincoln told Washington that he hoped "things will be better settled and I never shall be driven to the hard necessity of altercating with the civil power, than which nothing would be more disagreeable."[43]

Unfortunately South Carolina's proved unreliable because they refused to obey his orders or to be put under the same regulations as the Continental troops while in the field. Rather than attempt to impress the discipline necessary on the South Carolinians, Lincoln chose to use militia from North Carolina under Brigadier General John Ashe, which had recently arrived in the state as reinforcements.[44]

Ashe marched his troops to Augusta, forcing the British to withdraw from the town. Pushing south in pursuit of the enemy, Ashe's troops were joined by a small force of Georgia Continentals under the recently promoted Brigadier

General Samuel Elbert. Underscoring the provincialism prevalent at the time, Ashe insisted on having command of the combined force since there were more North Carolina troops present than Georgians. Elbert agreed, though his rank as a Continental brigadier technically gave him seniority over Ashe, who was only a state brigadier of militia. In November 1775, Congress had passed a regulation stating that Continental officers, "when acting in conjunction with officers of equal rank on the provincial establishment, take command of the latter, and also of the Militia." Lincoln was aware of the arrangement between Ashe and Elbert and yet chose not to enforce regulations. When the British counterattacked Ashe's troops at Briar Creek on March 3, 1779, Ashe had overall command with Elbert acting as a subordinate. The American militia fled, taking Ashe along with them. Elbert, however, was captured with the last Americans fighting on the field.[45]

In late April, Lincoln decided to move his carefully rebuilt Southern Army to Augusta. Lincoln believed this maneuver would "circumscribe" the limits of British power to lower Georgia, preventing them from forming a junction with backcountry Loyalists and allied Indians. The move to Augusta would also protect a meeting of the Georgia assembly there. Since many Georgia legislators still harbored ill-feelings toward the Continental army left over from Major General Robert Howe's "abandonment" of the state a few months earlier, the maneuver would show the Continental army's renewed commitment to the state.[46]

Lincoln believed the British would not be so bold as to take advantage of the absence of his army from lower South Carolina, but he underestimated British audacity. On April 29, 1779, Major General Augustine Prevost, the commander of the British forces in Georgia, crossed the Savannah River and slashed into lower South Carolina. By May 11, Lieutenant Colonel James Mark Prevost, the younger brother of the general, had laid "siege" to Charleston. Lincoln, having thought the British attack a feint to draw him out of Georgia, had delayed returning to South Carolina. His army was therefore days away from relieving the city.[47]

Civilian leaders jockeyed for command of the military forces in the city with the Continental and militia officers until Brigadier General William Moultrie arrived at a compromise. He would assume overall military command in the city, leaving the power of "parlies [and] capitulations" to the civilian leaders. The British were actually far too weak to take the town, having fewer than two thousand troops available to them, but the civilian leadership inside Charleston had come to believe the British numbered eight thousand men. In an attempt to save Charleston from an attack that they thought would destroy the town, John Rutledge (by then governor, rather than president, under the state's new constitution) and the majority of the state leadership sent a "neutrality proposal" to Prevost. This proposal offered to make Charleston an open city and the state neutral for the duration of the war, if the British would not assault the town.[48]

Refusing to negotiate with anyone but the city's military commander, Brigadier General Moultrie, the British commander rejected the neutrality proposal and instead demanded the city's unconditional surrender. Some of the civilian leaders were willing to capitulate, given their mistaken assumption of the odds, but Moultrie refused. With their bluff called, the British were forced to withdraw as Lincoln finally arrived to relieve the city, his army having made its way back from the frontier by way of forced marches. The surrender of the city had been narrowly avoided, but Major General Lincoln had discovered that the civilian leadership of South Carolina was far more willing to negotiate with the British than American leaders in the North had been when their cities were under threat. To keep the South Carolinians steadfast, Lincoln needed to keep his army in a position where Charleston could not be so easily endangered again.[49]

After forcing Prevost away from Charleston, Lincoln pursued the British as they marched slowly southward. A sharp rearguard action was fought at Stono Ferry in June, but this did not prevent the British from completing a successful withdrawal into Georgia by the end of the summer, leaving only a small garrison at Beaufort on Port Royal Island off the South Carolina coast. This suited Lincoln, who was biding his time waiting for a promised French expeditionary force under Charles-Hector, Comte d'Estaing, to come help besiege Savannah and drive the British from Georgia.[50]

The French arrived in September, but things did not go as Lincoln had planned. Misunderstandings between Lincoln and d'Estaing resulted in confused operations. For example the British garrison on Port Royal Island was allowed to escape and reinforce Major General Prevost's forces in Savannah because the French and the Americans each thought the other was primarily responsible for monitoring the island. Encouraged by the reinforcement, the British troops in Savannah dug in for a prolonged siege.[51]

The siege lasted more than three weeks and was concluded by an assault by the combined French and American forces on the British works on October 9, 1779. The attack was a disaster. The French and American troops were decimated, each army suffering hundreds of casualties. Lincoln wanted to renew the siege, but the French commander felt honor had been served. D'Estaing ordered his army to evacuate, and the French ships left with as much suddenness as they had arrived.[52]

The defeat at Savannah led to an atmosphere of defeatism in South Carolina. "Sorry I am to observe," wrote one of Lincoln's friends in Charleston, "that the people seem in general disposed to think . . . since Congress has exerted itself so little to our support in men, we ought to accept the best terms that can be obtained [from the British]."[53] Lincoln knew these sorts of comments had to be taken seriously after the neutrality proposal of the previous May.

In the early months of 1780, Charleston came under siege by Lieutenant General Sir Henry Clinton with an army of thirteen thousand men brought from New York. It was the greatest threat to southern security that any commander in the South had yet faced. There was no wisdom in defending the city against the land and naval forces that the British had arrayed against the Americans. But Lincoln—remembering the willingness of the South Carolinians to negotiate and capitulate when the British attacked their vulnerable capital the previous year—felt he had to make the attempt from political necessity. Lincoln, however, did plan to withdraw his garrison before the city became a death trap for his army.[54]

On April 13, 1780, after holding the British off for several weeks, Lincoln held a council of war with his officers to discuss whether they should consider "evacuating the garrison." Though uninvited, the lieutenant governor intruded on the meeting, annoyed that he had not been asked to attend when questions of such importance to the city were being discussed. The lieutenant governor happened to be Christopher Gadsden, the man who had caused Robert Howe so much grief during his tenure as Continental commander in the South. Now he was acting chief executive in the city because Governor Rutledge had gone into the countryside to attempt to organize the militia.[55]

Gadsden told Lincoln he was "surprised and displeased" that the military "had entertained a thought of capitulation or evacuating the garrison." Even more disturbing were the comments of South Carolina councilman Thomas Ferguson, who had accompanied Gadsden. He told Lincoln that if the Continentals attempted to leave the city, "He would be among the first who would open the gates for the enemy and assist them in attacking [the Continental troops]." Remembering the neutrality proposal made the previous year, Lincoln had to be wary.[56]

At the meeting Colonel Charles Cotesworth Pinckney, commander of the First South Carolina Continental Regiment and Lincoln's subordinate, also censured Lincoln in support of Gadsden's and Ferguson's positions. Pinckney's siding with Gadsden shows that this was not merely a crisis between civil and military authorities but one of state versus national authority. Lincoln tolerated all the verbal assaults without vigorous response, showing that he was too acquiescent to both the civilian authorities and the local military commanders. That Colonel Pinckney felt he could publicly take to task a superior officer without fear of repercussions shows Lincoln was something of a pushover.[57]

While Lincoln did not yield the power of "parlies [and] capitulations" to the civilian authorities, as Moultrie did during the 1779 siege, Lincoln did agree to allow Gadsden to have a say in all negotiations with the British. Gadsden was against giving up, but if they were to surrender, he wanted explicit language in the terms that protected civilian rights and property. Surrounded and facing impossible odds, Lincoln was eventually forced to open surrender negotiations with Clinton. The additional conditions insisted on by Gadsden prolonged the negotiations needlessly—as they were not granted by the British. Lincoln surrendered his fifty-six-hundred-man garrison as prisoners of war on May 12, 1780. British troops then immediately swept into the backcountry of South Carolina and Georgia, temporarily pacifying the two states and solidifying British control.[58]

A month after the fall of Charleston, Congress appointed Major General Horatio Gates as Lincoln's replacement. Gates had achieved heroic stature after his victory at Saratoga. In 1778, however, he was implicated—fairly or unfairly—in a supposed plot known to history as the "Conway Cabal," the purpose of which was to undermine George Washington and replace him as commander in chief of the Continental army. As a result Gates went without a significant command in the army for several years until the fall of Charleston, when it was decided that only he had sufficient stature to rescue the situation there. Since the Southern Department was an independent command, reporting directly to Congress and not Washington, there would be no political or personal issues that would hinder Gates's effectiveness.[59]

The Americans had early perceived the British "southern strategy" to use Loyalists as the basis of manpower for an army with which they would reclaim the South. The British army numbered more than thirteen thousand men in South Carolina when Charleston fell on May 12, 1780. Lieutenant General Clinton reduced this number to fewer than eight thousand at the end of June, when he turned control of British forces in the South over to Lieutenant General Charles, Earl Cornwallis, and returned to New York with the rest of his troops. Congressman Joseph Jones wrote that the number of troops Clinton left under Cornwallis "cannot be sufficient" to hold the South "unless increased by the accession of Tories." This was proof, he thought, that the British sought to get southerners to rise "in support of the British government." He believed, however, that the approach of an American army under Gates would afford the patriots "hopes of protection" and so foil British plans.[60]

This was indeed the line of logic that Gates followed as he advanced with his army into North Carolina. He issued printed proclamations and circulars directed at both civilians and patriot militia leaders informing them that he was coming, that he would support them, and that he expected their support too. Gates declared that those who professed a "temporary acquiescence" to the British government would be forgiven if they swore their allegiance to the American cause and turned out in its support.[61]

The government of South Carolina had for years borne the principal burden of supplying the Southern Army. But with that state in British hands, North Carolina and Virginia had to fill that logistical vacuum. Those states, however, had yet to get the financing or infrastructure in place to provide the foodstuffs and munitions that were needed. As a result, Gates's army was literally "famished" as it proceeded south. Local militia commanders exacerbated the problem. Gates complained that the North Carolina militia had "gleaned the country" ahead of him, while the Virginia militia "stick to my rear and devour all that comes forward."[62]

North Carolina general Richard Caswell proved the most problematic of the myriad of provincial militia commanders that Gates had to deal with. A former governor of North Carolina with tremendous political clout, Caswell was independent and always seemed to find a reason to delay implementing Gates's orders. In July, Caswell was ordered to link up with Gates's main army. Instead he led his militia force into South Carolina in pursuit of Loyalist forces. Gates was forced to follow to ensure the safety of Caswell's militia.[63]

Gates finally caught up with Caswell in northern South Carolina in early August. He then pushed on toward Camden, which was the primary British base in the region. It was there on August 16, 1780, that Gates encountered a British army commanded by Cornwallis. In the ensuing battle, the Americans were defeated in spectacular fashion. In addition to suffering hundreds of killed, wounded, and missing, Gates's whole army was routed. Whether his being drawn prematurely into South Carolina to protect Caswell contributed materially to the disaster at Camden is debatable, but in 1782 this point was mentioned by delegates of Congress as a reason why they did not think it necessary to conduct a court of inquiry into the matter.[64]

Fortunately for the Americans, illness in the British ranks prevented them from immediately pushing into North Carolina after their victory. Nevertheless Gates's reputation was damaged beyond repair by his poor performance at Camden and his precipitate retreat of 180 miles in three days after the battle. This unprecedented withdrawal separated him from the remnants of his army so completely that he did not even know the fate of the survivors who still bore arms. Gates lost the confidence of many southern political leaders if not that of the Southern Army. Knowing that "no good can be expected from his being continued in the command," Congress voted on October 5, 1780, to relieve Gates as soon as another officer could be appointed to replace him.[65]

After Camden, Gates was a lame duck. Even the American victory at Kings Mountain on October 7, 1780, seemed to underscore how little influence he had on the course of events in the South. While this American victory forestalled a renewed British advance into North Carolina, it was a battle fought without any guidance, assistance, or leadership from Gates.[66]

Gates's waning authority was undeniable, yet he did accomplish one act that incontestably changed the course of the war in the South: he recruited Daniel Morgan into the service of the Southern Army and helped secure his promotion to brigadier general. In 1781 Morgan won one of the most important battles in the southern theater. Sadly for Gates, Morgan won this battle under the command of a general other than Gates.

When Gates was appointed to command the Southern Army in June 1780, practically his first act was to request that Morgan be recalled to service. Morgan had gone into semiretirement after he lost a bid to command the elite Corps of Light Infantry in 1779. Gates knew from his experience in the Saratoga campaign that Morgan was exactly the right man to lead a "select corps" of light infantry and cavalry in independent operations in the South.[67]

Colonel Morgan, however, agreed to serve only if he would eventually be promoted to brigadier general. If Morgan were not made a brigadier in the Continental army, he would be outranked by other state officers, such as the recently promoted Brigadier General Edward Stevens of Virginia. Indeed the South was rife with militia brigadiers, and it was clear that without a promotion Morgan could not effectively command the independent corps of Continentals and militia that Gates had envisioned for him.[68]

Gates was Washington's political enemy. When Congress asked the commander in chief his opinion about the promotion Gates had requested for Morgan, Washington said, "considering the delicate situation in which I stand with respect to General Gates, I feel an unwillingness to give any opinion." Referring to Morgan's resignation the previous year, however, Washington said it "could not be justified on any ground" and that "the season and circumstances were totally opposed to the measure."[69]

Washington's unenthusiastic response to the proposed promotion caused Congress to table the resolve. The matter probably would have remained in legislative limbo had not Governors Thomas Jefferson and John Rutledge intervened by pressing for Morgan's promotion as well. The additional political pressure caused Congress to yield to Gates's request, and Morgan's promotion was approved on October 13, 1780. Gates had the pleasure of receiving the papers for Morgan's commission, which he forwarded to the new brigadier on October 27. Ironically Gates had already been technically relieved at that time though he did not get official notice until December, when Nathanael Greene arrived to take over the department.[70]

In a tacit admission that things had not gone so well with past appointments, for the first time Congress asked Washington to choose the general to command the Southern Army. The southern delegates to Congress did, however, recommend Major General Nathanael Greene for the position. A former Quaker from Rhode Island, Greene was a favorite of the commander in chief, who happily made the appointment on October 14. The new arrangement implied Greene would report to Washington instead of Congress, but if implication was not enough, Congress codified it by passing a resolution that stated Greene's command of the Southern Army was "subject to the control of the Commander in Chief."[71] The string of southern military disasters at Savannah, Briar Creek, Savannah again, Charleston, and Camden had apparently overridden the republican caution that had previously kept the Southern Department independent.

Greene believed "that General Washington's influence will do more than all the assemblies upon the continent" to help get the resources he needed from the southern states. While this hope proved overly optimistic, Washington was certainly more engaged in the affairs of the Southern Department than under earlier commanders. Another dramatic change to the department occurred when Congress added the states of Maryland and Delaware to Greene's jurisdiction. Troops from those states had been serving with the Southern Army since the summer. Greene noted, however, that since those states were not part of the Southern Department, he had no authority to call on them for "supplies and support." Greene requested and was granted this power. He put it to good use, writing many letters to the governments of Maryland and Delaware for assistance.[72]

On December 2, 1780, six weeks after his appointment, Greene finally arrived in Charlotte to take command from Gates. His greatest initial concerns were the same his predecessor had faced: lack of clothing, supplies, and soldiers. The loss of Charleston in May 1780 had destroyed the logistical infrastructure of the Southern Department, leaving shortages of everything. Yet there were some ironic advantages to this situation. Charles Lee, Robert Howe, and Benjamin Lincoln had seemingly endless disputes with the governments of Georgia and South Carolina over the disposition of their troops and the distribution of supplies. But with the power of these states broken, Greene could conduct a war of maneuver mostly unfettered by local political interference. It was true, however, that he did not have to bicker over the distribution of supplies mainly because there were no supplies to distribute.

Greene's early strategy was to conduct initially "a kind of partizan [*sic*] war," that is, engaging the enemy with small actions while avoiding a large direct confrontation, and at the same time building an army capable of meeting the primary British army on equal terms. The instrument that Greene saw as most useful to conduct this partisan war was a "flying army" made up of cavalry and light infantry. With this in mind, on December 16, 1780, Greene ordered Brigadier General Morgan to western South Carolina with a small force of light infantry and cavalry and orders to cooperate with the militia of that region. Greene meanwhile took the remainder of the army to Cheraw, South Carolina, to start the process of building a regular force that could take on the British regulars.[73]

Morgan had been ordered to add the South Carolina militia of Brigadier General Thomas Sumter to his force. However, the officers Morgan sent to requisition troops and supplies returned empty-handed, having been told by Sumter's men that they were "to obey no orders" from Morgan unless they came directly through Sumter, who was out of the state recovering from a wound. "I confess I have been under some embarrassment respecting General Morgan's command & the orders he has given," Sumter wrote, "as I have been concerned but little in either trust." Because of Sumter's intransigence, lack of supplies nearly forced Morgan to withdraw, and Sumter's militia failed to participate in the upcoming campaign. Greene decided it was better to "conciliate than aggravate matters," and he sent letters stroking Sumter's ego in an attempt to push him into the field to help the common cause. At the same time he insisted that the South Carolinian acknowledge Morgan's seniority as a Continental officer and his right to command Sumter's troops directly.[74]

Even without Sumter's men, sufficient numbers of southern militia turned out to support Morgan for him to defeat the British light troops under the command of Lieutenant Colonel Banastre Tarleton on January 17, 1781. Morgan won the one-sided action using innovative tactics, and the battle was a critical turning point of the war in the South. The event fully justified all Gates had done to get Morgan back into the army as brigadier, and Greene's decision to split his army and send Morgan west to conduct "partizan" operations was vindicated as well.[75]

Despite the successful employment of militia at Cowpens in January 1781, and earlier at Kings Mountain in October 1780, Greene was resolute in his belief that militia should not be "depended upon as a principal, but employed as an auxiliary" military force. This stemmed from his conviction that most militia, with a few exceptions, were "better calculated to destroy provisions than the enemy." States often relied on militia because they were less expensive and easier to recruit than regulars, not to mention that states had greater control over these forces. Greene thought that some southern states had "such a high opinion of the militia that I don't expect they will ever attempt to raise a single Continental soldier." He attempted to cure state officials of their addiction to militia by writing them letters extolling the virtues of professional troops.[76]

After the Battle of Cowpens, the Americans were forced to withdraw into North Carolina, pursued by British troops commanded by Lord Cornwallis. On March 15, 1781, a battle was fought at Guilford Courthouse. Greene's army consisted of more than 60 percent militia, and as the Quaker general had predicted, their performance in the battle was uneven, with hundreds fleeing the field. After a hard fight Greene was forced to withdraw, but for the British the battle's outcome was nearly the definition of a Pyrrhic victory. Suffering hundreds of casualties, Cornwallis had to retreat from North Carolina. The Americans had suffered a tactical defeat but won a strategic victory. After Guilford Courthouse, the war in the South divided. Cornwallis took his wounded army to Virginia, where a British force was already operating under the turncoat Benedict Arnold, now a brigadier in the service of the Crown. Greene, however, returned to South Carolina, where he began a campaign to reduce all the British posts outside Charleston and Savannah. There he again called on Brigadier General Sumter to rally the state militia to cooperate with the army.[77]

Despite many calls, however, Sumter failed to march with his troops in a timely fashion. As a result, on April 25, 1781, Greene was forced to fight a battle just north of Camden at Hobkirk's Hill without the benefit of the South Carolina militia as reinforcements. Sumter's failure to support Greene was probably not the reason for the American defeat that day, but it was a contributing factor. This pattern was repeated when Greene laid siege to the British fort on South Carolina's western frontier at the town of Ninety Six. He called on Sumter to raise his militia and interpose them between Ninety Six and Charleston, hoping they would be able to slow a British column commanded by Lieutenant Colonel Francis, Lord Rawdon, that was marching to the fort's relief. Once again, however, Sumter failed to gather his militia in time. Lacking the time to complete proper siege operations, on June 18, 1781, Greene chose to mount a bloody assault on the fort. The attack was repulsed, and Greene had to withdraw.[78]

While Sumter complained of various problems getting his militia to turn out quickly, Greene privately suspected that the local commander was more interested in finding plunder for his troops than in helping the common cause. Greene's commissary general, Colonel William R. Davie, later recalled his commander commenting: "Sumter refuses to obey my orders, and carries off with him all the active [militia] force of this unhappy state on rambli[ng] predatory expeditions."[79]

Further compounding the plundering problem was "Sumter's Law." This was the informal name given to General Sumter's method of recruiting soldiers by promising them a bounty of property (principally slaves) confiscated from Tories. Unfortunately many patriot soldiers saw the "law" as a financial incentive to identify enemies of the state in order to increase their loot. Greene may have been frustrated with Sumter on many occasions, but he always tried to maintain good relations with the South Carolinian. He understood the important role that Sumter played in providing local leadership in a state that had lost all semblance of government.[80]

Of course South Carolina was not the only place that Greene had difficulties. In January 1781 Benedict Arnold led an amphibious invasion of Virginia.

"Female Patriotism." In this engraving a Mrs. Steele is comforting Greene over his frustrations with supply shortages, stubborn subordinates, meddlesome state officials, and a string of battlefield defeats.

Greene was in South Carolina at the time, and like Charles Lee in 1776, he could be in only one place at a time. Greene wrote in February 1781, "I have always considered the incursions in Virginia as of no consequence if we could prevent their penetrating this way [to the Carolinas]."[81] Therefore he chose to let Major General Friedrich von Steuben handle the British in Virginia, while he remained in the Carolinas.

Virginia's governor, Thomas Jefferson, seemed to sense that Greene was not putting as much emphasis on his home state and desired better communications with and access to the Southern Department commander. He therefore sent Major Charles Magill to Greene's headquarters to file reports on the situation there. Greene was not pleased with the major's presence, and he informed the governor that he could not give Magill any substantive intelligence because of the "necessity for secrecy." Nevertheless Greene did try to communicate more frequently with Jefferson from that time forward.[82]

A few weeks after the Battle of Guilford Courthouse, Jefferson agreed to send two thousand Virginia militia to reinforce the Southern Army in response to a request from Greene. Difficulties arose, however, and the raising of the reinforcements was delayed for several weeks. When Cornwallis invaded Virginia in May, Jefferson decided that the militia he originally intended to send to Greene, who was now in South Carolina, were needed instead for the defense of his own state. The new levies, except a small portion, would be kept at home.[83]

Blaming the failed siege of Ninety Six on the absence of the Virginia reinforcements, Greene told Jefferson: "The tardiness, and finally the countermanding of the militia ordered to join this army has been attended with the most mortifying and disagreeable consequences." Had Jefferson sent the militia in a timely fashion "we should have completed the reduction of all the enemy's out posts in this country; and for want of which we have been obliged to raise the siege of 96."[84]

Thinking that a governor did not have the right to give orders to militia when it was "engaged upon a continental plan," Greene petitioned Congress to intervene. Congress decided that it did not have the authority to take action on the matter and instead appointed a committee to consider granting itself "additional powers" to do so. The committee ultimately reviewed constitutional matters that went far beyond the issue of state and national authority over militia. Questions debated included "erecting a mint," "establishing a Census," and adopting "one universal plan of equipping, training and governing the Militia." While Greene's specific question was never answered, and the resolution never fully acted upon, it is fascinating that it was at the prompting of Nathanael Greene that Congress began some of the first serious investigations into expanding the powers of a central government that preceded the debate over the Constitution.[85]

In the end Greene's disputes with Thomas Jefferson and Thomas Sumter over control of military forces were far less significant than the problems Charles Lee or Robert Howe had with southern governors such as John Rutledge or John Houstoun. While Greene was forced to give up the siege of Ninety Six, his army survived intact, which forced the British to withdraw from the post anyway. Similarly, after the Battle of Eutaw Springs on September 8, 1781, the British may have kept the field, but the Americans had the stronger army, and within a few days the British abandoned their post to withdraw to the environs of Charleston.

Greene's strategic victory at Eutaw Springs, along with the capture of Cornwallis's army at Yorktown by Washington and Lieutenant General Jean-Baptiste-Donatien de Vimeur, Comte de Rochambeau, on October 19, meant that the war was winding to a close. Greene had for all practical purposes won the military portion of the war in the Deep South, even if he was not yet aware of the fact. Because of this victory, many of the disputes Greene had with militia leaders such as Sumter were rendered moot in historical terms. In addition

Jefferson left office at the beginning of June 1781, thus ending any further potential conflict there as well.

Indeed for some months Greene had been looking to *increase* the power of local officials by reestablishing the civil governments of South Carolina and Georgia. Greene felt this was the only way to stop the rampant plundering and murder that was sweeping the backcountry of South Carolina and Georgia. In 1776 Charles Lee, the first commander of the Southern Department, had sought to increase the divisions between Whigs and Tories by relocating and arresting Loyalists. However, that was before bloody civil war ripped through the Carolinas and Georgia after the fall of Charleston in 1780. Now Greene sought to bring the two sides together and begin the process of reconciliation. He wished to stop "the horid practice of private murders and plundering which prevail among both Whigs [and] Tories" and to reestablish civilian courts.[86]

An even more important strategic reason underlaid Greene's rush to reestablish civilian government. He had received intelligence that foreign powers were possibly helping to negotiate peace between the United States and Britain, and he was anxious that the treaty might be concluded "upon the plan of *uti posseditis* [*possidetis*]," or "as you possess." This ancient treaty principle meant the two belligerents in the conflict would keep the territory they possessed at the conclusion of the war. By pressing the enemy as closely as possible while at the same time reestablishing South Carolina's and Georgia's civilian governments, Greene hoped to counter any possible claim that the United States had given up territory to the British in those states.[87]

In fact Greene's information proved false, and peace was ultimately concluded through bilateral treaty negotiations between Great Britain and the United States alone. The Treaty of Paris, which brought the war to an end in 1783, did not use *uti possidetis* to determine the borders of the new United States of America, but since Greene could not have known that in 1781, establishing civilian governments and confining the British to as small an area as possible stayed one of his top priorities while he commanded in the South.

Greene had sent a letter to Governor John Rutledge of South Carolina as early as May 1781 encouraging him to begin the process of reestablishing civilian government. Greene began sending similar letters to officials from Georgia the next month. Georgia moved quickly on his advice, holding its legislative elections in August. The next month South Carolina reconvened the governor's privy council, and finally, in December, the state held elections for a new legislature. Thus Major General Nathanael Greene was a critical figure in reestablishing the civilian governments of these two states. The relationship between commanders of the Southern Department and local southern officials, which had proved so competitive at times, was brought full circle by Greene's curative actions on this matter.[88]

After the British defeat at Yorktown in October 1781, the war began to wind down. Fighting continued through 1782, but at a much reduced tempo. Greene continued to spar with local civilian officials on matters such as the supplying of his troops and the raising of black regiments. The enlistment of black troops had proved unpopular in South Carolina and Georgia since it had been first introduced under Major General Lincoln in 1779. But with everyone looking forward to peacetime, Greene's influence began to wane, and his arguments gained little traction in the state governments, even those that he had helped to reestablish.

The British evacuated Savannah in July 1782, and the last redcoats left Charleston in December of that year. Greene dismissed his army on June 21, 1783, telling them they had succeeded "against the tide of misfortune." The war in the South was officially over. On August 11, 1783, when Greene left Charleston headed for the North, negotiations were still underway in Europe for the peace treaty, which was signed in September. Yet the outcome was certain, and the former Quaker from Rhode Island could look back satisfied that he had avoided the "disgrace" that had befallen all that had "gone that way" before him.[89]

NOTES

1. Greene to Griffin Greene, October 11, 1780, *The Papers of General Nathanael Greene*, edited by Richard K. Showman, Dennis R. Conrad, and Roger N. Parks, 13 vols. (Chapel Hill: University of North Carolina Press, 1976–2005), 6:422.

2. Greene to Alexander Hamilton, January 10, 1781, ibid., 7:88.

3. Worthington C. Ford et al., eds., *Journals of the Continental Congress*, 34 vols. (Washington, D.C.: U.S. Government Printing Office, 1904–37), 4:15 (cited hereafter as *JCC*).

4. *JCC*, 4:174; Samuel Adams to Elbridge Gerry, October 29, 1775, in Peter Force, ed., *American Archives*, 4th ser. (Washington, D.C., 1853), 3:1248, National Endowment for the Humanities and Northern Illinois University Libraries online edition, http://dig.lib.niu.edu/amarch/index.html (accessed August 23,2011).

5. *JCC*, 4:180–81; James Duane to William Alexander, March 1, 1776, in Paul H. Smith et al., eds., *Letters of Delegates to Congress, 1774–1789*, 25 vols. (Washington, D.C.: Library of Congress, 1976–2000), 4:316–17.

6. Charles Lee to Edmund Pendleton, May 10, 1776, *The [Charles] Lee Papers*, edited by George Moore, in *Collections of the New-York Historical Society for the Year 1872*, 4 vols. (New York: New-York Historical Society, 1873), 2:21; David Wilson, *The Southern Strategy: Britain's Conquest of South Carolina and Georgia, 1775–1780* (Columbia: University of South Carolina Press, 2005), 17; Force, ed., *American Archives*, 4th ser. 4, 6:682–83; *Virginia Gazette* (Williamsburg, Dixon and Hunter), June 1, 1776, 3; *Virginia Gazette* (Purdie), March 29, 1776, 2; *Virginia Gazette* (Dixon and Hunter), February 10, 1776, 3; ibid., May 4, 1776, 3; Isaac Reed to Andrew Lewis, May 25, 1776, *The Lee Papers*, 2:3 9; "Extract

of a Letter from a Member of the Continental Congress to his Friend in Virginia," October 16, 1775, Force, ed., *American Archives*, 4th ser., 3:1072; Walter Hatton to Nathaniel Coffin, November 21, 1775, ibid., 3:1622; "Ordinances Passed by the Convention . . . ," January 1, 1776, ibid., 4:131; K. G. Davies, ed., *Documents of the American Revolution 1770–1783: Colonial Office Series*, 21 vols. (Shannon: Irish University Press, 1972–81), 12:67.

7. William Hand Browne, ed., *Archives of Maryland: Journal of the Maryland Convention, July 26–August 15, 1775 and Journal and Correspondence of the Maryland Council of Safety, August 29, 1775–July 6, 1776*, vol. 11 (Baltimore: Maryland Historical Society, 1892), 11:339–40; Thomas Stone to Daniel of St. Thomas Jenifer, April 24, 1776, Smith et al., eds., *Letters of Delegates*, 3:581. Letter from the Provincial Council of North Carolina, March, 5, 1776; Charles Lee to Samuel Purviance, April 6, 1776; Virginia Committee of Safety to Baltimore Committee of Safety, April 6, 1776; George Germain to William Eden, December 23, 1775; Samuel Purviance to the Baltimore deputation at Annapolis, April 14, 1776; Force, ed., *American Archives*, 4th ser., 5:60, 800, 928, 929, 930.

8. "Proceedings of a Council [of War]" Charles Lee, president, Lee to Edmund Pendleton, May 9, 1776; Lee to George Washington, May 10, 1776; Lee to Edmund Pendleton, May 10, 1776; *The Lee Papers*, 2:8–9, 16, 19, 21; Lee to Samuel Purviance, April 6, 1776, Force, ed., *American Archives*, 4th ser., 5:800.

9. Lee to Samuel Purviance, April 6, 1776, Force, ed., *American Archives*, 4th ser., 5:800. John Richard Alden, *General Charles Lee: Traitor or Patriot?* (Baton Rouge: Louisiana State University Press, 1951), 114.

10. Lee to Samuel Purviance, April 6, 1776, Force, ed., *American Archives*, 4th ser., 5:800.

11. Ibid., 11:vii. Thomas Johnson to the Maryland Council of Safety, April 17, 1776; Minutes of the Maryland Council of Safety, April 24, 1776; Lee to Thomas Jenifer, May 6, 1776; ibid., 11:347–48, 373–88, 410–11.

12. Lee to James Moore, and Lee to Edmund Pendleton, June 1, 1776, *The Lee Papers*, 2:30, 51.

13. John Armstrong to Charles Lee, May 8, 1776, ibid., 2:10.

14. John Rutledge to William Moultrie, June 9, 1776, ibid., 2:57.

15. William Moultrie, *Memoirs of the American Revolution*, 2 vols. (New York: Longworth, 1802), 1:141.

16. Charles Lee to William Moultrie, June 11, 1776, *The Lee Papers*, 2:60–61.

17. R. W. Gibbes, ed., *Documentary History of the American Revolution*, 3 vols. (New York: Appleton, 1853–57), 2:10, 28; Charles Lee to William Moultrie, June 21, 1776, *The Lee Papers*, 2:77; John Drayton, *Memoirs of the American Revolution*, 2 vols. (Charleston: A. E. Miller, 1821), 2:312.

18. Wilson, *The Southern Strategy*, 36–57; Alden, *Charles Lee*, 134–35.

19. Moultrie, *Memoirs*, 1:184.

20. Charles Lee to Richard Peters, August 2, 1776; Lee to John Rutledge, August 3, 1776; minutes of a conference with the Georgia Council of Safety; *The Lee Papers*, 2:188–89, 199, 233–35; Alden, *Charles Lee*, 131–32; Charles Bennett and Donald R. Lennon, *A Quest for Glory: Major General Robert Howe and the American Revolution* (Chapel Hill & London: University of North Carolina Press, 1991), 57–58.

21. *JCC*, 5:462.

22. Charles Lee to John Rutledge, July 22, 1776, and Lee to the congressional Board of War and Ordnance, August 7, 1776, *The Lee Papers*, 2:156, 201–4.

23. Lee to John Rutledge, June 6, 1776, ibid., 2:200, 201–4; Alden, *Charles Lee*, 132; Drayton, *Memoirs*, 2:335.

24. Moultrie, *Memoirs*, 1:187.

25. John Armstrong to Charles Lee, July 1776, *The Lee Papers*, 2:184–85, 246; Robert Howe to John Rutledge, September 1776, George Washington Papers, Manuscript Division, Library of Congress, Washington, D.C. http://memory.loc.gov/mss/mgw/mgw4/038/0300/0338.jpg (accessed August 23, 2011).

26. *JCC*, 4:181, 5:761; Bennett and Lennon, *Quest for Glory*, 57–58.

27. Henry Laurens to John Rutledge, October 19, 1777, Smith et al., eds., *Letters of Delegates*, 8:144–45; Bennett and Lennon, *Quest for Glory*, 57.

28. Christopher Gadsden to William Drayton, September 9, 1778, *The Writings of Christopher Gadsden*, edited by Richard Walsh (Columbia: University of South Carolina Press, 1966), 151.

29. Bennett and Lennon, *Quest for Glory*, 57, 60; Christopher Gadsden to William Drayton, September 9, 1778, *The Writings of Christopher Gadsden*, 151.

30. Robert Howe to George Washington, May 14, 1777, George Washington Papers, Library of Congress, http://memory.loc.gov/mss/mgw/mgw4/041/0800/0893.jpg (accessed August 23, 2011); Kenneth Coleman, *The American Revolution in Georgia: 1763–1789* (Athens: University of Georgia Press, 1958), 103–4. Charles Francis Jenkins, *Button Gwinnett: Signer of the Declaration of Independence* (Garden City, N.Y.: Doubleday, Page, 1926), 220–21.

31. Jenkins, *Button Gwinnett*, 144, 215–21, Hugh McCall, *History of Georgia*, 2 vols. (Atlanta: A. B. Caldwell, 1909), 1:339–45.

32. George Walton to George Washington, August 5, 1777, and William Ellery to Oliver Wolcott, September 18, 1777, Smith et al., eds., *Letters of Delegates*, 7:199, 431.

33. *Proceedings of a General Court Martial . . . of Major General Howe* (Philadelphia: Hall & Sellers, 1782), facsimile reprinted in *Collections of the New-York Historical Society for the Year 1879* (New York: New-York Historical Society, 1880), 273.

34. Smith et al., eds., *Letters of Delegates*, 10:9n2; *JCC*, 11:553–54.

35. Coleman, *The American Revolution in Georgia*, 107; Charles Oscar Paullin, *The Navy of the American Revolution: Its Administration, Its Policy and Its Achievements* (Chicago: University of Chicago Press, 1906), 461.

36. Robert Howe to William Moultrie, July 5, 1778, and Charles Pinckney to Moultrie, July 10, 1778, Moultrie, *Memoirs*, 1:227–28, 230.

37. Hugh F. Rankin, *The North Carolina Continentals* (Chapel Hill: University of North Carolina Press, 1971), 18; Bennett and Lennon, *Quest for Glory*, 7–8.

38. Henry Laurens to Robert Howe, October 6, 1778, in Smith et al., eds., *Letters of Delegates*, 11:34; *JCC*, 12:951; Cornelius Harnett to Richard Caswell, 26 September 26, 1778, in Smith et al., eds., *Letters of Delegates*, 10:696; Cornelius Harnett to Richard Caswell, November 24, 1778, in Smith et al., eds., *Letters of Delegates*, 11:252.

39. Wilson, *The Southern Strategy*, 78–79. Benjamin Lincoln to George Washington, December 19, 1778, George Washington Papers, Library of Congress, http://memory.loc.gov/mss/mgw/mgw4/055/0000/0063.jpg (accessed August 23, 2010).

40. *Proceedings of a General Court Martial . . . of Major General Howe*, 267, 271; Wilson, *The Southern Strategy*, 79.

41. *Proceedings of a General Court Martial . . . of Major General Howe*, 217, 219, 310.

42. Jared Sparks, ed., *Correspondence of the American Revolution*, 4 vols. (Boston: Little, Brown, 1853), 2:241; Benjamin Lincoln to George Washington, December 19, 1778.

43. Sparks, ed., *Correspondence of the American Revolution*, 2:241; Benjamin Lincoln to George Washington, December 19, 1778.

44. Benjamin Lincoln to Rawlins Lowndes, January 6, 1779, Benjamin Lincoln Papers, Massachusetts Historical Society, Boston, reel 3, frame 69; *The State Records of North Carolina*, edited by Walter Clark, 16 vols., numbered 11–26 (Winston & Goldsboro, N.C.: State of North Carolina, 1895–1905), 14:52.

45. *JCC*, 3:326; Moultrie, *Memoirs*, 1:322.

46. Council of general officers, April 19, 1779, in Moultrie, *Memoirs*, 1:375.

47. Wilson, *The Southern Strategy*, 104, 106.

48. Moultrie, *Memoirs*, 1:426; Wilson, *The Southern Strategy*, 110.

49. Wilson, *The Southern Strategy*, 100–15.

50. Ibid., 121, 128–29.

51. Ibid., 145.

52. Ibid., 157.

53. Benjamin Lincoln to William Moultrie, June 10, 1779, and Peter Timothy to Lincoln, October 13, 1779, Benjamin Lincoln Papers, Massachusetts Historical Society.

54. Wilson, *The Southern Strategy*, 222, 240–41.

55. *Lachlan McIntosh Papers*, edited by Lilla Mills Hawes (Athens: University of Georgia Press, 1968), 101; Wilson, *The Southern Strategy*, 222.

56. *Lachlan McIntosh Papers*, 101, 104.

57. Ibid., 104; E. Stanly Godbold Jr. and Robert H. Woody, *Christopher Gadsden and the American Revolution* (Knoxville: University of Tennessee Press, 1982), 200.

58. Moultrie, *Memoirs*, 1:426. Wilson, *The Southern Strategy*, 240.

59. For Gates's appointment to command the Southern Department see *JCC*, 17:492, 508, 510–11; John Armstrong to Horatio Gates, June 6, 1780, June 15, 1780, Smith et al., eds., *Letters of Delegates*, 15:259, 319–20n1. For Gates's role in the "Conway Cabal," see Thomas Fleming, *Washington's Secret War: The Hidden History of Valley Forge* (New York: Smithsonian Books, 2005).

60. Joseph Jones to Thomas Jefferson, June 30, 1780, Smith et al., eds., *Letters of Delegates*, 15:393–94.

61. Horatio Gates to officers of South Carolina Militia, July and August 1780, in Thomas Addis Emmett, ed., "The Southern Campaign 1780: Letters of Major General Gates," *Magazine of American History* 5 (December 1880): 293–94.

62. Gates to Richard Caswell, August 3, 1780, and Gates to Abner Nash, August 3, 1780, ibid., 296.

63. Gates to Richard Caswell, July 30, 1780, and Gates to Richard Caswell, August 3, 1780 (two letters), ibid., 295, 296, 298.

64. John Rutledge to Horatio Gates, August 14, 1782, Smith et al., eds., *Letters of Delegates*, 19:66–67.

65. John Hanson to Thomas Sim Lee, October 3, 1780, Smith et al., eds., *Letters of Delegates*, 16:136. George Washington to Nathanael Greene, October 14, 1780, George Washington Papers, Library of Congress.

66. For a history of the Kings Mountain campaign, see Lyman C. Draper, *King's Mountain and Its Heroes* (Cincinnati: Peter G. Thompson, 1881), and H. L. Landers, ed., *Historical Statements Concerning the Battle of Kings Mountain and the Battle of Cowpens* (Washington: U.S. Government Printing Office, 1928).

67. Horatio Gates to Samuel Huntington, July 4, 1780, in Emmett, ed., "The Southern Campaign," 282; Gates to Daniel Morgan, June 23, 1780, Papers of General Daniel Morgan, Theodore Bailey Myers Collection, New York Public Library Manuscripts and Archives Collection, item 857.

68. Gates to Samuel Huntington, July 4, 1780, in Emmett, ed., "The Southern Campaign," 282.

69. George Washington to Joseph Jones, July 22, 1780, George Washington Papers, Library of Congress.

70. *JCC*, 18:920–21; Joseph Jones to George Washington, July 18, 1780, Smith et al., eds., *Letters of Delegates*, 15:468–70; George Washington to Joseph Jones, July 22, 1780, George Washington Papers, Library of Congress; Horatio Gates to Daniel Morgan, October 27, 1780, Morgan Papers, New York Public Library, item 860.

71. *JCC*, 18:995.

72. Greene to Alexander Hamilton, January 10, 1781, *The Papers of General Nathanael Greene*, 7:88–89; Greene to congressional committee, October 29, 1780, ibid., 6:441.

73. Greene to George Washington, October 31, 1780, ibid., 6:448; Theodore Thayer, *Nathanael Greene: Strategist of the Revolution* (New York: Twayne, 1960), 290, 299.

74. Daniel Morgan to Nathanael Greene, January 15, 1781; Greene to Morgan January 19, 1781; Greene to Thomas Sumter, January 19, 1781; Sumter to Greene, January 29, 1781; *The Papers of General Nathanael Greene*, 7:127–28, 146, 149, 217.

75. Greene to Daniel Morgan, December 16, 1780, ibid., 6:589. Greene to Robert Howe, December 29, 1780; Morgan to Greene, January 15, 1781; Greene to Morgan, January 19, 1781; Greene to Thomas Sumter, January 19, 1781; ibid., 7:18, 127, 146, 149.

76. Greene to Thomas Sim Lee, November 10, 1780, and Greene to Thomas Jefferson, November 20, 1780, ibid., 6:474, 492; Greene to Alexander Hamilton, January 10, 1781, and Greene to North Carolina legislature, February 17, 1781, ibid., 7:88, 90, 304.

77. Thayer, *Nathanael Greene* 329–30, 335.

78. Greene to Thomas Sumter, April 23, 1781; Sumter to Greene, April 25, 1781; Greene to Sumter, May 17, 1781; Greene to Sumter, May 21, 1781; Sumter to Greene, June 7, 1781; Greene to Sumter, June 10, 1781; Sumter to Greene, June 16, 1781; Sumter to Greene, June 19, 1781; *The Papers of General Nathanael Greene*, 8:135–36, 149–50, 278, 321, 360, 374, 403, 416–17.

79. Recollection of William R. Davie, May 9, 1781, ibid., 8:225.

80. Greene to Francis Marion, May 17, 1781, and Greene to Thomas Sumter, May 17, 1781, ibid., 8:276–77, 278; Richard Maxwell Brown, *Strain of Violence: Historical Studies of American Violence and Vigilantism* (New York: Oxford University Press, 1975), 77–78.

81. Greene to Baron Friedrich von Steuben, February 3, 1781, *The Papers of General Nathanael Greene,* 7:243.

82. Thomas Jefferson to Greene, February 18, 1781, and Greene to Jefferson, February 28, 1781, ibid., 7:312–13, 367, 367n2.

83. Greene to Thomas Jefferson, 23 March 23, 1781, ibid., 7:466, 466n1; Jefferson to Greene, March 30, 1781, and Greene to Samuel Huntington, June 9, 1781, ibid., 8:13, 363.

84. Greene to Thomas Jefferson, June 27, 1781, ibid., 8:463.

85. Greene to Samuel Huntington, June 9, 1781, ibid., 8:363, 365n4; *JCC,* 21:784, 790, 894–96.

86. Greene to James Mason, June 11, 1781, *The Papers of General Nathanael Greene,* 8:377.

87. Greene to Arthur St. Clair, November 21, 1781, ibid., 9:604.

88. Greene to John Rutledge, May 14, 1781, Greene to John Wilkinson, June 13, 1781, ibid., 8:256, 386.

89. Ibid. 13:45; Thayer, *Nathanael Greene,* 424.

"I am an independent spirit, and confide in my own resources"

Nathanael Greene and His Continental Subordinates, 1780–1781

GREG BROOKING

$\mathcal{B}$arely two weeks after Major General Nathanael Greene assumed command of the Continental army's Southern Department, the officers of the Maryland Line, the department's most dependable unit, submitted to him a list of grievances concerning their displeasure with their state for "Creat[ing] a new Corps and Commenc[ing] new Officers without regard to the service and sufferings of those in the field," thus diminishing the "relative rank" of Maryland's current Continental officers after the Battle of Camden. Greene's response encapsulates the manner of relationships he cultivated with subordinates, for he intimately understood their concerns and pledged himself to their redress. "As an officer I feel for you," Greene replied, "[and] as your commander it is my duty to represent your grievances, and to indeavor to procure you redress. It has ever been my study to render the service as agreeable to the feelings of Officers as possible."[1] He concluded with the assurance that a recent congressional decree affirmatively resolved their petition and personally contacted Governor Thomas Sim Lee of Maryland with suggestions to ameliorate the situation.[2] This brief exchange placed Greene's leadership style on full display: his response to the Marylanders was immediate, empathetic, and thorough. Most important, Greene fully exerted himself on behalf of his subordinates, a trait that became his modus operandi as commander of the Southern Department.

To a great degree Greene's relationships with his subordinates in the South replicated the rapport he had established with his own superior, General George Washington. Washington took an immediate liking to the inexperienced

Greene, whom he paternally groomed into a miniature version of himself. Greene more than reciprocated Washington's feelings, seeing in the Virginian a surrogate father worthy of devotion and emulation.[3] A Greene descendant commented on their relationship: "On the one side it was based upon profound respect and admiration, unquestioning loyalty, willing obedience, and unbounded faith; on the other, upon the fullest confidence, affection, and esteem."[4]

Throughout the long and arduous conflict, Greene occupied a position of great importance to Washington. Whether Greene directed a critical wing of the main army, lobbied Congress for support, piloted the underfunded Quartermaster Department, or commanded the much-maligned Southern Department, Washington considered him his "favorite officer."[5] In a letter to his wife, Greene noted, "I am exceeding happy in the full confidence of his Excellency General Washington, and I found [that confidence] to increase every hour, the more [difficult] and distressing our affairs grew."[6] Their relationship allowed Greene to express himself freely, and he took liberty in conveying his martial opinions to his commander.[7] Like Washington, Greene allowed his own subordinates to express their concerns and opinions.

Washington called on Greene's devotion throughout the war, but most notably in the fall of 1780, when he nominated Greene to succeed Major General Horatio Gates following the disastrous Battle of Camden. Congress had never before consulted Washington when determining the command of the Southern Department, but after losing two armies in a few months, that body asked Washington to choose the new commander.[8] Washington wrote his recommendation to Congress: "I beg leave to mention General Greene, upon this occasion, to Congress as an Officer, in whose abilities, fortitude and integrity, from a long and intimate experience of them, I have the most intire confidence."[9]

From headquarters at Passaic Falls, New Jersey, Washington notified Greene of his decision.[10] Washington later affirmed his belief in Greene's ability to "stop the progress of the evils which have befallen and still menace the Southern States."[11] In the formal appointment Washington afforded Greene the latitude to act as he saw fit.[12] Greene relished this autonomy and later afforded certain members of his own army similar autonomy—but with qualifications. Washington then made a concerted effort to provide Greene with the resources he could spare, namely the legion commanded by Major Henry Lee. In closing, Washington reminded Greene to keep him appraised of his "Affairs and of every material occurrence."[13] Greene demanded this same level of communication from his own subordinates. Comparing Washington's letter to Greene with appointment letters sent to Major Generals Benjamin Lincoln and Horatio Gates provides further insight into Greene's relationship with Washington. The letters to Greene regarding the southern command were replete with warm, fatherly sentiments and advice. With previous southern commanders, Washington maintained a distant, purely professional tone.[14]

Although Greene had longed for an independent command, he soon found himself effectively alone—with communication to Washington taking at least a month. Greene lamented the difficulties of waging war so "far removed from almost all my friends."[15] Ultimately, however, this arrangement suited Greene because, as he later admitted to Lee, "I am an independent spirit, and confide in my own resources."[16] Greene's conduct of the southern campaigns proved that he thrived in such a solitary situation.

Historians have liberally quoted—yet scarcely analyzed—Greene's comments about the utility of militia. Throughout the entirety of the war, Greene unleashed torrential criticism of the militia; however, by the time he arrived at Charlotte, North Carolina, on December 2, 1780, he understood their necessity. Although he preferred an established army to local partisans, Greene comprehended the need to "keep up a Partizan War" at least "Untill a more permanent Army can be collected."[17] There never arose a time during the southern campaigns in which Greene's Continentals were sufficient to engage the enemy alone; thus necessity mandated his continual reliance on partisans. Were it not for Greene's adroit management of the leading partisans, especially the contentious and self-serving General Thomas Sumter, the outcome of the southern phase of the war might have been quite different.[18]

More important than his capable handling of partisans, Greene's deft leadership of his Continental subordinates allowed him to implement strategies culminating in the near extirpation of the British army in the South. Most notable of these subordinates were the irrepressible Brigadier General Daniel Morgan, the flamboyant Major Henry Lee, the dependable Colonel Otho Holland Williams, the energetic Lieutenant Colonel William Washington, and the scapegoated Colonel John Gunby.

In examining Greene's leadership style and his relationships with these officers, four questions require resolution: How much autonomy did Greene allow his subordinates? To what extent did he rely on them for counsel? How did he soothe or discipline them? At what level did he support them? That is, did he avail himself to them; did he stand up for them; and did he equip them for success?

Best known for administering a "devil of a whiping" to Lieutenant Colonel Banastre Tarleton, Daniel Morgan was granted an independent command in December 1780.[19] Morgan was Greene's first detached subordinate, and their relationship provides valuable insight into Greene's command style. Although he afforded Morgan some independence, Greene also gave succinct instructions and—much like an overprotective and nagging parent—constantly warned Morgan to act cautiously and avoid surprise.[20]

Their correspondence also reveals that Greene afforded his subordinates ample latitude to express themselves, much as Washington afforded him. For example, with Tarleton nipping at his heels, a worried Morgan offered several strategic suggestions that would allow him to disengage with Tarleton.[21] Greene carefully considered such proposals. Sensing Morgan's insecurity, Greene acknowledged that although "Col. Tarlton is said to be on his way to pay you a visit. I doubt not but he will have a decent reception and a proper dismission."[22] On January 17, 1781, Morgan indeed dismissed Tarleton and "obtain[ed] a compleat Victory."[23]

Just hours after the battle, Morgan extricated himself from the region and made haste toward Greene's camp. General Charles, Lord Cornwallis, decided Morgan must be caught at all costs.[24] The British chased Morgan with relentless fury, and Greene deemed the situation too important for Morgan to handle alone.[25] On the thirty-first Greene held a brief, informal council of war with Morgan, General William Lee Davidson, and William Washington and formulated a plan that resulted in the army successfully crossing the Yadkin River.[26]

A formal council of war on February 9 unanimously decided to avoid a general action and called for a retreat into Virginia, initiating the final push in the race to the Dan River. Greene seldom convened councils of war, learning from Washington that leadership by committee could prove catastrophically inhibiting. Greene always preferred self-determination, boasting to Alexander Hamilton that "I call no councils of war; and I communicate my intentions to very few."[27]

Most likely Greene convened this rare council of war not for the purpose of seeking counsel but to protect himself from possible censure.[28] Shortly thereafter Morgan's tenure in the Southern Department ended, although neither he nor Greene knew this to be the case at the time because they believed his leave would be temporary. The next month, while preparing to return to Greene, Morgan received a request to join Marie Joseph Gilbert du Motier, Marquis de Lafayette, in anticipation of Cornwallis's arrival in Virginia, a request Morgan accepted.[29] Greene replaced Morgan with the reliable Colonel Otho Holland Williams,[30] directing Williams's corps of seven hundred men to serve as a screening force between the main army and Cornwallis so that the remainder of the army could safely cross the Dan River.[31]

On February 10, Greene tried to lure Cornwallis to the upper part of the Dan by dispatching Williams's light corps to Bruce's Cross Roads, seven miles northwest of Guilford Courthouse.[32] On the same day and with "great hopes [that Greene] would not escape," Cornwallis eagerly chased Williams.[33]

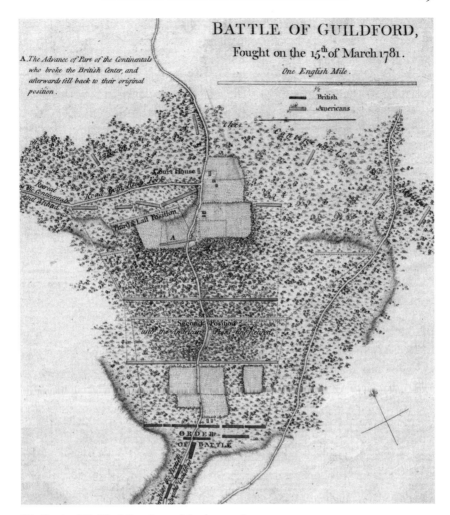

The Battle of Guilford Courthouse, March 15, 1781

Ordered by Williams to find Cornwallis, Henry Lee engaged the British vanguard and captured a few prisoners, who reported that Cornwallis and Tarleton were on their heels. With great celerity and deft management of his detachment, Williams hurried across the Haw River bridge, successfully avoiding a general action with Cornwallis.[34]

Details for the events of February 12–13 are murky because the contemporary accounts are inconsistent.[35] It is clear, however, that Lee's Legion, occupying the hazardous rear guard position of the light corps, was in constant contact with Tarleton's Legion.[36] The utter dearth of Greene correspondence during these days testifies to the harried nature of this trek across the Carolina back-country. In fact Greene did not have time to write Williams until February 13 when he cautioned his subordinate not to expose the "flower of the army." A dispirited Williams beseeched his commander to move with all alacrity to the lower fords because Cornwallis had gathered solid intelligence, "maneuvered us from our Strong position at Chambers Mill and then mov'd with great rapidity." Betraying a sense of doom, Williams lamented that the cost of Greene's crossing the Dan might be the loss of his own corps.[37]

Before daybreak on the fourteenth, Greene ordered Williams to follow the main army to the lower fords and expressed concern for the army's fate.[38] Later that day, however, Greene happily informed Williams that the troops had crossed the Dan, and the "stage is clear" for Williams to join them.[39] After a final hectic push for the crossing by Williams's force, the race to the Dan concluded around midnight on February 14. All told, Cornwallis chased Greene for three weeks and 250 miles, to no avail—Greene had bested him.[40]

Williams felt deeply the effects of the retreat. Writing to Greene four days later, he revealed that although "Rheumatism" in his "Breast, Neck & shoulders has been exceedingly painful," he hoped that a "few Days refreshment" would allow him to revel in the "Glories of a successful Campaign." He also predicted future success for the Southern Army and acknowledged a reluctance to "relinquish" his present command.[41] Williams did not have to relinquish command just yet and continued to lead the light corps until shortly before the Battle of Guilford Courthouse.

Much credit for the successful conclusion of the race to the Dan rests squarely on Williams's broad shoulders. Tarleton credited Greene and Williams for their "judiciously designed and vigorously executed" plan.[42] Greene expressed the utmost satisfaction in the performance of Williams, reporting to Washington, "His conduct upon the occasion does him the highest honor."[43] Greene's contentment with the performance of the screening force, however, paled in comparison to Williams's own evaluation. In a letter to Dr. David Ramsay, Williams opined, "the propriety of the retreat . . . has not been exceeded by any military manouvre practised this War."[44]

Williams had not yet completed his task. During the dramatic period between the conclusion of the race to the disbanding of the lights corps on March 9, Williams wrote Greene at least twenty times. The majority of this correspondence related to provisions and supplies, but it also provided sufficient examples of the easy nature with which Greene accepted suggestions from his subordinates, particularly regarding troop movements.[45]

Unlike Morgan, who tended to be lax in maintaining correspondence according to Greene's standards, Williams constantly kept his commander apprised. Not once during this period did Greene remind the Marylander to keep him informed.[46] In the last days of February, Williams expressed apprehension that the British had initiated a game of "Hide & Seek."[47] Even though Williams's concerns were unfounded, Greene failed to reply. In fact Greene did not send Williams one letter between February 26 and March 3. While this lack of correspondence must have frustrated Williams, Greene's correspondence during this period was uncharacteristically sparse.

On March 1 Williams suggested that a "brisk, unexpected attack" on Cornwallis's force "may be considerable and of great consequence to your future operations."[48] Because of an organizational breakdown, the proposed attack never materialized. The next afternoon, Williams reported a brief, intense exchange with Tarleton's Legion at Clapp's Mill, resulting in several dozen casualties on both sides.[49]

Greene finally responded to Williams's flurry of correspondence on March 3, simply "approv[ing]" of Williams's position.[50] The next day Williams notified Greene that his force had again engaged a British "Picquett near Tarleton's Legion," killing several and capturing two.[51] Williams forwarded the prisoners to the main camp where, after an interrogation, Greene determined that Williams should, if "practicable," attack Tarleton's detachment.[52] Williams assured Greene that he was "always mindful of your orders to attack the Enemy when any opportunity offers," especially in light of how Greene's "repe[ti]tion of this order imply's how solicitous you are to have it done."[53] Then in a moment of frustration, his feelings hurt, Williams added. "Perhaps I am to construe those frequent intimations as sufficiently expressive. Whenever an Opportunity offers I will embrace it if I can be justified by the circumstances . . . if anything more is expected I wo[ul]d thank you to be explicit."[54]

This exchange reveals much about their relationship. On March 6, Williams admitted that he "was perhaps too tenacious of [Greene's] approbation." He admitted that he had even questioned Greene's aide, Major Ichabod Burnet, "respecting your sentiments of my conduct."[55] Williams acknowledged that Greene's orders "gave me a latitude which manifested a confidence in my Capacity." On a personal note, Williams added, "I regard your Friendship as invaluable. . . . I will endeavour to deserve it by a rectitude of Conduct."[56] Williams was apparently the only subordinate to unabashedly express his feelings for Greene. While there is no record of Greene's response, he likely welcomed such attention, as he expressed himself similarly to Washington and maintained a close relationship with Williams throughout the rest of their short lives.

Williams's duty as an independent operator in the Carolina backcountry concluded shortly after the mysterious and controversial Battle of Weitzel's Mill on March 6. Attempting to bait Greene into a general action, Cornwallis had dispatched Lieutenant Colonel James Webster and Tarleton "to beat up [Williams's force] at Reedy Fork."[57] Clueless about Cornwallis's machinations,

Williams sent out his own party, only to learn then that the British were on the march.[58] By the time Williams learned of Cornwallis's intentions, the British were already within two miles of him. Williams sent patrols to delay the British and raced for Weitzel's Mill. Williams again won the race and preserved his men, although the British contested the crossing.[59]

Williams reported his losses as "very inconsiderable."[60] Contemporary accounts contradict this assessment, estimating at least two dozen rebel casualties.[61] Exacerbating the situation was the militia's claim that Williams had used them as human shields while the Continentals crossed the river.[62] In his memoir Colonel William R. Davie, Greene's commissary and former North Carolina partisan, spoke ill of Williams's performance: "Colo Williams was reproached for suffering so important a movement of the enemy to take place without observing it, 'till he had scarce time to escape himself, altho' he commanded a party of observation and the salvation of the Army depended upon his vigilance. . . . Gen. Greene was at that moment more exposed than he had ever been."[63]

Within two days Greene had dissolved Williams's light corps and reassigned most of his men into a reorganized Southern Army that would soon initiate offensive operations.[64] Although the action at Weitzel's Mill may have caused Greene to lose faith in Williams, Greene most likely believed William's job had been satisfactorily completed. In a letter to Joseph Reed, Greene noted that Williams "judiciously avoided" Cornwallis.[65] Adding support to this positive appraisal is Williams's continued important role in the Southern Army. Following this reorganization, Greene placed Williams in command of Maryland's Continental brigade, and he continued service as Greene's adjutant general.[66]

Attached to Williams's light corps, Henry Lee emerged as Greene's most trusted subordinate. The two were well acquainted, and Greene knew of Lee's sterling reputation.[67] While he desired Lee's transfer to the Southern Department, Greene repeatedly had to massage the temperamental and insecure Lee. Back in the fall, while Greene methodically trekked southward, Lee dallied around Philadelphia haggling Congress for a promotion.[68] Lee believed his present rank of major unsuitable "for any capital services."[69] Greene went to bat for Lee, declaring to Congress that the "merit and services of Major Lee . . . are so generally known and so universally confessed that . . . I beg leave to propose the promotion of Major Lee to a Lieutenant Colonel."[70]

Lee's most notable action prior to the Battle of Guilford Courthouse occurred near the Haw River when, on February 25, he and Andrew Pickens engaged Colonel John Pyle's Loyalist militia. In his memoir Lee stated that a "beautifully deceptive maneuver" resulted in the annihilation of Pyle's men.[71] Pickens, however, noted that their men had also been confused, thinking Pyle's troops to be a contingent of Whigs.[72] The ruse aside, the brutal nature of the event did not negatively impress Greene, who acknowledged that Lee's destruction of Pyle's corps "put a total stop to their recruiting service."[73]

In mid-March, Greene prepared for imminent conflict with Cornwallis. On March 10, he attached Colonel William Campbell's riflemen to Lee's Legion to monitor the British left flank.[74] Lee kept Greene apprised of Cornwallis's movements, writing, "It appears to me that his Lordship & army begin to possess disagreeable apprehensions. If you dare, get near him."[75] The next morning, Lee informed Greene that Tarleton engaged his patrols and might be on his way to visit Greene. Lee also expressed concern that he did not know where to reach Greene and that such knowledge "is material," lest they be caught ill prepared.[76]

Either on the twelfth or thirteenth, Lee suggested that Greene move the army, but timing made such a move difficult. Instead Greene ordered Lee to guard New Garden Road and maintain extreme vigilance to avoid a surprise. Greene added that, while he did not think the British would advance in the morning, if they did, it would be to "attack us."[77] At 2:00 A.M. on the fifteenth, Lee learned that the British were advancing toward Greene's force at Guilford Courthouse.[78]

Shortly after Greene asked Lee to ascertain the nature of Cornwallis's movement, Lee's vedettes encountered Tarleton's dragoons, initiating the Battle of Guilford Courthouse. Lee hurriedly withdrew toward the main army and sent a courier to inform Greene. Tarleton took this opportunity to press Lee's men but quickly found himself too extended and "retired with celerity" toward Cornwallis's main army. Attempting to intercept Tarleton, Lee became embroiled in a hot firefight along the New Garden and Great Salisbury Road, which lasted approximately two hours. Convinced a general action was imminent, both Tarleton and Lee broke off the engagement. Greene concurred, "not doubting," according to Lee, "that the long avoided, now wished-for, hour was at hand."[79]

As Greene prepared, he certainly remembered Daniel Morgan's letter of February 20, in which Morgan noted that the outcome of the contest would rest on the ability of the militia. He then advised Greene about utilizing the militia and deploying troops. Morgan's tactical suggestion mirrored that of his great battle at Cowpens. Morgan ended his letter with deference: "I hope you'll not take this as dictating but as my opinion."[80] In fact Greene's tactics resembled those Morgan suggested.[81]

Although Greene relinquished the field at Guilford Courthouse, the rebels dealt the British a severe blow, inflicting many more than five hundred casualties.[82] Lee's most active engagement during the battle occurred about one-quarter mile south of the main fighting line. The fighting in this sector proved disjointed and exceptionally ferocious. The seesaw affair turned in favor of the British on the arrival of Tarleton. After the war, Colonel Johan Du Buy related to Lieutenant Colonel John Eager Howard of Maryland that "his [Hessian] regiment would have been cut up if Tarleton had not so seasonably come to his relief."[83] Instead of Du Buy's Von Bose Regiment getting "cut up," it was Campbell's riflemen—in large part because Lee withdrew at, or just prior to, the arrival of Tarleton's dragoons. Campbell clearly believed Lee had deliberately deserted the Virginians. According to William C. Preston, "Lee's abandonment of Campbell's riflemen . . . without giving notice of his withdrawal, was long regarded by the survivors with the most bitter feelings."[84] Lee painted quite a different picture in his memoir, but it is plausible that his version was an attempt to preserve his reputation.[85]

Lee's action could have been cause for a court-martial, and Campbell failed to conceal his disgust for Lee's behavior. But Greene never mentioned the incident in his official correspondence.[86] Greene's gushing letter to Campbell three days later, praising his "faithful services" and "manly behavior," may have been an attempt to mollify the Virginian.[87] Greene made only two substantive comments about Lee in his official battle report. The first dealt with the prebattle encounter with Tarleton; the second was a brief compliment of Lee's performance as part of the corps of observation.[88] Despite his questionable conduct at Guilford, Lee had not lost favor with Greene.

As the army regrouped after the battle, Lee resumed his practice of offering unsolicited advice, advising Greene that it would be "best to attack the enemy on their march."[89] A few days later, on March 22, Greene informed Lee, "I am agreed in opinion with you that Lord Cornwallis don't wish to fight us, but you may depend upon it, he will not refuse to fight if we push him."[90] To that end Greene ordered Lee to harass the British commander. In spite of his aggressive efforts, circumstances required Greene call off his pursuit a week later.[91] Lee apparently agreed with the decision, suggesting that Greene "imitate the example of Scipio Africanus."[92] In this praising, if not sycophantic, letter Lee proffered several suggestions, some of which Greene had already addressed and some of which he ignored.

Four weeks after the battle, Cornwallis, "tired of marching about the country in quest of adventures," formulated a new plan, ordering his weakened force northward into Virginia.[93] About the same time, Greene drove his army in the opposite direction—back into South Carolina. In a letter to General Washington on March 29 Greene explained: "I am determined to carry the War immediately into South Carolina [for] the Enemy will be obliged to follow us or give up their posts in that State."[94] Lee later claimed credit for this strategy. He cited an April 5 council of war debate in which he suggested that the light corps break down all intermediate posts, demolishing communication between Camden and Ninety Six with Charleston.[95] Greene concurred, but he had already determined his course.

Accordingly Lee set out on the morning of April 6 to join Francis Marion's partisans heading for Fort Watson, an important communications post on the Santee River. Ever cognizant of placing his subordinates in a position where success seemed likely, Greene suggested Fort Watson because it was the most likely fort to succumb to attack. He then exhorted Lee to be both vigilant, because the army could not "afford to waste men without a valuable object in contemplation," and modest, because "you command Men, and their powers may not keep pace with your ambition."[96] While Greene maintained confidence in Lee's ability, he had become concerned that Lee's desire for laurels might impair his judgment.

Greene's correspondence during the next two weeks conveyed this concern. In contrast to the tone of his previous communications with Lee, Greene's three letters between April 1 and 14 (when Lee joined Marion) resemble the fatherly and patronizing tenor of his letters to Morgan in the days leading up to Cowpens, offering both suggestions and warnings to be careful.[97] On the eighteenth, Lee informed Greene that he and Marion had initiated the siege of Fort Watson. He also requested that Greene send one cannon to expedite the capitulation of the fort.[98] Greene believed that the utility of the cannon was dubious and that the risk in transporting it outweighed the benefit.[99] He agreed, however, to send the piece if Lee could detach a guard to retrieve it. Not having heard from Greene, Lee expressed his "unhapp[iness]" with the delay.[100] Two days later, Greene insisted he could not send a fieldpiece, but Lee persisted and felt no compunction about expressing his frustration: "I am miserable to find by your letr of yesterday that no field piece is on the way. I am confident you are losing by its delay great & certain advantages." Lee continued, if "you do not permit us to improve this opportunity you will get very little advantage by coming into this state" because "passive advantages will not arouse the people."[101]

Later that day Lee informed Greene that the fort had been taken and apologized for his tone concerning the cannon.[102] On April 28, Greene rebuked Lee for his lack of discretion, reminding him that he had "run every hazard to promote your plan of operations, as well to oblige you."[103] Nevertheless Greene congratulated Lee on his success in bringing about the capitulation of Fort Watson. Prior to this letter, however, Greene had more pressing concerns than Lee's ego and temperament. Greene was on the eve of a general engagement with Lieutenant Colonel Francis, Lord Rawdon.

After weeks of posturing, Greene placed his army one-half mile north of Camden at Hobkirk's Hill. The British works in Camden were formidable, and neither Sumter's militia nor reinforcements from Virginia had arrived. Rather than risk an assault on Camden, Greene attempted to "induce the Enemy to sally" from their stronghold, but Rawdon did not budge until he heard that Marion, Sumter, and Lee were "coming to Greene."[104] The battle began at 11

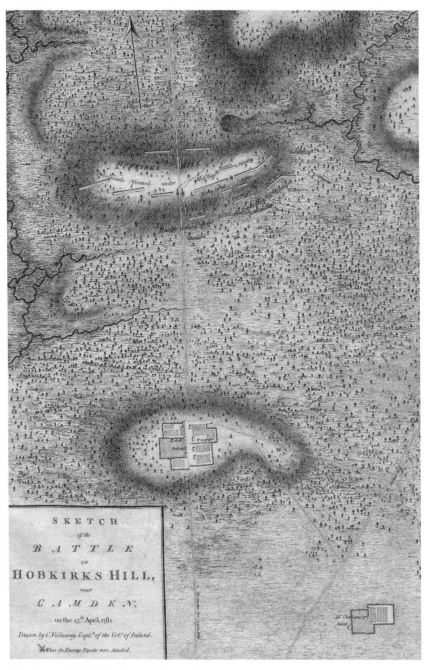

The Battle of Hobkirk's Hill, April 25, 1781

A.M. on April 25 when the Americans were "alarmed by a firing from the Piquets located 300 yards in front of the infantry, many of whom were cooking or washing their clothes." Rawdon's force pushed Greene's pickets into their camp in "not more than six, eight, or ten minutes," according to John Eager Howard.[105]

With the British advancing along a narrow front, Greene ordered an all-out assault, attacking both British flanks and their front. Greene ordered Colonel John Gunby's First Maryland "to advance down the Hill and charge them in front." This maneuver staggered the British, forcing their left to retire. At that moment two companies on the right of the First Maryland got disordered, and "Colo Gunby gave an order for the rest of the Regiment then advancing to take a new position in the rear, where the two Companies were rallying." This retrograde movement resulted in a full-scale retreat by the First Maryland. While both Maryland regiments ultimately rallied, the "fortune of the Day" could not be recovered. Despite the loss, Greene reported that his army was in good spirits and that the general plan of operation would not be affected.[106] Moreover the long-term effect proved catastrophic for Rawdon as the loss of Fort Watson necessitated his withdrawal from Camden on May 10.[107]

The Battle of Hobkirk's Hill sheds light on another of Greene's relationships and on his leadership limitations. After the battle Greene vociferously blamed John Gunby for the American defeat. Although there is no reason to debate this issue fully, it is important to mention that there were other possible culprits. Greene's army had been caught off guard, a factor Gunby believed was the primary cause of the defeat. Howard later stated that, because of the surprise, Gunby's regiment "never perfectly formed."[108] Might not Greene have been better served by first absorbing the British assault and then using his numerical superiority to inflict a decisive counterattack? What about William Washington's dragoons? Why did he encumber himself with gathering wounded prisoners instead of striking a decisive blow into the British rear?[109] Moreover Greene never received reinforcements either from Sumter or from the various states that had promised to send them; could Greene, as Lee wrote later, have fallen victim to the "deranging effects of unlimited confidence?"[110] One must wonder if Lee would have dared to write this criticism had Greene been alive. For the most part, present-day historians exonerate Gunby, concluding that the sum of the aforementioned issues resulted in a British victory.[111]

Following the battle Greene blamed Gunby in his official report to the Continental Congress and in letters to virtually everyone else with whom he communicated.[112] Greene told Baron Friedrich von Steuben that they would have been victorious "had it not been for the unfortunate orders of Colo Gunby."[113] Likewise Greene's letter to Henry Lee on the twenty-ninth blamed "an order of Col Gunby's."[114] The court-martial of Gunby concluded that although his "spirit and activity were unexceptionable . . . his order for the regiment to

retire . . . was in all probability, the only cause why we did not obtain a complete victory."[115]

Later that day Greene's tone had calmed slightly when he wrote North
Carolina Governor Abner Nash that "the fortune of the day would have been
favorable had it not been for Col Gunbies order and it was only an error in
judgment in him as his courage and activity are unquestionable."[116] Two days
later, to the president of the Pennsylvania Council, Joseph Reed, Greene wrote
that, were it not for Gunby, a "Victory was certain."[117] On May 5, Greene informed Sumter, whose absence from the battlefield certainly played a role in the
loss, that Gunby's order triggered the American repulse at Hobkirk's Hill.[118]

Months later, still smarting from his defeat, Greene whined to Joseph Reed:
"we should have had Lord Rawden and his whole command prisoners in three
Minutes, if Col Gunby had not orderd his Regiment to retire." Four months
later Greene even believed Gunby more blameworthy than represented in his
public letter.[119] Two months later, with the siege of Yorktown well under way in
Virginia, Greene informed General Horatio Gates that "I was almost sure of
capturing the whole garrison, and nothing prevented, but Colonel Gunby."[120]

Gunby believed he had been unjustly singled out for the loss and spent years
trying to clear his name. In March 1782 he enlisted John Eager Howard's support. Howard's unequivocal reply simply stated that Gunby "exerted [himself]
as much as possible."[121] Gunby died without recovering his reputation. His
most ardent supporter, descendant Andrew Augustus Gunby, wrote an apologia
for his tarnished forebear, arguing that his ancestor's order in fact saved the
American army from further disaster, that Greene's surprise proved catastrophic,
and that the loss of the battle resulted from Greene's bad judgment in sending
his cavalry on "a wild goose chase."[122] While many of his arguments betray his
motive, Andrew Gunby made some valid points and his conclusion that his
ancestor had been unfairly scapegoated has been adopted by many modern
historians.

One final question remains: why did Greene scapegoat Gunby instead of,
for example, Washington or Sumter? It would have been difficult for Greene to
attach blame to William Washington, with whom he had built a strong working relationship and who had previously served with distinction. Also many of
those present lauded Washington's performance at Hobkirk's Hill. Captain
William Pierce, one of Greene's aides, informed Lee that "Washington made a
timely charge and cut down a number of them besides taken about 40 Prisoners."[123] Greene's official report and general orders also praised Washington's
performance. Greene's operations in the South depended on the mobility provided by cavalry. He thus needed Washington's services in the future. Likewise
placing blame on Sumter would have been problematic as one of Greene's most

important tasks was winning the proverbial hearts and minds of southerners, and Sumter played a crucial role in that aspect of the war.

According to Greene's most capable modern biographer, Terry Golway, this episode reveals Greene at his worst, "petulant, filled with self-pity, and desperately trying to protect his reputation from those confounded critics who were ever so willing to find fault with him."[124] In spite of the mountain of variables that contributed to his defeat, Greene chose Gunby as the scapegoat to protect his own reputation. Self-pity led to hyperbole, as Greene compared his disappointment to Gates's disgrace at Camden. He wrote Gates, "How cruel fortune! How uncertain military Fame! [Gunby's gaffe] mingled our misfortunes together, and as ours was last, it drew a veil over yours."[125] Thus Greene's own desire for glory and reputation required him to betray his sense of decency, both in his thoughtless letter to Gates and in his relentless persecution of a subordinate who had served the cause from its inception.[126] Did not Greene remember the depth of the pain he felt when the Kentish Guards, a Rhode island militia unit, publicly rejected him because he walked with a limp? To James Varnum in 1774, Greene had confided: "I feel more mortification than resentment, but I think it would have manifested a more generous temper to have given me their Oppinions in private than to make a proclamation of it in publick . . . for nobody loves to be the subject of ridicule however true the cause."[127] Unfortunately for Gunby, Greene did not extend this courtesy following Hobkirk's Hill.

Fortunately for Greene, his direct superior was more loyal and more forgiving than he.[128] In November 1776 Greene served as the overall commander of Fort Washington in Manhattan. He convinced George Washington that reducing the fort would cost the British another Bunker Hill and that ferrying the garrison to safety could be easily accomplished. The British proved Greene terribly wrong. Watching the capitulation through his telescope, Washington became so overwhelmed with emotion that he wept "with the tenderness of a child."[129]

Greene bore much of the blame for the loss of the fort, and he knew it. To General Henry Knox he wrote, "This is a most terrible Event. Its consequences are justly to be dreaded. Pray what is said upon the occasion?"[130] Greene had reason to worry about what others might say. Washington's adjutant desperately implored General Charles Lee to join the retreating army and provide a bit of decisive and inspirational leadership because Washington seemed paralyzed by Greene's counsel.[131] Lee asked Washington why he would "be overpersauded by men of inferior judgment to your own?"[132]

Washington did not, however, fully shield Greene from criticism. In his official report he informed Congress that he directed Greene "to govern himself by Circumstances"—a decision that resulted in the loss of the fort. He added that Greene was "struck with the Importance of the Post, and the Discouragement which our Evacuation of Posts must necessarily have given" to both the citizenry and the Congress.[133] To his brother, Washington felt more comfortable expressing himself: "this is a most unfortunate affair and has given me great Mortification," especially because the fort "was held contrary to my Wishes and opinion."[134] But Washington admitted again that his order had been discretionary. While many called for Greene's head, Washington understood that the loss of the fort was ultimately his own responsibility.[135] Now a commander in his own right, Greene reacted differently from Washington. Greene refused to accept any responsibility for the outcome at Hobkirk's Hill and protected his honor by ruining Gunby's reputation.

Intrigue aside, Greene had to focus on the situation on the ground. With Camden in his hands, British control of South Carolina was tenuous, and he decided to pursue Rawdon. On April 28 Lee, perhaps desirous of military laurels, offered a variety of opinions about the upcoming campaign, namely that he hoped Greene would afford him the opportunity to "pursue the conquest of every post & detachment."[136] Greene concurred and detached Lee from Marion with the admonition to avoid "running great hazards."[137] Lee replied that it gave him pleasure to know his sentiments coincided with Greene's intentions and thanked Greene for "calling the adopted plan of operations mine."[138]

A few days later, Lee was in great spirits, confident "of [a] brilliant success, which will be [especially] pleasing" because "it must tend to make happy a General."[139] Greene did not share Lee's ebullience. Fearing that Cornwallis might return to Camden, Greene ordered Lee to return immediately.[140] If Cornwallis did move into Virginia, however, Greene considered a plan in which he would take charge of the forces in Virginia, and leave a subordinate in charge of the Carolinas. Lee adamantly opposed such a plan, fearing that the Southern Army would be greatly reduced by desertion as a result of Greene's departure.[141] Greene's thoughts about Virginia were well-considered: "Which will be more honourable," he asked, "to be active [in Virginia], or laying, as it were, idle here?" Greene disagreed with Lee about mass desertions and expressed confidence that Steuben would manage "matters very well" in his absence.[142]

Rawdon evacuated Camden on May 10, and Lee notified Greene that the capture of Fort Motte, the primary supply depot between Camden and Charleston, was imminent unless Rawdon interfered. Lee also communicated his desire to remain in the Carolinas until "things are properly [lined?] in this country."[143] Believing Cornwallis to have completely abandoned the Carolina campaign, Greene initiated his "war of posts." The day after the successful investment of Fort Motte on the twelfth, Greene ordered Lee to take Fort Granby at Friday's Ferry. "Wishing to save the effusion of blood," Greene ordered Lee to inform the commander that he would receive only one summons for its surrender and that he depended on Lee to push "matters vigirously."[144] And this Lee did, securing the capitulation of Fort Granby in a matter of days, although the terms of the capitulation became controversial.[145]

The British commander at the fort, Major Andrew Maxwell, had accumulated a pile of plunder. Lee, "solicitous to hasten" the surrender of Granby, allowed Maxwell to keep two wagons loaded with spoils.[146] Sumter and his militiamen were infuriated and requested Lee's recall. Greene's refusal prompted Sumter's resignation.[147] Lee and Sumter were not friends, and their cooperation during the southern campaigns had been tenuous at best.[148] Historians have often debated Lee's motives and criticized him for rushing the negotiations, but Greene's directive clearly expressed his desire to "save the effusion of blood." Greene, according to Lee, had been delighted with this happy event."[149]

Pursuing his "war of posts," Greene ordered Lee to Augusta, Georgia, to "demand the Surrender of those posts" with the caveat "that none of the Stores [be] plunder'd."[150] Concerned that his troops would encounter a detachment from Rawdon, Lee asked for Greene's route to Ninety Six so he could quickly respond to disaster. Lee also asked Greene to write Rawdon concerning the terms of the capitulation of Fort Watson, fearing that the plundering by American forces would give the British "full reason" to violate the terms.[151] Although there is no evidence concerning Lee's reference to plundering, a Loyalist officer captured at Fort Motte claimed that Lee himself had violated the terms by hanging several prisoners. According to that Loyalist, only Francis Marion's intervention prohibited further executions.[152] These extracurricular issues related to Lee's conduct must have caused Greene some concern.

On the twenty-first, Greene notified Lee that he was approaching Ninety Six and hoped it would "fall into our hands." Greene also urged Lee to cultivate an understanding with General Pickens and the militia as some of "your Legion behaved greatly amiss at" Fort Granby.[153] While Greene noted that he did not blame Lee, he began micromanaging Lee more and more. The next day Greene complimented Lee's rapid march to Augusta but chided him for overexerting his troops. Greene then pressed him to take Fort Dreadnought quickly.[154] By the time Greene wrote, however, Lee had already captured the fort, procured a large quantity of stores, and enabled the Americans to "adopt the most vigorous operations" readily to liberate Augusta.[155]

On May 22 Greene began the siege of Ninety Six, another important British post on the old Cherokee trading path in the Carolina backcountry.[156] At the end of the month he dispatched Major Ichabod Burnet to consult with Pickens and Lee about the situations at Augusta and Ninety Six. The siege at Ninety Six had become more problematic than anticipated, and Greene needed them to conclude their "present business" at Augusta with all deliberate speed.[157] Lee replied that the operations would likely last longer "than you can wish or expect" although he would pursue any opportunity to expedite the process.[158] Greene warned that any attempt to storm the fort should be attempted with caution.[159]

On June 4 Lee expressed his growing concern that Fort Cornwallis (one of the two Augusta posts) might not fall. He sought Greene's assistance should Rawdon attempt to come to the fort's defense and warned Greene that, if he did not establish civil authority in Georgia, he "will loose all the benefit from it" because the Loyalists "exc[eed] the Goths & Vandals in their schemes of plunder murder & iniqu[ity]."[160]

After an arduous siege, Lee and Pickens completed "a perfect circumvallation" of Forts Cornwallis and Grierson (the other Augusta fort) on June 5. The besiegers recorded that their loss was not too considerable, "and by no means proportionate to the warmth of the contest" that recovered the "capital of Georgia." Lee's star still shone brightly, and Greene told Samuel Huntington that Lee's Legion "deserve the highest honor."[161]

After completing his business in Georgia, Lee raced to Ninety Six to help reduce that post. Greene ordered Lee and Pickens to focus their energies on a wooden fort west of a vital spring. Lee positioned his troops in a way that denied the defenders access to the spring, but the Loyalist commander, Lieutenant Colonel John Harris Cruger, countered Lee by sending naked slaves to the creek at night. The measure worked, providing life-sustaining water for the garrison. Finding the defenders more numerous and defiant than expected, Greene eventually resolved to storm the fortifications. However, the Loyalist defenders proved too resolute. News that Rawdon was approaching forced Greene to lift the siege.[162]

The day after the siege ended, Lee suggested changes that would make his legion "doubl[y] serviceable" by mounting his infantry and arming them with dragoon swords and "carbines with bayonets."[163] Greene agreed and submitted the proposal to Congress, which lacked the funds to implement the plan.[164] A couple of days later, Lee reported that Rawdon had reached Ninety Six and planned to burn the town and either chase Greene or return to Charleston. Lee then suggested that Greene always "preserve the appearance of fighting."[165] Later that same day, he reported Rawdon's force was in dire straits and recommended a move against him.[166] Greene agreed and ordered the army to march immediately.[167] In fact Rawdon later noted that he had not planned on chasing Greene, who "had then so much the [head]start."[168]

On learning that Rawdon was retreating, Greene urged Lee to "annoy them on their return" and move into the "Lower Country," acting as his "judgment may direct."[169] The next day, Lee reported that Rawdon had continued his retreat and would likely destroy Ninety Six. He then proposed that Greene "give the color of a pursuit, & cause suspicion" that Greene was driving toward

Charleston. He also recommended that Greene send William Washington's troops to Virginia because Lee's cavalry "is sufficient here."[170] As June wound down, Greene still maintained confidence in Lee's ability and afforded him latitude in his independent operations although not as much as he had earlier in the campaign.

Lee could not act fully independent of Greene, however. On the twenty-ninth, Greene asked him to form a junction with Washington and harass Rawdon's army near Orangeburg or to act on his own "if you think" it advisable. But Greene urged Lee "not to hazard too much."[171] Interpreting Greene's message as offering free reign, Lee devised a plan of action to "gain [Rawdon's] front" and keep "a party of horse" in his rear.[172]

The next day, however, Lee received Greene's letter desiring him to unite with Washington. Lee "instantly moved in the direction" Greene had "commanded," but he then complained that Greene's orders to him and to Washington were contradictory. For some reason Lee still considered Captain Robert Kirkwood and his Delaware infantry to be under his orders; yet Greene had ordered Kirkwood to join Washington. As a result, Lee bemoaned that such "confusion in orders must detriment the service."[173] Lee did not seem to appreciate being corralled by Greene.[174]

On July 2, Lee reported the locations and conditions of Rawdon's forces at Fort Granby and Cruger's forces at Ninety Six. Never lacking confidence, Lee stated his desire to fight Rawdon and then advised Greene to gather his forces so he could "ruin the enemy."[175] Prior to receiving this letter, Greene's patience may have been growing thin; he complained to William Washington that he had not heard from Lee "since day before yesterday."[176] There was perhaps good reason for Lee's failure to communicate. He had initiated a plan to engage the British at Granby and Ninety Six. On the morning of the third, Captain Joseph Eggleston, whom Lee detached to follow Rawdon to Fort Granby, encountered the "main body of the British horse" and "entirely defeated" them, capturing nearly fifty British soldiers.[177] Meanwhile Lee prepared to "throw" himself "between his Lordship & [Lieutenant Colonel Alexander] Stewart to break down bridges."[178]

During the first week of July, Greene stated his desire to Washington and Lee to prevent Stewart from joining Rawdon.[179] Greene's request proved prescient; Washington's men intercepted a letter from Stewart stating that he was marching to do just that. Washington informed Greene that he would soon join with Lee and that they would "get up with Rawdon" with great celerity.[180] They were unable, however, to prevent Rawdon from joining Stewart, which prompted Greene to establish a camp in the High Hills of the Santee.[181]

This move initiated the partisan "Dog Days Expedition," in which Greene hoped to force the evacuation of the British posts in the upper country. Lee operated as a partisan during much of this campaign, but the frequency with which he communicated with Greene noticeably diminished because Marion and Sumter took the lead. Greene implored him, however, to "prosecute your operations with the utmost industry."[182]

During this phase of operations, Lee maintained Greene's confidence and often suggested tactical and strategic advice.[183] In early August, Lee notified Greene that in spite of "much toil," his troops had met "with very little success" in two minor engagements. He also informed Greene that Stewart probably had no "intention of retiring," but will "advance up to the Congaree," and suggested that Greene make a retrograde movement to Camden to draw the British "farther in the country."[184] Greene believed Lee "rather fortunate" in his recent maneuvers as the consequences would be grave if "misfortune attend you at a critical hour."[185]

Greene's message fell on deaf ears. Lee replied that his corps "tr[ies] to deserve the approbation of their country & the eulogisem of their general." Additionally he wished that the operations of his corps could be "more important, but such is the paucity of [Greene's] numbers, that an officer of common consideration & common enterprize cannot venture."[186] He then proposed that Greene cross the Congaree and send his infantry so he could venture toward the coast, unless Greene disapproved of such an action. Greene replied that he wished Lee to postpone his movement southward as there "will be time enough to play the small game" if we "cannot play a greater."[187] Lee again lamented Greene's insufficient numbers because "there was [never] so glorious an opportunity of giving a fatal stab to the British tyrant."[188] Greene agreed with Lee's "account of the strength and temper of the British Army" and also expressed growing frustration with the condition of his army, admitting his desire to "put all to the hazard with the regular troops" because if augmented by the cavalry the result could be positive.[189]

On the seventeenth Lee again pressed Greene to move against Stewart before reinforcements arrived and later reported that the British hoped to surprise Greene. He then proposed to harass the British because his zeal might "encrease the spirit of desertion so prevalent in the enemy."[190] Greene again found it necessary to remind Lee gently to maintain his focus. On one hand he had to tell Lee to be cognizant of the fragile nature of civil-military relations. On the other it became necessary to repeat that, while Lee's "zeal for the service are truly laudable," it "must be bounded by considerations of a higher nature."[191] This admonition is similar to one Greene delivered to Daniel Morgan in January. While Greene wished for Morgan the opportunity to acquire "laurels," he proved "unwilling to expose the common cause" to afford him that prospect.[192] This last clause would be a common thread in Greene's correspondence with his subordinates, Continental or otherwise. He wished for them personal glory, but not at the expense of the greater cause.[193] Lee responded as if a scolded child, stating that it was inconceivable that he would place personal glory over the public good.[194]

Lee still hoped Greene would "act on the great scale."[195] He suggested that Greene order the burning of the jail at Orangeburg and the bridge over the Edisto River to limit Stewart's options. Greene soon notified Lee that he planned to break camp and pursue Stewart and that Lee's Legion would "have to act a very capital part."[196] Greene then advised Lee to have his legion as strong as possible, for "we must have victory or ruin."[197] The next week Lee notified Greene that Stewart had camped at Eutaw Springs and suggested Greene position himself at Colonel Richard Richardson's.[198] In fact Greene had already determined to pursue this course. On August 26, he told George Washington that he planned to "make an attack on the enemy" because "we must risque more here."[199]

The topography forced Greene to take a circuitous route and, unbeknownst to Stewart, Greene's troops camped within seven miles of Stewart's army, which was at Eutaw Springs. The next morning, on September 8, Greene initiated the final full-scale battle in the southern campaigns. The fighting became intense, likely the hottest in the campaigns, and lasted four hours. American victory seemed imminent as, according to Greene, the "Enemy were routed in all quarters," but the attack hit a literal brick wall at the two-story Roche house, described by Otho Holland Williams as a "Citadel," where the British halted Greene's advance.[200]

Greene persisted and ordered Lee's Legion forward on the American right, past the British encampment. Unfortunately Lee's Legion advanced without Lee, who had personally led his infantry toward the Roche house. The leaderless legion was driven back by Major John Coffin's cavalry.[201] This spelled the end for Greene, who withdrew with substantial casualties. Fortunately for Greene, Stewart's losses topped 40 percent—another Pyrrhic victory for the British. Greene marched his weary soldiers back to the High Hills to recuperate. Just as at Guilford, British losses necessitated their retreat. Stewart marched back to Charleston, with Greene nipping at his heels.

Following the battle, Lee endured heavy criticism for his conduct. Childish, temperamental, and hypersensitive, he augmented real criticism with perceived censure. Lee's friends informed Greene that Lee believed his merit had been publicly misrepresented and that Greene's public accounts had given him insufficient praise. Greene disagreed, claiming that his letters had "done ample justice both to the friend and officer."[202] Lee subsequently offered his resignation. Contrary to his castigation of John Gunby, Greene came to Lee's aid and twice attempted to dissuade Lee from leaving the army: "I have beheld with extreme anxiety for some time past a growing discontent in your mind . . . what ever may .

be the source of your wounds I wish it was in my power to heal them." He added, "From our earliest acquaintance I had a partiality for you which progressively grew into a friendship. . . . Every body knows I have the highest opinion of you as an officer and you know I love you as a friend."[203] Lee quickly responded: "I ever have, & shall consider myself bound to you by the strongest obligations of friendship" and that I will take this "attachment to you" to the grave. Nevertheless Lee acknowledged he felt "distress" upon reading "some of your public reports." Lacking any self-awareness, he claimed not to seek "private or public applause."[204]

By the middle of February 1782, Greene had grown tired of this discourse. "I am exceeding sorry," Greene said, "you harbor sentiments respecting me no less groundless than unfriendly. I do not expect therefore that any thing that I can say will either convince your judgment or correct your prejudice. I shall leave you at liberty to think of me as you please and what ever sentiments you may entertain of me I will always do justice to your merit, and shall always be happy to share your friendship and confidence when it can be had on terms reciprocal and honorable."[205] It is unclear what so upset Lee. Greene's official report of the Battle of Eutaw Springs stated that "Lee had with great address, gallantry, and good conduct, turned the Enemy's left flank." Greene acknowledged that Lee's Legion struggled but that Lee "exhibited uncommon acts of heroism."[206] Greene asked Lee to reflect on the situation, and if after that, "your ambition is not satisfied, If the rights of friendship have been violated, I shall be ready to submit to any censure that justice may dictate. I love and esteem you, and wish you not to think meanly of me, as some of your insinuations seem to impart."[207] Lee's problem likely rested with Greene's omission of Lee from a list of officers to whom he was "obligated."[208]

Lee's reply indicates his inner turmoil and inability to deal with it. "I am much mortified," he lamented, "at the trouble which my stupid conduct gives you. . . . I now repent . . . [because] My friendship & high respect for you is as firm & warm this moment as it ever was."[209] Lee had become controlled by his passions. In October 1782 Greene finally acquiesced, saying, "There was no man that deserved greater credit than you that day [Battle of Eutaw]; and if you are not so represented, it is my fault."[210]

Greene's words to Lee serve as a final illustration of his close relationship with his Continental subordinates. He loved his principal subordinates, and their well-being remained a constant concern. Writing a few weeks before the penultimate battle of the southern campaigns, Greene noted: "Great Generals are scarce; there are few Morgans to be found."[211] In recommending that Williams be promoted to brigadier general, Greene stated, "few Officers merit more, or will be more studious to discover such honor as Congress may think proper to bestow."[212] He added that Williams's "zeal and long services, give him just claim" to the promotion, and from a personal perspective, Greene was "under many and singular obligations" to his subordinate.[213] Williams fully understood the depth of their friendship: "I am too fully perswaded of the sincerity of your Friendship for me . . . that I feel myself principally indebted to you for my late very Honorable promotion."[214]

In Greene's opinion, Henry Lee and William Washington were the "heroes of the South."[215] In February 1782, after Lee returned to Virginia, Greene wrote: "I shall be always happy to do you every friendly office in my power."[216] A few months later, Greene remained touched by the depths of Lee's pain. He asked if Richard Henry Lee had seen the legionnaire, stating that Henry Lee had been "gloomy from reports propagated to his prejudices." Greene carefully explained that such opinions resulted from malice, and "There was no officer or Corps ever in service that had an equal number of honorable reports of important services as Col Lee had last campaign."[217]

Greene even lavished praise on lesser-known subordinates. For example he effusively praised the services of Lieutenant Colonel John Eager Howard of the Maryland Line. Greene admiringly wrote, "Colonel Howard [is] as good an officer as the world affords. He has great ability and the best disposition to promote the service. My own obligations to him are great—the public's still more so. He deserves a statue of gold no less than the Roman and Grecian heroes."[218] Howard, who later became a man of substantial national influence, fully appreciated Greene's friendship. "Whatever may be my fortune," he wrote in 1782, "I shall always remember your polite behavior at all times."[219] Only praise for John Gunby is absent from Greene's letters. Gunby would always be the scapegoat of Hobkirk's Hill, the exception to Greene's normally positive relations with leading subordinates, relations that proved critical to the American victory in the South.

Notes

The author wishes to dedicate this essay to his first high school history teacher, Kevin Dockrell, who is still imparting historical and life lessons twenty-five years later.

1. Greene to the officers of the Maryland Line, December 18, 1780, *The Papers of General Nathanael Greene*, edited by Richard K. Showman, Dennis R. Conrad, and Roger N. Parks, 13 vols. (Chapel Hill: University of North Carolina Press, 1976–2005), 6:595–96.

2. Greene to Thomas Sim Lee, December 30, 1780, ibid., 7:28–29.

3. Greene to Ward, Senior, July 14, 1775, ibid., 1:98–100. See also Terry Golway, *Washington's General: Nathanael Greene and the Triumph of the American Revolution* (New York: Holt, 2004), 48–58, and John Ferling, *The Ascent of George Washington: The Hidden Political Genius of an American Icon* (New York: Bloomsbury Press, 2009), 208–9.

4. Francis Vinton Greene, *General Greene* (New York: Appleton, 1897), 25.

5. George Washington Greene, *The Life of Nathanael Greene, Major-General in the Armies of the Revolution,* vol. 1 (New York: Putnam, 1867); vols. 2 and 3 (New York: Hurd & Houghton, 1871), 1:448. See also Greene to Henry Marchant, July 25, 1778, *The Papers of General Nathanael Greene,* 2:470–72.

6. Greene to Caty Greene, January 20, 1777, *The Papers of General Nathanael Greene,* 2:7.

7. See Greene to George Washington, November 24, 1777, ibid., 2:209; John Ferling, *Almost a Miracle: The American Victory in the War of Independence* (New York: Oxford University Press, 2007), 257.

8. Worthington C. Ford et al., eds., *Journals of the Continental Congress,* 34 vols. (Washington: U.S. Government Printing Office, 1904–37), 18:906. For Greene's appointment to the southern command, see Douglas Southall Freeman, *George Washington,* 7 vols. (New York: Scribners, 1948–57), 5:226–32; Golway, *Washington's General,* 230–35; George Washington Greene, *The Life of Nathanael Greene,* chapter 3; and William Johnson, *Sketches of the Life and Correspondence of Nathanael Greene,* 2 vols. (Charleston, S.C.: A. E. Miller, 1822), 1: chapter 8.

9. George Washington to the president of Congress, October 22, 1780, *The Writings of George Washington, from the Original Manuscript Sources, 1745–1799,* edited by John C. Fitzpatrick, 39 vols. (Washington, D.C.: U.S. Government Printing Office, 1931–44), 20:244. Washington added that the situation on the ground in the Carolinas required that Congress grant Greene "extensive powers." Greene also possessed the confidence of a cadre of southern congressmen. See John Mathews to Washington, October 6, 1780, in Paul H. Smith et al., eds., *Letters of Delegates to Congress, 1774–1789,* 26 vols. (Washington, D.C.: Library of Congress, 1976–2000), 16:159; quoted in *The Papers of General Nathanael Greene,* 6:386n.

10. George Washington to Greene, October 14, 1780, *The Papers of General Nathanael Greene,* 6:385–87.

11. George Washington to Greene, October 18, 1780, ibid., 6:410–11.

12. George Washington to Greene, October 22, 1780, ibid., 6:424–26. For Greene's official appointment, see Samuel Huntington to Greene, October 31, 1780, ibid. 6: 450–52.

13. George Washington to Greene, October 22, 1780, ibid., 6:424–26.

14. George Washington to Benjamin Lincoln, October 3, 1778, *The Papers of George Washington, Revolutionary War Series,* edited by Philander Chase et al., 20 vols. (Charlottesville: University Press of Virginia, 1985–2010), 17:240; Washington to Horatio Gates, June 4, 1780, in *The Writings of George Washington,* 18:473.

15. Greene to George Washington, November 19, 1780, *The Papers of General Nathanael Greene,* 6:488–89.

16. Greene to Henry Lee, February 8, 1781, ibid., 7:257. While this is true of Greene, he did rely on councils of war, especially in the early days of his command. For example Don Higginbotham has noted that Morgan "may have been surprised and pleased to find that the ex-Quaker deferred to his opinion." See Higginbotham, *Daniel Morgan: Revolutionary Rifleman* (Chapel Hill: University of North Carolina Press, 1961), 120. See also Greene to Thomas Sumter, December 12, 1780, *The Papers of General Nathanael Greene,* 6:563–64.

17. Greene to Francis Marion, December 4, 1780, *The Papers of General Nathanael Greene*, 6:519–21.

18. See John Buchanan's examination of Greene's partisans in this volume.

19. Daniel Morgan to William Snickers, January 19, 1781, in Higginbotham, *Daniel Morgan*, 142; Lawrence Babits, *A Devil of a Whipping: The Battle of Cowpens* (Chapel Hill: University of North Carolina Press, 1998), 10.

20. For examples of Greene's reminders to Morgan, see Greene's letters to Morgan, dated January 3, 4, 8, 13 (two letters), and 19, 1781, *The Papers of General Nathanael Greene*, 7:41–42, 48, 72–74, 106, 107, and 146–47.

21. Morgan to Greene, January 15, 1781, ibid., 7:127–29.

22. Greene to Morgan, January 13, 1781, ibid., 7:106.

23. Babits, *A Devil of a Whipping*, 160. For the quote and Morgan's battle report to Greene, see Morgan to Greene, January 19, 1781, *The Papers of General Nathanael Greene*, 7:152–61. See also, Lawrence E. Babits and Joshua B. Howard, *Long, Obstinate, and Bloody: The Battle of Guilford Courthouse* (Chapel Hill: University of North Carolina Press, 2009), 11.

24. Cornwallis to Francis, Lord Rawdon, January 21, 1781, in Franklin B. Wickwire and Mary B. Wickwire, *Cornwallis and the War of American Independence* (London: John Dickens, 1970), 269. See also Cornwallis to Lord George Germain, March 17, 1781, in Babits and Howard, *Long, Obstinate, and Bloody*, 15; Charles O'Hara to Augustus Henry Fitzroy, Duke of Grafton, April 20, 1781, "Letters of Charles O'Hara to the Duke of Grafton," edited by George C. Rogers Jr., *South Carolina Historical Magazine* 65 (July 1964): 174; and Morgan to Greene, January 29, 1781, *The Papers of General Nathanael Greene*, 7:215.

25. For Morgan's strategic concerns, see Morgan to Greene, January 23, 24, 25, and 28, 1781, *The Papers of General Nathanael Greene*, 7:178–79, 192–93, 199–200, 201, and 211–14. For Greene's decision to join Morgan, see Greene to Lee, January 26, 1781, ibid., 7:202–3. See also Johnson, *Nathanael Greene*, 1:394; See Edward Stevens to Thomas Jefferson, February 8, 1781, quoted in *The Papers of General Nathanael Greene*, 7:209n. At the time Greene did not know Morgan felt unable to continue. See Morgan to Greene, January 24, 1781, ibid., 7:190–91.

26. For this impromptu discussion, see William Alexander Graham, *General Joseph Graham and His Papers on North Carolina Revolutionary History* (Raleigh, N.C.: Edwards & Broughton, 1904), 289–90. See also Greene to Baron Friedrich von Steuben, February 3, 1781, *The Papers of General Nathanael Greene*, 7:242–44; Higginbotham, *Daniel Morgan*, 150–51; and John Buchanan, *The Road to Guilford Courthouse: The American Revolution in the Carolinas* (New York: Wiley, 1997), 342–44. For the action at Cowan's Ford and Torrence's Tavern, see Greene to Baron Friedrich von Steuben, February 3, 1781, *The Papers of General Nathanael Greene*, 7:242–44; John Eager Howard to William Johnson, c. 1822, James Bayard Papers, MS 109, Maryland Historical Society, Baltimore.

27. Greene to Alexander Hamilton, January 10, 1781, *The Papers of General Nathanael Greene*, 7:87–91.

28. Proceedings of a council of war, February 9, 1781, ibid., 7:261–62.

29. Morgan to Greene, April 11, 1781, ibid., 8:84–85.

30. Otho Holland Williams to Elie Williams, February 15, 1781, Otho Holland Williams Papers, MS 908, Maryland Historical Society, Baltimore. See also *The Papers of General Nathanael Greene*, 7:282n, and Arnold W. Kalmanson, "Otho Holland Williams and the Southern Campaign, 1780–1782," M.A. thesis, Salisbury State University, 1990, chapter 5.

31. Greene to George Washington, February 9, 1781, *The Papers of General Nathanael Greene*, 7:267–70.

32. Williams to Greene, February 11, 1781, ibid., 7:282.

33. Cornwallis to Germain, March 17, 1781, in Tarleton, *A History of the Campaigns of 1780 and 1781 in the Southern Provinces of North America* (London: T. Cadell, 1787), 264.

34. Williams to Greene, February 11, 1781, *The Papers of General Nathanael Greene*, 7:283.

35. Babits and Howard, *Long, Obstinate, and Bloody*, 34; Henry Lee, *Memoirs of the War in the Southern Department of the United States*, edited by Robert E. Lee (1869; reprint, New York: Da Capo Press, 1998), 237–50; *The Papers of General Nathanael Greene*, 7:283n.

36. Tarleton, *A History of the Campaigns*, 229. Tarleton wrote that "many skirmishes took place."

37. Greene to Williams, February 13, 1781, *The Papers of General Nathanael Greene*, 7:285.

38. Greene to Williams, 4:00 A.M., February 14, 1781, ibid., 7:287.

39. Greene to Williams, 2:00 P.M., and Greene to Williams, 5:30 P.M., February 14, 1781, ibid., 7:287. In the second letter, Greene stated that he was ready to give Williams a "hearty welcome."

40. Babits and Howard, *Long, Obstinate, and Bloody*, 36.

41. Williams to Greene, February 18, 1781, *The Papers of General Nathanael Greene*, 7:315. For a detailed description of the physical difficulty of the march, see Williams to Elie Williams, February 21, 1781, Otho Holland Williams Papers. For Greene's comments about the physical difficulties accompanying such a retreat, see Greene to Jefferson, February 15, 1781, *The Papers of General Nathanael Greene*, 7:289–90.

42. Tarleton, *A History of the Campaigns*, 229.

43. Greene to George Washington, February 15, 1781, *The Papers of General Nathanael Greene*, 7:293–95.

44. Williams to David Ramsay, February 2, 1782, Otho Holland Williams Papers.

45. See, Williams to Lee, 8:00 A.M., February 22, 1781, and Williams to Lee, 4:00 P.M., February 22, 1781, *The Papers of General Nathanael Greene*, 7:334

46. For examples of Williams's steadfast reporting of Cornwallis's movements, see Williams to Greene, February 22, 25, 26, 27, 28, March 1, 2, 3, 4, 6, 7, and 8, 1781, ibid., 7:334, 349–51, 360–62, 366, 373–74, 378–79, 381–82, 387, 391, 393–94, 406–7, 409, and 413–14. On March 5 Greene mentioned that he had not heard from Williams "or the enemy" since the evening before. See Burnet to Williams, March 5, 1781, ibid., 7:397.

47. Williams to Greene, February 28, 1781, ibid., 7:373–74.

48. Williams to Greene, March 1, 1781, ibid., 7:378–79.

49. Tarleton, *A History of the Campaigns*, 234–36; *The Papers of General Nathanael Greene*, 7:381–82.

50. Ichabod Burnett to Williams, March 3, 1781, *The Papers of General Nathanael Greene*, 7:388.

51. Williams to Greene, March 4, 1781, ibid., 7:391.

52. Burnett to Williams, March 4, 1781, ibid., 7:391.

53. Williams to Greene, March 4, 1781, ibid., 7:393–94.

54. Ibid. Greene expressed a similar frustration with Washington on many occasions. See Greene to George Washington, July 21, 1778, ibid., 2:461–64.

55. Williams to Greene, March 6, 1781, ibid., 7:406–7. Greene felt similar desires for Washington. See Greene to Catharine Greene, May 20, 1777, ibid., 2:85–86; Greene to Griffin Greene, May 25, 1778, ibid., 2:405–7.

56. Williams to Greene, March 6, 1781, ibid., 7:406–7.

57. Roger Lamb, *A British Soldier's Story: Roger Lamb's Narrative of the American Revolution*, edited by Don A. Hagist (Baraboo, Wis.: Ballindalloch Press, 2001), 83.

58. Williams to Greene, March, 7, 1781, *The Papers of General Nathanael Greene*, 7:407–8.

59. For the action at Weitzel's Mill, see Graham, *General Joseph Graham*, 342–46.

60. Williams to Greene, March 7, 1781, *The Papers of General Nathanael Greene*, 7:407–8.

61. Graham, *General Joseph Graham*, 346–47; *The Papers of General Nathanael Greene*, 7:408n.

62. Pickens noted the deleterious effect on the militia in Pickens to Lee, August 28, 1811, *The Papers of General Nathanael Greene*, 7:408n.

63. William R. Davie, *The Revolutionary War Sketches of William R. Davie*, edited by Blackwell P. Robinson (Raleigh: North Carolina Division of Archives and History, 1976), 30. Davie also criticized Williams's performance at the Battle of Guilford Courthouse. Perhaps there was personal animosity between the two. Davie, *The Revolutionary War Sketches*, 31.

64. Greene to Lee, March 9, 1781, *The Papers of General Nathanael Greene*, 7:415–16.

65. Greene to Reed, March 18, 1781, ibid., 7:448–51. See also Greene to Jefferson, March 10, 1781, ibid., 7:419–21.

66. Ibid., 7:119n and 130n.

67. Marie Joseph Gilbert du Motier, Marquis de Lafayette, called Lee the "best officer of light infantry" in America. Lafayette to Anne-César, Chevalier de La Luzerne, October 28, 1780, ibid., 6:431.

68. Lee did not arrive at the southern camp in South Carolina until January 9, 1781. See Lee to Greene, October 23, 1780, ibid., 6:427.

69. Lee to Greene, October 25, 1780, and October 29, 1780, ibid., 6:430–31, 444–45.

70. Greene to Samuel Huntington, November 2, 1780, ibid., 6:459–60. Congress concurred. See, Ford et al., eds., *Journals of the Continental Congress*, 18:1023–24.

71. Lee, *Memoirs*, 254–59; Babits and Howard, *Long, Obstinate, and Bloody*, 38–39; Charles Royster, *Light-Horse Harry Lee and the Legacy of the American Revolution* (Baton Rouge: Louisiana State University Press, 1981), 37–38; Buchanan, *The Road to Guilford Courthouse*, 362–65.

72. Pickens to Greene, February 26, 1781, *The Papers of General Nathanael Greene*, 7:355–59. Lee failed to mention this detail in his report. See Lee to Greene, February 25, 1781, ibid., 7:347–48.

73. Greene to Joseph Reed, March 18, 1781, ibid., 7:448–51.

74. Greene to Lee, March 10, 1781, ibid., 7:421.

75. Lee to Greene, March 11, 1781, ibid., 7:427–28.

76. Lee to Greene, March 12, 1781, ibid., 7:428. For Greene's reply see Nathanael Pendleton to William Washington and Lee, March 13, 1781, ibid., 7:429.

77. Greene to Lee, March 14, 1781, ibid., 7:430–31. The details of Lee's suggestions are unknown because the letter has not been found.

78. Lee, *Memoirs*, 270–72.

79. Babits and Howard, *Long, Obstinate, and Bloody*, 51–56; Lee, *Memoirs*, 275.

80. Morgan to Greene, February 20, 1781, *The Papers of General Nathanael Greene*, 7:324–25. For Greene's alignment and battle report, see Greene to Huntington, March 16, 1781, ibid., 7:431–33.

81. Greene to Morgan, March 20, 1781, ibid., 7:455–56.

82. Babits and Howard, *Long, Obstinate, and Bloody*, appendix B. See also O'Hara to Augustus Henry Fitzroy, Duke of Grafton, April 20, 1781, in "Letters of Charles O'Hara to the Duke of Grafton," 177.

83. John Eager Howard to John Marshall, c. 1804, James Bayard Papers, MS 109, box 4, folder 2, Maryland Historical Society, Baltimore. For Howard see Greg Brooking, "'As Good an Officer as the World Affords': John Eager Howard and the American Revolution," M.A. thesis, Georgia College and State University, 2009; Jim Piecuch and John Beakes, *"Cool Deliberate Courage": John Eager Howard in the American Revolution* (Charleston, S.C.: Nautical and Aviation Publishing, 2009).

84. Lyman C. Draper, *King's Mountain and Its Heroes* (Cincinnati: Peter G. Thompson, 1881), 395.

85. For Lee's version see Lee, *Memoirs*, 281. See Babits and Howard, *Long, Obstinate, and Bloody*, 138. The authors state: "While his account might be a reflection of a failing memory, it might also be an attempt to save face." They believed that Lee did indeed "abandon" Campbell (177). See also Buchanan, *The Road to Guilford Courthouse*, 380. Buchanan states that Lee "left Campbell and his Virginians to fend for themselves."

86. Babits and Howard, *Long, Obstinate, and Bloody*, 209.

87. Greene to William Campbell, March 18, 1781, *The Papers of General Nathanael Greene*, 7:445. Campbell resigned from his current assignment and died of camp fever five months later. See Babits and Howard, *Long, Obstinate, and Bloody*, 209.

88. Greene to Huntington, March 16, 1781, *The Papers of General Nathanael Greene*, 7:433–41.

89. Greene to Lee, March 19, 1781, ibid., 7:454. Lee's letter suggesting the attack has not been found. See also Greene to Morgan, March 20, 1781, ibid., 7:455–56, and Greene to Lee, April 21, 1781 (two letters), ibid., 7:456–57. Williams had acted as Greene's adjutant since Greene's arrival, but did not sign his official correspondence as such until April 1, 1781. See Williams to Robert Lawson, April 1, 1781, ibid., 8:19.

90. Greene to Lee, March 22, 1781, ibid., 7:461.

91. Greene to Abner Nash, March 29, 1781, ibid., 7:480.

92. Lee to Greene, April 2, 1781, ibid., 8:28–29.

93. Cornwallis to William Phillips, April 10, 1781, in Babits and Howard, *Long, Obstinate, and Bloody*, 180. See also *Correspondence of Charles, First Marquis Cornwallis*, edited by Charles Ross (London: Murray, 1859), 1:88.

94. Greene to George Washington, March 29, 1781, *The Papers of General Nathanael Greene*, 7:481–82.

95. Lee, *Memoirs*, 315–25, especially 320.

96. Ibid., 325. See also Greene to Lee, April 4, 1781, *The Papers of General Nathanael Greene*, 8:46–47, and Greene to Lee, April 4, 1781, ibid., 8:47, regarding Greene's suggestion for "the best route to surprise Watsons Corps."

97. See Greene to Lee, April 4 (two letters) and April 12, 1781, ibid., 8:46–47 and 85–86.

98. Lee to Greene, April 18, 1781, ibid., 8:113.

99. Greene to Lee, April 19, 1781, ibid., 8:117–18.

100. Lee to Greene, April 20, 1781, ibid., 8:125.

101. Greene to Lee, April 22, 1781, ibid., 8:133–34. Greene later agreed to send the piece, but by then the fort had already been captured. See Greene to Lee, April 24 and 28, 1781, ibid., 8:143–44; 168–69.

102. For a detailed report of siege of Fort Watson, see Francis Marion to Greene, April 23, 1781, ibid., 8:139–41, and Lee, *Memoirs*, 331–32. See also Lee to Greene, April 23, 1781 (second letter of that date), *The Papers of General Nathanael Greene*, 8:139.

103. Greene to Lee, April 28, 1781, *The Papers of General Nathanael Greene*, 8:168–69. See also, Greene to Lee, April 29, 1781, ibid., 8:171–73.

104. Greene to Huntington, April 27, 1781, ibid., 8:155–60, which was Greene's official account of the Battle of Hobkirk's Hill. For Rawdon's quotation, see Rawdon to Cornwallis, April 26, 1781, ibid., 8:157n.

105. John Eager Howard to John Gunby, March 22, 1782, MS 109, box 1, folder 10, Maryland Historical Society. See also Howard to John Marshall, no date, MS 109, box 4, folder 2, Maryland Historical Society.

106. Greene to Huntington, April 27, 1781, *The Papers of General Nathanael Greene*, 8:155–60.

107. Rawdon to Cornwallis, May 24, 1781, in Piecuch and Beakes, *John Eager Howard*, 108–9. See also Brooking, "As Good an Officer as the World Affords," 194.

108. Howard to Marshall, no date, MS 109, box 4, folder 2, Maryland Historical Society.

109. Even William Washington's biographer admitted that "Washington's time consuming action among the enemy non-combatants may also have contributed somewhat to the American reverse." Stephen E. Haller, *William Washington: Cavalryman of the Revolution* (Bowie, Md.: Heritage Books, 2001), 132.

110. Lee, *Memoirs*, 340. Lee added that this was the "only instance in Greene's command, where this general implicitly yielded to its [overconfidence] delusive counsel." See also Freeman, *George Washington*, 4:368, which states that Greene's defects were of his own making—a haste in decision, an *overconfidence* [emphasis added] in judgment."

111. For the exoneration of Gunby, see John S. Pancake, *This Destructive War: The British Campaign in the Carolinas, 1780–1782* (Tuscaloosa: University of Alabama Press,

2003), 187–203; Piecuch and Beakes, *John Eager Howard*, 99–111; Babits and Howard, *Long, Obstinate, and Bloody*, 180–81; Henry Lumpkin, *From Savannah to Yorktown: The American Revolution in the South* (Columbia: University of South Carolina Press, 1981), 182; Golway, *Washington's General*, 269.

112. Greene to Samuel Huntington, April 27, 1781, *The Papers of General Nathanael Greene*, 8:155–60.

113. Greene to Baron Friedrich von Steuben, April 27, 1781, ibid., 8:161–62.

114. Greene to Lee, April 29, 1781, ibid., 8:172–74.

115. General Greene's orders, May 2, 1781, ibid., 8:187.

116. Greene to Abner Nash, May 2, 1781, ibid., 8:190–91.

117. Greene to Joseph Reed, May 4, 1781, ibid., 8:199–202.

118. Greene to Sumter, May 5, 1781, ibid., 8:208.

119. Greene to Reed, August 6, 1781, ibid., 9:134–38.

120. Greene to Horatio Gates, October 4, 1781, ibid., 9:425–26. One of John Gunby's descendants stated that "there is a singular resemblance in the conduct of General Greene to that of Gates on nearly the same battleground. Both were surprised, both were too ready to accept defeat, and both left before the fight was finished." Andrew A. Gunby, *Colonel John Gunby of the Maryland Line* (Cincinnati: Robert Clarke, 1902), 84.

121. Howard to Gunby, March 22, 1782, MS 109, box 1, folder 10, Maryland Historical Society. In a letter to Greene biographer William Johnson, written c. 1822, Howard had difficulty either supporting or denying Greene's accusations against Gunby. He also failed to support fully Gunby's claim that Greene's being surprised caused the defeat because that mistake "may not excuse the conduct of our men." See Howard to Lee, January 19, 1819, Henry Lee, *The Campaign of 1781 in the Carolinas, with Remarks Historical and Critical on Johnson's Life of Greene* (Philadelphia: E. Littell, 1824), 262.

122. Gunby, *Colonel John Gunby*, 76, 104.

123. William Pierce to Lee, April 25, 1781, *The Papers of General Nathanael Greene*, 8:146. See also Pierce to John Butler, May 2, 1781, Library of Congress, Manuscript Division, MSS 386. Pierce also blamed Gunby, who "lost us the honor of a victory."

124. Golway, *Washington's General*, 269.

125. Greene to Gates, October 4, 1781, *The Papers of General Nathanael Greene*, 9:425–26.

126. Gunby, *Colonel John Gunby*, 26; Francis B. Heitman, *Historical Register of Officers of the Continental Army during the War of the Revolution* (Washington: Rare Book Shop Publishing, 1914), 265; Rieman Steuart, *A History of the Maryland Line in the Revolutionary War* (Towson, Md.: Metropolitan Press, 1969), 89.

127. Greene to James Varnum, October 31, 1774, *The Papers of General Nathanael Greene*, 1:75–77.

128. That is not to say that Washington was incapable of such behavior himself, for he was, especially early in his career, capable of Machiavellian machinations. Washington, however, proved especially loyal to those closest to him, most notably Greene, Henry Knox, and Alexander Hamilton.

129. Washington Irving, *George Washington: A Life*, edited by Charles Neider (New York: Da Capo Press, 1994), 295.

130. Greene to Henry Knox, November 17, 1776, *The Papers of General Nathanael Greene*, 1:351–59. For a thorough treatment of the postbattle blame game, see 353–60n2.

131. Joseph Reed to Charles Lee, November 21, 1776, in John Richard Alden, *General Charles Lee, Traitor or Patriot?* (Baton Rouge: Louisiana State University Press, 1951), 148.

132. Lee to George Washington, November 19, 1776, in Alden, *Charles Lee*, 148. See also Freeman, *George Washington*, 4:253.

133. Washington to the president of Congress, November 16, 1776, *The Writings of George Washington*, 6:284–87. The last qualifier in this sentence is important because Greene surely knew that Congress wished Washington to hold the fort.

134. George Washington to John Augustine Washington, November 6, 1776, *The Writings of George Washington*, 6:242–47. Note that the date of the letter is November 6 but that Washington later appended the date November 19.

135. For recent historians' observations on this issue, see Golway, *Washington's General*, 103. Golway declared that Washington "declined the chance to make him a public scapegoat." David Hackett Fischer, *Washington's Crossing* (New York: Oxford University Press, 2004), 114. Fischer stated that Washington "blamed no one else for what had happened, took all the responsibility on his own shoulders." David McCullough, *1776* (New York: Simon & Schuster, 2006), 245. McCullough opined that "Washington never blamed himself for the loss of Fort Washington, but then he never openly blamed Greene either, which he could have." General Washington also had another opportunity to blame Greene for a military misfortune. According to historian William Gordon, Washington had been asked shortly after the Battle of Germantown if he blamed the defeat on Greene's tardiness. Washington replied: "No, not at all; the fault lay with" himself. William Gordon, *The History of the Rise, Progress, and Establishment of the Independence of the United States of America*, 4 vols. (London: Printed for the author, 1788), 2:527.

136. Lee to Greene, April 28, 1781, *The Papers of General Nathanael Greene*, 8:171–72.

137. Greene to Lee, April 29, 1781, ibid., 8:172–74.

138. Lee to Greene, April 30, 1781, ibid., 8:178–79.

139. Lee to Greene, May 2, 1781, ibid., 8:192–93.

140. Greene to Lee, May 4, 1781, ibid., 8:198.

141. Lee to Greene, May 8, 1781, ibid., 8:222–23.

142. Lee to Greene, May 9, 1781, ibid., 8:227–30. Greene also believed the remainder of the Carolina conflict would be a "war of posts" with the "glory" belonging to subordinates.

143. Lee to Greene, May 10, 1781, ibid., 8:237–38.

144. Greene to Lee, May 13, 1781, ibid., 8:249. For the siege of Fort Motte, see Greene to Huntington, May 14, 1781, ibid., 8:250–54.

145. Lee to Greene, May 15, 1781, and Sumter to Greene, May 15, 1781, ibid., 8:262–66, 269–70.

146. Lee, *Memoirs*, 349–52.

147. Thomas Sumter to Greene, May 15 and 16, 1781, *The Papers of General Nathanael Greene*, 8:269–70, 274.

148. Lee to Greene, July 29, 1781, ibid., 9:102. See also Sumter to Greene, July 22, 1781, and Lee to Greene, August 20, 1781, ibid., 9:62–64, 214–16.

149. Lee, *Memoirs*, 352.

150. Greene to Lee, May 16, 1781, *The Papers of General Nathanael Greene*, 8:272.

151. Lee to Greene, May 16, 1781, ibid., 8:273–74.

152. Levi Smith's narrative, *Royal Gazette* (Charleston), April 13–17, 1782, *The Papers of General Nathanael Greene*, 8:273–74. See also Greene to Huntington, May 14, 1781, ibid., 8:250–54 (especially note 8).

153. Greene to Lee, May 21, 1781, *The Papers of General Nathanael Greene*, 8:290.

154. Greene to Lee, May 22, 1781, ibid., 8:291–92.

155. Lee to Greene, May 22, 1781, ibid., 8:293–94. See also Greene to Lee, May 29, 1781, ibid., 8:326.

156. For the siege of Ninety Six, see Robert D. Bass, *Ninety-Six: The Struggle for the South Carolina Backcountry* (Lexington, S.C.: Sandlapper, 1978), and Jerome A. Greene, *Ninety Six: A Historical Narrative* (Denver: Eastern National, 2005).

157. Lee to Greene, June 1, 1781, *The Papers of General Nathanael Greene*, 8:334. See also Greene to Lee, May 22, 1781, Greene to Pickens, May 29, 1781, and Greene to Lee, May 29, 1781, ibid., 8:291–92, 326, 328.

158. Lee to Greene, June 1, 1781, ibid., 8:334.

159. Greene to Lee, June 3, 1781, ibid., 8:340.

160. Lee to Greene, June 4, 1781, ibid., 8:346–47.

161. Andrew Pickens and Lee to Greene, June 5, 1781, ibid., 8:351–52. For Greene's report, see Greene to Huntington, June 9, 1781 (two letters), ibid., 8:363–65.

162. For Greene's official report of the siege, see Greene to Huntington, June 20, 1781, ibid., 8:419–26.

163. Lee to Greene, June 20, 1781, ibid., 8:430.

164. Greene to Huntington, June 23, 1781, ibid., 8:444–45. Congress approved the plan on September 29.

165. Lee to Greene, June 22, 1781, ibid., 8:442.

166. Lee to Greene, June 22, 1781 (second letter of that date), ibid., 8:443.

167. General Greene's orders, June 23, 1781, ibid., 8:443. See also William Pierce to Sumter, June 23, 1781, ibid., 8:450. Lee was as yet unaware of Rawdon's movement and exact intentions. See Lee to Greene, June 23, 1781, ibid., 8:451–52.

168. Rawdon to Cornwallis, August 2, 1781, ibid., 8:453n. By the twenty-fourth of June, Greene had surmised the same. See Greene to Lee, June 24, 1781, ibid., 8: 452–53.

169. Greene to Lee, June 25, 1781, ibid., 8:455–56. See also Greene to Lee, June 25, 1781 (second letter of that date), ibid., 8:456–57.

170. Lee to Greene, June 26, 1781, ibid., 8:462.

171. Greene to Lee, June 29, 1781, ibid., 8:473–74.

172. Lee to Greene, June 29, 1781, ibid. 8:475–76.

173. Lee to Greene, June 30, 1781, ibid., 8:477–78.

174. Lee to Greene, July 3, 1781 (second letter of that date), ibid., 8:487–88.

175. Lee to Greene, July 2, 1781, ibid., 8:481–82. See also Lee to Greene, July 3, 1781, ibid., 8:487–88.

176. Greene to William Washington, July 3, 1781, ibid., 8:486.

177. Lee to Greene, July 3, 1781, ibid., 8:486–87. See also Lee, *Memoirs*, 381–82. For Greene's response see Greene to Lee, July 4, 1781, *The Papers of Nathanael Greene*, 8:489–90.

178. Lee to Greene, July 3, 1781 (second letter of that date), *The Papers of Nathanael Greene*, 8:487–88.

179. Greene to Lee, July 4, 1781, ibid., 8:489–90.

180. William Washington to Greene, July 4, 1781, and July 5, 1781, ibid., 8:494, 499–500.

181. Greene's orders and after orders, July 11, 1781, ibid., 9:3. See also Marion to Greene, July 7, 1781, and Williams to Greene, July 8, 1781, ibid., 8:505, 511–12.

182. Greene to Lee, July 18, 1781, ibid., 9:38.

183. Lee to Greene, July 30, 1781, ibid., 9:114–15, and Lee to Greene, July 30, 1781, ibid., 9:115.

184. Lee to Greene, August 8, 1781, ibid., 9:150–51.

185. Greene to Lee, August 9, 1781, ibid., 9:152–53.

186. Lee to Greene, August 10, 1781, ibid., 9:162.

187. Greene to Lee, August 12, 1781, ibid., 9:170–72.

188. Lee to Greene, August 13, 1781, ibid., 9:177.

189. Greene to Lee, August 14, 1781, ibid., 9:181. Greene also admitted that a defeat could be disastrous.

190. Lee to Greene, August 17, 1781, and August 18, 1781, ibid., 9:195–96, 203–4.

191. Greene to Lee, August 19, 1781, ibid., 9:205–6.

192. Greene to Morgan, January 19, 1781, ibid., 7:146–47.

193. Lee, *Memoirs*, 504. Lee acknowledged that Greene required his officers to maintain "that happy mixture of caution and ardor."

194. Lee to Greene, August 23, 1781, *The Papers of General Nathanael Greene*, 9:226–27.

195. Lee to Greene, August 20, 1781 (two letters), ibid., 9:214–15.

196. Greene to Lee, August 21, 1781, ibid., 9:218–19.

197. Greene to Lee, August 22, 1781, ibid., 9:222–23.

198. Lee to Greene, September 1, 1781, ibid., 9:278.

199. Greene to George Washington, August 26, 1781, ibid., 9:257–58. See also Greene's orders, September 4–7, 1781, ibid., 9:291, 298, 302 (includes order of battle), and 305.

200. See Greene's official report. Greene to Thomas McKean, September 11, 1781, ibid., 9:328–38. See also Otho Holland Williams to Edward Giles, September 23, 1781, Otho Holland Williams Papers, MS 908, Maryland Historical Society, Baltimore.

201. For an analysis of the cavalry action at Eutaw Springs, see Lee F. McGee, "Most Astonishing Efforts: William Washington's Cavalry at the Battle of Eutaw Springs," *Southern Campaigns of the American Revolution* 3 (March 2006): 15–33.

202. Greene to Williams, September 17, 1782, *The Papers of General Nathanael Greene*, 10:669–71.

203. Greene to Lee, January 27, 1782, ibid., 10:268–70.

204. Lee to Greene, January 29, 1782, ibid., 10:282–83.

205. Greene to Lee, February 18, 1782, ibid., 10:378–80.

206. Greene to McKean, September 11, 1781, ibid., 9:328–38.

207. Greene to Lee, February 18, 1782, ibid., 10:378–80. Greene explicitly stated that he favored Lee over William Washington.

208. Greene to McKean, September 11, 1781, ibid., 9:328–38.

209. Lee to Greene, February 19, 1782, ibid., 10:389–91.

210. Greene to Lee, October 7, 1782, ibid., 12:35–42.

211. Greene to Morgan, August 26, 1781, ibid., 9:256–57.

212. Greene to McKean, October 30, 1781, ibid., 9:496.

213. Greene to George Washington, October 30, 1781, ibid., 9:497–98.

214. Williams to Greene, June 1, 1782, ibid., 11:279–82. See also Williams to Greene, February 20, 1783, ibid., 12:466–69.

215. Greene to Anthony Wayne, July 24, 1781, ibid., 9:75.

216. Greene to Lee, February 12, 1782, ibid., 10:358–59.

217. Greene to Richard Henry Lee, April 25, 1782, ibid., 11:114–17.

218. Greene to [George Lux?], November 14, 1781, ibid., 9:571–72.

219. Howard to Greene, December 12, 1782, ibid., 12:283–84.

"We must endeavor to keep up a Partizan War"

Nathanael Greene and the Partisans

John Buchanan

"*I* have not the Honor of your Acquaintance but am no Stranger to your Character and merit."[1] What a felicitous sentence. The writer, Major General Nathanael Greene, was the newly arrived commander of the Southern Department. The recipient, Colonel Francis Marion, led a mounted brigade of South Carolina militia. Yet two months later, on arriving in Salisbury, North Carolina, during the long retreat to Virginia with British Lieutenant General Charles, Lord Cornwallis, in hot pursuit, Green exploded when he found almost seventeen hundred militia muskets nearly useless because of poor storage conditions. "These are some of the happy effects of defending the country with Militia; from which the good lord deliver us."[2]

Greene had been expressing similar sentiments since early in the war. In 1776, following the American debacles on Long Island and at Kip's Bay on Manhattan, with reference to formal, open-field engagements, he wrote to his brother Jacob: "The policy of Congress has been the most absurd and ridiculous imaginable, pouring in militia men who come and go every month. A military force established upon such principles defeats itself. People coming from home with all the tender feelings of domestic life are not sufficiently fortified with natural courage to stand the shocking scenes of war. To march over dead men, to hear without concern the groans of the wounded, I say few men can stand such scenes unless steeled by habit or fortified by military pride."[3]

How do we explain the apparent contradiction between praising a militia colonel and heatedly criticizing militia behavior and the policy of depending on militia for the war effort? That Greene was buttering up a key militia officer is beyond question, but the real answer is contained in another sentence in the

*Lieutenant General Charles,
Earl Cornwallis*

same December 4, 1780, letter to Marion: "Untill a more permanent Army can be collected than is in the Field at present, we must endeavor to keep up a Partizan War and preserve the Tide of Sentiment among the People as much as possible in our Favour."[4]

"Untill a more permanent Army can be collected": that is the key phrase. Whatever he thought of militia—and his attitude overall was negative—Nathanael Greene was a realist. South and North, the Continental army was never large enough to fight the war by itself. At times it required militia units to join in formal, set-piece battles, as occurred in the South at Camden, Cowpens, Guilford Courthouse, and Eutaw Springs. But the chief mission of militia was to control the countryside: keep the Tories in check, protect lines of communication and supply, deny the enemy provisions and forage, gain intelligence of enemy intentions and movements, and, in George Washington's words, "harrass their troops to death."[5]

Although Greene's letters written from both theaters of war contain far more criticism than praise of militia, he never hesitated to give kudos when they were earned. In a letter to Thomas Paine, Greene paid tribute to the Philadelphia militia for their behavior under fire during the 1776–77 Trenton-Princeton campaign and for their bearing "a winter's campaign with a soldier like patience." In the winter and spring of 1777, he played an active role in a partisan campaign that was begun by Jersey militia, joined by Washington's Continentals, and ended with the British evacuation of New Jersey. So the general who came south in late 1780 to assume the southern command was well aware that "Partizan War" was critical to the eventual triumph of the cause.[6]

Immediately after writing to Marion, Greene turned to another important partisan leader, with whom his relations would steadily deteriorate, the commander of the South Carolina militia, General Thomas Sumter, of whom his leading biographer wrote: "In war he was a politician, and in politics he was an old soldier." Prior to Greene's assuming command of the Southern Department, Sumter was the peerless partisan commander in the South. He had taken the field at a time when British forces seemed invincible. His ability to raise large numbers of men in the darkest hours, even after his debacle at Fishing Creek on August 18, 1780, was one of the reasons Cornwallis considered Sumter his most dangerous foe. Sumter must be given full credit for his role during the first phase of the insurgency in frustrating the British pacification effort. But he was also a deeply flawed commander, both in temperament and ability, and his refusal to cooperate with Greene fully seriously hampered the second phase of the Carolina campaign.[7]

The exiled rebel governor of South Carolina, John Rutledge, who was in Greene's camp in Charlotte, wrote to Sumter on December 3, 1780, informing him of Greene's arrival and urging that he "come to or near this place as fast as your Health and the Weather will permit." Rutledge even sent his carriage and driver to fetch the general, but Sumter declined. In all fairness Sumter was still suffering from the terrible wound he had received at the Battle of Blackstock's on November 20, when he had inflicted on Banastre Tarleton the first defeat of the young cavalryman's career. Sumter could neither ride a horse nor wield a sword. But he controlled too many men to be ignored, and on December 8, five days after Greene had taken over his new command, the general and the governor rode west to Tuckasegee Ford on the Catawba River, where Sumter was recuperating in the fortresslike stone house of his armorer, John Price.[8]

At their conference Sumter, who was no strategist, urged Greene to attack Cornwallis. Given the state of Greene's Continentals, that would have been suicidal. Nevertheless, on Greene's return to Charlotte, he told Generals Daniel Morgan and William Smallwood of Sumter's proposal. Morgan could never be accused of not being a fighter, but he joined Smallwood in arguing against the attack, pointing out that the army in its present condition was in no state to take on Cornwallis's regulars. Greene knew this, but when he wrote to Sumter to inform him of the reaction of Morgan and Smallwood, Greene added, "I am not altogether of this opinion, and therefore wish you to keep up a communication of intelligence, and of any changes of their disposition that may take place." The only explanation for Greene's words can be his desire to keep Sumter as contented as possible, for he had no intention of attacking or even accepting battle until his army was fit and he could choose the ground.[9]

Greene soon began preparations to divide his army and wage partisan war. Even before starting south from Philadelphia, he had made clear his intentions in a November 2 letter to Samuel Huntington, president of the Continental Congress: "As it must be some time before the southern Army can be collected and equipped in sufficient force to contend with the Enemy in that quarter upon equal ground, it will be my object to endeavour to form a flying army to consist of Infantry and horse. It appears to me that Cavalry and Partizan Corps are best adapted to the make of the Country and the state of war in that quarter, both for heading and encouraging the Militia as well as protecting the persons and property of the Inhabitants."[10]

When Greene referred to "Cavalry and Partizan Corps" he meant regular forces waging irregular war, a type of fighting well known to American, British, and European soldiers. Lieutenant Colonel Henry "Light-Horse Harry" Lee Jr., and his legion of horse and foot arrived in Greene's camp at Charlotte on January 8, 1781, and the following day Greene detached Lee's Legion eastward to join Francis Marion's partisan brigade. The two forces thereafter waged the "Partizan War" that Greene had in mind. Marion and Lee operated well together, which is surprising, as Hugh Rankin pointed out in his biography of Marion. Lee was egotistical and eager for glory, Marion moody and prickly. Yet on the whole there was little friction between the two. Marion made it clear to Greene that "I expect to command, not from the Militia Commission I hold, but from an Elder Continental Commission"; yet he also wrote to Greene a week later, "Colo Lee's Interprising Genuis promises much." Lee and Marion almost immediately undertook on attack on the British garrison at Georgetown, South Carolina. They achieved limited success, but because of the lack of artillery they could not take the town. One sour note emerged from this action: in his report to Greene, Lee failed to mention Marion's role. He rectified that error in judgment on subsequent occasions.[11]

With regard to Thomas Sumter, however, Brigadier General Daniel Morgan was unable to emulate Lee's relationship with Marion, for Greene and Sumter had different concepts of Morgan's role west of the Catawba River. On December 21 Morgan left Charlotte with the cream of the army: 600 light troops comprising 320 Maryland and Delaware Continentals, 80 Continental

Nathanael Greene. Engraving after a portrait by Alonzo Chappel.

light dragoons, and 200 Virginia militia who were discharged Continental veterans and could be counted on to behave as regulars. In a December 14 letter
to Governor Rutledge, Sumter had written that if Greene "thought proper to
send over a party of horse or foot or both, they might well be supplied at my
Camp and would be of very great service in supporting the foragers." This
makes it clear that Sumter expected the detachment to operate if not under his
command at least with his forbearance, out of his camp, under his observation,
for the purpose of providing escort service for foraging parties. Greene's orders
to Morgan flew in the face of Sumter's assumptions. Morgan was ordered to
"proceed to the West side of the Catawba River where you will be joined by a
body of Volunteer Militia under the command of Brig'r Genl Davidson of this
State [North Carolina], and by the Militia lately under the command of Brig'r
Genl Sumter." The phrase "lately under the command" seems a strange choice
of words. There is no evidence that Sumter, despite his serious wound, had relinquished his command or that he and Greene had even discussed the possibility. Greene gave Morgan freedom to act "offensively or defensively" against
the enemy in order "to give protection to that part of the country and spirit up
the people, to annoy the enemy in that quarter" and deny them provisions and
forage by collecting them himself and storing them in magazines established in
his rear. If all this were not enough to provoke Sumter's wrath, the key sentence
certainly did. "For the present," Greene wrote Morgan, "I give you the entire
command in that quarter, and do hereby require all Officers and Soldiers engaged in the American cause to be subject to your orders and command."[12]

Governor Rutledge sought to mollify Sumter by writing to him on January
21, 1781, "Genl Greene and you understand the matter, with respect to you
not having any command at present, in a very different way." In other words
Greene believed that, until Sumter could take the field, he had temporarily
relinquished command west of the Catawba, whereas Sumter assumed the
opposite.[13] Making matters worse, two weeks earlier Greene had conveyed to
Sumter his thoughts on the nature of militia and partisan warfare that angered
the Gamecock: "The salvation of this country don't depend on little strokes;
nor should this great business of establishing a permanent army be neglected to
pursue them. Partizan strokes in war are like the garnish of a table, they give
splendor to the Army and reputation to the Officers, but they afford no substantial national security. They . . . should not be neglected, & yet they should
not be pursued to the prejudice of more important concerns. You may strike a
hundred strokes, and reap little benefit from them. The enemy will never relinquish their plan, nor the people be firm in our favor untill they behold a better
barrier in the field than a Volunteer Militia who are one day out and the next
home."

If this statement were not enough for Sumter to swallow at one sitting, Greene added another paragraph that must have stung: "Plunder and Depredation prevails so in every quarter that I am not a little apprehensive all this Country will be laid waste. Most people appear to be in pursuit of private gain or personal glory. I persuade myself though that you may set a just value on reputation, your soul is filled with a more noble ambition."[14]

In his letter Greene did praise the men who followed Sumter, contrasting them with the "shoals of useless militia" raised by North Carolina, who "are not worth one of your men, whose all depend upon their own bravery." This was not empty flattery, for Greene was correct in his judgment of the fighting abilities of the partisan riders of the backcountry as opposed to eastern militia. In a well-known letter to Alexander Hamilton, Greene wrote: "There is a great spirit of enterprise among the back people; and those that come out as Volunteers are not a little formidable to the enemy. There are also some particular corps under Sumpter Marion and Clarke that are bold and daring; the rest of the Militia are better calculated to destroy provisions than oppose the Enimy."[15]

Although Greene was right in all particulars in both letters, the letter to Sumter reveals one of Greene's faults. Coupled with his tendency to micromanage, his letters often took on the tone of a schoolmaster lecturing to his pupils. Yet probably even the subtlest of language to express Greene's well-taken points would have offended Sumter, whose large ego was matched by the size of the chip on his shoulder.

In his reply of January 29, Sumter denied "any injudicious thirst for enterprise, private gain, or personal Glory" and apologized if he had given that impression when he and Greene had met. He also denied being "arrogant and designing" but confessed that "I have been under some embaressment respecting Gen. Morgans command, & the orders he has given," although "I have been guilty of no Impropriety." Throughout the letter Sumter stressed that his actions were always designed for the "Publick Good."[16]

But had Sumter the "Publick Good" in mind, had he been "guilty of no Impropriety" when he had earlier refused to cooperate with Daniel Morgan unless Morgan went through him? Morgan had sent his commissary officer, Captain C. K. Chitty, to meet with Colonel William Hill, one of Sumter's regimental commanders, with orders that Hill furnish Chitty with enough men to assist him in collecting and storing provisions. Morgan wrote to Greene that to his "great surprise," Captain Chitty returned empty-handed, reporting that Colonel Hill had "assured him that General Sumpter directed him to obey no orders from me, unless they came though him."[17]

Two days after he wrote to Greene, Morgan and his mixed force of Continentals, state troops, and partisans won the tactical masterpiece of the war, the

*Brigadier General
Daniel Morgan*

critical Battle of Cowpens, crushing Cornwallis's light troops commanded by
Lieutenant Colonel Banastre Tarleton. The partisans, commanded by Colonel
Andrew Pickens of South Carolina, were from North Carolina, South Carolina,
and Georgia, but the South Carolina partisans did not include men from Sumter's regiments. Thirty years after the battle, Colonel Pickens wrote to Light-
Horse Harry Lee with regard to Sumter: "He was I believe pressed much by
Green and Morgan to join the Latter at Grindals Shoals on the Pacolet river
before the Battle of Cowpens. He was excuseable in some measure to himself
he had received a wound in his shoulder not long before, tho he ought to have
ordered those who were attached to him or under his orders." Pickens final
comment is damning: "None of them were with us."[18]

Following the Battle of Cowpens, Greene's relations with Sumter improved
marginally, and the issues between them had to be temporarily set aside as the
American and British armies raced northward through North Carolina and out
of the area of Sumter's operations. Greene asked Sumter to call up the militia
and go on the offensive in South Carolina and gave Sumter command of all the
militia in the state. Sumter decided to roll up the British posts on the Congaree and Santee Rivers. He called his men to him and wrote to Marion to gather

his men and join him. Marion, however, had little enthusiasm for the venture, while Sumter, previously accustomed to leading 1,000-odd men on operations, was able to assemble only 280 riders. With his usual slipshod planning and inattention to detail, Sumter marched on February 16. He attacked three British posts, was repulsed at each, and ended his three-week swing through the lower Piedmont with a quarter of his men lost and the rest sullen and rebellious.[19]

Northward in the meantime, Nathanael Greene was having his own problems with the militia. He knew that eventually he had to meet Cornwallis in battle, for continual retreat would devastate rebel morale. As he wrote to Virginia governor Thomas Jefferson, "I know the People have been in anxious suspence waiting the event of an Action." But he would risk a general engagement only if he had enough men. It was imperative, therefore, that militia turn out in large numbers in order to reinforce the Continentals for a formal, open-field battle. This need brought to a head a highly contentious matter that Morgan had raised in his letter of January 15 to Greene. Morgan wrote that he was "apprehensive that no part of this state accessible to us, can support us long. Could the militia be persuaded to change their fatal mode of going to war, much provision might be saved, but the custom has taken such deep root that it cannot be abolished."[20]

Morgan was referring specifically to the mounted backcountry partisans, who insisted on riding their horses to war and keeping them while serving. When dismounted for action and required to move to another position, their first thought was to retrieve their horses and vanish. Furthermore, when large numbers of mounted men came together, the impact on forage for the horses became critical. Supplying an army was an enormous task, as indicated in the statistics for a later war in which horses were still vital for military operations. The American Civil War general William Tecumseh Sherman wrote in his memoir: "To be strong, healthy, and capable of the largest measure of physical effort, the soldier needs about three pounds gross of food per day, and the horse or mule about twenty pounds." At one point during the campaign, Andrew Pickens commanded about seven hundred mounted militia. Under Sherman's formula, their horses required fourteen thousand pounds of forage per day, ninety-eight thousand pounds per week. That amount of forage was practically impossible to obtain in the sparsely populated Carolina backcountry, and we can be certain that men and horses rarely if ever came close to meeting Sherman's standard. Morgan was right. The countryside could not support them for long.[21]

Despite Morgan's admonition that the custom of riding to war had "taken such deep root that it cannot be abolished," Greene later made a serious effort to dismount the backcountry and frontier militia. Following the death of the North Carolina militia general William Lee Davidson, Greene had given

Colonel Andrew Pickens of South Carolina command of the militia that re-
mained behind in North Carolina after Greene and the army crossed the Dan
River into Virginia. Morgan had earlier described Pickens as "a valuable, dis-
creet, and attentive officer" who "has the confidence of the militia." Pickens
lived up to Morgan's praise. He had with him about thirty Georgians and South
Carolinians when the militia officers of backcountry North Carolina supported
Greene's decision to give Pickens command of the militia that had been led by
Davidson. By February 19 Pickens had about seven hundred riders behind him.
His mission, wrote Greene, was to "continue to pursue the Enemy and harrass
them as much as possible." The faithful Pickens carried out his orders but with
much difficulty. He reported to Greene that those from south of the Catawba
had followed him reluctantly and were interested in an "expedition to South
Carolina where their thoughts seem universally bent." In addition the Salisbury,
North Carolina, militia "are continually deserting, and no persuasion can prevail with them." Pickens considered them "among the worst Men" he had ever
commanded.[22]

But Pickens's troubles with his backcountry riders had just begun, and they
were partially precipitated by two of Greene's key subordinates, who undoubtedly were acting on behalf of their chief. Colonel Otho Holland Williams of
Maryland, an officer of high merit, had been given command of the Continental light troops after Morgan had been forced to leave the army because of ill
health. The North Carolina militia officer Joseph Graham recalled long after
the war that Williams and Lee proposed that half the mounted militia, dismounted and "organized as infantry[,] would be of more service to the cause
than all of them as they were." But the two Continental officers met a stone wall
of opposition. Their proposal was meant to augment Greene's regulars in an
engagement against Cornwallis. Williams and Lee were also probably in despair
over the wanderings of the mounted partisans in search of forage. Greene's secretary and aide, Captain William Pierce Jr., informed General John Butler of
the North Carolina militia how the forage situation had become so critical that
almost one thousand horses had been sent away and advised Butler to dismount
his troops "who are not properly equipped with swords etc." and to send their
horses home.[23]

In addition the partisan riflemen, including officers, serving under Colonel Williams "decline obeying" the officer sent to command them, Williams
reported to Greene. They actually named the officer they would serve under
and reminded Williams that they had the right to appoint their own commander. "They say they are Voluntiers," Williams continued, "and shod be
treated with distinction." Eight days later Andrew Pickens, who then had about
533 partisans under him, wrote to Greene that "I am sorry to acquaint you of
the fast desertion rate that prevails and am afraid that in a very few days there

*Lieutenant Colonel
Banastre Tarleton*

will hardly be a man belonging to the Salisbury district remaining. The plan of dismounting them, altho it seemed to take, has proved a bone of contention for them; not only with those of Salisbury, but, likewise those from the Mountains and several of the last have absconded." Pickens also brought to Greene's attention the "miserable plight" of his South Carolinians and Georgians, who had been in the field since Charleston had fallen to the British in May 1780. There was no commissary for these men. They lived hand to mouth off the land, and Pickens claimed that not one of them had a spare shirt.[24]

The coming and going of militia during this period vexed the commander of the Southern Department. Five days after Pickens reported his problems, Greene wrote to Thomas Jefferson: "Every Day has given me hopes of being stronger, but I have been as constantly disappointed." Within a period of a few weeks some five thousand militiamen had been "in motion." But when Greene wrote to Jefferson only eight hundred to nine hundred were with him. Pickens, who was accustomed to commanding militia, became so frustrated that he asked Greene to be allowed to return to South Carolina. Pickens wanted to be in on the expected clash with Cornwallis, writing, "I must confess I want to see what becomes of Cornwallis," but he thought himself "capable of doing more good there [South Carolina] than here."[25]

With regard to the refusal of the backcountry partisans to give up their horses, one must take into account the first, and critical, phase of their partisan campaign, which began in June 1780 and ended with the Battle of Cowpens in January 1781. That campaign stymied the efforts of the British to pacify the South Carolina backcountry and thereby bought the time necessary for the arrival of a fighting general to command the Southern Department: Nathanael Greene. It was a classic guerrilla campaign in which frustrated British and Loyalist regulars reinforced by Loyalist militia tried in vain to bring their foe to bay. Not even the debacles suffered by two regular American armies at Charleston and Camden and Sumter's blunder at Fishing Creek discouraged the partisans enough to give up the struggle. Their success, however, would have been impossible had they not been mounted. Writing after the war, Tarleton's deputy, Major George Hanger, put his finger on the tactical problem faced by the British: "The crackers and militia in those parts of American are all mounted on horseback, which renders it totally impossible to force them to an engagement with infantry only. When they chuse to fight, they dismount and fasten their horses to fences and rails, but if not very confident in the superiority of their numbers, they remain on horse-back, give their fire, and retreat, which renders it useless to attack them without cavalry: for though you repulse them and drive them from the field, you can never improve the advantage, or do them material detriment."[26]

Lieutenant Colonel Francis, Lord Rawdon, Cornwallis's able deputy and commander of British forces in South Carolina following Cornwallis's departure, made the same point during the war: the superior mobility of the partisans was the reason why "we have never been able to force them to a decisive action." The British in the Carolinas had only some 240 regular cavalry, not enough to fight the type of war chosen by the elusive partisans, especially as the Loyalist mounted militia and their leaders, who were supposed to provide the riders necessary to combat the common foe effectively, were in general inferior to the rebel horsemen and their leaders. Is it any wonder then that the partisans so vigorously resisted Greene's efforts to dismount them? Yet at the same time, Greene desperately needed auxiliary infantry. It was a problem without solution.[27]

The dispute over horses was not the only "bone of contention" between partisans and Continental officers. The bad feelings came to a head after the action at Weitzel's Mill, North Carolina, on March 6, 1781, when Cornwallis pursued and tried to cut off Colonel Otho Holland Williams's light troops. Cornwallis's advance was engaged by backcountry riflemen, who provided covering fire while Williams's light infantry crossed Reedy Ford Creek. During the militia's withdrawal, Captain Joseph Graham of North Carolina, who fought at Weitzel's Mill, later recalled the "militia running down the hill from under the smoke. The ford was crowded, many crossing the watercourse at other places. Some, it was said, were drowned." Although Colonel Williams reported "very few were kill'd & most of our wounded were brought off," Captain Graham estimated light-infantry casualties at two killed and three wounded, but partisan casualties at "between twenty and twenty-five . . . killed and wounded." The South Carolina and Georgia riflemen were furious. As Charles Magill reported to Thomas Jefferson, they complained that the "burthen, and heat, of the Day was entirely thrown upon them, and that they were to be made a sacrifice by the Regular Officers to screen their own Troops." Several years later Pickens, wrote to Lee that, when he rode into the partisan camp that evening, he found that the men "were determined to stay no longer." In addition to their attitude toward the attempt to dismount them, they probably had other reasons too, with the action at Weitzel's Mill being the final straw. Partisans rarely ventured as far from home as they had, and they had been away from their families for almost two months in uncertain and perilous times. They were adamant, Pickens reported to Greene and Governor Rutledge, and on March 8 Greene ordered Pickens to return with the South Carolina and Georgia men to South Carolina, to notify Thomas Sumter of his return, and to request Sumter's orders.[28]

Despite his travails with the partisans, in the absence of a regular army large enough to undertake reconquest on its own, Greene did not deviate from his determination to wage a "Partizan War," in which the two forces available to him, regulars and partisans, complemented each other in the struggle to drive the British from the lower South. A mere three weeks after the March 1781 Battle of Guilford Courthouse, Greene ordered Lee and his legion, reinforced by a company of Maryland Continentals, to march for South Carolina, where, Greene hoped, Lee could "effect a surprise upon the enemies posts on the Santee" River. On the same day Lee left, Greene and the main army also headed for South Carolina but directly toward the British post at Camden. Thus began the second phase of the campaign to drive the British from South Carolina and Georgia, during which Greene struggled to put an end to the freewheeling independence of partisan commanders and convince them to join "some general plan of operation."[29]

The Battle of the Cowpens

Greene had written to Sumter on March 30, "I am in hopes by sending forward our Horse and some detachments of light infantry to join your militia, you
will be able to possess yourself of all their little out posts before the Army
arrives." He also informed Sumter that he would probably arrive in the vicinity
of Camden about April 20 and asked the Gamecock to collect provisions, "for
on this our whole operation will depend," and to "please inform me of your
prospects, and the probable force I may expect to cooperate with us." He followed up with a letter of April 7, again alerting Sumter of plans to proceed
against Camden and judging that "if we can get provisions, and you can raise a
considerable force to co-operate with us, I think we shall perplex the enemy not
a little, and perhaps do them an irreperable injury." In neither letter did Greene
present his wishes as orders. He was asking for Sumter's cooperation. On the
same day Sumter replied to Greene's letter of March 30 that he expected to have
six hundred or seven hundred men gathered by the twentieth, and he assured
Greene that "you may Rely upon my unremitted endeavours to Promote and
facilitate your Designs." In the final sentence of his letter, Sumter repeated his
promise of support: "Nothing in the Summit of my Power Shall be Neglected
that may in the least tend to further your opperations against the Enemy." On
receiving this information, Greene wrote to Lee on April 12 that Sumter was
gathering men, and "if you go over the Santee you will fall in with him." Yet
Lee, following an eight-day forced march, instead joined Marion's brigade on
the Santee on April 14.[30]

Was this by design or chance? Greene had not ordered Lee to join Sumter but observed that, if Lee crossed the Santee, "you will fall in with him." Had Greene in discussion with Lee left it up to him, depending on which partisan commander he met first? We know that Greene had shared his thoughts on the coming campaign with Lee, who wrote to Greene four days before leaving his chief's camp, "As you have been pleased to honor me with your confidence, I take the liberty to communicate to you my Sentiments respecting your plan of operations." We can also be sure that Greene and Lee had discussed Thomas Sumter and the difficulty of dealing with him.[31]

Whatever led Lee to Marion it was a lucky happenstance. Marion was in a funk, at least partly brought on by an order from Sumter to carry out a movement, "which is very necessary to not only prevent the stock from being drove to Camden, but also to facilitate my plans and designs on the west side of the Wateree. The more speedy your movements are, the better they will answer." Determined not to follow Sumter's orders, uncertain of what he might do, Marion immediately took heart when he learned of Lee's approach. The joint force marched the next day to Fort Watson on the Santee and laid siege. Eight days later the fort fell, and both Marion and Lee wrote triumphant letters (two each) to Greene. Lee expressed admiration and his willingness to serve under the partisan officer, not wholly but "in some degree." Marion—whose four hundred men according to Lee had "not four hund'd cartridges" before the siege—was able to resupply his troops from the large quantity of ammunition taken at Fort Watson. Marion praised Lee for his "advice and indefatigable diligence" during this "tedious operation against as strong as a Little post as could be made on the most advantageous spot that could be wished for." Marion also informed Greene that he had made arrangements to gain intelligence of Cornwallis's "first movements." Marion and Lee then demolished the fort, moved immediately to the High Hills of the Santee, and there awaited Greene's orders. If only Greene had experienced similar cooperation from Thomas Sumter, with whom Greene's relations took a steady downward spiral.[32]

Following Sumter's April 7 letter stating that Greene could rely on the writer "to Promote and facilitate your Designs," Greene wrote back on April 14 and ordered Sumter to "collect your force with all possible speed, and endeavour to take a position . . . where you may be enabled to cut off, or interrupt the communication between Camden and the other posts of the enemy." But Sumter, despite his promise, ignored the order and went his own way. On April 25 Greene's army met the British army under Lord Rawdon at the Battle of Horbkirk's Hill, just outside of Camden. Rawdon's bold attack—combined with the death and wounding early in the battle of key American officers, the mishandling of the First Maryland Regiment by Colonel John Gunby, and the failure of Colonel William Washington's cavalry to forego minor triumphs over stragglers and noncombatants and quickly attack Rawdon's rear—led to an American defeat. Greene also blamed the loss on Sumter's failure to cooperate. Four days after the battle, Greene wrote to Lee that he had sent Major Edmund Hyme to Sumter, "if possible to get him to join us, but this I know he will avoid if he can with decency, for the same reasons that you wish to act separately from the Army." Here Greene was all but saying that both Sumter and Lee wished to act separately from the main army in order to gain personal glory. Although after the battle Greene kept his correspondence with Sumter on a friendly basis and even released him from the order to "to cross the Wateree and join me," Greene's commissary general, Colonel William Richardson Davie, who saw Greene often during this period, wrote many years after the war that "General Greene was deeply disgusted with the conduct of General Sumter," that Greene considered Sumter a "mere freebooter, whose sole object was plunder, and who would therefore neither act under" Greene "nor in concert with him." Davie thought that Greene "would certainly have arrested him but from considerations arising from the State of the Country at the time, and the hope that these rambling expeditions of Sumter might arrest the attention of the enemy, and be considered by them as connected with some plan of general operations, and thereby attract more attention than they really deserved."[33]

According to Davie, Greene's defeat at Hobkirk's Hill left the general in a gloomy state of mind. On the evening of May 9, he conferred with Davie over a map of the Carolinas. Davie recalled that Greene felt Lord Rawdon had superior force and could push Greene's army back to the mountains. He felt that he also had insufficient militias for "convey and detachment service," and once again charged that "Sumter refuses to obey my orders, and carried off with him all the active force of this unhappy State on rambling predatory expeditions unconnected with the operations of the army." Greene intended to "dispute every inch of ground in the best manner we can—but Rawdon will push me back to the mountains; Lord Cornwallis will establish a chain of posts along the James River and the Southern States, thus cut off, will die like the Tail of a snake." Davie recalled, "These are his very words, they made a deep and melancholly impression, and I shall never forget them." Yet there is nothing to indicate such gloom in Greene's letters of the same date to Lee, Marion, and Andrew Pickens. In fact his tone in all of them is upbeat, and his letter to Pickens alerted the partisan commander to "Collect all the force you can and hold them in perfect readiness for the close investiture of Ninety Six which will soon be undertaken."[34]

Whatever Greene's state of mind at the time, Lord Rawdon's decision to evacuate Camden and begin a retreat to the lowcountry around Charleston, which began on May 10–11, changed the situation on the ground. Rawdon had defeated Greene and pursued him but failed to destroy him. As a result Rawdon found himself deep in the backcountry. In front of him was a beaten but unbroken foe in a strong defensive position, and behind him was a hostile territory swarming with partisans. It was an old story in this frustrating war. In the vast American backcountry, South and North, British armies could march where they pleased and win most of their battles along the way, but after they passed, implacable enemies who had gotten out of the way reappeared from their sanctuaries and once again took control of the countryside. Rawdon later wrote to Cornwallis, "The situation of affairs in this Province had made me judge it necessary, for a time, to withdraw my force from the back country, and to assemble what troops I can collect at this point." The tactical victor of Hobkirk's Hill had been in strategic peril. Davie recalled that he was summoned to Greene's headquarters tent on May 10 and given the good news. He wrote that Greene "instantly changed his plan of operations and assumed the offensive."[35]

But Greene would have to do it without Sumter. In a letter of May 6, Sumter raised various reasons why he could not join Greene and dismissed the possibility that militia and regulars could act together in formal combat. "How far the Militia Could be Depended upon to act With Regular Troops, I am also at a Loss to Determin. But am Rather of oppinion They Would Not behave well as they have Never been accustomed to oppose the enemy openly." Yet Daniel Morgan had combined regulars and militia brilliantly in formal battle at Cowpens, and although Greene at Guilford Courthouse had not been as successful as Morgan, his mix of militia and regulars had used similar tactics to inflict grave damage on the British army. Sumter was certainly familiar with the details of those two battles. It is therefore difficult to deny that his real reason was his obsessive desire to act independently.[36]

Militia recruitment also became a problem during the second phase of the insurgency. Sumter was known for his ability to raise men during the first phase, but in 1781 he fell so short that in late March he announced the controversial scheme that came to be known as "Sumter's Law." It invited plunder, although it must be admitted that plundering was already out of control. Sumter's Law spelled out that men who signed up for ten months in state regiments would receive bounty payments in the form of slaves and other booty taken from Loyalists. The bounty received depended on rank. The plan was not a success. Sumter hoped to raise five ten-month regiments, but he ended up with only three undersized regiments. Andrew Pickens joined the scheme, but Francis Marion disapproved and refused to have anything to do with it. Greene reluctantly approved the plan, but in an earlier letter to Sumter he had noted that he was "a great enemy to plundering," and he urged that for "any horses, or any other kind of property whether taken from Whig or Tory, certificates ought

*Colonel Otho
Holland Williams*

to be given, that justice may be done to the inhabitants hereafter." Eventually
Governor John Rutledge, also deeply concerned with the problem of plundering, ended the experiment.[37]

In the meantime Marion and Lee continued their offensive against the British posts. Following the capture of Fort Watson, their joint force moved against
Fort Motte, located high on a hill overlooking the Congaree River a few miles
before it joins the Wateree to form the Santee. They arrived on May 6, and
on that same day Marion received a letter that Greene would have better left
unwritten. Again horses were involved, but in this case Greene needed good
dragoon horses. He had applied to Sumter, who replied that he could procure
horses only with "Great difficulty" but that "Genl Marian is also in Way of
Getting Good horses, but how far I May Succeed by applying to him I Know
Not." Greene replied that he too understood that Marion had many good
horses, on which he mounted his militia, and stated, "It is a pity that good
horses should be given into the hands of people who are engaged for no limited time." In his offending letter to Marion, Greene accused Marion's men

of taking horses from the inhabitants for their own use instead of for public service. Marion was incensed. He denied that he had many horses and insisted that the few taken were "never for private property." (They were undoubtedly used for both purposes.) If Greene wanted the militia dismounted, Marion would give the necessary order, but in that case he was "certain we shall never git their service in the future." Then he informed Greene that such a development would not bother him as he intended to resign his command as soon as Fort Motte either fell or was abandoned by the enemy.[38]

Greene immediately scrambled to retrieve the situation. He assured Marion, "It is not my wish to take horses from the Militia if it will injure the public service, the effects and consequences you can better judge of than I can." He stressed the "important services" Marion had rendered and the "great honor" he had thereby secured, arguing that, after seven years of war, "What has been done will signify nothing unless we preserve to the end." Marion replied, "I am very serious" about resigning and blamed "such men as I have, who Leave me very Often at the very point of Executing a plan." He did, however, send Greene a horse for his own use and promised to send more if possible. Apparently it was not until the two men met at Fort Motte for the first time that Greene was able to dissuade Marion from resigning.[39]

Rawdon's retreat to the environs of Charleston and the British decision to abandon their backcountry posts led to rapid developments. Fort Motte surrendered to Marion and Lee on May 12. An incident that occurred on that occasion revealed Marion's sensitivity over the prerogatives of his command. He came upon some of his victorious troops about to hang a Loyalist, one Levi Smith, who not long after related that he saw General Marion ride up "with his sword drawn. He asked in a passion what they were doing there. The soldiers answered, 'We are hanging them people, Sir.' He then asked them who ordered them to hang any person. They replied, 'Col. Lee,' whereupon the little Swamp Fox took over. 'I will let you know, damn you, that I command here and not Col. Lee.'" Marion ordered Levi Smith returned to the quarter guard.[40]

Sumter, meanwhile, had begun a siege of Fort Granby on the Congaree River on May 2, but believing that he could not take it without artillery, he left a small force under Colonel Thomas Taylor to invest it while he moved against Orangeburg. Sumter arrived at Orangeburg on May 10, and Fort Granby surrendered the following day. Following the surrender of Fort Motte, however, Greene believed that Rawdon would attempt to relieve Fort Granby. He therefore ordered Lee to march "immediately with the van of the Army . . . and demand an immediate surrender of that post"; he further conveyed the urgency of the matter with his final sentence: "I depend upon your pushing matters vigirously." Sumter got word of Lee's being at Fort Granby and wrote Greene on the fourteenth asking that he "recall Colonel Lee, as his services cannot be wanted at that place." Sumter then clearly revealed his attitude about his own role and about the Continental army: "I have been at great pains to reduce that place, I have it in my power to do it, and I think it for the good of the public to do it without regulars." Even if Greene had been agreeable to recalling Lee, which is doubtful, it was too late. On the fifteenth Lee negotiated the surrender of Fort Granby, allowing the garrison to keep its plunder and march to Charleston under escort as prisoners of war.[41]

Sumter was furious. On May 16 he wrote Greene a letter of resignation and enclosed his commission. Greene answered the following day. He refused to accept Sumter's resignation, returned his commission, flattered him with "how important your services are to the interest & happiness of this country," and begged him "to continue your command." In a follow-up letter the same day, Greene gave Sumter part of the booty taken at Fort Granby and any slaves belonging to Loyalists for the men recruited under Sumter's Law. According to an early historian, Greene "compelled" Lee "to apologize to Sumter," even though Greene had ordered Lee to take Fort Granby in the first place. Assuaged, South Carolina's prima donna returned to service, offering other opportunities for him to plague the commander of the Southern Department and send many men to unnecessary deaths.[42]

It must have been with great relief that Greene was able to turn temporarily from stroking the ruffled feathers of the Gamecock to one of the finer characters of the Revolution: Andrew Pickens. Greene valued him highly, writing a little later to Lee, "I am happy to hear that you and General Pickens are upon a perfect good footing; and I beg you will cultivate it by every means in your power. He is a worthy good Man and merits great respect and attention; and no Man in this Country has half the influence that he has."[43]

Greene had ordered Pickens to lay siege to the British post of Augusta, Georgia, just across the Savannah River from South Carolina, and the key to the Georgia backcountry. Pickens reported to Greene on May 3 that Georgia militia were besieging Augusta, and a few days later wrote that he was on his way to Augusta with his command. Demonstrating an attitude toward Continentals that ran contrary to Sumter's, Pickens urgently requested from Greene some "regular troops." Greene acted quickly. On May 16, the day after Fort Granby fell, he ordered Lee to "march immediately for Augusta as the advance of the Army," to "report your arrival to" General Pickens, and to "cooperate with him until the army arrives." Greene with the main force would march by way of Ninety Six. Lee marched rapidly. He left Fort Granby on the seventeenth and covered the seventy-five miles in three days. Lee decided to first take Fort Dreadnought (also known as Fort Galphin), about twelve miles downriver from Augusta. Reinforced by two regiments from Pickens's command, Lee cleverly combined the respective strengths of regulars and partisans. Keeping his regulars out of sight, he had the militia attack and then feign retreat. The Loyalist rangers inside the fort rushed out in pursuit of the militia, whereupon Lee's regulars dashed forward, cut them off, and forced the Loyalist militia inside to surrender. This was the key to the subsequent surrender of Forts Grierson and Cornwallis, which guarded Augusta, for Dreadnought yielded a rich supply of arms, powder, ammunition, salt, blankets, and other stores that were in short supply in the rebel camp. Greene gave Pickens authority to distribute the supplies as he thought best and warned Lee, "If you have appropriated any part of the Stores to the use of your Corps, which I hope you have not, as it will increase prejudicial jealousies, let the things be received as part of the continental proportion." This is further evidence of Greene's efforts to maintain a smooth working relationship with the partisans, whose contribution to the cause was vital for eventual success. Pickens later informed Greene that the booty had been distributed by thirds to Continentals, South Carolina militia, and Georgia militia, "reserving the arms, Ammunition, Rum and Salt entirely for the publick Service."[44]

Lee, Pickens, and Colonel Elijah Clarke, who commanded the Georgia militia, conferred and decided to first attack Fort Grierson. That post fell quickly, and most of the garrison was either killed or captured, but Fort Cornwallis, commanded by the able Loyalist officer Colonel Thomas Brown, held out until June 5. Given the vicious nature of the civil war in the backcountry, what followed was not surprising. Brown had waged vigorous war against the rebels for several years and was hated by the partisans, but Lee and Pickens were determined to keep him from harm. Lee wrote in his memoir that Brown was given parole and "sent down the river to Savannah, under the care of Captain [Joseph] Armstrong, with a party of infantry, who had orders to continue with Lieutenant-Colonel Browne until he should be placed out of danger." Their fears were not misplaced. The South Carolina partisan Tarlton Brown confided in his memoir that he and others followed the escort, looking for a chance to kill Thomas Brown, but they failed to find an opening. Colonel James Grierson was not so fortunate. After Lee left for Ninety Six on June 6, Pickens reported to Greene the following day "a very disagreeable and Melancholly affair," the murder of Grierson by a man who "rode up to the door of the room where Colo Grierson was confined, and without dismounting Shot him." The killer was pursued but escaped. Pickens gave orders to bury Grierson "with Military honors." Greene, furious, issued a proclamation offering one hundred guineas for the capture of the "perpetrator of this horid crime." The assassin was never caught.[45]

While all this was going on, Francis Marion was on the move. Although his relations with Greene were generally good, every now and then Marion's independent streak appeared. In letters to Greene on May 19 and 20, Marion suggested that Georgetown was lightly defended and requested "the Liberty of going against it," but he awaited Greene's orders. Greene gave him the go-ahead in a letter of May 26, provided conditions elsewhere did not dictate otherwise; for example, if "General Sumter don't think himself exposed in consequence of your moving to George Town of which I have desird him to inform you." Marion, however, usually ignored Sumter, and in fact he was marching on Georgetown before receiving Greene's letter of permission. Marion arrived on May 28. The following day the British evacuated by sea, and Marion took control of the town. Now the only important British post outside Charleston was Ninety Six, but Greene's efforts to take it were not going well.[46]

Greene had neither training nor experience in siege warfare, and he was faced with a tough, able, determined enemy, a former mayor of New York City, Lieutenant Colonel John Harris Cruger, whose garrison included two battalions of northern provincial regulars. Cruger had been ordered to evacuate Ninety Six and withdraw to Savannah if he learned that Camden had been evacuated. But Cruger either never heard of the evacuation of Camden or for his own reasons decided to sit tight, and subsequent orders to evacuate Ninety Six were intercepted by the rebels. When Greene learned that Rawdon with reinforcements of regulars from Ireland was marching upcountry to the relief of Ninety Six, he ordered Marion and Sumter to get in Rawdon's way and "have the Militia constantly employed in galling them as they advance." But Marion lingered in the lowcountry, and Sumter was outmaneuvered by Rawdon. Greene was forced to raise the siege and march away. Rawdon, however, had decided before relieving the post that Ninety Six, alone in a vast backcountry increasingly controlled by rebels, could not be permanently held. Cruger was given the job of destroying what he could and then escorting a long, sad column of Loyalist refugees to a miserable, pestilence-ridden collection of huts outside Charleston, derisively called Rawdontown. Ill and physically worn down, Rawdon gave up his command and sailed for home. Greene kept losing fights but winning the campaign, in no small part because he successfully combined the respective talents of regulars and partisans. Yet Greene felt that—had he been able to gather to him the partisan regiments of Marion, Sumter, and Pickens—he could have met and defeated Rawdon. In a letter to Marion, Greene complained, "I am surprised the people should be so averse to joining in some general plan of operation. It will be impossible to carry on the war to advantage or even attempt to hold the Country unless our force can be directed to a point, and as to flying parties here and there they are of no consequence in the great events of war. If the people will not be more united in their views they must abide the consequences for I will not calculate upon them at all unless they will agree to act comfortable to the great plan of recovering all parts of the Country and not particular parts."[47]

Subsequently Sumter's proposal for an expedition against British forces in the lowcountry fit into Greene's "general plan of operation," and he ordered Lee and Marion to cooperate with Sumter. Greene's specific instructions to each differed in interesting ways. To Lee, the Continental officer, Greene wrote, "Let your movements be correspondent with his [Sumter], in so far as you may find them consistent with the good of the service." Marion the militia commander, however, was given no such leeway: "You will . . . call out all the force you can and cooperate with him in any manner he may direct." The expedition was a strategic and psychological success, showing that the rebels could move at will throughout almost all South Carolina. But, following several engagements and a steady British retreat down the Cooper River, at the final action on July 17 at Quinby Bridge on the Shubrick Plantation, about thirty miles west of Charleston, blunders by Sumter, Lee, and other officers—as well as timely maneuvering and disciplined musketry by British regulars—led to a tactical failure and heavy casualties. Marion's men, who absorbed most of the casualties, felt that they had been ill-used, and on the night of the action at Biggins Bridge, many left Sumter's camp. Lee and his legion also left that night. Colonel Thomas Taylor, one of Sumter's regimental commanders, was so incensed by Sumter's tactic of a frontal assault against the strong British position that he faced the Gamecock, berated him, and said, "I will never more serve under you." Greene wrote a letter of praise to Sumter, but he criticized the operation in letters to Pickens and Marie Joseph Gilbert du Motier, Marquis de Lafayette, and to Daniel Morgan, Greene wrote, "Had you been with me a few weeks past, you would have had it in your power to give the world the pleasure of reading a second Cowpen affair."[48]

The expedition was Sumter's last hurrah. To Greene's astonishment, in August without warning, Sumter disbanded his brigade and retired from the field. "It would be little less than madness to grant the indulgences General Sumter requires," Greene wrote to Colonel William Henderson and ordered Henderson to collect the troops "as fast as possible." Sumter returned briefly to his command, but his glory days were long behind him. The following February, Sumter resigned from the militia. It was a sad end, largely of his own making, to the military career of the man who was the most important partisan commander during the first phase of the insurgency but whose attitude and activities during the second phase hampered Greene's operations.[49]

Sumter did not participate in the last major engagement in the lower South, but some of his men were at the Battle of Eutaw Springs on September 8, 1781. In this long and bloody fight, Greene followed his custom, learned from Morgan's deployment at Cowpens, of placing the militia in the front line and his regulars in the second line. Marion was given overall command of the militia line, and Pickens commanded the left wing. Greene reported that the "Militia fought with a degree of spirit and firmness that reflects the highest honor upon this class of Soldiers," and his adjutant general, Colonel Otho Holland Williams, wrote, "It was with equal astonishment, that both the second line and the enemy, contemplated these men, steadily, and without faltering, advance with shouts and exhortations into the hottest of the enemy's fire, unaffected by the continual fall of their comrades around them."

Williams attributed their behavior to their trust in Francis Marion and Andrew Pickens. Thus we have come full circle from Greene's statement in 1776: "To march over dead men, to hear without concern the groans of the wounded, I say few man can stand such scenes unless steeled by habit or fortified by military pride." Some fifteen months of often vicious partisan warfare had hardened men to accept such scenes—provided they were well led.[50]

The British also behaved with conspicuous gallantry at this fierce battle and denied Greene the battlefield victory he never gained. Their army, however, the last British army in the lower South, was no longer fit to remain in the field. The British withdrew to the environs of Charleston, and thereafter the fighting consisted of raids and counterraids by fast moving bands of horsemen until the British evacuation of Charleston in December 1782. Nathanael Greene had reconquered the Carolinas and Georgia for the new nation.

Although Nathanael Greene was a revolutionary intent on overthrowing the monarchy and establishing a republic in North America, he was also a moderate conservative with an instinctive horror of disorder and random violence. When necessary, violence could be meted out in measured fashion by duly established authority, in America by the states or the Continental army under congressional sanction, and by militia operating either under Continental army or state authority and direction. A good example is Greene's reaction to Pyle's massacre in North Carolina. When Lee and his legion horse, joined by militia under Andrew Pickens, closed with Loyalist militia by subterfuge and attacked without warning, killing an estimated ninety largely unresisting Loyalists commanded by Colonel John Pyle, Greene wrote to Thomas Jefferson "It has had a very happy effect on those disaffected Persons, of which there are too many in this country." But uncoordinated operations by predatory bands roaming the countryside were unacceptable. Francis Marion accepted Greene's authority and in most cases followed his orders. Andrew Pickens's record was unblemished. Thomas Sumter usually marched to a different drummer. It was Greene, however, who prevailed.[51]

Nathanael Greene was second only to Washington in determining the outcome of the American Revolution. Without Greene's strategic vision and mastery of the military arts, without his joint emphasis on engaging the enemy and establishing civil government, without his insistence on coordinated operations of regular forces and partisans, the war in the Carolinas and Georgia would have remained a standoff between British forces and uncoordinated partisan bands. Notwithstanding Sumter's freelancing, other plundering bands, and the occasional killing of prisoners by out-of-control partisans, it was Greene's military and political strategy that led to victory in the lower South. A "Partizan War" it was. Fortunately for the republic, it was a "Partizan War" as Nathanael Greene dictated.

NOTES

1. Greene to Francis Marion, December 4, 1780, *The Papers of General Nathanael Greene,* edited by Richard K. Showman, Dennis R. Conrad, and Roger N. Parks, 13 vols. (Chapel Hill: University of North Carolina Press, 1976–2005), 6:519.

2. Greene to Baron Friedrich von Steuben, February 3, 1781, ibid., 7:243.

3. Greene to Jacob Greene, September 28, 1776, ibid., 1:303.

4. Greene to Francis Marion, December 4, 1780, ibid., 6:520.

5. George Washington to William Heath, February 3, 1777, *The Papers of George Washington. Revolutionary War Series,* edited by Philander D. Chase et al., 20 vols. (Charlottesville: University Press of Virginia, 1985–2010), 8:230.

6. Greene to Tom Paine, January 9, 1777, *The Papers of General Nathanael Greene,* 2:3.

7. See Anne King Gregorie's biographical sketch of Sumter in *Dictionary of American Biography* (18:219–21) for the shrewd and succinct description of Sumter.

8. Rutledge, quoted in Robert D. Bass, *Gamecock: The Life and Campaigns of General Thomas Sumter* (New York: Holt, Rinehart & Winston, 1961), 115.

9. Greene to Thomas Sumter, December 12, 1780, *The Papers of General Nathanael Greene,* 6:564.

10. Greene to Samuel Huntingdon, November 2, 1780, ibid., 6:459.

11. Greene to Daniel Morgan, January 8, 1781; Francis Marion to Greene, January 20, 1781, and January 27, 1781; Henry Lee to Greene, January 25, 1781; ibid., 7:73, 165, 207, 197–98. Henry Lee, *Memoirs of the War in the Southern Department of the United States,* edited by Robert E. Lee (1869; reprint, New York: Arno Press, 1969), 223. Hugh F. Rankin, *Francis Marion: The Swamp Fox* (New York: Crowell, 1973), 152.

12. Bass, *Gamecock,* 116; Greene to Daniel Morgan, December 16, 1780, *The Papers of General Nathanael Greene,* 6:589.

13. John Rutledge to Thomas Sumter, January 21, 1781, quoted in ibid., 7:129n4.

14. Greene to Thomas Sumter, January 8, 1781, ibid., 7:74–75.

15. Greene to Thomas Sumter, January 8, 1781, and Greene to Alexander Hamilton, January 10, 1781, ibid., 7:75, 88.

16. Thomas Sumter to Greene, January 19, 1781, ibid., 7:217–18.

17. Daniel Morgan to Greene, January 15, 1781, ibid., 7:127.

18. Andrew Pickens to Henry Lee, August 28, 1811, Draper Manuscripts (microfilm), Wisconsin Historical Society, Madison, 1VV107.

19. Greene to Thomas Sumter, February 3, 1781; Greene to Francis Marion, February 11, 1781; Sumter to Greene, March 9, 1781; *The Papers of General Nathanael Greene,* 7:246, 281, 417. Sumter to Marion, February 10, 1781, February 28, 1781, March 4, 1781, in R. W. Gibbes, ed., *Documentary History of the American Revolution,* 3 vols. (New York:

Appleton, 1853–57), 3:23–24, 27–28, 49. Anne King Gregorie, *Thomas Sumter* (Columbia, S.C.: R. L. Bryan, 1931), 136–43. Rankin, *Francis Marion*, 162–64. Bass, *Gamecock*, 126–35.

20. Greene to Thomas Jefferson, March 10, 1781, and Daniel Morgan to Greene, January 15, 1781, *The Papers of General Nathanael Greene*, 7:420, 127–28.

21. William Tecumseh Sherman, *Memoirs of W. T. Sherman* (1886; reprint, New York: Library of America, 1990), 880.

22. Greene to Andrew Pickens, February 3, 1781; Greene to Francis Lock and others, February 9, 1781; Daniel Morgan to Greene, January 15, 1781; Pickens to Greene, February 19, 1781; Greene to Pickens, February 20, 1781; Pickens to Greene, February 20, 1781; *The Papers of General Nathanael Greene*, 7:241, 262, 128, 320, 322, 325. Clyde R. Ferguson, "General Andrew Pickens," Ph.D. diss., Duke University, 1960, 156. William A. Graham, *General Joseph Graham and His Papers on North Carolina Revolutionary History* (Raleigh, N.C.: Edwards & Broughton, 1904), 203.

23. Graham, *General Joseph Graham*, 334; William Pierce to John Butler, March 4, 1781, *The Papers of General Nathanael Greene*, 7:388.

24. Otho Holland Williams to Greene, February 26, 1781, and Andrew Pickens to Greene, March 5, 1781, *The Papers of General Nathanael Greene*, 7:360, 399.

25. Greene to Thomas Jefferson, March 10, 1781, and Andrew Pickens to Greene, March 5, 1781, ibid., 7:420, 399.

26. Major George Hanger, *An Address to the Army in Reply to Strictures by Roderick M'Kenzie . . . on Tarleton's History of the Campaigns of 1780 and 1781* (London, 1789), 82.

27. Francis, Lord Rawdon, to Sir Henry Clinton, March 23, 1781, *The American Rebellion: Sir Henry Clinton's Narrative of His Campaigns, 1775–1782, with an Appendix of Original Documents*, edited by William B. Willcox (New Haven: Yale University Press, 1954), 501. For the difficulties of the British in fighting a guerrilla war and the superiority of rebel partisans, see John Buchanan, *The Road to Guilford Courthouse: The American Revolution in the Carolinas* (New York: Wiley, 1997), especially 137–40, 176–86, 245–48; and a candid Tory account of the problems of the Tory militia and its inferior leadership in Robert Gray, "Colonel Robert Gray's Observations on the War in the Carolinas," *South Carolina Historical and Genealogical Magazine* 11 (July 1910): 1–159.

28. Graham, *General Joseph Graham*, 242–46; Otho Holland Williams to Greene, March 7, 1781, and Greene to Andrew Pickens, March 8, 1781, *The Papers of General Nathanael Greene*, 7:407–8; Charles Magill to Thomas Jefferson, March 10, 1781, *The Papers of Thomas Jefferson*, edited by Julian P. Boyd et al., vol. 5 (Princeton: Princeton University Press, 1952), 5:115; Andrew Pickens to Henry Lee, August 23, 1811, Draper Manuscripts, 1VV107; for British accounts and estimates, see Banastre Tarleton, *A History of the Campaigns of 1780 and 1781 in the Southern Provinces of North America* (London: T. Cadell, 1787), 238; Charles Stedman, *The History of the Origin, Progress, and Termination of the American War*, 2 vols. (London, 1794), 2:336.

29. Greene to Henry Lee, April 4, 1781; Lee to Greene, April 4, 1781; Greene to Francis Marion, June 15, 1781; *The Papers of General Nathanael Greene*, 8:46–47, 457.

30. Greene to Thomas Sumter, March 30, 1781, April 7, 1781; Sumter to Greene, April 7, 1781; Greene to Henry Lee, April 21, 1781; ibid., 8:12–13, 64, 66–67, 85–86.

31. Henry Lee to Greene, April 2, 1781, ibid., 8:28.

32. Rankin, *Francis Marion*, 182–83; Thomas Sumter to Francis Marion, March 28, 1781, Gibbes, ed., *Documentary History*, 3:46; Henry Lee to Greene, April 23, 1781 (two letters), and Marion to Greene, April 23, 1781 (two letters), *The Papers of General Nathanael Greene*, 8:138–42.

33. Greene to Thomas Sumter, April 14, 1781; Greene to Henry Lee, April 29, 1781; Greene to Sumter, April 30, 1781; *The Papers of General Nathanael Greene*, 8:94, 173, 176–77; William R. Davie, *The Revolutionary War Sketches of William R. Davie*, edited by Blackwell P. Robinson (Raleigh: North Carolina Department of Cultural Resources, Division of Archives and History, 1976), 44.

34. Davie, *Revolutionary Sketches*, 44–45; Greene to Henry Lee, Greene to Francis Marion, and Greene to Andrew Pickens, all May 9, 1781, *The Papers of General Nathanael Greene*, 8:227–28, 230–32.

35. Rawdon to Charles, Earl Cornwallis, May 24, 1781, in Gibbes, ed., *Documentary History*, 3:77; Davie, *Revolutionary Sketches*, 46.

36. Thomas Sumter to Greene, May 6, 1781, *The Papers of General Nathanael Greene*, 8:218.

37. Richard Hampton to John Hampton, April 2, 1781, and Thomas Sumter to Francis Marion, March 28, 1781, in Gibbes, ed., *Documentary History*, 3:48, 45; Sumter to Greene, April 7, 1781; Greene to Sumter, April 15, 1781, and May 17, 1781; Greene to Marion, May 17, 1781; *The Papers of General Nathanael Greene*, 8:66, 100–101, 276–78.

38. Thomas Sumter to Greene, May 2, 1781; Greene to Sumter, May 4, 1781; Greene to Francis Marion, May 4, 1781; Marion to Greene, May 6, 1781; ibid., 8:193–94, 202, 198–99, 214–15.

39. Greene to Francis Marion, May 9, 1781, and Marion to Greene, May 11, 1781, ibid., 8:231, 242; Rankin, *Francis Marion*, 208–9.

40. Rawdon to Cornwallis, May 19, 1781, in Gibbes, ed., *Documentary History*, 3:76–77; Catherine S. Crary, *The Price of Loyalty: Tory Writings from the Revolutionary Era* (New York: McGraw-Hill, 1973), 288–90.

41. Greene to Henry Lee, May 13, 1781; Thomas Sumter to Greene, May 2, 1781, May 11, 1781, May 14, 1781; Greene to Samuel Huntingdon, May 14, 1781; Lee to Greene, May 15, 1781; *The Papers of General Nathanael Greene*, 8:249, 193–94, 244, 258–59, 250–53, 262–64. Lee, *Memoirs*, 349–52.

42. Thomas Sumter to Greene, May 16, 1781, and Greene to Sumter, May 17, 1781 (two letters), *The Papers of General Nathanael Greene*, 8:274–78; William Johnson, *Life and Correspondence of Nathanael Greene, Major General of the Armies of the United States*, 2 vols. (Charleston, S.C.: A. E. Miller, 1822), 2:123.

43. Greene to Henry Lee, May 29, 1781, *The Papers of General Nathanael Greene*, 8:326.

44. Greene to Samuel Huntingdon, May 14, 1781; Andrew Pickens to Greene, May 3, 1871, May 8, 1781, May 12, 1781, May 25, 1781, and June 1, 1781; Greene to Henry Lee, May 16, 1781; Greene to Pickens, May 16, 1781; Lee to Greene, May 22, 1781; Greene to Lee, May 29, 1781; ibid., 8:250, 197–98, 223–24, 246–47, 310–11, 335, 272, 293–94, 328 326. Lee, *Memoirs*, 352–55. Edward J. Cashin, *The King's Ranger: Thomas Brown and the American Revolution on the Southern Frontier* (Athens: University of Georgia Press, 1989), 131.

45. Henry Lee to Greene, May 22, 1781; Andrew Pickens to Greene, May 25, 1781, and June 7, 1781; proclamation, June 9, 1781; *The Papers of General Nathanael Greene*, 8:293, 310–11, 359, 370. Lee, *Memoirs*, 370. Tarlton Brown, "Memoirs of Tarlton Brown," edited by Charles Bushnell, *Magazine of History with Notes and Queries* extra no. 101 (1924): 25. See also Steven J. Rauch, "A Judicious and Gallant Defense: The Second Siege of Augusta, Georgia [the battles of Forts Grierson and Cornwallis], 22 May–5 June 1781," *Southern Campaigns of the American Revolution* 3 (June–July–August 2000): 32–52. For the negotiations leading to the surrender of Fort Cornwallis and the articles of capitulation, see Gibbes, ed., *Documentary History*, 3:82–88.

46. Francis Marion to Greene, May 19, 1781, and May 20, 1781; Greene to Marion, May 26, 1781; Marion to Greene, May 19, 1781; *The Papers of General Nathanael Greene*, 8:285, 287, 313, 329.

47. Greene to Thomas Sumter, June 17, 1781, and Greene to Francis Marion, June 25, 1781, ibid., 8:405, 457–58; Andrew Pickens to Henry Lee, November 25, 1811, Draper Manuscripts, 1VV108.

48. For events leading up the expedition, see Greene to Henry Lee, June 24, 1781; Greene to Francis Marion, June 25, 1781; Greene to Thomas Sumter, June 25, 1781; *The Papers of General Nathanael Greene*, 8:452, 456–59. For reports and Greene's critiques, see "Headnote on the Dog Days Expedition"; Sumter to Greene, July 15, 1781, July 17–19, 1781, and July 22, 1781; Marion to Greene, July 19, 1781; Greene to Sumter, July 21, 1781; Greene to Andrew Pickens, July 22, 1781; Greene to Lafayette, July 24, 1781; Greene to Thomas McKean, July 26, 1781; Greene to Daniel Morgan, August 26, 1781; ibid., 9:17–18, 47–48, 50–56, 60–64, 71–72, 83–85, 256–57; Gregorie, *Thomas Sumter*, 79n83; and, if used with caution, Lee, *Memoirs*, 387–93.

49. William Henderson to Greene, August 14, 1781, and Greene to Henderson, August 16, 1781, *The Papers of General Nathanael Greene*, 9:182, 188–89; John Mathews to Greene, February 27, 1782, ibid., 10:416.

50. Greene to Thomas McKean, September 11, 1781, ibid., 9:328–38, containing Greene's report on the battle, and the accompanying notes; Williams, quoted in Gibbes, "Battle of Eutaw," in *Documentary History*, 3:148.

51. Greene to Thomas Jefferson, February 29, 1781, *The Papers of General Nathanael Greene*, 7:367.

Nathanael Greene and Republican Ethics

JOHN M. MOSELEY AND ROBERT M. CALHOON

*F*ollowing the Battle of Guilford Courthouse, Major General Nathanael Greene faced a series of decisions, the difficulty of which has been unappreciated by scholars. The scale of his eventual success has conversely hidden the less-than-obvious size and scope of his achievement. He had the option of following the retreating British army of Charles, Lord Cornwallis, or returning to the lower South for a campaign to recover Georgia and South Carolina. He chose the latter course. Beyond the military hazards of that undertaking, however, Greene sought to build a civil order from the bloodied ruins of that region even while a civil war, including what today would be called "ethnic cleansing" with the worst atrocities, still raged. Friend and critic alike could argue that military success for the American cause would have been achieved eventually, but the societal outcome, also dependent on Greene's republican ethics, might well have been different. His decision to return to the lower South involved strategic considerations, but it was also informed by a moderate ethics that influenced his approach to fighting the war and building a peace constructed on civic harmony. To examine the strategic thinking behind this crucial decision and the conjunction between Greene's military practices and his moderate ethics is the purpose of this essay.

The foundation for the internecine warfare of those years harkened back to before the American Revolution, a burden that made Greene's tasks all the more difficult. In the colonial period, there had been revolts by slaves, atrocities by and against Indians, the Regulator rebellions, intolerance of ethnic and religious groups, and even levels of class conflict. During the Revolution, British East and West Florida, never having rebelled, provided safe havens for Tory partisans, and Georgia, having the largest percentage of Loyalist population of any of the thirteen states, became the only state reduced to colonial status, complete with royal governor and colonial assembly. Members of its state government, before partial British reconquest, had been more involved in internal class warfare than in fighting a common foe. Almost the only patriot military forces left in South Carolina after May 1780 consisted of various bands and types of guerrillas, some of whom were motivated by plunder or revenge. A cynical joke went that the murder of prisoners of war had come to be called "granting a Georgia parole."[1] In the midst of this chaos, Greene had to battle the British army at the same time that he had to restore not just civil government but basic civility, not only to win battles for the present but also to salvage a future for this region in turmoil.

In a remarkable body of work on the moral economy, as well as the political and military history of the lower Revolutionary South, the late Edward J. Cashin and the late Heard Robertson explored revolutionary and counterrevolutionary history from the perspective of political ethics. Nathanael Greene, Cashin wrote, "encouraged Georgia Whigs to resist the British occupation; he sent Continental troops toward Georgia to 'spirit up' the fainthearted; he courted the allegiance of the wavering by a generous reconciliation policy; he gave Georgia tangible existence by setting up a Georgia Legion and by supervising the restoration of civil government; [and] he nursed the infant government toward self-sufficiency with tact and patience." Professor Cashin's verbs— *resist, spirit-up, courted, nursed*—reveal Greene's actions as an exercise in moral philosophy by which Greene and other patriot leaders inserted ideology into a revolutionary situation while managing mobilization and exercising self-constraining discipline such as "tact and patience." Leaders such as Greene acted this way not for pragmatic reasons but because of an ethical commitment toward rationalism in the conduct of their statecraft. "Greene's strategy," Cashin concluded, "worked better than even he had hoped. Upon his return to [South] Carolina the backposts began to collapse like a house of cards." Those defeats were not so much military as they were cultural because Greene coupled aggressiveness with sensitivity to the novelty of unconventional warfare. On hearing that loyalist prisoner James Grierson had been summarily executed, Greene reacted with outrage: "The idea of exterminating the Tories is not less barbarous than unpolitical." Private executions delayed reconciliation of the Tory faction, which should instead "be won over to the Whig cause" by persuasion and kindness. Gaining that political high ground was for Greene more important than simply killing British regulars or sending Tory militia fleeing for their lives. Cashin depicted the Rhode Islander as "continu[ing] to hover over Georgia like some better angel," inspiring battle-hardened Whigs to believe that "it is better to save than to destroy. . . . The preservation of morals and an encouragement to honest industry should be the first object of [republican]

Government. I wish the cause of liberty may never be tarnished, nor the morals of people bartered in exchange for wealth."[2]

Greene was able to talk in such terms to Georgia officials and soldiers because the British had, ever since 1775, led the way in instituting a counterrevolutionary regime based on opportunism, on excellent intelligence about rebel behavior, and on a seesaw relationship between Tory elation and Whig dejection when the war was going well and the exact reverse with the emergence of new patriot forces backed by an outraged populace. "This, my Lord," wrote East Florida governor Patrick Tonyn to Lord George Germain, "is not a very honorable way of making war, but it is . . . the only one left for supplying this town and garrison [St. Augustine] with fresh provisions as the Georgians would not allow the cattle belonging to the Butchers who supply their market to be drove hence." Heard Robertson has painstakingly reconstructed the process of waging a "not very honorable" kind of war with the materials at hand. Loyalists in arms had to be entrusted to the leadership of vengeful, embittered, violent, but implacably determined men such as Thomas Brown; then after training in Florida, they had to be organized into forty-man units and equipped with the clothing and accouterments of frontier hunters ("hats, hunting shirts, belt, breeches, buckles, blanket, and leggings" and "riffle guns" or American hunting rifles rather than British smooth-bore muskets). These small, maneuverable units then performed varied tasks—scouts for British regulars, guerrilla forces along the Florida-Georgia border, intelligence gatherers, dispatch carriers, custodians of Whig prisoners, and cattle thieves. All this incessant activity became self-justifying for the simple reason that, as East Florida governor Patrick Tonyn put it, "it is cruel to continue doing nothing, it is always a losing game."[3]

Patriot partisan commanders such Thomas Sumter and Elijah Clarke understood that logic and made a veritable cottage industry out of staving off boredom among their rank-and-file partisans. Under Colonel Clarke, the Georgia militia "were so exasperated by the cruelties mutually inflicted in the course of the war . . . that they were disposed to sacrifice every man taken [prisoner], and with great difficulty was this disposition now [June 1781] suppressed."[4] No one expressed the realities of counterrevolutionary warfare better than the Augusta Tories who belted out these verses of "The Volunteers of Georgia" to the tune of "The Lilies of France":

> Come join my brave lads, come all from afar,
> We're all Volunteers, all ready for war;
> Our service is free, for honour we fight,
> Regardless of hardships by day or by night.

Chorus: Then all draw your swords, and constantly sing,
    Success to our Troop, our Country and King.

The rebels they murder—Revenge is the word,
Let each lad return with blood on his sword;
See Grierson's pale ghost point fresh to his wound,
We'll conquer, my boys, or fall dead to the ground.
Chorus: Then brandish your swords, and constantly sing,
    Success to our Troop, our Country and King.

They've plunder'd our houses, attempted our lives,
Drove off from their homes our children and wives;
Such plundering miscreants, no mercy shall have.
Chorus: Then chop with your swords, and constantly sing,
    Success to our Troop, our Country and King.[5]

For patriot leaders, success meant something different from exultant shouts and flashing swordplay. The revolutionary calculus of war required a sober reckoning of means versus ends. In early June 1780, British commander Lieutenant Colonel Francis, Lord Rawdon, sent his agents fanning out across the upcountry offering paroles to local Whigs who would lay down their arms and cease resistance against the authority of the Crown. At a settlement west of the Broad River called New Acquisition, a scattering of Ulster Scots farmers gathered to discuss their situation. Major Joseph McJunkin described the scene: "Here after enumerating our dangers and trials past & thinking of future dangers and hardships, with the offers of British protection before us, the question came up, what shall be done. 'Shall we join the British or strive like men to gain the noble end for which we have striven for years past?' . . . The question was put—all who were in favor of fighting the matter out were to clap their hands & throw up their hats. The question came. The hats flew upwards and the air resounded with clapping of hands and shouts of defiance."[6]

In much the same way, Greene and his army, marching south from Guilford Courthouse toward the Waxhaws and South Carolina, asked themselves whether they should hunker down or rise up.[7] To answer that question, Greene had at his disposal a remarkable cohort of staff officers he had nurtured in periodic councils of war—Lieutenant Colonels Henry Lee and William Washington, Colonels Otho Williams and William R. Davie, and Captain Robert Lockwood, as well as Greene's civilian confidant, South Carolina governor John Rutledge. Greene had apprenticed in such an advisory body under General George Washington in Pennsylvania in 1777.[8] According to Greene's grandson George Washington Greene, the general was "patient in hearing everything offered, never interrupting or slighting what was said, and having possessed

*Lieutenant
Colonel William
Washington*

himself of the subject fully, he would enter into a critical comparison of the opposite arguments convincing his hearers, as he progressed, with the propriety of the decision he was about to pronounce."[9]

A common thread running through Greene's planning for his return to South Carolina was what his Quaker forebears and their Revolutionary-era successors called "discernment": a centered search for truth that entailed listening and speaking with discipline and circumspection. Breaking free of professional military secretiveness, Greene's councils of war were permeated with candor, openness, respect, and shared understanding. Greene acquired some of his modesty and patience from his apprenticeship under Washington in New York, New Jersey, and Pennsylvania during 1776–79, but his democratic command style owed much to his Quaker upbringing, which taught that "meekness, diffidence, & doubt accompany the true gospel" even though many Friends were "impatient of contradiction and very apt to smite" those with whom they disagreed. "An appearance of zeal," Philadelphia Friend and lifelong educational reformer Anthony Benezet cautioned fellow Friends, "makes the creature imagine it is on the Mount when its fruit, its spirit, and . . . its religious sense declares that it is not."[10]

The choice of the majority of the officers with whom Greene talked was to continue to follow Cornwallis and attempt to force him into another battle or to besiege him in Wilmington, North Carolina, where he had gone to resupply his army. This option, however, did not provide a realistic prospect for the decisive victory Greene desired. Cornwallis would be left the opportunity of maintaining offensive operations at will against American armed forces and local Whigs and militias.

Understandably Greene rejected this recommendation of opportunistically tracking after Cornwallis, knowing the best the Americans could hope for was to catch the British at an inopportune moment and present a challenge on a field of Greene's choosing. But the likelihood of that happening was not strong, especially since Greene had received intelligence of the arrival of a British fleet in the Chesapeake. A decisive engagement might have resulted in ensnarement by fresh British forces and a resupplied Cornwallis. Greene did not have the strength to conduct a siege of Wilmington, so trapping Cornwallis was not a viable alternative. North Carolina, chronically short of supplies, also had political problems. "The confusion which prevails in North Carolina," Greene wrote to Joseph Reed, "put almost a total stop to all business."[11] Greene confided the same information to Colonel Timothy Pickering, explaining that, because courts were unable to meet and recorders of deeds could not function, "the powers of Government are feeble in North Carolina, and their property is held by the most precarious tenure."[12]

The conventional wisdom correctly predicted that, if Cornwallis moved out of North Carolina, he would head north toward Virginia. If the British secured Virginia while also controlling Georgia and South Carolina, they would put pressure on North Carolina to submit to royal authority. A move into Virginia by the army of the Southern Department would present Greene with an opportunity to correct deficiencies that had hobbled him ever since taking over as commander. With the British offloading forces already in Virginia, Greene could move north and unite his command with a force commanded by Baron Friedrich von Steuben. A stronger American force might lure the British into a battle in which victory might be achieved. The fresh Continental army and militia forces available in Virginia, added to his veteran units, would give Greene the needed troop strength to assault Cornwallis. Greene praised the courage and effectiveness of the Virginia militia in the second line at Guilford Courthouse. His after-action reports to Congress and to his own correspondents underscored their recent superior performance. Most important, by marching his army to Virginia, Greene could keep the number of his troops high. Because "Virginia has given me every support I could wish or expect," "the chief source of his hopes and expectations as to troops, provisions, and military store"[13] came from Virginia, the nearest point of replenishment. With supply depots easier to reach, Greene could proceed to supply the desperate needs of his army.[14]

The major drawback to this plan was the perceived notion that Greene's forces were retreating after their encounter with Cornwallis. Armed patriots in Georgia and South Carolina might feel abandoned. Rutledge saw his chance to persuade Greene of an altogether different strategy. He hinted that "if he did go to Virginia he would loose all chance for individual glory." The South Carolina governor wanted to "make it even more attractive for Greene [by placing] all of his [Rutledge's] officers directly under orders to Greene."[15] Rutledge would leave for the North, and therefore his officers would have no other option but to obey Greene's commands. On the downside, the tactical situation Greene would encounter in South Carolina would not leave room for him to maneuver easily because he would be bounded by superior British forces on land and by a British navy in control of the sea. In the British numerical superiority, however, lay an advantage for Greene, as the vast majority of redcoats were assigned to garrison duty or to guarding supply convoys. As a result, British forces in South Carolina were unable to resume offensive operations. They were locked into fixed fortifications, which left the vast majority of land and population to the will of Whig forces. This defensive arrangement hobbled British plans to subdue the southern theater.

Recovering South Carolina had been a part of Greene's thinking in December 1780 and January 1781. Offensive operations in the state piqued his interest because this option would cause the British to drop further plans for a southern offensive. Since June 1780, the partisan militias of Sumter, Pickens, and Clarke had been raiding supply trains and outposts but had been unable to affect British plans. What worked better was co-opting the militia system in South Carolina as a political entity with a mission to suppress Tory supporters of the British. By remaining active in the face of superior British forces, the partisans were able to forestall any major Loyalist uprising. Unable to defeat the British and Loyalist troops, Whig militias seized the initiative by using hit-and-run tactics. In the end these tactics worked so well that one Tory commander wrote to Cornwallis that "the whole district had determined to submit as soon as the rebels should enter it."[16] With Greene's acknowledgment and support, Whig partisans kept the British distracted and many Loyalists in hiding. However, a more substantial military intervention was needed.

Cornwallis had eluded Greene's pursuit on March 28–29, 1781, by constructing a makeshift bridge across the Deep River at Ramsay's Mill, then heading southeast toward Cross Creek, and thence to Wilmington, but Greene did not let this lull suspend his strategic consultations with his subordinates. With Lee

*Lieutenant Colonel
Henry "Light-Horse
Harry" Lee*

detached from his army and trailing Cornwallis, Greene asked him for his input. "As you have been pleased to honor me with your confidence," Lee prefaced his reply, "I take the liberty to communicate to you my sentiments respecting your plan of action."[17] Greene apparently left the door open for Lee to propose his own idea utilizing his "favorite tactic in war: the daring stratagem."[18] A move into South Carolina was just the sort of daring and bold maneuver that would energize Lee.

What Lee deferentially called "your plan of action" was designed to move Greene's troops toward the South Carolina backcountry, placing much space between himself and Cornwallis until the British made their move against the American army. Greene's moving into the backcountry might induce Cornwallis to leave the supply net provided by the coast and in part subsist off the land. Throughout the war, Greene realized, "Lee was given commands that enabled him to exercise independent initiative outside routine military operations and the ordinary hierarchy of command."[19] A return to South Carolina would continue this mode of operation for Lee. Both Greene and Lee had met some of the partisan leaders in South Carolina and understood their ability to fight and stir up the South Carolina population for the Whig cause.

Lee later wrote that he appeared at the last of the councils of war called by Greene while the decision was still being discussed by senior officers. Lee referred to himself in the third person throughout his book, but when the plan of moving to South Carolina came up, Lee attributed it ambiguously to "the proposer." Could Lee have been "the proposer"? He implied as much. Detractors point out that in late March, Lee was no longer available for Greene's councils of war. Historian M. F. Treacy said "Lee was not even in the American camp" when Greene assembled his officers. Although Lee could not have proposed the return to South Carolina verbally, Greene and Lee maintained contact throughout his detachment from the main body of the army. These communications could have included ideas discussed in councils of war by Greene and his subordinates. One of the problems in trying to figure out Lee's actual input is that the records kept by Colonel Otho Williams were lost at sea—something Lee knew by the time he wrote his memoir.[20] While Lee's letter does allude to a plan for returning to South Carolina, Greene's April 28, 1781, letter to Lee reported that "I have run every hazard to promote your plan of operations," evidence Lee's supporters cite as conclusive proof that he was the impetus behind the campaign.[21]

In addition to attributing the plan for the South Carolina campaign to Greene's war councils with officers encamped with him in late March 1781 or to Lee, there is probably a third interpretation. It is obvious that Greene planned to move to South Carolina at some time during the campaign, but it was also possible that Greene and Lee came up with the idea at the same time and independently of one another. And what if Greene's original plan was to consolidate the entire American force around Camden with the intention of provoking a battle or laying a siege? What if Lee convinced Greene to modify his tactical plan, allowing Lee and Francis Marion to engage the British outposts.

In this scenario the other partisan leaders would have been requested to reduce the flow of reinforcements being sent to the posts close to Camden. Lee and Marion had worked together in January and February 1781, before the race to the Dan River. The mutual respect between the two leaders manifested itself in Lee's subordinating himself, a Continental army officer, to Marion a South Carolina militia leader, an unheard-of occurrence. Lee had always been enamored with the idea of an independent command, and separation from the main American force played right into his desires. For Greene another advantage that would result from the reentrance of the army into South Carolina was the ability to "deny the enemy resources to which they previously ha[d] uncontested access." He fully expected that "Cornwallis would follow him back into South Carolina and not hazard the loss of that state."[22] This is what Greene saw as the possibility of returning in strength to South Carolina. As he wrote to General Friedrich von Steuben, the maneuver would force the "enemy to follow us or give up their posts." On March 29, 1781, Greene started notifying others of his intention to "carry the war immediately into South Carolina."[23]

Greene's choice to set out for Camden further illuminates his strategic thinking. As Don Higginbotham observed in *The War of American Independence*, Camden presented the best opportunity for success in South Carolina. By positioning the main American army outside Camden, Greene freed smaller detachments to attack British outposts.[24] The British forces in South Carolina under Lord Rawdon had to choose between attacking Greene or protecting their outposts. Just as he had done prior to the Battle of Cowpens three months previously, Greene split his tiny army into two parts in close proximity to one another. On April 4, Lee and his legion, marching toward Wilmington, turned south into South Carolina and headed for Marion's camp on Snow Island. Lee and Marion joined forces on April 14 and set out to invest Fort Watson on the Santee River (at present-day Scott's Lake). Greene, still collecting supplies, left a couple of days later and camped outside Camden on April 20. The movements on Fort Watson and Camden demonstrate that Greene was determined to force a classic "turning point/deciding moment" in the southern campaign.

Previous American victories in the region—Huck's Defeat in July 1780, Kings Mountain in October 1780, Blackstock's plantation in November 1780, Cowpens in January 1781, and to a lesser extent Guilford Courthouse in March 1781—had each been accomplished without major offensive troop movements. Huck's Defeat initiated the bloody civil war in the backcountry; Kings Mountain destroyed the left wing of Cornwallis's army, delaying British movement northward; Blackstock's plantation showed that Lieutenant Colonel Banastre Tarleton could be beaten by militia if it were well led and defending a protected area; Cowpens initiated the American retreat to the Dan River and Virginia; the results of Guilford Courthouse gave Greene the opportunity to change the course of the war by inducing Cornwallis into offensive maneuvers in Virginia. It was the decision to move into South Carolina and adopt an offensive strategy there that created the "turning point/decisive moment" in the South. Short of supplies in North Carolina, Greene understood that abandoning South Carolina would doom the entire lower South. Thus Greene decided to survive off of stockpiles of supplies captured from the British posts. The move toward Fort Watson was the test of this new strategy.

In the end the move into South Carolina was hailed as a brilliant stroke, ranking among the great exploits in military history. Virginia delegate to Congress Richard Henry Lee likened Greene's invasion of South Carolina to Scipio's invasion of Carthage during the Second Punic War because it compelled Corn-wallis "to relinquish his prospects or find his southern conquests wrenched from him. Comparing small things with great, this plan may save Virginia."[25] The return to South Carolina, contemporary historian David Ramsay declared, was "one of those times when more is to be done by a wise plan of operations than by numbers."[26] After much deliberation, Greene had chosen the uncon-ventional plan of attacking British posts in South Carolina over any other viable alternative. In making this decision, Greene changed the course of the war. His next victory came at the ancient Indian burial mound that had been converted into Fort Watson.

The move to South Carolina highlighted Greene's strategic brilliance, but underneath the decision lay a moderate ethics that guided his approach to win-ning the war and establishing civic peace in the South. The symbolism and immediacy of violent death hovered over Greene's command in the Southern Department. "The two opposite principles of Whiggism and Toryism," his aide William Pierce observed, "have set the people of this country to cutting each other's throats, and scarce a day passes but some poor deluded Tory is put to death at his door."[27] Just as war had driven his Quaker ancestors to radical reli-gious activism, so the most savage and horrifying acts of military brutality drove Greene deep into the resources of radical Whig ideology and into the tradi-tion of historic moderation. "I have always observed both in religion and poli-tics [that] moderation answers the most valuable purposes," Greene cautioned North Carolina militia general Griffith Rutherford in January 1782. The Brit-ish evacuation of Wilmington created a delicate civil and military situation in lowcountry North Carolina, and Greene wanted to sensitize Rutherford that the persecution of Tories was almost always counterproductive.[28] "If we pursue the Tories indiscriminately and drive them to a state [of] desperation, we shall make them, from a weak and feeble foe, a sure and determined enemy."[29] Two years later, the slowly healing wounds of partisan warfare in postrevolutionary Charleston convinced Greene that "Providence must have intended . . . that men should be local in their views and limited in politics." Society, he under-stood, could not exist without passionate localism, and this social condition was self-correcting: "the struggles which happen from this temper serve to animate the [more farsighted] view of mankind and purge off the dissocial passions." Localists sought vengeance against the Loyalists, and the people whom histo-rian Jackson Turner Main called "cosmopolitans" considered leniency toward former internal foes the defining characteristic of a mature regime.[30] "In poli-tics," Greene recommended, "we should be neither too local or too general in our policy." Both localism and centralization of national authority, Greene admonished the Georgia localist John Collins, "lead away from the high road of political happiness."[31]

*Lieutenant Colonel Francis,
Lord Rawdon*

Considering Greene as a moderate—neither a nationalist nor a localist but a moderate problem solver during the bloody fighting in the southern backcountry—and examining his ethics in the light of his own desperate circumstances—provides a prism through which to examine the entire American Revolution. Greene was not just a moderate, he was a *historic* moderate. His Quaker background, his Universalist religious convictions, his self-education in Enlightenment writings, and his difficult apprenticeship in command under Washington from 1776 to 1779 all made him conscious of his political heritage.

Of all his commanders, Washington concluded, Greene best understood how to navigate the new terrain of a conventional army operating in irregular circumstances.[32] Greene's openness to competing religious, political, and military dictates, and his ability to juggle them motivated Washington to influence, with exquisite tact, Congress's selection of Greene to succeed the discredited Horatio Gates after the Battle of Camden in August 1780. Washington may have realized that Greene knew how to coordinate movements of main force units, which he considered essential to civilized warfare, with the guerrilla warfare he distrusted and loathed. According to Richard Showman, Washington also saw in Greene a protégé who at Trenton, Brandywine, and Germantown had displayed "a keen retentive mind, a large measure of common sense, a capacity for organization, and a genius for comprehending . . . geography and topography,"[33] qualities essential to keeping in view all of the factors impinging on any given military situation.[34]

The self-educated son of a Rhode Island iron founder, Greene taught himself moral philosophy, religious skepticism as well as spirituality, and Whig history and politics. During his adolescence and early adulthood, he struggled to attain a sense of moral autonomy, reading widely in books his unlettered Quaker father considered spiritually suspect. At the same time Greene felt certain that his crabbed Quaker heritage was an unavoidable distortion of an admirable intention in the founders of the Society of Friends "to cultivate youthful minds to be subservient to their after purposes [that is, their eternal salvation]." He inhabited an oral and psychological universe bounded on one side by Quaker moral prescription and on the other side by a force no less frightening that he called "Self." In his late twenties he concluded that both pressures—that is, his "education . . . amongst the most superstitious sort" of Quakers in "a fine nursery of ignorance and superstition instead of piety"[35] and his realization that "self, uniformly and connectively considered," was "the original cause and spring of all action or motion"—acted in concert to make him a morally accountable being: "Does not the mind . . . bring two prospects in contrast and by its power of comparing and considering with itself which measure will more effectually conduce to it happiness, form a resolution . . . which to pursue? I am apt to believe it does and that . . . all our thoughts and actions flow from a selfish principle. . . . All of our religious dispositions and moral conduct is fundamentally established upon a self exalting principle or a natural desire to promote our own happiness."[36] The serious Rhode Islander who in the early 1770s sketched this map of human nature, based on a smattering of Enlightenment reading and a determination to make his own way in the world, depended for his self-education on eighteenth-century moral philosophy in what a recent historian of philosophy calls a "self conscious effort . . . to create a theory of morality as self-governance."[37]

The Continental army in the South, over which Greene assumed command in December 1780, presented him with the opportunity to test in combat the "self exalting principle" that a "natural desire to promote our own happiness" empowered soldiers to be brave and resourceful. He decided at once to incorporate partisan guerrilla bands into his strategy of harassing the British, but he wanted partisan commanders to know that military success depended less on spreading mayhem than on institutionalizing in the Continental army and state militias the palpable embodiment of the determination of the people to have their freedom. "When I was with you" in South Carolina, he reminded Thomas Sumter, "your soul was full of enterprise. The salvation of this country don't depend upon little strokes, nor should this great business of establishing a permanent army be neglected to pursue them. Partisan strokes are like the garnish of a table, they give splendor to an army and reputation to the officers, but they afford no national security. . . . There is no mortal more fond of enterprise than myself, but this is not the basis upon which the fate of this country depends. It is not a war of posts but a contest of states dependent upon opinion."[38] In his last four words, Greene echoed one of the new axioms of eighteenth-century moral philosophy: that political regimes cannot depend on force to secure obedience because, as David Hume put it, in the long run "governors have nothing to support them but opinion."[39] Making his army the visible guarantor of order and the embodiment of republican government while at the same time unleashing the demons of irregular partisan warfare in the southern backcountry, Greene endorsed Sumter's zeal for "enterprise" but bluntly warned partisan commanders that "plunder and depredation . . . in pursuit of private gain or personal glory"[40] would blemish their immortal reputations. He continually urged Abner Nash, North Carolina governor from April 1780 to June 1781, to energize state government as the organizer, financier, and manager of the war against Cornwallis.[41] Greene thus sustained his lifelong belief that "if great and exalted spirits undertake pursuit of hazardous actions for the good of others, . . . they have in view the gratification of their passion for glory."[42]

Nowhere did Greene's passion for glory motivate hazardous action more fully than at the Battle of Guilford Courthouse on March 15, 1781. Just as Daniel Morgan had gone from campfire to campfire the night before the Battle of Cowpens explaining the new tactics they would execute in the morning, so Greene spent the night making sure his troops understood the strategic window of opportunity that an engagement at Guilford Courthouse would offer.

"My Dear Nancy," one of his soldiers, Richard Harrison, wrote to his wife at dawn; "General Greene has published in camp [what turned out to be a false report] that Comte de Estaing has taken six British ships of the line, three frigates, and forty five transports with troops for America" in naval action in the Caribbean[43] and that "Great things have been done by Marion and Sumter. We daily expect to hear of the surrender of [Benedict] Arnold in the Chesapeake. . . . If we succeed against Cornwallis, we expect to be discharged instantly, for by that time the Continentals will have eaten up all the provisions that this country and South Carolina affords." In short, with Britain's strategic opportunities running out and with the Carolinas' capacity to support organized armed resistance nearly exhausted, soldiers such as Harrison knew that history would turn on the battle they were about to fight. Within a few hours, for all he knew, Nancy would go into labor to give birth to their first child. "This is the very day [March 15, 1781]," he said, "that I hope will be given to me a creature capable

Colonel William Washington's cavalry charge at the Battle of Hobkirk's Hill, April 25, 1781

of enjoying what its father hopes to deserve and earn, the sweets of liberty and grace."[44]

After the war ended, Delaware Quaker Warner Mifflin pressed Greene to reflect on his Quaker origins and on the ethical dilemmas he had faced commanding troops in the struggle against the British. "Whether wars originate from . . . human nature or from lusts that creep into the soul . . . is difficult to determine," Greene told Mifflin, positioning himself between a Calvinist view of human depravity and a Quaker understanding of the nature of violence; "we feel in ourselves strong affections and resentments, forcible sympathies and powerful antipathies; and all these inhabit the same soul and have their operation upon our conduct. They form the dark and light shades of human life, and like alternate seasons of day and night, may have their use. To say more, would be presumption; and to say less would be to draw into question the perfection and plan of universal government [that is, Providence as understood by the Universalists]."[45]

Greene's moderate ethics arose from his observation that "forcible sympathies and powerful antipathies . . . inhabit the same soul," pulling men simultaneously toward, and away from, violent conflict. In performing the immoderate task of ordering the execution of plunderers and deserters, Greene distinguished

The Battle of Eutaw Springs, September 8, 1781

the "impudence" of the "perpetrators" from the "patience, moderation, and good conduct under every species of suffering" of his rank and file, considered their suffering and provocation before judging as "unprincipled" the conduct of theft and desertion at West Point in October 1780.[46] He appealed to the Lockean idea that sensory experience pacifies and civilizes the human psyche, even in the face of tyranny or anarchy, as a controlling moral principle: "affections and resentments . . . form the dark and light shades of human life." Richard Harrison had sensed in Greene a commander disciplined by detestation of killing. Greene himself invoked "a social principle" wherein "the happiness of one is disturbed by inroads of another" as an axiom of human behavior that made "opposition" by force of arms "both just and necessary."[47]

Greene's return to South Carolina in April 1781 mirrored his republican ethics. His ethics arose from two clusters of sources, one dominant and the other recessive. The dominant influences were his radical Whiggery and the Universalist religious faith he embraced following his abandonment of the Society of Friends. But mingled subtly with his political and religious radicalism were habits of the heart he had earlier acquired from Rhode Island Quakers. A Quaker theory of "legal discernment" understood fundamental law as a gift of

God and something to be treasured and preserved within the conscience.[48] In Greene, as in the case of Thomas Paine, son of an English Quaker, discernment may have imparted irenic moral certainty to radical Enlightenment education.[49] Greene acted boldly in the southern campaigns of 1780–82, but he also husbanded finite American resources of manpower, supplies, military initiative, and morale. There were resources for one attempt to lure Tarleton into a tactical trap, one race to the Dan, one Battle of Guilford Courthouse, and one post–Guilford Courthouse shadowing of Cornwallis's army—but not two. The resource Greene possessed in somewhat more plentitude, and that he used with skill and effectiveness, was time and opportunity to plan. And as the late Don Higginbotham observed almost four decades ago, Greene's planning of the war of posts in South Carolina in the late spring and summer of 1781 was done with well-practiced care.

Greene's radical faith in the people and his clear-eyed understanding of human limitation arose from his Enlightenment rationalism and his skills at observation of the natural world and its human creatures. By 1781 Greene's military training and experience had no doubt toned down his "doubt and diffidence," but the spirit of Benezet's caution about being impatiently transfixed by the "melody" of ones "own voice" continued to describe the way Greene wrote and spoke to trusted associates. "You are in a State [South Carolina] which is disposed to fear the power of Congress," Gouverneur Morris, in the Congressional Office of Finance, wrote to Greene on May 18, 1783:

> In every State shortly after the enemy leave it or are driven away there succeeds a Period of moral anarchy, in which they are sure to act wrongly, but there succeeds again another Season in which as the Minds of Men tranquilize *the orders and Ranks* become more clearly designated. The People who can always feel and who never Reason (for such is that Creature Man all our Boastings) have felt for their folly in trusting Power to improper Hands look round for those who ought to hold the Reins. *These* are to be found only among the *more elevated ranks* and the *graver order of citizens.* And such as these love Peace, Quiet, solid Establishments and permanent Security. Such as these will therefore by Degrees endeavor to cement the American Union. *Happily for us the Southern States are so exposed* that they will soon be sensible of their own Extravagance. Other States will not find themselves too much at Ease. However I will not say more on this Subject for I hope we shall soon see each other.[50]

Morris's appreciative anticipation of his forthcoming conversation with Greene about republican virtue expressed in its purest form is the subject Sarah Knott addresses in *Sensibility and the American Revolution*—what she identifies as "the fundamental link of self and society" in the Revolutionary experience.[51] Revolutionary sensibility arose directly from cognitive dissonance, what Morris called "moral anarchy," the wild, uncontrolled force of nature domesticated by "the *more elevated ranks* and the *graver order of citizens*" characterized by "peace, quiet, solid establishments, and permanent security," which only statecraft and national institutions could guarantee. In moving to South Carolina in the spring of 1781, Greene turned the lower South toward a path that ultimately led to peace rooted in the security of established governments based on popular consent. Greene's rational Universalism, his radical Whig ideology, and his Quaker discernment of divine legal truth in the midst of a revolution thus came together to change the course of history.

NOTES

1. Robert S. Davis, "A Georgia Loyalist's Perspective on the American Revolution: The Letters of Dr. Thomas Taylor, 1776–1782," *Georgia Historical Quarterly* 81 (Spring 1997): 138.

2. Edward J. Cashin, "Nathanael Greene's Campaign for Georgia in 1781," *Georgia Historical Quarterly* 61 (Spring 1977): 43, 48, 50–51, 54.

3. Heard Robertson, "Unpublished Ms. on the Loyalists in Revolutionary Georgia, Augusta State University Library, Augusta, Georgia, ch. 6:1–9, ch. 5:1.

4. Edward J. Cashin and Heard Robertson, *Augusta and the American Revolution: Events in the Georgia Backcountry, 1773–1783* (Darien, Ga.: Ashantilly Press, 1975), 59.

5. Ibid., 63–65.

6. Michael C. Scoggins, *The Day It Rained Militia: Huck's Defeat and the Revolution in the South Carolina Backcountry, May–July 1780* (Charleston: History Press, 2005), 71–73.

7. George Washington to Greene, March 21, 1781, *The Papers of General Nathanael Greene*, edited by Richard K. Showman, Dennis R. Conrad, and Roger N. Parks, 13 vols. (Chapel Hill: University of North Carolina Press, 1976–2005), 7:458–83.

8. Greene to Joseph Reed, January 9, 1781; Otho Holland Williams to Greene, March 4 and 8, 1781; Henry Lee to Greene, March 5, 1781; Greene to Samuel Huntington, March 16, 1781; ibid., 7:84, 393–94, 398, 413–14, 415–17, 436–37.

9. George Washington Greene, *Life of Nathanael Greene, Major-General in the Army of the Revolution*, 3 vols. (New York: Hurd & Houghton, 1871), 3:43. Greene learned from George Washington how to conduct councils of war with his subordinates. See Greene to Washington, November 24, 1777, and December 3, 1777, *The Papers of George Washington: Revolutionary War Series*, edited by Philander Chase et al., 20 vols. to date (Charlottesville: University Press of Virginia, 1985–2010), 12:379–81, 516–18.

10. Benezet, quoted in Richard Bauman, *For a Reputation of Truth: Politics, Religion, and Conflict among Pennsylvania Quakers, 1750–1800* (Baltimore: Johns Hopkins University Press, 1971), 57.

11. Greene to Joseph Reed, March 30, 1781, *The Papers of General Nathanael Greene*, 8:11–12.

12. Greene to Timothy Pickering, April 4, 1781, ibid., 8:48–49.

13. Greene to George Washington, March 18, 1781, ibid., 7:451–52.

14. Charles Caldwell, *Memoirs of the Life and Campaigns of . . . Nathanael Greene* (Philadelphia, 1819), 223; Henry Lee, *Memoirs of the War in the Southern Department of the United States* (Philadelphia, 1812), 220.

15. Rutledge understood that "Greene's strategy . . . was sensitive to public confidence as a key to support for the army and ultimate victory. . . . For the time being the war in the South had to be one of continued partisan raids to keep the enemy from consolidating its hold on the country. But Greene knew that partisan warfare alone could not bring victory. While keeping the British off balance, he needed to raise and support a regular army strong enough to meet the enemy in the field with a good chance of success, which would not be easy. . . . While trying to reinforce and supply his army, Greene would have to do his best with the materials at hand." James Haw, *John and Edward Rutledge of South Carolina* (Athens: University of Georgia Press, 1997), 149–50.

16. Clyde R. Ferguson, "Functions of the Partisan Militia in the South during the American Revolution: An Interpretation," in *The Revolutionary War in the South: Power, Conflict, and Leadership*, edited by W. Robert Higgins (Durham: Duke University Press, 1979), 257.

17. George Washington Greene, *Life of Nathanael Greene*, 3:216.

18. Charles Royster, *Light-Horse Harry Lee and the Legacy of the American Revolution* (New York: Knopf, 1981), 20.

19. Royster, *Light-Horse Harry Lee*, 14.

20. M. F. Treacy, *Prelude to Yorktown: The Southern Campaigns of Nathanael Greene, 1780–1781* (Chapel Hill: University of North Carolina Press, 1963), 194–95.

21. Greene to Henry Lee, April 28, 1781, *The Papers of General Nathanael Greene*, 8:168.

22. Dennis R. Conrad, "Nathanael Greene and the Southern Campaigns, 1780–1783," Ph.D. diss., Duke University, 1979, 166–68.

23. Greene to George Washington, March 29, 1781, *The Papers of General Nathanael Greene*, 7:481.

24. Don Higginbotham, *The War of American Independence: Military Attitudes, Policies, and Practice* (New York: Macmillan, 1971), 371.

25. James Curtis Ballagh, *The Letters of Richard Henry Lee*, vol. 2: *1779–1794* (New York: Macmillan, 1914), 217–18.

26. David Ramsay, *The History of the Revolution in South Carolina, from the British Province to an Independent State* (Trenton, N.J.: Isaac Collins, 1785), 225.

27. Charles Royster, *A Revolutionary People at War: The Continental Army and American Character* (Chapel Hill: University of North Carolina Press, 1979), 278.

28. Greene to Griffith Rutherford, January 29, 1782, *The Papers of General Nathanael Greene*, 10:277.

29. Greene to Griffith Rutherford, October 18, 1781, ibid., 9:452.

30. Jackson Turner Main, *Political Parties before the Constitution* (Chapel Hill: University of North Carolina Press, 1973), 348–53.

31. Greene to John Collins, April 22, 1783, *The Papers of General Nathanael Greene*, 12:631–32.

32. Mark V. Kwasny, *Washington's Partisan War, 1775–1783* (Kent, Ohio: Kent State University Press, 1996), 329–39.

33. Richard N. Showman, "Nathanael Greene," in *Blackwell Encyclopedia of the American Revolution*, edited by Jack P. Greene and Jack R. Pole (Oxford: Blackwell, 1991), 727.

34. Robert M. Calhoon, *Dominion and Liberty in the Anglo-American World, 1660–1801* (Arlington Heights, Ill.: Harlan Davidson, 1994), 79–101.

35. Greene to [Samuel Ward], October 9, 1770, *The Papers of General Nathanael Greene*, 1:47.

36. Greene to [Samuel Ward], September 24, 1770, ibid., 1:16–17.

37. J. B. Schneewind, *The Invention of Autonomy: A History of Moral Philosophy* (Cambridge: Cambridge University Press, 1998), 5.

38. Greene to Thomas Sumter, January 28, 1781, *The Papers of General Nathanael Greene*, 7:74–75.

39. Edmund S. Morgan, *Inventing the People: The Rise of Popular Sovereignty in England and America* (New York: Norton, 1988), 13.

40. Greene to Thomas Sumter, January 8, 1781, *The Papers of General Nathanael Greene*, 7:75.

41. Greene to Abner Nash, January 7, 1781, ibid., 7:61–65.

42. Greene to [Samuel Ward], September 24, 1770, ibid., 1:17.

43. Editorial note, ibid., 7:373.

44. Richard Harrison to Nancy Pattillo Harrison, March 15, 1781, Henry Pattillo Papers, Southern Historical Collection, University of North Carolina at Chapel Hill.

45. Nathanael Greene to Warner Mifflin [November 1783], *The Papers of General Nathanael Greene*, 13:191.

46. Greene's orders, October 13, 1780, *The Papers of General Nathanael Greene*, 6: 372–73.

47. Warner Mifflin to Greene, October 21, 1783, and Greene to Mifflin, November 1783, ibid., 13:155–58, 191–92.

48. Jane E. Calvert, "The Quaker Theory of a Civil Constitution," *History of Political Thought* 27, no. 4 (2006), 586–619 ("Discernment of Fundamental Law"), 589–93.

49. Jonathan I. Israel, *Radical Enlightenment: Philosophy and the Making of Modernity* (Oxford: Oxford University Press, 2001), 343–44, discusses the Dutch friends of Spinoza, Pieter Balling and Jarig Jelles, who absorbed Quaker spirituality into radical enlightenment thought, associating the "inner light" as a "bridge" between "a mystical emanation of God and the philosophical reason of the Cartesians."

50. Gouverneur Morris to Nathanael Greene, May 18, 1783, *The Papers of Robert Morris*, vol. 8: *May to December 31, 1783*, edited by Elizabeth M. Nuxell and Mary A. Gallagher (Pittsburgh: University of Pittsburgh Press, 1995), 92.

51. Sarah Knott, *Sensibility and the American Revolution* (Chapel Hill: University of North Carolina Press, 2009), 1.

Nathanael Greene

Soldier-Statesman of the War of Independence in South Carolina

James R. Mc Intyre

*N*athanael Greene is rightly credited with conducting a brilliant military campaign in the Southern Department that achieved two extremely significant results. First and foremost, it eventually pushed General Charles, Earl Cornwallis, down the road that led him to surrender his army at Yorktown, Virginia, in October 1781. Cornwallis's defeat sent shockwaves through the halls of British government, bringing on the collapse of Frederick, Lord North's ministry and culminating in the end of hostilities. Second, and of no less significance, Greene's continued activities in South Carolina in the aftermath of the March 1781 Battle of Guilford Courthouse were largely responsible for securing the membership of both that state and its southern neighbor, Georgia, in the United States at the end of the war. In South Carolina, Greene simultaneously conducted successful military and political campaigns to upset the British and their Loyalist supporters and reinstall a working Whig government,[1] using a measured combination of diplomacy and force. An examination of three separate but related lines—use of militia, restraint of violence, and cooperation with civilian authorities—reveals much about how Greene effected a positive outcome in South Carolina in particular and the southern states in general.

Historians have often characterized Greene's actions in South Carolina as an insurgency of sorts. Using the framework of insurgency-counterinsurgency, or guerrilla warfare, as an interpretive model for analyzing the American War of Independence certainly does not constitute a new methodological approach. It first reached a peak in popularity during the years just after the American involvement in Vietnam, so much so that the noted historian Don Higginbotham published pieces decrying the comparison. Still the search for analogies across centuries continues to hold seemingly irresistible temptations for some. At least one recent work compares the War of Independence and the Iraq War, with the United States cast in the role of Great Britain in the latter conflict.[2]

Such assessments can certainly draw out important parallels. At the same time, these comparisons can be quite dangerous, running the risk of being reductionist to the point of complete falsehood. For instance an insurgency-counterinsurgency framework assumes that the British military reinstated a legitimate, working civilian government. On a broader level, while one dimension of the American War of Independence definitely encompassed an insurgency, it was only one of several layers in a complex, multitiered conflict. Certainly a part of the War of Independence included a civil war between Whigs and Loyalists for political control, which played out at the local level up and down the Atlantic Seaboard. Simultaneously there occurred a struggle for national liberation from the British government and a war of colonial expansion along the frontier.[3] Too much emphasis on the insurgency aspect ignores these other dimensions of the conflict, and therefore reduces and distorts our overall understanding of the War of Independence.

Likewise, and especially in the case of South Carolina, the insurgency-counterinsurgency approach misses a key feature: there was no effective civilian government in the state, at the latest from the fall of Charleston to British forces under Sir Henry Clinton in May 1780. After this point the Whig government led by Governor John Rutledge was quite literally on the run. At the same time, the British, while installing a military occupation, never erected a functioning civilian government loyal to the Crown. Clinton did set up a board of police in Charleston to oversee civil matters, but he stopped short of reinstating a full civilian authority, feeling that the time was not yet opportune to do so.[4] With neither side in full control, political legitimacy, the acceptance of the government by the governed, became a contested zone. Whichever side could win that contest would gain control of South Carolina. The British challenge was aptly summed up by Robert M. Calhoon when he observed, "British success in the southern campaign depended not only on Loyalist military success but also on the capacity of Loyalist administrators and British officers to re-establish normal patterns of civic life."[5] The Whigs' challenges were slightly more complex. They did not have any regular military forces in the state, nor did they have any working governmental apparatus. Restoring Whig control over South Carolina therefore required both political and military action. This action had to come from a national agency, as there remained the lurking concern over a peace negotiated on the basis of *uti possidetis*, the principle that the combatants held on to whatever territory they controlled at the conclusion of peace negotiations, an arrangement that would leave South Carolina and Georgia in British hands.[6]

South Carolina in 1779

This was the strategic situation Nathanael Greene marched into after the Battle of Guilford Courthouse. In order to place Greene's actions in their proper context, his campaign must be understood within the context of the war itself. From 1775 until 1779, the southern states of North Carolina, South Carolina, and Georgia stood as a relatively quiet zone. Certainly some skirmishes occurred, especially in South Carolina, and the British launched a major naval assault on the important port city of Charleston in 1776, which was repulsed. In North Carolina, the Battle of Moore's Creek Bridge in February 1776 broke the back of organized Loyalist activity in that state for several years. Also in 1776 contingents from both of the Carolinas, as well as Georgia and Virginia, took part in a brief but extremely successful war against the Cherokee.[7] Still the British army made no sustained organized military attempt on any of these states comparable to the operations in the North, where the British sought to break the rebellion. Yet the British ministry did not fail to consider the South in devising their strategy. Though the region always figured in the strategic thinking of the king's ministry, that thinking did not always translate into positive actions. Among the reasons for this inaction was the uncertainty over whether to back potential allies—Loyalists, African slaves, or Native Americans—or to shun them. Each of these groups possessed strategic assets as well as liabilities.[8]

While the southern states remained predominantly quiescent in the military sense, the same could not be said in regards to their internal politics. The Whig faction in South Carolina erected a functioning government, but it fell far short of achieving the universal consent of the governed. Certainly across the entire Southern Department, the militant Loyalists had been dealt some heavy blows at battles such as Great Bridge, Virginia, Moore's Creek Bridge, North Carolina, and in particular during the Snow Campaign in South Carolina.[9] Still, even with these military setbacks, the Loyalists' acceptance of Whig political supremacy was grudging at best. Although the Palmetto State did stand among the first to alter its instrument of government once independence was declared, promulgating a new constitution in March 1776 and another in 1778, neither of these documents achieved the unanimous consent of the governed. In the early phases of the Revolution, the South Carolina backcountry was so divided that it was deemed necessary to dispatch a diplomatic mission to gain support for the Whig faction. The ministers Oliver Hart and William Tennent and Whig political representative William Henry Drayton traveled through the region in the summer of 1775, attempting to drum up support for the Whig cause and trying to convince the residents of the region to sign an Association, essentially a loyalty oath to the Whig government. Their mission met with only limited success. A refusal to sign one of the Associations, which circulated in South Carolina and other colonies, stood as a clear indication that a person supported the Crown at least passively. That representatives of the Whig government had to lobby the backcountry for support implies strongly that political legitimacy remained a point of great contention, even internally.[10] Political dissension continued to plague the state throughout the early years of the conflict. As late as 1778, constituents elected several known Loyalists to the legislature, and some of these representatives even took their seats.[11]

For the most part, however, the Whig faction secured a certain level of control of the state, and set up a working government based in Charleston. Realizing the precarious nature of their political situation, the Whigs sought to either win over those sympathetic to the Crown, or to drive them out. Even early in the conflict, those who did not sympathize with the Whigs faced political ostracism at the very least. Likewise, local Whigs seemed more than willing to denounce neighbors for perceived unpatriotic speech or activity. There are many examples in the correspondence between the Whig government in Charleston and the local Committees of Safety and other officials denouncing local Loyalists. One example comes in a letter from Henry Laurens to Lieutenant Colonel William Thomson, dated August 31, 1775: "Your Zeal in dismissing Several disaffected Captains from Service in your Regiment of Militia merits commendation, the vacancies occasioned thereby ought to be forthwith filled up."[12] Loyalists were removed from service to the state. With no real ability to organize, no flag to rally around, the South Carolina Loyalists could do little to challenge the Whig government. They could form their own government and create their own military organizations, but without British succor they did not pose a major threat to the Whigs and would be opening themselves up for severe repression. There was also the option of leaving South Carolina and making the long trek to Florida, which some did voluntarily, and others did under coercion.[13] Taken as a whole, the situation in the South Carolina backcountry was one of bristling resentment toward the Whig government. The repression of the Loyalists by the Whigs, in turn, bred an undercurrent of resentment as the war progressed.

The seething undercurrent of discontent with Whig rule burst forth in a full-fledged tsunami when the British invaded the South in late 1778. The Loyalists first gained an opportunity when France entered the war in support of the American revolutionaries in 1778 and Sir Henry Clinton implemented a revamped version of the southern strategy. This strategy encompassed the reduction of the southern colonies, where the ministry believed large numbers of friends to royal government stood waiting for the arrival of British forces before taking the field. These loyal Americans would then erect a new government friendly to the Crown, in turn releasing British regulars for duties elsewhere. The idea of using Americans to prosecute the war was certainly appealing to Clinton, as his own manpower resources were dwindling as detachments were siphoned off from his forces to guard important British interests in the West Indies.[14]

The possibilities in the southern theater seemed all the more appealing when Georgia, the first colony to face the British onslaught, fell quickly to the forces of the Crown in December 1778. Then, after a month long siege, Charleston surrendered in May 1780, the largest single defeat inflicted on American arms down to the present day. Among the consequences attending the capitulation of Charleston was the loss of the majority of the organized Whig military forces in the Southern Department. These included some four thousand militia and approximately one thousand Continental troops. In addition large quantities of weapons and supplies fell into British hands—equipment the Whigs could ill-afford to lose. Finally the Whig government of the colony essentially ceased to exist as anything resembling organized authority during the siege. Governor John Rutledge was ordered to leave Charleston to preserve a government in absentia should the city fall. Thus the closest thing to a legitimate Whig political entity in the region now stood as severely compromised, if not wholly ineffectual.[15]

Following quickly on the heels of the fall of Charleston, Clinton dispatched Lieutenant Colonel Banastre Tarleton and his British Legion to scour the countryside and mop up any remaining Whig resistance. Simultaneously Clinton ordered other troops into the hinterlands of South Carolina. These detachments secured a series of key outposts for the British, including Camden, Georgetown, and Ninety Six. These strategically significant sites formed a ring of bases that the British could utilize as strongpoints in order to control the backcountry. Likewise these posts could serve as recruiting centers to bring Loyalist militia units into the field. At the same time that the British hold on South Carolina seemed to be strengthening, the qualities of British occupation underwent a fundamental change. As Clinton prepared to return to New York City, he publicized a proclamation altering the terms under which many of the Whig militia who had fought in the defense of Charleston received paroles. As a result of the change in conditions of their paroles, they now had to be ready to fight for the Crown when summoned or be deemed as active rebels once again.[16] This change in terms pushed many who would willingly have waited out the rest of the war in peace into partisan groups then forming in the backcountry. Still no organized regular force represented the United States in the South.

In addition to the change in the terms of parole, British actions provided the necessary catalyst for many backcountry Whigs to once again take up arms. The most prominent incident of what were considered British atrocities derived from the battle alternately know as Waxhaws or Buford's Defeat: the defeat of a contingent of some 350 to 400 Virginia Continentals under the command of Colonel Abraham Buford. On the march to reinforce Charleston during the siege, these troops received word of the city's capitulation and began falling back to North Carolina to join other Continentals mustering in that state. The British Legion under the command of Tarleton came upon this group at the Waxhaws on May 29, 1780, and there followed a fairly one-sided engagement in which the British were victorious. At one point in the confused encounter, the troops under Tarleton's command thought enemy fire had killed their leader. They proceeded to exact vengeance on some of the surrendering Continentals until Tarleton restored order. The treatment meted out to some of the surrendering Americans led to allegations of a massacre. Historians continue to keep the controversy over the fight at the Waxhaws alive down to the present day. One of the most recent and objective discussions of the encounter convincingly argues that whether or not an atrocity occurred is secondary in importance to the perception that one did. This belief was one of the primary contributing factors in the rising of the backcountry. It is worthy of note that, while Buford's Defeat certainly served as a catalyst, there occurred many other, more verified examples of British and Loyalist excesses in the South Carolina backcountry.[17]

Responding to British depredations, real or perceived, many small bands of local partisans took to the field and initiated a guerrilla war that destabilized the British occupation.[18] These partisan actions, while they successfully denied the British anything resembling complete control of South Carolina, came nowhere near the magnitude necessary to force them to abandon the state altogether. In order to reclaim South Carolina for the Whig cause, regular troops would be necessary. A commitment of the Continental army on the part of the national political authority, the Continental Congress, would be indispensable for political as well as military reasons. There were several factors that made Continental troops essential for reclaiming the South. Their presence would prove to the local populace that the national government had not turned its back on the state, a rumor all too common in the weeks after the fall of Charleston and tending to spread under the guise of a peace negotiated according to *uti possidetis.* In a military sense the commitment of Continentals would bolster and reinforce militia efforts. Historian John Pancake perhaps best described the importance of having troops from the national army in the South: "The regulars also had a symbolic value. They constituted a national army that epitomized the nation's resistance to England; in a word, the army *was* the United States."[19]

Reacting to the deteriorating situation in the Southern Department, the Continental Congress ordered Major General Horatio Gates, the "victor of Saratoga," southward in the hope he would work another miracle like the one he had in upstate New York against the invasion led by General John Burgoyne in 1777. At Hillsborough, North Carolina, Gates met the battered remnants of those fortunate enough to escape the Whig defeats in South Carolina. For reasons that remain obscure, Gates, who most contemporaries recognized more for his administrative abilities than his lust for battle, immediately ordered his troops to advance on the British post at Camden, South Carolina.[20] Gates's advance continued even after one of his subordinates, Colonel Otho Holland Williams, informed the general that he had barely half the forces Gates believed were under his command. The end of this movement came at the Battle of Camden on the morning of August 16, 1780. The engagement amounted to another debacle for the Whig forces, and yet another American army disintegrated, though the Maryland and Delaware troops fought well, with their commander Baron Johann de Kalb falling mortally wounded on the field.

After Camden no effective regular force remained to resist British expansion in the region. The Continental Congress found itself in a dire situation. This time the delegates solicited George Washington's choice for a new theater commander to replace Gates. Washington recommended Nathanael Greene, who was unpopular in Congress. During his recently completed two-year stint as the quartermaster general, he had often fought with Congress, and the delegates currently had his accounts under review. In the end Congress overcame its current troubles with Greene and ordered him to take over the Southern Department.[21]

Greene assumed command over a force that resembled more the specter of an army than a true military command. There were roughly nine hundred Continentals huddled around Hillsborough, North Carolina, an area desolate of the provisions necessary to support them. Some of the men were survivors of the Camden debacle; others were reinforcements dispatched to the army from the North.[22] With this small, poorly supplied force, Greene would have to stem the tide of British advance and begin the process of retaking South Carolina and Georgia for the Whigs. Clearly the meager numbers under his command would not allow Greene to wage a traditional offensive campaign according to eighteenth-century standards, even with further reinforcements, which included the crack troops of Henry "Light-Horse Harry" Lee.

Facing the prospect of waging a campaign on a virtual shoestring, Greene approached the challenges of the Southern Department from a radically different perspective. First and foremost he understood that he would have to rely in large measure on local militia and partisan units. Second he would have to make sure that the Continental troops under his command set a standard of behavior through example, with regard to both the restraint of violence and the protection of private property. Finally he would have to work with local Whig political leaders, both to keep militia in the field and to maintain the semblance of a political organization in the state. Keeping the militia active presented some concerns in and of itself.

Washington's top generals commonly viewed militia units as unreliable. Their lack of discipline was well known to the officers of the Continental army.

In addition it was commonly accepted opinion that they would just as often run away as stand the field, especially when pitted against British regulars. As a group, the militia remained keenly aware of the duration of their commitment to serve. When their time in the field expired, they returned home; often they began their journey home prior to the end of their term of service.[23] They were known to plunder as well, especially in the South, where old personal or familial quarrels tended to mix with the military conflict. Here the lines that separated militia or partisan troops from simple bands of armed thieves blurred—to say the least.[24] By the same token, it is worth noting that at least one scholar has recently challenged these common contemporary assumptions regarding the militia, especially those from South Carolina.[25]

In many instances Greene relied on the militia to take the lead in bringing the war to the British and Loyalists. To be successful in the South, these partisans had to operate within the parameters he set and worked diligently to enforce. They had to conduct themselves with some restraint and abide by the rules of war as understood in the eighteenth century, especially with regard to the treatment of noncombatants and respect for private property.[26] Murderers, rapists, and thieves stood no chance of retaking the South. They could in fact bolster support for the British and the Loyalists and undermine the perceived legitimacy of the Whig cause. In order to reinstate the authority of the Congress and bring South Carolina as well as Georgia back into the Whig fold, militiamen had to represent the side of law and order and thus earn legitimacy in the eyes of the local populace.[27]

Because he relied on them to supplement his numbers in the field and to provide important intelligence and logistics service, Greene could not enforce anything resembling iron discipline on these partisan fighters for fear of alienating them and losing their support. They were not directly under his control, and their local commanders zealously guarded their own status in the theater. Greene had to deal delicately with the militia and needed to frame his directives in the form of requests rather than orders. He had to strike a delicate balance between working to get the partisans to abide by the rules of war and not pushing so hard as to alienate them and keep them from turning out to support the Continentals. Certainly some of the partisan leaders in South Carolina were more amenable to cooperation with Greene than others. Thomas Sumter exemplifies the more difficult type of local commander, as he was often more ardent in the preservation of his own independence than he was to act in support of the greater good of the Whig cause. Sumter's reticence to cooperate with the Continentals created a strained relationship with Greene. Francis Marion by contrast stands as a model of those most willing to work with the national authority.

Greene's first communication with Marion is indicative of the commanding general's comprehension of his tenuous role in the department. Writing from

Charlotte on December 4, 1780, Greene began by complimenting Marion on his conduct of operations: "I like your plan of frequently shifting your Ground. It frequently prevents a Surprise and perhaps a total Loss of your Party. Untill a more permanent Army can be collected than is in the Field at present we must endeavor to keep up a Partizan War and preserve the Tide of Sentiment among the People as much as possible in our Favour."[28] Greene realized he could not come into the area and dictate to local military leaders. Such compliments laid the foundation for a positive working relationship with militia commanders such as Marion, one in which both sides felt that they were contributing successfully to the outcome of the campaign. Once this relationship was established, the Whig forces in the South possessed a powerful combination.

When working in tandem with the Continentals—at least on a strategic level—the militia, or partisans, created an extraordinarily difficult situation for the British, putting them in the position of dealing "concurrently with regulars and guerrillas existing in a symbiotic relationship, a genuine quandary for an army operating over vast expanses of less-than-friendly territory."[29] If the British chased after Greene and his Continentals, the local Whig militia could and did wreak havoc with the redcoats' logistics. In order to make such a scenario a reality, however, Greene required a reliable force of regulars who could take the field against the forces of the Crown—he needed a respectable army.[30]

The core of regular troops under Greene's command consisted of the survivors of the Maryland and Delaware Continentals left after the Battle of Camden, augmented by some reinforcements who had arrived in the interim.[31] The supply situation for these troops was precarious at best. Writing to the Baron Friedrich von Steuben on October 12, 1780, Otho Holland Williams reported only twenty-five tents and roughly twenty camp kettles available for the "army."[32] The desperate supply situation was more poignantly illustrated by William Seymour of the Delaware Regiment: "At this time the troops were in a most shocking condition for the want of clothing, especially shoes, and we having kept open campaign all winter the troops were taking sick very fast. Here the manly fortitude of the troops of the Maryland Line was very great, being obliged to march and do duty barefoot, being all the winter the chief part of them wanting coats and shoes, which they bore with the greatest patience imaginable."[33]

Their lack of supplies led these men into the twin evils of plunder and indiscipline. On assuming command Greene took immediate steps to restore discipline, executing the first men caught plundering under his regime. Though his action may appear harsh, Greene possessed a keen appreciation that the stakes were extremely high. The Continentals, the manifestation of the legitimate government of the Continental Congress, had to set a high standard of behavior in order to project the perception of themselves as the force of law and order. The maintenance of discipline, even among the Continental troops under his command, remained a difficulty that dogged Greene's actions in the department through the remainder of the war.[34]

In confronting the daunting strategic situation, Greene was not bereft of all assets. In fact he possessed several significant advantages, especially in the realm of leadership. Greene quickly utilized the talents of Brigadier General Daniel Morgan, one of the most tactically proficient Whig military leaders.[35] Thinking beyond the conventions of eighteenth-century warfare, Greene split his forces, sending Morgan into northwestern South Carolina with a corps of troops, which included some of the Maryland and Delaware Continentals as well as Lieutenant Colonel William Washington's cavalry. As Greene explained to Morgan, "The object of this detachment is to give protection to that part of the country and spirit up the people, to annoy the enemy in that quarter; collect the provisions and forage out of the way of the enemy." Greene cautioned Morgan to "prevent plundering as much as possible . . . giving receipts for whatever you take to all such as are friends to the independence of America."[36] While Greene charged Morgan with galvanizing Whig support, he also made certain that his subordinate knew to respect law and order, but selectively. He was to refrain from plundering those *friendly* to the cause. While some would argue that any plunder breeds indiscipline, the realities of warfare in the region necessitated some confiscation in order to keep the army supplied and in the field.[37] Selective plundering aided the Whig cause because it reduced the likelihood of alienating the local support they already possessed.[38] It stands as a tribute to Morgan's leadership that he achieved such an amazing outcome despite an uncertain logistical situation and the difficulties of campaigning in winter.

The campaign Morgan embarked on eventually resulted in the Battle of Cowpens on January 17, 1781, probably the clearest tactical victory for the Whigs in the entire War of Independence.[39] This victory held tremendous importance for the Whig cause in the South. Battlefield victories were important for morale, and Cowpens certainly offered a much needed tonic to the Whigs. Still it would not have been possible—nor would Morgan's escape have occurred without substantial support—from the countryside. Many partisans were turning out to aid the regular forces. The winds of war were shifting in favor of the Whigs.[40]

Morgan's victory at the Cowpens set off the race to the Dan River and eventually led to the Battle of Guilford Courthouse, North Carolina, on March 15, 1781. On this occasion Greene tried with less success to mimic the sort of defense that Morgan had employed to such advantage at the Cowpens.[41] After this engagement, Greene made what would prove to be one of the key decisions of the entire conflict—he marched back into South Carolina. It is clear from his writings that he felt motivated as much by political as by military considerations. For instance, in a March 29, 1781, letter to George Washington explaining his decision, Greene first laid out the advantages and disadvantages and then summed up: "All things considered, I think the movement is warranted by the soundest reasons, both political and military."[42] Writing to Baron von Steuben shortly thereafter, Greene expressed his intentions as follows: "From a persuasion that the Enemy wish to get full possession of this State [North Carolina], and are making every effort to effect it; and as their advance northward secures their possessions Southward I think it will be our true plan of policy to move into South Carolina, notwithstanding the risque and difficulty attending the maneuver."[43]

As Greene moved into South Carolina, Cornwallis attempted to shore up what he perceived as his victories in the Carolinas by advancing into Virginia. Returning to South Carolina, Greene eventually began a campaign aimed at reducing the various Loyalist strongholds that dotted the state's interior. Thus followed a series of actions fought both by Continentals and militia, culminating in the Battle of Eutaw Springs on September 8, 1781. Although this battle is sometimes seen as either a tactical defeat or a draw for Greene, it was certainly a strategic victory because the British fell back to Charleston, leaving most of the remainder of the state in Whig hands. In addition this engagement helped Greene win the approval of many South Carolinians, as the presence of his army clearly demonstrated his determination to liberate the state from British control and clearly represented the national government in the region.[44]

By the same token, now that he occupied most of South Carolina, Greene's mission grew much more complicated. He faced not only a British army but also local Loyalist forces and an all-out guerrilla war with all its attendant horrors. During the summer of 1781, Loyalist forces in South Carolina continued to put forth a determined military effort.[45] In order to succeed, Greene needed to ratchet down the violence prevalent between the two factions and to restore respect for private property. Greene and his Continentals needed to serve as a force for law and order. To accomplish these tasks, Greene had to maintain discipline within his own ranks and work effectively with local political and military authorities.

A crucial test of Greene's overall command in the theater as well as his ability to work with local leaders arose with the case of Colonel Isaac Hayne, a Whig militia leader who had taken the proffered British parole after the fall of Charleston. He returned to the field in an attempt to capture the noted loyalist leader General Andrew Williamson. Shortly after completing this mission, Hayne was captured by the British. Lieutenant Colonel Nisbet Balfour, the commandant of Charleston, where Hayne was incarcerated, refused all calls for a prisoner exchange and had Hayne executed on August 4, 1781.[46]

Balfour was acting on a policy he had established some months previously. Writing to Henry Clinton in May 1781, Balfour stated, "This Spirit of Revolt is, in some measure, kept up by the many Officers Prisoners of War here, and I should therefore think it advisable to remove them, as well as to make the most striking examples of such as having taken protection, snatch every occasion to rise in arms against us."[47] Once Hayne was in British custody, Balfour enacted his policy.

Hayne's capture and execution developed into a cause célèbre among the other partisan leaders, and Greene's reaction to it would either cement or lose their adherence. Militia leaders sought to exact vengeance by reciprocal treatment for any captured British officer. If Greene failed to act, he might discourage the militia from taking the field, a motive often attributed to Balfour for Hayne's execution.[48] By the same token Greene had to keep in mind that the British still held many more captives, including Continentals and prominent South Carolina Whigs taken when Charleston fell. Greene's correspondence on the subject shows a profound grasp of the complexities of the situation. Writing to Colonel William Henderson of the South Carolina militia on August 12, 1781, Greene informed him of Hayne's execution and advised, "Should you take any british officers keep them close prisoners until you hear farther from me on the subject. I shall explain my self more in a few days."[49] Several days later Greene sought Henderson's opinion on the possibility of retaliation on British officers, which Greene placed in a strategic perspective: "If retaliation is not had the Militia will [be] all discouraged and quit the service." At the same time, he saw the possible negative effects of such a policy: "But [if] we begin to retaliate it involves the life of an Officer or its consequences may terminate finally in giving no quarter," he noted.[50] In the end, after consulting various local leaders, as well as Henry Lee, Greene opted for the policy of retaliation. As he informed Congress in a letter dated August 25, 1781, "I conceive retaliation highly necessary and doubt not Congress will approve of the steps I have taken let them lead to what consequences they may."[51] While Greene did adopt such a policy, he never implemented it. He accepted that local militia leaders would not settle for anything less than revenge and would not remain in the field otherwise, but his predilection for restraint continued to win out. A key feature of Greene's command in the South was his judicious restraint of violence in order to bring about a return to law and order. This approach helped him achieve legitimacy for the Whig cause in South Carolina. Likewise the British handling of incidents, such as the execution of Hayne, alienated the local populace, who viewed British authority as illegitimate.

At the same time the British were losing military and civil control in South Carolina, Cornwallis sought to close the supply conduit from the North that in some measure helped to keep the Whig forces in the field.[52] This strategy of expanding the scope of his conquests in order to consolidate his previous gains and cut his enemy's logistical supports eventually led Cornwallis down the road to Yorktown, though not before he adopted a hard war policy in Virginia.[53] The siege of Yorktown did not spell the end of active combat operations in the War of Independence. Neither side issued an immediate ceasefire in the period following Cornwallis's surrender. There were still substantial numbers of British and Loyalist troops based in both New York and Charleston, and they were available to continue fighting. Finally many Loyalist units in South Carolina in particular continued to pursue a military campaign with the hope of salvaging the situation in the southern states.[54]

Throughout his campaign, Greene confronted the challenges of defeating the remaining British forces and their Loyalist supporters in South Carolina. Greene's reliance on Whig militia brought with it some real political dangers because they often seized the property of Loyalists and frequently took vengeance on their persons. Greene's correspondence abounds with injunctions to local commanders to restrain both themselves and their troops from perpetrating what could later be construed as war crimes of varying degrees. For example, when Colonel Stephen Drayton, a former commissary officer, questioned whether or not his parole remained binding, Greene responded, "Paroles should be treated with respect and delicacy otherwise military operations become cruel and barbarous as it will be for the interest of the parties to put such to death as cannot be conveniently carried off."[55] Greene's position was an attempt to redirect the conduct of the belligerents from the nadir it had reached. Likewise requiring Whig troops, even irregulars, to abide by paroles would go a long way in developing their image as the side of law and order.

Of the various partisan leaders, Francis Marion was the most restrained in this regard while Thomas Sumter often disregarded these sorts of instructions. One example of the manner in which Marion sought to reimpose the rule of law is contained in a communication from Greene dated January 16, 1781. Marion had sought permission to try some men he had caught marauding, and Greene wrote: "Since writing you this morning I have been with Governor Rutledge who informs me you had written to him for authority to try by a Court Martial some offenders who were taken marauding. If you will acquaint me with the circumstances and whether you mean to try them capitally I will give you Authority to hold the Court. The Governor can give you no legal authority and therefore don't choose to give any at all. Military Courts are upon a different principle and may be in some sort accommodated to the nature of the offence."[56]

When civil authority did not extend to soldiers who abused property rights, Greene was more than willing to bridge the gap with military justice. Marion, a Continental officer himself, often worked in tandem with Henry Lee, a

uncement was the statement that "should any of them hereafter be claimed
proved as the property of any inhabitants of this State, and Congress should
mine, that such property shall be restored to the former owners, they are
given up, and the purchase money will be returned by the public to the
hasers."[66] Such statements went a long way to show the Continental army
he cause it fought for was the side of law and order.

the end Greene's efforts were successful, and the contest for political
ilitary control of the South was concluded in favor of the Whigs. Much
achievement stemmed from the perceived legitimacy of their forces. By
me token the perception of legitimacy stemmed in part from the restraint
e worked to impose on the troops under his command, both regulars and
. All these actions eventually bore fruit as South Carolina and Georgia
etaken by the Whigs, and in each state the government was legitimate in
se that it possessed the support of the majority of the enfranchised white
tion.

eene's conduct of simultaneous military and political contests for the
acy of the Whig cause in South Carolina stands as the reason his cam-
as attracted so many modern students. Though one must keep in mind
is conflict was waged in a specific social-political-cultural context—and
ngs were done differently, and for their own reasons, in the eighteenth
—some general lessons may emerge

first and foremost lesson is that the support of the local populace was
unt to Greene's triumph in South Carolina. They provided material sup-
well as troops. Certainly many of Greene's decisions in the theater were
ed at least in part by the need to supply his army.[67] It is unclear whether
possessed an understanding of this concept when he assumed command
outhern Department or whether it developed from practical experience
eld. In either case he came to rely a great deal on the fighting and intel-
capabilities of the various militia units. Likewise he knew or quickly
that the support of local inhabitants would be forthcoming only if they
they stood to benefit under Whig rule through the restoration of law
r. The role of the Continentals was important in the traditional mili-
e: they had to win on the battlefield. But they could not engage in the
wless behavior that was often seen as characteristic of the militia or the
d their Loyalist supporters. Thus plunder and the treatment of pris-
re key issues Greene attended to constantly and necessarily.
dition Greene managed to strike the fine balance of discipline and
on necessary to have the local partisans work as an effective para-
rce. They took the field, and Marion at least coordinated many of his
with Greene, demonstrating the support of the local population in the
ningful sense. As the military tide turned in favor of the Whigs, the

commander in the Continental army, and this partnership may have helped
instill a greater level of restraint, as Lee's troops were known as among the most
disciplined in the army.[57] Sumter, on the other hand, often created great difficulties for Greene, as exemplified in their correspondence.

Sumter charged that Greene showed favoritism in distributing equipment
to Marion's troops. Greene responded, "I do not know of any partial respecting
the Militia, nor do I give any o[rders] in the matter; but General Marion being
ne[ar] the enemies lines I suppose led to the indulgence if any was granted."
Greene added a reminder that "you know the nature of service must always
govern the mode of equipping troops."[58]

Assuaging hurt feelings over such minor details could seem a pitiful waste
of time for someone shouldering the burdens Greene bore. At the same time,
this sort of diplomacy toward the local troops remained essential if he were to
keep a commander as potent as Sumter in the field. It was through preserving
good relations with the militia that Greene was able to rely on them to keep
British and Loyalist forces off balance. In addition, through garnering the
support of local commanders, Greene demonstrated that he was a supporter of
local government rather than an invader. He could thus work through these
men to restore law and order and do so in a manner that promoted positive relations between the national military force and the local partisans. These efforts
resulted in stronger ties between the national polity and local political leaders.

One last area in which Greene demonstrated great skill, and one that was
likewise a key in building the legitimacy of the Whig cause in South Carolina,
was his relationship with the civilian authority. Greene developed a close and
productive relationship with John Rutledge, the fugitive governor of the state,
and later with his successor, John Mathews. The siege of Charleston forced
Rutledge and other important figures in the Whig government to abandon the
city. After that Rutledge had continued to fulfill his duties as governor in absentia.[59] Greene included Rutledge in his planning for future actions. One example of this confidence dates from December 5, 1781: "From the preparations
making in Charleston for its defense and from the measures taken to incorporate the tories, and embody the negroes, as well as spirit up the Savages, it
appears the Enemy have farther designs upon this country. It is difficult to tell
what will be their plan; nor can we form an idea how far European politicks
may affect our operations here. Our attention is naturally directed to two objects, one is to cover this country, the other, to drive the Enemy from their
strong holds[;] an additional force to our present may become necessary for
either or both."[60]

This communication brought Rutledge into Greene's process of weigh-
ing the options in preparation for future operations. In addition Greene presented the governor with his input on what the goals of these operations should

encompass. The last line also implies the possibility of arming the slaves, something that Rutledge opposed and a measure that the Whigs did not adopt.

Not only did Greene bring the political authorities into his ruminations when discussing strategy, he also took an active role in the debate over confiscating and dividing Loyalist property. Many among the Whig leadership sought to recoup their property losses by sequestering the estates of Loyalists. Greene took a balanced approach to questions concerning the nature and disposition of Loyalist property. Writing to Mathews from Ashley Hill, South Carolina, on October 14, 1782, Greene suggested, "In deciding upon the present question I only wish that original claims may not supersede such new rights as appear to be authorized by the Law of Nations and are conformable to practice of most; if not all of the States in the progress of this war." Greene supported the idea of sequestering some Loyalist property. He did impose limitations on the practice, limits set by practical necessity, a point he made clear in the same letter: "Since I have had the command in the Southern department I flatter my self every body who has had any connection with me in the order of business will do me the justice to say that I have always been as attentive to the rights of the Citizen as to the claims of the Army and that the property of the people has suffered as little depradation from the army as could be expected from the Nature of the war and the manner of subsisting it."[61]

Greene continued his support for civil authority in general and of Mathews in particular on November 7, 1782, when he wrote the governor to clear up a misunderstanding concerning access to Charleston, then still occupied by the British: "I did not know until I received your letter of the 6th that it is known that the enemy intended to evacuate Charlestown to prohibit any person from having the benefit of a flag to settle such private concerns with those that were going away as might be necessary for their domestic happiness. Nor did I conceive that granting passports for this purpose was counteracting the wishes of those in power much less bringing the Government into contempt and placing you in an unfavorable light with the people."[62]

Greene's concern for the legitimacy of the civil authority comes through clearly in these comments. Beyond taking Rutledge into the process of making strategy and presenting Mathews with suggestions as to how to dispose of Loyalist property, Greene worked to give the appearance of acting as a servant to the civil authority. The term "appearance" is applied consciously because for much of the period of Greene's command in the Southern Department, the power of the civil authority stood as more perceived than real. So much is demonstrated in the earlier communication between Marion and Greene concerning the treatment of the soldiers caught marauding. Still the Continental general labored ceaselessly to return the beleaguered state to some semblance of civilian rule. Likewise Greene's efforts were not tied lina, but under the auspices of his command, they stre well.

When General Anthony Wayne went to command ir vided advice on how to reestablish Continental control instructions contained wisdom gained through his exp lina. In many ways his words summarize his overall c every means in your power, to soften the malignity ar subsisting between Whig and Tory; and put a stop, as i cruel custom of putting them to death after they have prisoners. The practice of plundering, you will endea possible; and point out to the militia, the ruinous con Let your discipline be as regular and as rigid as the n your troops will admit."[63]

Stopping the execution of prisoners was a key to the side of law and order. If soldiers, even paramilitari be treated as prisoners of war, with all the rights thereto, they were more likely to surrender than figl those [passion and resentment] to influence us, a s hurry us into acts of the most horrid cruelty; and, wl of people respecting severity, both philosophy and secution does but confirm the error it is meant to think those measures highly unwarrantable, which and in fact only increase our enemies."[64]

The notion that the use of indiscriminate or un the number of enemies is common sense. Further essary combination of political and military thinkir actions in South Carolina. Thinking of this sort wa hoped to retake the South. By restraining the n activities vis-à-vis the Loyalists, Greene and the C herents to the Whig cause.[65] The same held true f it helped to create a certain level of stability and tl where a civil government could develop.

In addition to insisting that militia leaders abi the indiscriminate use of violence, Greene worl environment of law and order, one where a sta could resume functioning. One means of achievi of private property. In the later stages of the cor proponent of such protections. In October 178 the announcement of a sale of horses taken f

British found it increasingly difficult to get Loyalist support for military ventures. Finally, in order to be perceived as legitimate and law abiding, the military had to facilitate the installation of a legitimate civilian government and then act in a subordinate role to that government. Even if the government were merely a skeleton, it could claim legitimacy dating back to the days prior to the British invasion, which gave Greene something to work with. By the same token, the British never set up a civilian government, a point often criticized even by the Loyalists. Likewise, in their backing of the Loyalist military apparatus, the British simultaneously refrained from integrating African Americans and Native Americans in their overall strategy for conquering and holding South Carolina.[68] Thus some portion of the credit for Greene's success is owed to the British for the actions they failed to take.

Greene and his subordinates developed a climate where a civil government could reassert itself. As historian Russell F. Weigley phrased it, "Behind Greene's protective lines the South Carolina Assembly resumed its sessions."[69] With the meeting of thirteen senators and sixty-nine representatives at Jacksonborough on January 18, 1782, civil government began to return to South Carolina. Shortly thereafter the state's leaders recognized Greene's contribution to its autonomy. Hugh Rutledge, speaker of the South Carolina House of Representatives, wrote that his colleagues were "impressed with a Sense of the very signal Service which you have rendered to this State, & which fully entitled you to the most grateful Acknowledgements of a free & generous People."[70] Thus the Whig political leadership identified Greene as one of the key factors in their return to power. As soon as a civilian government began to coalesce, Greene made it seem that the men under his command were under civil control. As one historian aptly phrased it, "The extent of Greene's intervention in civil affairs directly correlated to the amount of social order. . . . Once state government began functioning, however, Greene interfered with its operation as little as possible."[71] By standing for law and order, the rights of prisoners, and protection of property, Greene made the Continentals and their partisan allies the choice of the majority of the people and thus gained legitimacy for the Whig cause in the South.

NOTES

The author would like to thank Lawrence Babits, Charles Baxley, Joanna Craig, Dennis Conrad, John Maass, Curtis Morgan, Jim Piecuch, and all the others who participated in or helped to organize the 2006 Nathanael Greene Symposium in Camden, South Carolina, for creating a fantastic environment for the exchange of information and discussion of the highest caliber on Greene and his efforts in the southern campaigns.

1. Since the experiences of both states have their own complexities, South Carolina will be the sole focus of the present examination.

2. For comparisons between the American War of Independence and the Vietnam conflict, see John M. Dederer, *Making Bricks without Straw: Nathanael Greene's Southern Campaign and Mao Tse-Tung's Mobile War* (Manhattan, Kans.: Sunflower Press, 1983), 19; among other works in this genre are Ray L. Bowers Jr., "The American Revolution: A Study in Insurgency." *Military Review* 46 (July 1966): 64–72; Thomas C. Barrow, "The American Revolution as a Colonial War for Independence," *William and Mary Quarterly*, 3rd ser., 25 (July 1968): 452–68. Louis D. F. Frasche, "Problems of Command: Cornwallis, Partisans, and Militia, 1780," *Military Review* 57 (April 1977): 60–74; and John Shy, "The Military Conflict Considered as Revolutionary War," in *A People Numerous and Armed: Reflections on the Military Struggle for American Independence* (New York: Oxford University Press, 1976), 193–224. These comparisons finally reached a point where they drew criticism from Don Higginbotham in "Now and Then: The Vietnamization of the American Revolution," *American Heritage* 32 (October/November 1981): 79–80; Higginbotham developed his critique further in "Reflections on the War of Independence, Modern Guerrilla Warfare, and the War in Vietnam" in *Arms and Independence: The Military Character of the American Revolution*, edited by Ronald Hoffman and Peter J. Albert (Charlottesville: University Press of Virginia, 1984), 1–24. To date, the earliest work I have found that looks at the conflict as an insurgency is John B. Landrum, *Colonial and Revolutionary History of Upper South Carolina* (Greenville, S.C.: Printed by Shannon, 1897), 65. For the comparison of the War of Independence to the Iraq War, see Michael Stephenson, *Patriot Battles: How the War of Independence was Fought* (New York: HarperCollins, 2007), xix. An extended examination of this comparison between the War of Independence and the Iraq War serves as the premise of Michael Rose, *Washington's War: The American War of Independence to the Iraq Insurgency* (New York: Pegasus, 2007).

3. Stephen Conway makes the case for such a tiered approach to the conflict in his *The War of American Independence* (London: Arnold, 1995).

4. Jim Piecuch, *Three Peoples, One King: Loyalists, Indians, and Slaves in the Revolutionary South, 1775–1782* (Columbia: University of South Carolina Press, 2008), 183.

5. Robert M. Calhoon, *The Loyalists in Revolutionary America, 1760–1781* (New York: Harcourt Brace Jovanovich, 1973), 487.

6. *The Papers of General Nathanael Greene*, edited by Richard K. Showman, Dennis R. Conrad, and Roger N. Parks, 13 vols. (Chapel Hill: University of North Carolina Press, 1976–2005), 8:xiii.

7. Hugh F. Rankin, "The Moore's Creek Bridge Campaign, 1776," *North Carolina Historical Review* 30 (January 1953): 23–60. For information on the Cherokee War, see John Grenier, *The First Way of War: American War Making on the Frontier* (New York: Cambridge University Press, 2005); John Oliphant, *Peace and War on the Anglo-Cherokee Frontier, 1756–1763* (Baton Rouge: Louisiana State University Press, 2001); Tom Hatley, *The Dividing Paths: Cherokees and South Carolinians through the Era of Revolution* (New York: Oxford University Press, 1993); David H. Corkran, *The Cherokee Frontier: Conflict and Survival, 1740–1762* (Norman: University of Oklahoma Press, 1962); and Corkran, *The Carolina Indian Frontier* (Columbia: University of South Carolina Press, 1970). See also Clyde R. Ferguson, "General Andrew Pickens," Ph.D. diss., Duke University, 1960,

11–13, for an excellent discussion on the impact of service in this war on one of the future partisan leaders.

8. David K. Wilson, *The Southern Strategy: Britain's Conquest of South Carolina and Georgia, 1775–1780* (Columbia: University of South Carolina Press, 2005), xi. For an excellent and concise discussion of the failures of British strategy in regard to which groups they should employ, see Jim Piecuch, "Incompatible Allies: Loyalists, Slaves, and Indians in Revolutionary South Carolina," in *War and Society in the American Revolution: Mobilization and Home Fronts*, edited by John Resch and Walter Sargent (DeKalb: Northern Illinois University Press, 2007), 191–214, which is a much abridged version of the argument he elaborates in his *Three Peoples, One King*.

9. For information on these engagements, see Rankin, "Moore's Creek Bridge Campaign"; Ferguson, "General Andrew Pickens," 21–28, contains some discussion of the Snow Campaign, as does Walter Edgar, *Partisans and Redcoats: The Southern Conflict That Turned the Tide of the American Revolution* (New York: Morrow, 2001), 32–38.

10. For the Drayton peace mission, as it is sometimes called, and the implications of the associations, see Edgar, *Partisans and Redcoats*, 31–32, and J. Russell Snapp, "William Henry Drayton: The Making of a Conservative Revolutionary," *Journal of Southern History* 57 (November 1991): 637–58. Jerome D. Nadelhaft, *The Disorders of War: The Revolution in South Carolina* (Orono: University of Maine Press, 1981), provides an excellent account of the political transformations occurring within South Carolina during and after the War of Independence. See also Wayne E. Lee, "The American Revolution" in *Daily Lives of Civilians in Wartime Early America from the Colonial Period to the Civil War*, edited by David S. Heidler and Jeanne T. Heidler (Westport, Conn,; Greenwood Press, 2007), 35–37.

11. The Little River District returned three open Tories, Robert Cunningham, Jacob Bowman, and Henry O'Neall, the last of whom actually appeared and participated in the legislative session of 1779. Robert Stansbury Lambert, *South Carolina Loyalists in the American Revolution* (Columbia: University of South Carolina Press, 1987), 74.

12. Council of Safety to William Thomson, August 31, 1775, in David R. Chesnutt, ed., *The Papers of Henry Laurens*, vol. 10 (Columbia: University of South Carolina Press, 1985), 353.

13. Piecuch, *Three Peoples, One King*, 60, 101.

14. Wilson, *The Southern Strategy*, 61–64.

15. Carl P. Borick, *A Gallant Defense: The Siege of Charleston, 1780* (Columbia: University of South Carolina Press, 2003).

16. Michael C. Scoggins, *The Day It Rained Militia: Huck's Defeat and the Revolution in the South Carolina Backcountry, May–July 1780* (Charleston, S.C.: History Press, 2005), 49; Edgar, *Partisans and Redcoats*, 54–55.

17. The most recent account is James Piecuch, "Massacre or Myth: Banastre Tarleton at the Waxhaws, May 29, 1780," *Southern Campaigns of the American Revolution* 1 (October 2004): 3–9. Other important discussions include Thomas A. Rider, "Massacre or Myth: No Quarter at the Waxhaws," M.A. thesis, University of North Carolina, 2002; and Edgar, *Partisans and Redcoats*, 55–57, 69; see also Dan L. Morrill, *The Southern Campaigns*

of the American Revolution (Mount Pleasant, S.C.: Nautical & Aviation Publishing, 1993), 77–80.

18. Scoggins, *The Day It Rained Militia*. This work provides an excellent account of not only Huck's Defeat but also the other small clashes that took place in the backcountry after the fall of Charleston.

19. John S. Pancake, *The Destructive War: The British Campaign in the Carolinas, 1780–1782* (University: University of Alabama Press, 1985), 50.

20. Gates's aggressive stance remains controversial. Paul D. Nelson asserted that it was owing in part to contemporary criticisms of Gates's conduct during the Saratoga campaign. See Paul D. Nelson "Horatio Gates in the Southern Department, 1780: Serious Errors and a Costly Defeat," *North Carolina Historical Review* 50 (July 1973): 256–72. For Gates's role in the Battle of Camden, see John R. Maass, *Horatio Gates and the Battle of Camden — "That Unhappy Affair," August 16, 1780* (Camden, S.C.: Kershaw County Historical Society, 2001).

21. Terry Golway, *Washington's General: Nathanael Greene and the Triumph of the American Revolution* (New York: Holt, 2005), 204–5.

22. For information on the reinforcements received by the Delaware Continentals, see Christopher Ward, *The Delaware Continentals* (Wilmington: Historical Society of Delaware, 1941), 356–57. Though dated, this work remains the best source of information on the unit. Also useful is C. P. Bennett, "The Delaware Regiment in the Revolution," *Pennsylvania Magazine of History and Biography* 9 (January 1886): 451–62.

23. This penchant to begin the journey home prior to the end of their time in the field stemmed from different understandings as to what their time of service entailed, whether it was actual time in the field, or the total of time marching from home and back.

24. Harry M. Ward, *Between the Lines: Banditti of the American Revolution* (Westport, Conn.: Praeger, 2002).

25. Scoggins, *The Day It Rained Militia*, 155–59.

26. The rules of war and their effect on the conduct of conflicts in the eighteenth century constitute a separate but related topic. The principle work that delineated what were considered the proper practices at the time was Hugo Grotius, *De Jure Belli ac Pacis* (1646). A very good overview article of notions of what constituted just warfare practices in the period can be found in Dan Edelstein, "War and Terror: The Law of Nations from Grotius to the French Revolution," *French Historical Studies* 31 (Spring 2008): 229–62.

27. This argument concerning the winning of the support of the local populace is made in a more general sense by John A. Lynn, "Patterns of Insurgency and Counterinsurgency," *Military Review* 84 (July–August 2005): 22–27.

28. Greene to Francis Marion, December 4, 1780, *The Papers of General Nathanael Greene*, 6:520.

29. David Keithly, "Poor, Nasty and Brutish: Guerrilla Operations in America's First Civil War," *Civil Wars*, 4 (Autumn 2001): 46.

30. On this point see James Kirby Martin and Mark Edward Lender, *A Respectable Army: The Military Origins of the Republic, 1763–1789* (Wheeling, Ill: Harlan Davidson, 1982). They argue that Washington sought to create a European-style army from early in the war.

31. Ward, *Delaware Continentals*, 350–57.

32. Otho Holland Williams to Baron Friedrich von Steuben, October 12, 1780, Otho Holland Williams Papers, Maryland Historical Society, Baltimore.

33. William Seymour, "A Journal of the Southern Expedition," *Pennsylvania Magazine of History and Biography* 7 (July 1883): 292.

34. Richard J. Batt, "The Maryland Continentals, 1780–1782." Ph.D. diss., Tulane University, 1974, 71–72. It is worth noting that this policy paid dividends later in the war. For example, while the Americans did plunder the British camp at the Battle of Eutaw Springs, the regulars, such as Lee's Legion, and more to the point, John Eager Howard's Maryland troops, held their places in the line. See Batt, "The Maryland Continentals," 202.

35. Don Higginbotham, *Daniel Morgan Revolutionary Rifleman* (Chapel Hill: University of North Carolina Press, 1961). See also Lawrence E. Babits, *A Devil of a Whipping: The Battle of Cowpens* (Chapel Hill: University of North Carolina Press, 1998), 10–25.

36. Greene to Daniel Morgan, December 16, 1780, *The Papers of General Nathanael Greene*, 6:589–90.

37. Mark A. Clodfelter, "Between Virtue and Necessity: Nathanael Greene and the Conduct of Civil-Military Relations in the South, 1780–1782," *Military Affairs* 52 (October 1988): 173.

38. Scoggins, *The Day It Rained Militia*, 64–65.

39. Babits, *A Devil of a Whipping*, is the best treatment of this campaign.

40. Certainly the initiative had already begun to shift with the defeat of Patrick Ferguson at Kings Mountain in October 1780. It was an important victory, but it was one gained by the militia, and the focus here is on the Continentals and Greene.

41. John Buchanan, *The Road to Guilford Courthouse: The American Revolution in the Carolinas* (New York: Wiley, 1997), 372–83. The most recent history of the battle is Lawrence E. Babits and Joshua B. Howard, *Long, Obstinate, and Bloody: The Battle of Guilford Courthouse* (Chapel Hill: University of North Carolina Press, 2009).

42. Greene to George Washington, March 29, 1781, quoted in William Johnson, *Sketches of the Life and Correspondence of Nathanael Greene*, 2 vols. (Charleston, A. E. Miller, 1822), 2:37.

43. Greene to Baron von Steuben, April 2, 1781, *The Papers of General Nathanael Greene*, 7:24.

44. Clodfelter, "Between Virtue and Necessity," 173.

45. Piecuch, *Three Peoples, One King*, 280–85.

46. David K. Bowden, *The Execution of Isaac Hayne* (Lexington, S.C.: Sandlapper Store, 1977), 29–32.

47. Nisbet Balfour to Henry Clinton, Letterbook of Lieutenant Colonel Nisbet Balfour, British Commandant of Charleston, S.C. Charleston, S.C., 1 January–1 December 1781, MSS L2001F617 (bound), 68, Robert Charles Fergusson Collection, Society of the Cincinnati, Washington, D.C.

48. Bowden, *The Execution of Isaac Hayne*, 34.

49. Greene to William Henderson, August 12, 1781, *The Papers of General Nathanael Greene*, 9:169.

50. Greene to William Henderson, August 16, 1781, ibid., 9:189.

51. Greene to Thomas McKean, August 25, 1781, ibid., 9:242.

52. The main organizer of Greene's supply lines from Virginia was General von Steuben. For a detailed discussion of his efforts, see Paul Lockhart, *The Drillmaster of Valley Forge: The Baron de Steuben and the Making of the Continental Army* (Washington, D.C.: Smithsonian Books/New York: Collins, 2008), 229–57.

53. Gregory J. W. Urwin, "Cornwallis and the Slaves of Virginia: A New Look at the Yorktown Campaign," *Proceedings of the 28th Congress of the International Commission of Military History*, August 11–17, 2002, 172–92.

54. Piecuch, *Three Peoples, One King*, 278–88.

55. Greene to Stephen Drayton, December 9, 1781, *The Papers of General Nathanael Greene*, 10:16.

56. Greene to Francis Marion, January 16, 1781, ibid., 7:132. The letter continues: "If the trial is not meant to be capital, you have sufficient authority to try for less offenses, as brigadier General of the State. But if the trial is meant to be capital I will forward you a commission for holding such a Court."

57. Charles Royster, *Light-Horse Harry Lee and the Legacy of the American Revolution* (Baton Rouge: Louisiana State University Press, 1981), 18. On Francis Marion as a Continental officer and also on his restraint in warfare, see Hugh F. Rankin, *Francis Marion: The Swamp Fox* (New York: Crowell, 1973), 9–10, 127.

58. Greene to Thomas Sumter, December 27, 1781, *The Papers of General Nathanael Greene*, 10:120.

59. On John Rutledge's tenure as governor during the British invasion and occupation of South Carolina, see James Haw, *John and Edward Rutledge of South Carolina* (Athens: University of Georgia Press, 1997), 111–61.

60. Greene to John Rutledge, December 5, 1781, *The Papers of General Nathanael Greene*, 6:20–21.

61. Greene to John Mathews, October 14, 1782, ibid., 11:57–58.

62. Greene to John Mathews, November 7, 1782, ibid., 11:156.

63. Johnson, *Sketches*, 2:277.

64. Ibid., 2:250–51.

65. Even with Greene's measures, the problem of switching sides remained endemic in the South until after the British surrender at Yorktown. See Jac Weller, "The Irregular War in the South," *Military Affairs* 24 (Autumn 1960): 134.

66. Greene to John Mathews, October 20, 1782, *The Papers of General Nathanael Greene*, 11:94.

67. Lawrence E. Babits, "Greene's Strategy in the Southern Campaign, 1780–81," in *Adapting to Conditions: War and Society in the Eighteenth Century*, edited by Maarten Ultee (University: University of Alabama Press, 1986), 135–44.

68. Lambert, *South Carolina Loyalists*, 146. See also Piecuch, "Incompatible Allies."

69. Russell F. Weigley, *The Partisan War: The South Carolina Campaign of 1780–1782* (Columbia: University of South Carolina Press, 1970), 71.

70. Hugh Rutledge to Greene, February 26, 1782, *The Papers of General Nathanael Greene*, 10:420.

71. Clodfelter, "Between Virtue and Necessity," 174.

"With humanity, justice and moderation"

Nathanael Greene and the Reconciliation of the Disaffected in the South, 1780–1783

John R. Maass

*A*fter the British decided to concentrate offensive operations in the southern states in late 1778, the struggle for American independence there was principally a civil war.[1] While there was a traditional military contest between regular armies in the field, the primary conflict was a bloody internecine struggle between Loyalists and rebels—a civil war marked by plundering, property destruction, violence, and murder. The concurrent conflicts created great difficulties for patriot military and civilian leaders in the nascent southern states, who were attempting to establish political legitimacy through the restoration of order and stability. No American leader was more aware of these challenges than Major General Nathanael Greene, the Rhode Islander who assumed Continental command in the South in December 1780. The need to rebuild the southern states was of paramount importance to Greene, who recognized the necessity of ending uncontrolled violence among the citizenry. Greene and other patriot leaders had to balance the need for an end to the chaos through some reconciliation with the region's Loyalists as the war ended, with the strong desire among many Whigs to resort to violence, retribution, and property confiscation against their enemies. Greene consistently sought to limit retributive violence and calls for vengeance. He worked to foster a spirit of conciliation in order to bring peace, prosperity, and order to the South. This position, however, was not universally shared by all supporters of the American cause, often frustrating Greene's efforts to ensure leniency toward Loyalists during the war's final years.

Disaffection from the American independence movement among a large number of the inhabitants of the southern states often resulted in violent behavior, which served to undermine the authority and even the existence of the Revolutionary movement, particularly in the early 1780s. As Governor Thomas Burke of North Carolina complained, "it is our misfortune to have among us a large Settlement of people who were never thoroughly United with us, and who have always become very dangerous Instruments in the hands of the Enemy."[2] Much the same could be said as well of South Carolina and Georgia, where lawless hostility produced thousands of victims, many of whom were civilians. Shocking barbarities produced bitter resentment against the Tories who committed them and were followed all too often by reprisals of equal savagery. These outrages, few of which were officially countenanced by American or British authorities, created an unstable and chaotic military, political, and social situation. Examples of these outrages have been provided in several recent studies of the American Revolution.[3] A brief overview of the Loyalist presence in the South is a useful background for an examination of Greene's efforts to end destructive violence and reestablish order by reintegrating the Tories into society.

The daunting prospect of a large number of estranged Loyalists faced patriots from the beginning of the war. As Carole W. Troxler has suggested, this disaffection may be seen as early as 1774 in opposition to the colonies' nonimportation movement to protest the British government's "abuses" of their North American provinces.[4] North Carolina encountered a large insurgency of Loyalists at the start of the war but managed to defeat their uprising in late February 1776 at the Battle of Moore's Creek Bridge. Many Loyalist insurrections occurred in North Carolina through 1782. Tories attacked Whig soldiers and civilians, burned their homes, committed murders, raided supplies, conspired to kill state officials, and even managed to capture the state's governor, Thomas Burke, in 1781. Large sections of the state were controlled almost completely by Tories, notably the lower Cape Fear region. One historian has claimed that "North Carolina probably contained a greater number of Loyalists in proportion to its population than did any other colony." Although this statement is unverifiable, it suggests the level of disaffection within the state.[5]

Beginning in 1775, South Carolina had a similar experience with conflicts between Loyalist and Whig militia units. In that year Loyalists laid siege to the Whig stronghold at Ninety Six, forcing its surrender, but the Tories suffered defeat themselves a few months later in the so-called Snow Campaign of November and December, during which they were defeated at the Big Cane Brake.[6] Sporadic violence along these lines remained a worrisome problem for South Carolinians, especially in the backcountry.[7] Once the British began their southern campaign at the end of 1778, matters took a turn for the worse for the patriots. Not only did Charleston and its large garrison fall to British arms in May 1780, but a second American army suffered a devastating defeat at Camden, South Carolina, three months later. British military success in the state increased Tory activities, which quickly degenerated into a destructive and murderous civil war that caused incalculable destruction across the land. By 1782 part of northeastern South Carolina contained so many active Loyalists that a truce was arranged with them, in effect creating an enclave, which the Whigs under General Francis Marion pledged not to attack. The state remained burdened by violence and disorder until the British evacuated Charleston in December 1782.[8]

Georgia too had its share of internal violence and destruction, in part because of its proximity to the British base at St. Augustine in East Florida, from which many Tory partisans operated to the dismay of Georgia's Whigs. The most notable of these troublesome Tories was Thomas Brown, who came to command a regiment of Loyalists known as the King's Rangers. Brown's partisans and others like them caused great chaos in the Georgia and South Carolina too and incited retaliation by Whigs. Much of the violence occurred in the backcountry, while three abortive American invasions of East Florida did nothing to encourage Tories to switch sides. Adding to the mayhem in Georgia were three key American defeats: the British capture of Savannah in 1778 under Lieutenant Colonel Archibald Campbell, followed closely by his capture of Augusta in January; a disastrous Whig defeat at Briar Creek in March 1779; and the failure of a Franco-American force to retake Savannah in October 1779. These military setbacks for the revolutionaries further emboldened Tory insurgents as both sides sought to establish governments that would be perceived as legitimate in the eyes of the inhabitants—often at the same time.[9]

With consistent and widespread Tory violence in the Carolinas and Georgia by December 1778, reaction to the savagery on the part of those favoring independence was multifaceted. Whigs responded to Loyalist depredations with equal acts of violence and cruelty, such as the hanging of several Tory leaders captured at the Battle of Kings Mountain in October 1780, many "Tory hunting" campaigns conducted by vengeful militiamen in the war's last years, and reprisals often carried out by Whigs with little or no legitimate authority to do so. While the details of properly authorized military efforts by Francis Marion, Andrew Pickens, Griffith Rutherford, Elijah Clarke, and others against Loyalist forces are well-known, smaller local campaigns not sanctioned by state governments or Continental commanders were commonplace. Many state and local leaders advocated harsh treatment of the enemy within their midst. Moreover, during the war and its immediate aftermath, states enacted laws—many punitive in nature—discriminating against the Loyalists. Taken together, these various attempts to rid their states of these violent, disaffected men demonstrate that many southern patriots were inclined to eschew lenient treatment of their internal foes.[10]

In North Carolina, Loyalists quickly observed that the state did not intend to allow them to remain there quietly. From the beginning of the Revolution, patriots required that inhabitants take oaths of allegiance (known as the Association) to the new state governments and reacted harshly to those who refused to do so.[11] In 1776 North Carolinians passed an ordinance for punishing those within the state "bearing evil minds, disaffection and Enmity against the Freedom thereof," particularly those subversives who incited insurrections "and Conspiracy."[12] Starting in April 1777, the new state government passed several punitive acts regarding the Loyalists, beginning with a treason law enacted "for preventing the Dangers which may arise from the Persons disaffected to the State."[13] Those found guilty under this and similar subsequent acts were liable to have their property seized and sold for the benefit of the state, a practice that began in 1776 and was widespread by the early 1780s.[14] Worse yet, the state executed some of those convicted of treason, though the application of this ultimate punishment appears to have been uneven.[15] More commonly Loyalists were whipped by local authorities.[16] Many Tories who sought pardons were obliged to serve twelve-month tours as Continental soldiers before being granted amnesty. While the state did pass the Act of Pardon and Oblivion in 1783 "for past offenses . . . in the course of the late unhappy war," it specifically excluded several notable Tory leaders, anyone who had accepted Crown commissions or who had committed "murder, robbery, rape, or house burning," and barred them from state office holding. Others who tried to reenter the state after the hostilities concluded were not permitted to do so, though some exceptions were later made. As one Cape Fear valley resident noted in 1783, those Loyalists "who went away at the [British] evacuation of Wilmington may return in safety unless they have done something to exasperate the people; in which case there is no answering what violences may be committed."[17]

Many South Carolinians were also inclined to harsh measures against Tories, including vigilante violence. This vindictive spirit extended at times to British merchants, to whom many South Carolina planters were indebted. In addition, during the war's later years, the South Carolina assembly passed harsh measures against those who remained loyal to King George III, including such punishments as banishment, financial liens on estates, and property confiscation.[18] Many Whigs held that "the Peace and safety of this State require that proper examples be made of such offenders," as the language of a confiscation act made clear.[19] Governor John Rutledge offered some leniency to the disaffected in a 1781 proclamation but included such conditions as service in a Whig militia unit for six months. However, those Loyalists who had served as commissioned civil or military officers were not eligible for this pardon. As historian Robert

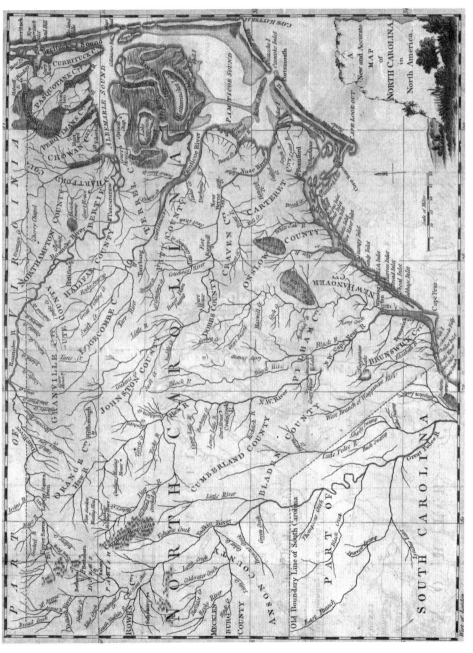

North Carolina in 1779

Weir has noted, other state leaders who seemed to favor reconciliation with the Tories by allowing them some mercy were often sharply criticized for doing so by vindictive South Carolinians, mostly from the backcountry.[20] In a spirit of revenge, the state's assembly established special courts of oyer and terminer to hear cases against Loyalists accused of barbarous crimes. As observers reported in the 1780s, Carolinians—particularly those in the western part of the state—were set on revenge. Incidents of Loyalists being abused in 1783 and 1784 were not unheard of. Assemblymen from coastal regions were somewhat more forgiving, but even as late as 1787, the legislature refused to pass a bill that would have repealed the confiscation acts.[21]

A penchant for punitive treatment of active Loyalists was to be found in Georgia as well. The patriot state government demanded oaths of allegiance from its citizens, and forced those who refused that requirement to leave the state. Since the redcoats were successful at reestablishing their authority over much of Georgia during the war, authority there swung back and forth between British and American control; the result was that both sides confiscated the estates and property of their foes. Georgia revolutionaries passed confiscation acts in 1778 and 1782 against those behind British lines, those who refused militia service, and anyone suspected of being inimical to the cause of liberty. Rebel legislative acts in 1782 declared several Loyalist men guilty of treason, summarily banished them, and forbade them from returning to the state on pain of death. Many disaffected Georgians were thus forced to flee the state for St. Augustine, already overcrowded by refugees. As in the Carolinas, Whigs in Georgia did allow some Loyalists to remain in the state with their property but made it conditional on military service.[22]

Thus, not only did the southern states experience a vicious civil war, one that was intensified when British troops began their attempt to subjugate the South in 1778, these states also contained within them a powerful element of vengefulness, a spirit against conciliatory measures aimed at bringing the Loyalists back into the political and social fold. Inhabitants who saw their homes burned, their friends and families injured or killed, and their prosperity ruined, could not readily be counted on to reconcile with their Tory enemies or allow them to reintegrate unpunished into a postwar society. Likewise depredations against the disaffected often pushed them to support the enemy. A North Carolinian concluded that "barbarous and unjust treatment has driven many to the Tories who would gladly have remained peaceful."[23] Such animosities served to increase the escalating violence in Georgia and the Carolinas, which made the task of restoring order and creating legitimate, effective state governments all the more difficult for those charged with doing so, especially Nathanael Greene.

If the Rhode Island general had been unaware of the chaotic situation in his new southern bailiwick prior to his assumption of command, he quickly came to appreciate the magnitude of the violence as well as the clamor for revenge. From South Carolina in late December 1780, Greene wrote that "the whole country is in danger of being laid waste by the Whigs and Torrys, who pursue each other with as much relentless fury as beasts of prey."[24] In similar language two weeks later he noted the dangers such violence posed for the southern states and their inhabitants. "The whigs and tories pursue one another in this country with little less than savage fury," he observed, "and such a spirit for plundering prevails, as threatens the depopulation of the whole country."[25] Such brutality continued unabated into 1781 and beyond. In May 1781 Greene lamented that "nothing but blood and slaughter have prevailed among the Whigs and Tories [of North Carolina], and their inveteracy against each other, must if it continues depopulate this Country."[26] The potent Loyalist threat was never far from Greene's mind as he campaigned in South Carolina during the spring and summer of 1781. "The Majority [of people] is greatly in favor of the Enemies interest now," he wrote, and "the Whigs and the Tories are butchering one another hourly."[27] The general also received many reports of outrages committed by both sides, such as that from Colonel Thomas Wade of North Carolina, who reported that "this Country will be Ruined . . . by the Whiggs [and] Torys that form small parties under no Orders and plunder the Country." Wade opined that "nothing short of hanging will put a stop to that pernicious practice."[28] Writing from South Carolina, Greene concluded that the "animosity between the Whigs and the Tories of this State render their situation truly deplorable. There is not a day passes but there are more or less who fall a sacrafice to this savage disposition." The violence was reciprocal. "The Whigs seem determined to extirpate the Tories and the Tories the Whigs," Greene noted, as "thousands have fallen in this way in this quarter, and the evil rages with more violence than ever. . . . If a stop cannot soon be put to those private massacres[,] this Country will be depopulated in a few months more, as neither Whig nor Tory can live."[29]

Thus General Greene came to understand the brutal nature of the internecine war in the lower South during the early 1780s by observing or hearing about the atrocities so common in that theater. Yet, while some on the patriot side called for vengeance and punitive measures against the Loyalists, Greene instead advocated a moderate course of action distinguished by humane treatment of and leniency toward these enemies as a way of bringing order to the ravaged southern states.

Order was certainly much needed there. Loyalists and patriots frequently plundered each other's homes, which not only resulted in lost or destroyed property but destabilized the states as well. The "spirit of plundering which prevails among the inhabitants adds not a little to our difficulties," Greene complained.[30] He deplored this all-too-common practice, which lasted until the end of the war and served to provoke bitter feelings among the populace. Such vindictive larceny was "very destructive to the morals and manners of a people. Habits and dispositions founded on this practice soon grow obstinate, and are difficult to restrain. Indeed it is the most direct way of under mining all Government, and never fails to bring the laws in contempt."[31] Therefore Greene sought to curb the practice among his own Continental troops and the states' militia forces as well, as a way to establish order and to stop alienating the disaffected in the department. "The practice of plundering" Greene sought "to Check as much as possible," in that it resulted in "ruinous Consequences," particularly when committed by undisciplined militiamen, who were often subject to less severe discipline than Continental regulars.[32]

In addition to plundering, the impressment of supplies by state and military officials caused many inhabitants to become alienated from the revolutionary cause. Greene sought to minimize the impact of impressment, to show Loyalists that so long as they remained peaceful, his army would treat them with fairness. If foraging, he advised his officers, take "care not to distress the Inhabitants; and give receipts for what is taken . . . all marading and plundering you will punnish on the spot with not less than fifty stripes for each offence."[33] In another situation, regarding the impressment of dragoon horses, Greene instructed General Thomas Sumter of the South Carolina militia to "give certificates for the whole, whether taken from Whig or Tory and if any discrimination is necessary, [let] Government make that hereafter."[34] Similarly, to Colonel Henry "Light-Horse Harry" Lee, Greene wrote, "don't neglect to take all the good horses you may come across; give receipts for all you take to both Whig and Tories."[35] In the field of course, commissary agents and quartermasters did not always comply with these instructions, but they do demonstrate Greene's philosophy of dealing fairly and leniently with those who opposed the Whigs, primarily so as not to alienate these opponents and drive them toward the enemy. Otherwise, as he well knew, "the Inhabitants will become our enemies when they find they are subject to oppression instead of finding protection."[36]

In addition to his attempts to stop the looting of Tories' property, Greene also strove to reduce the level of violence directed toward them. Such a policy, he hoped, would convince the Loyalists to abandon their support of the British. "Try by every means in your power," he ordered General Anthony Wayne in early 1782, "to soften the malignity and deadly resentments subsisting between the Whigs and the tories, and put a stop as much as possible to that cruel custom of putting people to death after they have surrendered themselves prisoners."[37] These efforts were not only in the interests of reducing violence, but would go a long way toward establishing order within the states, as well as the legitimacy of the new revolutionary governments. As Greene noted to Griffith Rutherford, a North Carolina militia general not known for benevolent treatment of Tories, "it has ever been my wish to avoid cruelty and the dignity of our cause requires that it should be marked with humanity, justice and moderation."[38] Greene frequently advised his subordinates to put an end to what he called "private murders," by which he meant the killing of Tories (and for that matter Whigs as well) outside the traditional limits associated with legitimate warfare. "I have, both from motives of Policy, as well as humanity, opposed every measure all in my Power, which had for its object, nothing but revenge and Persecution," he declared in February 1782, a clear statement of his principle that such violence undermined civil and military authority and increased chaos and bloodshed certain to impede reconciliation with the Loyalists.[39]

In Greene's view the most effective way to bring order and stability to the South—and to end abuses such as murder, plunder and house burning—was to adopt a conciliatory stance toward the disaffected of all stripes, save only those who had committed the most flagrant abuses and barbarous acts. He favored pardons for those Tories who took up arms against their Whig neighbors, provided they had served in a military capacity but not as banditti or lawless marauders. Regarding British and Loyalist activities in North Carolina, especially around Wilmington, Greene advised Governor Thomas Burke "to Strike at the root of the evil by removing the British [from Wilmington], and offer these poor deluded [Tory] Wretches some hopes of forgiveness, and you will feel little injury from this class of People."[40] Greene recognized that illegal acts of retribution, such as the execution of Tory officers following the Battle of Kings Mountain, served only to engender even more retributive violence.[41] Greene instead called for leniency as a way to begin to bring peace to the southern states, so that civil institutions might have a better chance to be reestablished. He consistently recommended moderation to all who would listen, "as men may be often reformed by soft means when persecution will only confirm them in their opposition."[42] Moreover, if the disaffected could see that the budding revolutionary governments were acting in a conciliatory manner toward them, it would clearly demonstrate that the southern states were the safer, less costly alternative to support, rather than the British, whose garrisons at Charleston, Savannah, and Wilmington seemed only to perpetuate the destructive war. Convincing the Loyalists that the patriot side had more to offer them in terms of ending the conflict and establishing order became a significant part of Greene's plan to end the chaos in the South and bring about a revolutionary settlement.

Greene certainly recognized that malice toward the disaffected was counterproductive: "Cruelty always marks the authors with disgrace and is generally attended with disadvantage. . . . I would always recommend moderation, not from any regard to the Tories but for our own sakes, cruelty being dishonorable and persecution always increasing the number and force of our enemies."[43] As Greene noted, there was a benefit to be derived from humane treatment of one's enemies,. He objected to making prisoners of those not taken in arms, which "can only lead to increase the Miseries of war without producing any advantage."[44] Not only would such behavior by the Whigs produce few benefits, it would also undermine the efforts of the revolutionaries to establish their own civil institutions, tasks which were made infinitely more difficult amidst these "miseries" of war. "Don't spare any pains to take off the Tories from the british interest," Greene advised Sumter at the end of 1781, "for though we have great reason to hate them, and vengeance would dictate one universal slaughter, yet when we consider how many of our good people must fall a sacrifice in doing it we shall find it will be more in our interest to forgive than to persecute."[45] A few weeks later he elaborated on this theme to Sumter. "Go ahead with the good work of trying to bring them in," he encouraged the South Carolinian, as "it will save the lives of so many people, and perhaps hereafter they may prove good Citizens."[46]

Greene's 1782 correspondence with Georgia governor John Martin provides an illuminating example of the general's position that violence merely begat violence and would ultimately undermine patriot efforts to establish strong, legitimate state governments and peaceful societies. The exchange also shows that not everyone in the South was of the same indulgent mind. "I cannot help recommending it to the consideration of your Excellency," Greene wrote to the governor in January, "to open a door for the disaffected of your state to come in with particular exceptions. . . . It is always dangerous to push people to a state of desperation; and the satisfaction of revenge has but a momentary existence; and is followed by pity and remorse."[47] Martin agreed that leniency was the proper course to adopt and issued a proclamation in February offering pardons and protection to most Georgia Loyalists, flagrant offenders excepted. As the war neared its end, the Georgia legislature was instead inclined to take punitive actions against the Loyalists, such as banishment and confiscation.[48] Martin responded to Greene that "your observations respecting the opening a door for the reception of the disaffected Citizens of our state with particular Restrictions, are in my opinion extremely Just and humane, and such as good policy as this crisis would undoubtedly dictate." With disappointment, however, he continued, "I have more than once urged those very measures during the sitting of the late house of the assembly, which were entirely disregarded, and not the least attention paid to them, owing to the repeated injuries & distresses those very characters have brought upon the Virtuous Citizens of this state. Nature would not be nature, could it immediately forget injuries like these, which impressions are only to be erased by time."[49] Thus, despite the high-mindedness of Greene and Martin, many citizens (in this case Georgians) refused to let bygones be bygones so easily and called instead for punishment for those who opposed them. A piqued Greene could only write back that "legislatures should follow policy[,] not their own private resentments."[50]

While Greene certainly advocated reconciliation with regard to the Loyalists, this did not necessarily mean forgiving and forgetting. As part of their atonement, Loyalist militiamen who left the British lines were to serve militarily in the patriot ranks and take oaths of allegiance.[51] This was especially necessary by 1782, when recruiting efforts to get men to serve in the Continental battalions had stalled all over the South. In the beginning of that year, Greene advised General Wayne that, "when you get into the lower Country [of Georgia] you will invite all the people to join you, and such as shall engage in the service under your command, afford them protection and security."[52] This conditional approach held out the hand of peace, and also attempted to make the American forces more formidable, though with limited success.[53] Along these lines, North Carolina governor Alexander Martin issued a proclamation in December 1781 offering pardons to Tories who would surrender by March 10, 1782, and would "expiate their offence by serving in our Continental Battalions" for twelve months. Those who would be found guilty of murder, robbery, and similarly egregious offenses were not eligible for such clemency.[54]

After Martin's proclamation, Governor Burke (who had recently resumed his post after escaping British captivity) continued this mixed policy of exculpation and atonement. Burke reported to Greene that he "found upon my arrival in the State [North Carolina] that Several persons had been Convicted by the Court of Justice for Treason and Some for other Offences: three have been executed . . . four who are under Sentence of death I propose pardoning on Condition of their faithfully Serving twelve months in the Continental army."[55] Records from state officials and several North Carolina county courts of common pleas and quarter sessions also record this type of judgment in the form of military service for the disaffected who "came in," as contemporaries termed it.[56] In January 1782 Sumter advised Greene that hundreds of Loyalists had surrendered to him during the past two months and that he allowed them to keep their arms so long as they actively served against the British. He was unconcerned that these men might rejoin the British, as he had made them "conspicuous and obnoxious to the enemy" and continuously active in the field, so they had everything fearful to apprehend if they were captured. Greene strongly approved of this "divide and conquer" measure[57] as it coincided with his own policies expressed clearly the year before in a proclamation he issued to backcountry South Carolinians: "Those who have been in the British interest and by their past conduct have rendered themselves obnoxious to their Country have now an opportunity in part to atone for their past conduct by joining the American Army and manifesting by their future conduct a sincere repentance for what is past. . . . It shall be my study upon their behaving properly to afford them all the security in my power from improper resentments and depredations of individuals or plundering parties."[58] Thus, if those who had opposed the revolutionaries abandoned their allegiance to the Crown and actively supported the revolutionary cause, Greene was willing to protect them from retribution at the hands of their former Whig neighbors. Without this assurance few Loyalists would have accepted Greene's offer.

Having returning Loyalists enter the ranks to fight the enemy on behalf of the American cause was, however ironic, an important but secondary benefit to Greene. He was far more insistent that clemency would not only bring a successful conclusion to the war more quickly but also make for a smoother transition to peace once the hostilities were finally over. "Principles of humanity as well as good policy require that proper Measures should be immediately taken to restrain . . . abuses, heal the differences, and unite the people as much as possible," Greene suggested in the summer of 1781, referring to both Whigs and Tories. He recommended that "all parties ought to be strictly prohibited under the penalty of capital punishment from plundering and that no violence should be offered to any of the Inhabitants let their political sentiments be as they may unless they are found in arms." At the same time, the general considered armed men in legitimately established units to be prisoners of war not traitors. There were exceptions, but he insisted that punishments be handled by civil officials, not by vindictive men acting outside the bounds of authority. "If charactors unfriendly to our cause have committed anything which renders them obnoxious to the laws of the land, let Civil Government hereafter inflict such punishments as they may think proper. The idea of exterminating the Tories is not less barbarous than impolitick; and if persisted in, will keep this Country in the greatest confusion and distress." Greene observed that "the disaffected cry for Mercy" and wrote to South Carolina partisan leader Andrew Pickens, "I hope you will exert yourself to bring over the Tories to our interest, and check the growing enormities which prevail among the Whigs in punishing plundering as private avarice or a bloody disposition stimulates them." Greene knew that there would surely be opposition to his conciliatory polices, "sensible [that] the most worthless part of the Whigs will think themselves injured in being restrained; but I am perswaded in doing it you will do honor to the cause of humanity and promote essentially the interest of your country."[59]

A conciliatory policy was not always easy to bring about in the field as not all soldiers concurred with Greene's belief in pardoning the disaffected. Although in 1781 he had "given directions . . . to all the militia officers to promise pardon and forgiveness to the tories that will come in and give up their Arms,"[60] South Carolina's notable partisan Francis Marion, reported in the following year that it was difficult to make arrangements for Loyalists to retire to within the British lines at Charleston. "I found there was some men who had Committed so many Enormaties that my men would kill them though they had been pardoned."[61] Greene received word in the fall of 1781 that North Carolina militia general Griffith Rutherford was harassing Loyalists and burning their homes. Unsure of the veracity of such reports, Greene wrote to Governor Alexander Martin in October; "I hope the report is not true," Greene penned, "for this mode of carrying on the war is so cruel and barbarous that if there were no other objection those would be sufficient. But the policy is not less pernicious than the mode is savage." He knew that such measures might harden the hearts of the disaffected rather than win them over. "Driving away the Tories without discrimination will render their situation desperate and make them from a feeble and partial enemy a firm and determinate foe. . . . The infidelities of the Tories may be sufficiently punished without having recourse to such desperate measures."[62]

Shortly thereafter, a concerned Greene wrote directly to Rutherford and enunciated his thoughts on the treatment of Tories: "Persecution does but confirm the cause it is meant to destroy; and therefore I think those measures highly unwarrantable which carries the mark of cruelty and increases our enemies." He reminded the militia commander that "to detach the disaffected from the British interest is our true policy and this can be done by gentle means only." For those who resisted such methods and remained "stubborn and obstinate there is ways and means of bringing them to punishment far more consistent with the dignity of the Government."[63] Greene meant, of course, that Loyalists must be countered by legitimate means (either civil or military) not by wantonness and cruelty. A few months later, as he continued to implore Rutherford to adopt lenient measures to reconcile the disaffected in North Carolina, Greene declared that "I have always observed both in religion and politicks moderation answers the most valuable purposes."[64]

Greene was tireless in his efforts to convince authorities in the southern states to win over the loyalty of the disaffected by eschewing harsh, punitive measures. In December 1781 for example he briefly corresponded with two South Carolina Loyalist militia officers, who inquired about obtaining pardons. Although Greene responded that this was a civil matter, not a military one, he did advise the two that he thought such an act of forgiveness would be granted them. "I . . . recommend your leaving the Enemy as soon as possible and that you communicate it to all your friends and indeed to the whole body of the Tories," he advised them.[65] In the same month, he applauded Sumter's efforts to offer leniency to South Carolina Loyalists. "I entirely approve of your plan of receiving the Tories," Greene encouraged Sumter, "I think it perfectly consistent with humanity and sound policy."[66] A few months later, Greene recommended to General Wayne in Georgia that he make a plan "for drawing off the disaffected from the Enemy; granting such persons pardon as have not been extremely obnoxious. At any rate hold out as much encouragement as you can, and treat those kindly who come over to your party."[67] Such leniency would go a long way toward bringing about peace and an end to the disorders of war.

Yet Greene was not unmindful of the dangers Loyalists still posed for the American cause, nor did he seek to overlook their abuses. Instead, he said, "I wish to show them mercy but if they continue obstinate after all these favorable overtures they may expect to suffer all the miseries that war can inflict."[68] Nor was Greene above threatening the use of severe measures as a means of reprisal for British depravity. Writing on the subject of the "barbarous custom" of the British "burning houses & desolating the countryside," Greene informed the enemy at Charleston that "I have made it my study ever since I had the honor to command in this department, to conduct the war upon the most humane principles, and it is my wish to continue to do so; but if your people persist in the practice of burning, I will change the plan and let savage cruelty rage in all the horrors of war."[69] Fortunately he did not have to resort to such extreme measures.

Nevertheless Greene was not uniformly successful in persuading all civil and military leaders of the necessity of granting pardons to those Loyalists who sought them. While Governor John Martin of Georgia was of one mind with the general in this regard, Greene had particular difficulties with North Carolina's governors during the last two years of the war, especially Thomas Burke. An exchange of letters between the two regarding Greene's attempt to arrange a prisoner-of-war exchange, or cartel, highlights the challenges faced by the general and others who sought to bring a close to the chaos of war through lenient means of reintegration of the disaffected into society.[70]

Greene and Burke disagreed notably over the workings of a prisoner-exchange cartel in 1782. The governor wanted to treat Loyalists captured while under British arms as traitors and punish them accordingly. If convicted, these men could face death by hanging, according to civil law. This was a long-held position of Burke's, who was of the opinion as early as 1778 that those North Carolinians who took up arms against the state in the service of the British should be subject to "municipal laws," not treated as prisoners of war.[71] Burke's position interfered with Greene's attempts to get Whigs released from British captivity in the Carolinas, many of whom were held in appalling conditions on prison ships in Charleston harbor. Greene expressed to Burke his belief that "it is much better to effect the relief of our good Citizens by considering the

Tories prisoners of war, than trying them for treason, and leave our best friends in captivity and distress."[72] In other words, by considering those Loyalists captured while serving in a military manner as prisoners, they could be exchanged for captured Whig militiamen, but if the state tried and executed them, they could not be used in the cartel. Such harsh treatment would also inspire retaliation by the British and Loyalists, adding to the chaos in the Carolinas and Georgia.

Burke's position differed from the general's to a degree. He reminded Greene of the many "Outlaws" within North Carolina, "who have always become very dangerous Instruments in the hands of the Enemy." He refused to treat these Loyalists as prisoners of war, because they would then be exempt from civil punishment, whereas the Whigs who did the same thing would not be. The governor also predicted that if every Tory found under arms when captured could claim to be acting under British military authority, such men would then use this protection as a cover for their crimes and abuses. This would, of course, "Increase our domestic Evils and distresses." He continued, "I intend to pardon all who should appear to me guilty of no Offence but bearing Arms with the Enemy and Acting agreeably to the Character of Soldiers, reserving them only as prisoners of War. But those who Should be found to have Committed atrocious Crimes before adhering openly to the Enemy, Or inhuman Barbarities such as the Laws of War will not Justify, afterwards, I intended to resign Altogether to the Civil Magistrate." These men, if convicted in a civil court, would face death. Burke also reported that "Great Numbers [of Loyalists] have Submitted themselves Voluntarily to the Civil Magistrate and now . . . stand tryal for their lives." These men, Burke had decided, would be required to serve in the state's regiments if not condemned by a court, unless they had committed heinous crimes prior to their requests for pardon. He was also clear that if any Carolinians were found to be "devoted to the Enemy," they would need to be banished from the state.[73]

In April 1782 Burke did show that he was willing to treat Loyalists captured in arms as prisoners of war if they had been soldiers serving with the British. Thus he reprieved three Loyalist officers on trial in Salisbury for high treason after the court's judges advised him that the men were not guilty of murder, looting, or other acts of barbarity. (It is telling, however, that the jury did find them guilty of treason despite the judges' opinion to the contrary.) Burke, however, advised Greene that he would order the removal of their families to the British lines as was typically the case with other Loyalists: "This is a necessary, but Severe Consequence of their being admitted on the footing of Prisoners of war and I assure you, Sir, that no part of my duty gives me more sensible pain in the Execution than this, because I foresee it must involve wretched mothers, and helpless infants in cruel want and distress."[74] Doubtless Greene did not regard Burke's insistence on forcibly removing the families of Loyalists from the state as a conciliatory policy.

Burke's successor, Alexander Martin,[75] was less opposed to Greene's position with regard to exchanging Loyalists and showing leniency than Burke had been, or at least he was more pragmatic. Martin reported to Greene in May 1782 that the three Loyalist officers in Salisbury, who by this time had been condemned to death under the state's treason laws, would not be executed "while our Friends are in Captivity," for the "rigor of Laws must give way to policy." These men were by convention recognized as British regular officers and could be exchanged in the cartel for American officers. Martin, however, also advised Greene with regard to other captured Loyalist officers in the custody of North Carolina. If the British refused to exchange them for Carolinians held in Charleston, then the "Treason Laws of this state are to have their full effect."[76] Martin seems to have agreed with Burke regarding Loyalist prisoners; that is to say they were traitors subject to the ultimate punishment, even though many of them committed no atrocities or other crimes. Only the Loyalists' value within the arrangements of the prisoner cartel made Governor Martin decide not to punish the three officers at Salisbury for treason. Greene later responded to Martin that mercy should be shown to those who sought it from the Whig governments so long as it did not leave dangerous individuals within the states to continue to perpetrate violence and destruction. "The interests of the Country will be promoted more by clemency than severity," he concluded.[77] Nevertheless Burke and Martin rejected Greene's suggestions of leniency and used pardons and prisoner exchanges primarily for the practical purpose of gaining the release of as many of their own men as possible from British captivity.

By the end of the war, Greene's persistent admonitions to bring the Loyalists back into the fold seemed to have mixed results. On the one hand, he received some encouraging reports, such as that of North Carolina general John Butler in September 1782 from Chatham County, long an area of disaffection and Tory sympathies, that several Loyalists had recently "surrendered themselves prisoners of war" with no reports of violence against them.[78] Later that year Greene recommended to South Carolina governor John Mathews that he and the legislature consider pardoning Andrew Williamson, a Whig leader earlier in the war who subsequently took British protection once Charleston fell in 1780. Since Williamson later provided the patriot forces with valuable intelligence of British actions "to extenuate the transgressions of his former offences," Greene recommended his pardon. "I hope the political offences of an individual may be cancelled where he employs all his powers for the safety of that people whom he may have offended," the general wrote. Williamson was eventually forgiven, and his confiscated estate returned to him.[79]

Other reports were not so sanguine. By May 1782 Greene had heard that the North Carolina legislature would not adopt moderate treatment of the Loyalists. With regard to this state, a correspondent in Charlotte advised Greene that "I know not what laws they will pass in favor of the tories, but they will be certainly unavailing; for the people seem more than ever occupied with the idea of their distruction."[80] Greene also knew of the deplorable state of the Loyalists in Charleston, most of whom had reason to worry that once the redcoats evacuated the city, they would be at the mercy of their enemies. He noted that "many are wandering in the Streets and fields cursing their former friends for leading them into such distress and ruin. Many in Charlestown beg for mercy but cannot obtain it. The resentment of the people runs so high that the voice of humanity and the falling tear has little or no effect. Perhaps hereafter they will give them a hearing, but at present they will not."[81]

Greene's lamentation about the sad condition the Loyalists were reduced to in Charleston suggests that his implorations for pardon and reconciliation met with only mixed results. At least in the cases of Georgia and South Carolina the state assemblies did show some leniency. In Georgia some Loyalists named in a late-war banishment act were removed from the list of offenders and had their citizenship restored. In both Carolinas many prominent Whigs were sympathetic to their Loyalist neighbors and opposed violence and punitive legislation against them. Some petitioners for clemency received favorable treatment from the assemblies as well. Yet for the most part, Greene's advice went unheeded. The states actively pursued confiscation of Loyalist property, refused to allow many Tories to return to their states after the conclusion of hostilities, and passed punitive legislation to the Loyalists' disadvantage.[82] Nevertheless, in the interest of peace and humanity, Greene appears to have remained fixed in his ideas. He expressed this sentiment in the summer of 1782 in a letter to North Carolina governor Alexander Martin. "Considering the frailties of human nature[,]" Greene concluded, "charity and mercy should be extended in all cases not opposed to the peace and safety of the people."[83]

NOTES

1. For the origins of this strategy, see Paul H. Smith, *Loyalists and Redcoats: A Study in British Revolutionary Policy* (Chapel Hill: University of North Carolina Press, 1964), 79–99; Ira D. Gruber, "Britain's Southern Strategy," in *The Revolutionary War in the South: Power, Conflict, and Leadership,* edited by W. Robert Higgins (Durham: Duke University Press, 1979), 208–14; Don Higginbotham, *The War of American Independence: Military Attitudes, Policies, and Practice, 1763–1789* (New York: Macmillan, 1971), 352–55;

David K. Wilson, *The Southern Strategy: Britain's Conquest of South Carolina and Georgia, 1775–1780* (Columbia: University of South Carolina Press, 2005), 59–64; and Piers Mackesy, *The War for America, 1775–1783* (Cambridge, Mass.: Harvard University Press, 1964), 232–34, 253–70.

    2. Thomas Burke to Nathanael Greene, March 28, 1782, *The Papers of General Nathanael Greene,* edited by Richard K. Showman, Dennis R. Conrad, and Roger N. Parks, 13 vols. (Chapel Hill: University of North Carolina Press, 1976–2005), 10:549–50.

    3. See Wayne E. Lee, *Crowds and Soldiers in Revolutionary North Carolina: The Culture of Violence in Riot and War* (Gainesville: University Press of Florida, 2001), 176–211; Robert M. Calhoon, *The Loyalists in Revolutionary America, 1760–1781* (New York: Harcourt Brace Jovanovich, 1973); Carole Watterson Troxler, *The Loyalist Experience in North Carolina* (Raleigh: North Carolina Division of Archives and History, 1976); Michael A. McDonnell, "Resistance to the American Revolution," in *A Companion to the American Revolution,* edited by Jack P. Greene and J. R. Pole (Malden, Mass.: Blackwell, 2000), 342–51; Robert M. Calhoon, "Loyalism and Neutrality," in *Companion to the American Revolution,* 235–38, 244–46; Ronald Hoffman, "The Disaffected in the Revolutionary South," in *The American Revolution: Explorations in the History of American Radicalism,* edited by Alfred F. Young (DeKalb: Northern Illinois University Press, 1976), 273–316; Ronald Hoffman, Thad Tate, and Peter J. Albert, eds., *An Uncivil War: The Southern Backcountry during the American Revolution* (Charlottesville: University Press of Virginia for the U.S. Capitol Historical Society, 1985); Charles Royster, *A Revolutionary People at War: The Continental Army and American Character, 1775–1783* (Chapel Hill: University of North Carolina Press, 1979); Jerome J. Nadelhaft, *The Disorders of War: The Revolution in South Carolina* (Orono: University of Maine at Orono Press, 1981); Don Higginbotham, *War and Society in Revolutionary America: The Wider Dimensions of Conflict* (Columbia: University of South Carolina Press, 1988); Harry M. Ward, *Between the Lines: Banditti of the American Revolution* (Westport, Conn.: Praeger, 2002); Rachel N. Klein, *Unification of a Slave State: The Rise of the Planter Class in the South Carolina Backcountry, 1760–1800* (Chapel Hill: University of North Carolina Press, 1990); John S. Watterson III, "The Ordeal of Governor Burke," *North Carolina Historical Review* 48 (April 1971): 95–117; Kenneth Coleman, *The American Revolution in Georgia, 1763–1789* (Athens: University of Georgia Press, 1958); and Leslie Hall, *Land and Allegiance in Revolutionary Georgia* (Athens: University of Georgia Press, 2001).

    4. Troxler, *The Loyalist Experience in North Carolina,* 1–3.

    5. Robert O. DeMond, *The Loyalists in North Carolina during the Revolution* (Durham, N.C., Duke University Press, 1940), vii; A. Roger Ekirch, "Whig Authority and Public Order in Backcountry North Carolina, 1776–1783," in *An Uncivil War,* 99. The subject of Loyalism during the American Revolution has been discussed in studies beyond those of Troxler and DeMond. See also Smith, *Loyalists and Redcoats;* North Callahan, *Flight from the Republic: The Tories of the American Revolution* (Indianapolis: Bobbs-Merrill, 1967); Robert M. Calhoon et al., *The Loyalist Perception and Other Essays* (Columbia: University of South Carolina Press, 1989); Calhoon, *The Loyalists in Revolutionary America;* Harry M. Ward, *The War for Independence and the Transformation of American Society* (London: University College London Press, 1999); Watterson, "The Ordeal of Governor Burke," 95–117; Claude Halstead Van Tyne, *The Loyalists in the American Revolution*

(Gloucester, Mass.: Peter Smith, 1902; reprint 1959); Jeffrey J. Crow, "Tory Plots and Anglican Loyalty: The Llewelyn Conspiracy of 1777," *North Carolina Historical Review* 55 (January 1978): 1–17; Laura Page Frech, "The Wilmington Committee of Public Safety and the Loyalist Rising of February 1776," *North Carolina Historical Review* 41 (January 1964): 1–20; William S. Powell, *North Carolina: A Bicentennial History* (New York: Norton, 1977), 78–82; Gregory De Van Massey, "The British Expedition to Wilmington, January–November 1781," *North Carolina Historical Review* 66 (October 1989): 387–411.

6. Lindley S. Butler, "David Fanning's Militia: A Roving Partisan Community," in *Loyalists and Community in North America*, edited by Robert M. Calhoon, Timothy M. Barnes, and George A. Rawlyk (Westport, Conn.: Greenwood Press, 1994), 149–50; Robert Duncan Bass, *Gamecock: The Life and Campaigns of General Thomas Sumter* (New York: Holt, Rinehart & Winston, 1961), 30–31; Calhoon, *Loyalists in Revolutionary America*, 448–57.

7. Klein, *Unification of a Slave State*, 83. The defeat of a combined British naval and land attack against Charleston's defenses in June 1776 dampened Loyalist activities within the state until the British renewed their efforts against the southern provinces at the end of 1778.

8. Nadelhaft, *The Disorders of War*, 45–86. See also John W. Gordon, *South Carolina and the American Revolution: A Battlefield History* (Columbia: University of South Carolina Press, 2003); John S. Pancake, *This Destructive War: The British Campaign in the Carolinas, 1780–1782* (Tuscaloosa: University of Alabama Press, 1985); Edward McCrady, *The History of South Carolina in the Revolution*, 2 vols. (New York: Macmillan, 1902); John Buchanan, *The Road to Guilford Courthouse: The American Revolution in the Carolinas* (New York: Wiley, 1997); Walter Edgar, *Partisans and Redcoats: The Southern Conflict That Turned the Tide of the American Revolution* (New York: Morrow, 2001); and David Ramsay, *The History of the Revolution of South-Carolina, from a British Province to an Independent State* (Trenton: Printed by Isaac Collins, 1785). For the truce area in South Carolina, see Hugh F. Rankin, *Francis Marion: The Swamp Fox* (New York: Crowell, 1973), 216–17; *The Papers of General Nathanael Greene*, 9:380n; and William A. Graham, *General Joseph Graham and His Papers on North Carolina Revolutionary History* (Raleigh: Edwards & Broughton, 1904), 56. A similar enclave existed in North Carolina as well, along the state's southeastern border with South Carolina.

9. For details on the war in Georgia, see Hall, *Land and Allegiance in Revolutionary Georgia*; Edward J. Cashin, *The King's Ranger: Thomas Brown and the American Revolution on the Southern Frontier* (Athens: University of Georgia Press, 1989); Coleman, *The American Revolution in Georgia*; Gary D. Olson, "Thomas Brown, Loyalist, Partisan, and the Revolutionary War in Georgia, 1777–1782," *Georgia Historical Quarterly* 54 (Spring 1970): 1–19, and (Summer 1970): 183–208; and Martha Condray Searcy, *The Georgia-Florida Contest in the American Revolution, 1776–1778* (Tuscaloosa: University of Alabama Press, 1985).

10. Lee, *Crowds and Soldiers*, 176–211; John Shy, *A People Numerous and Armed: Reflections on the Military Struggle for American Independence* (Ann Arbor: University of Michigan Press, 1990), 163–80, 229–44; Anthony Allaire, "Extract from a Letter from an Officer," *Royal Gazette* (New York), February 24, 1781; Adelaide Fries, *Records of the Moravians in North Carolina*, vol. 4 (Raleigh: Edwards & Broughton, 1930), 1906–7; pension

declaration of James McBride, in *The State Records of North Carolina*, edited by Walter Clark, 16 vols., numbered 11–26 (Winston & Goldsboro, N.C.: State of North Carolina, 1895–1905), 22:144–45 (hereafter cited as *NCSR*). McBride used the term "Tory hunting" himself.

11. DeMond, *Loyalists in North Carolina*, 154–156; Troxler, *The Loyalist Experience*, 3; Fries, *Records of the Moravians in North Carolina*, 3:1144; Powell, *North Carolina*, 66.

12. William L. Saunders, ed., *The Colonial Records of North Carolina*, 10 vols. (Raleigh: Josephus Daniels, 1887), 10:476, 545; *NSCR*, 23:998–99.

13. DeMond, *Loyalists in North Carolina*, 154–55; *NCSR*, 24:9–12.

14. Archibald McClaine to Thomas Burke, March 27, 1782, *NCSR*, 16:247; DeMond, *Loyalists in North Carolina*, 156–57, 170–74; Hugh T. Lefler and Albert R. Newsome, *North Carolina: The History of a Southern State* (Chapel Hill: University of North Carolina Press, 1973), 232–33, 257–58; Norman K. Risjord, *Chesapeake Politics, 1781–1800* (New York: Columbia University Press, 1978), 197–201.

15. Thomas Burke to John Rutledge, February 15, 1782, *NCSR*, 16:511.

16. Fries, *Records of the Moravians in North Carolina*, 4:1564, 1626.

17. *NCSR*, 24:85, 123–24, 489–90; Thomas Burke to Major Thomas Hogg, March 13, 1782, *NCSR*, 16:229–30; Archibald McClaine to George Hooper, April 29, 1783, *NCSR*, 16:957.

18. Klein, *Unification of a Slave State*, 121–26; James Haw, *John and Edward Rutledge of South Carolina* (Athens: University of Georgia Press, 1997), 162–65. The body that enacted these measures was known as the Jacksonborough assembly because the legislature met at that village in lieu of occupied Charleston.

19. Robert M. Weir, "'The Violent Spirit,' the Reestablishment of Order, and the Continuity of Leadership in Post Revolutionary South Carolina," in *An Uncivil War*, 79–82, 89. Weir found that, although these harsh measures were passed, the lawmakers had adopted an overall policy of leniency by 1783. Rachel Klein concurs. Klein, *Unification of a Slave State*, 120.

20. Nadelhaft, *Disorders of War*, 71; Weir, "'The Violent Spirit,'" 81, 87.

21. Klein, *Unification of a Slave State*, 120–21; Nadelhaft, *Disorders of War*, 73–85. Nadelhaft concludes that the South Carolina Assembly's 1782 measures were harsh but not radical and certainly understandable in light of the destruction visited upon the state by the British and Tories.

22. Hall, *Land and Allegiance in Revolutionary Georgia*, 69–71, 121, 125–28, 133–34, 160–61, 167. Hall points out, however, that perhaps one third of those listed in the banishment act of 1782 eventually gained pardons. See also Edward J. Cashin, "'But Brothers, It Is Our Land We Are Talking About': Winners and Losers in the Georgia Backcountry," in *An Uncivil War*, 240–75.

23. Fries, *Records of the Moravians in North Carolina*, 4:1572.

24. Greene to Samuel Huntington, December 28, 1780, *The Papers of General Nathanael Greene*, 7:9.

25. Greene to John Cox, January 9, 1781, ibid., 7:82.

26. Greene to Samuel Huntington, March 30, 1781, ibid., 8:8.

27. Greene to Joseph Reed, May 4, 1781, ibid., 8:199–200.

28. Thomas Wade to Greene, April 29, 1781, ibid., 8:175.

29. Greene to William Davies, May 23, 1781, ibid., 8:298.

30. Greene to Samuel Huntington, December 28, 1780, ibid., 7:9; Lee, *Crowds and Soldiers in Revolutionary North Carolina*, 180–85.

31. Greene to John Martin, January 9, 1782, *The Papers of General Nathanael Greene*, 10:173. Martin was governor of Georgia.

32. Greene to Anthony Wayne, January 9, 1782, ibid., 10:175; Lee, *Crowds and Soldiers in Revolutionary North Carolina*, 180–85.

33. Greene to Captain Griffin Faunt le Roy, December 25, 1780, *The Papers of General Nathanael Greene*, 6:612. See also Greene's orders, August 16, 1781, August 27, 1781, ibid., 9:187, 259, for his admonitions to the army against depredations against civilians.

34. Greene to Thomas Sumter, April 30, 1781, ibid., 8:176–77.

35. Greene to Colonel Henry Lee, June 25, 1781, ibid., 8:455.

36. Greene to Isaac Shelby, August 2, 1781, ibid., 9:127.

37. Greene to Anthony Wayne, January 9, 1782, ibid., 10:175.

38. Greene to Griffith Rutherford, January 29, 1782, ibid., 10:277. For Rutherford's reputation, see Fries, *Records of the Moravians in North Carolina*, 3:1376.

39. Greene to General Alexander Leslie, February 1, 1782, *The Papers of General Nathanael Greene*, 10:295. Leslie was the British commander in South Carolina during the end of the war. Pancake, *This Destructive War*, 237.

40. Greene to Thomas Burke, August 12, 1781, *The Papers of General Nathanael Greene*, 9:166.

41. Lee, *Crowds and Soldiers in Revolutionary North Carolina*, 186–92.

42. Greene to Marie Joseph Gilbert du Motier, Marquis de Lafayette, June 9, 1781, *The Papers of General Nathanael Greene*, 8:368.

43. Greene to Griffith Rutherford, October 20, 1781, ibid., 9:456–57. For South Carolina governor John Rutledge's harsh proclamation of pardon in 1781 for the disaffected in that state, see ibid., 9:458.

44. Greene to Francis Marion, October 30, 1781, ibid., 9:497.

45. Greene to Thomas Sumter, November 28, 1781, ibid., 9:634.

46. Greene to Sumter, December 12, 1781, ibid., 10:40.

47. Greene to John Martin, January 9, 1782, ibid., 10:173. On the subject of retributive violence, about which Greene was concerned, see Fries, *Records of the Moravians in North Carolina*, 4:1629.

48. John Martin to Anthony Wayne, January 19, 1782, *The Papers of General Nathanael Greene*, 10:268n.

49. John Martin to Greene, February 9, 1782, ibid., 10:343.

50. Greene to John Martin, March 12, 1782, ibid., 10:488.

51. Fries, *Records of the Moravians in North Carolina*, 4:1576, 1627; Greene to Francis Marion, December 12, 1781, *The Papers of General Nathanael Greene*, 10:38.

52. Greene to Anthony Wayne, January 9, 1782, *The Papers of General Nathanael Greene*, 10:175.

53. Fries, *Records of the Moravians in North Carolina*, 4:1743.

54. Alexander Martin to Greene, February 10, 1782, *The Papers of General Nathanael Greene*, 10:351.

55. John S. Watterson, *Thomas Burke: Restless Revolutionary* (Washington, D.C.: University Press of America, 1980), 198; Thomas Burke to Greene, February 15, 1782, *The Papers of General Nathanael Greene*, 10:370.

56. Senate Joint Resolutions, General Assembly Session Records, June–July 1781, box 1, North Carolina State Archives; Jane S. Hill, *Guilford County North Carolina Court Minutes* (Greensboro: Guilford County Genealogical Society, 1999); A. B. Pruitt, *Abstracts of Confiscated Loyalists Land and Property in North Carolina* (N.p.: A. B. Pruitt, 1989), 115; Thomas Burke to Major Hogg, March 12, 1782, *NCSR*, 16:229–31; Thomas Burke to Nathanael Greene, February 15, 1782, *The Papers of General Nathanael Greene*, 10:370.

57. Thomas Sumter to Greene, January 2, 1782, Greene to Sumter, January 8, 1782, *The Papers of General Nathanael Greene*, 10:152, 168.

58. Greene's Proclamation to the Inhabitants upon the Saluda, June 5, 1781, ibid., 8:349.

59. Greene to Andrew Pickens, June 5, 1781, ibid., 8:349–50.

60. Greene to Henry Lee, July 29, 1781, ibid., 9:103.

61. Francis Marion to Greene, June 9, 1782, ibid., 11:313.

62. Greene to Alexander Martin, October 9, 1781, ibid., 9:438–39.

63. Greene to Griffith Rutherford, October 18, 1781, ibid., 9:452–53.

64. Greene to Rutherford, January 29, 1782, ibid., 10:277.

65. Greene to Colonel William Ballentine and Major John Robinson, December 20, 1781, ibid., 10:82–83.

66. Greene to Thomas Sumter, December 27, 1781, ibid., 10:121.

67. Greene to Anthony Wayne, January 29, 1782, and February 2, 1782, ibid., 10:279, 311.

68. Greene to Thomas Sumter, November 25, 1781, ibid., 9:627.

69. Greene to General Paston Gould, November 9, 1781, ibid., 9:551.

70. Lefler and Newsome, *North Carolina*, 256.

71. *The Papers of General Nathanael Greene*, 11:163n.

72. Greene to Thomas Burke, February 24, 1782, ibid., 10:406–7.

73. Burke to Greene, March 28, 1782, ibid., 10:549–51.

74. Blackwell P. Robinson, *William R. Davie* (Chapel Hill: University of North Carolina Press, 1957), 157–58; Thomas Burke to Greene, April 9, 1782, *The Papers of General Nathanael Greene*, 11:24–25.

75. Martin had acted as governor during Burke's captivity and was elected to that office in his own right in 1782.

76. Alexander Martin to Greene, May 12, 1782, *The Papers of General Nathanael Greene*, 11:185–86.

77. Greene to Alexander Martin, June 27, 1782, ibid., 11:375.

78. John Butler to Greene, September 13, 1782, ibid., 11:654.

79. Greene to John Mathews, December 22, 1782, ibid., 12:331–32; Kathy R. Coker, "The Punishment of Revolutionary War Loyalists in South Carolina," Ph.D. diss., University of South Carolina, 1987, 253; Henry Lumpkin, *From Savannah to Yorktown* (New York: Paragon House, 1981), 248; Bass, *Gamecock*, 58–59, 207.

80. Captain Nathaniel Pendleton to Greene, May 1, 1782, *The Papers of General Nathanael Greene*, 11:150.

81. Greene to George Weedon, October 1, 1782, ibid., 12:4.

82. Hall, *Land and Allegiance in Revolutionary Georgia*, 108–34, 160–74; Weir, "'The Violent Spirit,'" 91–98; DeMond, *Loyalists in North Carolina*, 158–69; Jeffrey J. Crow, "Liberty Men and Loyalists: Disorder and Disaffection in the North Carolina Back-country," in *An Uncivil War*, 125–78.

83. Greene to Alexander Martin, June 27, 1782, *The Papers of General Nathanael Greene*, 11:375.

The Evolving Tactician

Nathanael Greene at the
Battle of Eutaw Springs

JIM PIECUCH

*M*ajor General Nathanael Greene has earned widespread praise from historians as the premier strategist of the American Revolutionary War—a reputation resulting from his successful campaign against the British in the South. When Greene took command of the Continental army in the Southern Department in December 1780, the British army controlled South Carolina and Georgia and was poised to invade North Carolina. Ten months later, British forces were confined to the environs of Charleston and Savannah, and the British commander in the South, Lieutenant General Charles, Earl Cornwallis, had taken his army from South Carolina to Virginia, where it shortly capitulated to a combined French and American force. Greene has been rightly credited with engineering this spectacular reversal of American fortunes although other factors, including some key errors on the part of Cornwallis, contributed to Greene's success.[1]

Despite his abilities as a strategist, Greene has garnered few accolades as a tactician. Four times he led his troops into combat against British and Loyalist forces, and on every occasion the American army suffered defeat, even though in each battle Greene had the advantage of numerical superiority over his opponents. Greene's string of defeats led one of his biographers, M. F. Treacy, to conclude that, while "he was an excellent planner," Greene "seems to have been unable to realize the fruition of his plans in actual tactical operations on the field of battle." Treacy attributed Greene's inability to defeat his enemies to a "lack of self-assurance and personal force."[2] These aspects of Greene's personality may have played a role in his string of battlefield failures, as did the fighting ability of the British army. At the time Greene took charge of the Southern Army, he had never exercised supreme command on the battlefield. Thrust into the difficult position of having to learn from experience how to command an army in combat, Greene proved adaptable and continually learned from his mistakes. By the time he fought the Battle of Eutaw Springs, South Carolina, Greene had become a much better tactician than he had been just six months earlier. In his planning, in maneuvers before the battle, and in much of the fighting at Eutaw Springs, Greene showed considerable tactical skill, which brought his army to the verge of a decisive victory. Only the failures of two key subordinates, Greene's own misunderstanding of the final British position, and the stubborn resistance of his British and Loyalist opponents deprived Greene of success in his final battle.

The first battle in which Greene led the Southern Army against the British was fought at Guilford Courthouse, North Carolina, on March 15, 1781. Aware that he would eventually have to come to grips with the pugnacious Cornwallis, Greene sought advice in advance from his able subordinate Brigadier General Daniel Morgan. An adept tactician, Morgan was the architect of the spectacular American victory over a detachment of Cornwallis's troops at the Cowpens, South Carolina, on January 17, 1781. Illness had forced Morgan to give up his command and return home to Virginia, but before departing he had given Greene the benefit of his counsel. On locating a suitable position at Guilford Courthouse, Greene followed Morgan's suggestion to employ the tactics that had worked so well at Cowpens and meet a British attack with multiple lines of defenders; however, Greene found it necessary to make some adjustments to suit his own larger force and the different terrain. On the morning of March 15, as the British army approached, Greene deployed his force of more than 4,400 men in three lines: the North Carolina militia in front, the Virginia militia on higher ground in the North Carolinians' rear, and on the highest terrain in the third line, the backbone of the army: Continental troops from Maryland, Virginia, and Delaware. Greene assigned light infantry and cavalry units to protect his flanks.[3] On reaching the field, Cornwallis positioned his own troops, numbering about 1,950. He opted for his favorite tactic, a frontal assault.

Early in the afternoon the British advanced, fighting their way through the North Carolina militia. These men were not expected to hold their ground indefinitely, but to delay the British assault and inflict casualties before they were driven back. Greene did not think that the North Carolinians fulfilled their assignment, reporting afterward that when the British line came within 140 yards of the militia, "part of them began a fire, but a considerable part left the ground without firing at all; some fired once, and some twice, and none more, except a part of a Battalion. . . . The General and field Officers did all they could to induce the Men to stand their Ground, but neither the advantages of the position nor any other consideration could induce them to stay. They left the ground and many of them threw away their Arms." Most observers, along with later historians, believed that the North Carolinians performed better than Greene indicated, with some units resisting until the British were nearly upon them and inflicting considerable casualties on their attackers.[4]

Greene's second line performed to his satisfaction. Posted in the woods, the Virginia militiamen were unable to see the fighting between the North Carolinians and the British, but they heard it and occasionally felt the effects of British cannon balls that overshot the first line. The British units did not cross the four hundred yards between Greene's first and second lines at a uniform pace, as some regiments were slowed by greater opposition from the Americans in their front or by difficult terrain. As each British unit entered the woods, they engaged the Virginians, who, Greene noted, "gave the Enemy a warm reception and kept up a heavy fire for a long time" before the second line was finally broken. Greene's tactics appeared to be working well, with the British having been slowed and weakened by the militia's resistance.[5]

Then it was up to the Continentals to blunt the British thrust. In theory Greene's regulars held all the advantages. In addition to being fresh and occupying the high ground, they faced only piecemeal attacks rather than a coherent assault along their entire front because "the British battle line had been broken" by the earlier fighting "into six separate elements that would arrive at different times."[6]

First to emerge from the woods was the British Thirty-Third Regiment, which charged the Virginia Continentals and was repulsed. The British fell back to a strong position and traded fire with the Virginians at a distance. Next came the Second Battalion of the King's Foot Guards, the elite of the British army. They struck the green Second Maryland on Greene's left flank, and that regiment fled, abandoning two pieces of artillery. The Continentals were in danger of being outflanked, and the unit posted alongside the routed Second Maryland did not see their comrades' flight because their view was blocked by trees and the uneven ground. Fortunately a staff officer who observed the collapse of the Second Maryland rushed over to warn Lieutenant Colonel John Eager Howard, second in command of the adjacent First Maryland. Howard relayed the information to his superior, Colonel John Gunby, who repositioned his regiment. After exchanging several volleys with the Guards, the First Maryland counterattacked. Gunby's horse was shot, and he was pinned beneath it, but Howard assumed command and in hand-to-hand fighting repulsed the Guards with the help of Lieutenant Colonel William Washington's cavalry. The First Maryland's advance had left the regiment in an exposed position, however, and on observing two other British units emerging from the woods, Howard ordered a withdrawal to the Marylanders' original place in the line.[7]

Greene, who had been trying to rally the Second Maryland and was nearly captured while so engaged, did not see the repulse of the Guards. Having failed to rally the Marylanders, he believed that his flank had collapsed. Greene then rode to the other end of his line, where he found the Virginia Continentals still engaged and decided that the line could not be held any longer without risking the destruction of his army. He ordered a retreat. The battle, according to official reports, cost the Americans 79 killed, 184 wounded, and 1,046 missing, while Cornwallis lost more than one-fourth of his own army: 93 killed, 413 wounded, and 26 missing. A careful study by Lawrence E. Babits and Joshua B. Howard concludes that the actual losses of both armies were higher than the reported figures.[8]

The Americans had suffered a tactical defeat; yet in the process they had badly weakened Cornwallis's army. The British held the field until March 18, when they withdrew to refit. Eventually Cornwallis marched to the British post at Wilmington.[9] In his debut as an army commander, Greene had performed fairly well. He had made a serious tactical error by placing the inexperienced Second Maryland Regiment on the left flank of his third line, rather than entrusting that important position to the veterans of the First Maryland. Greene's second tactical mistake occurred when he lost touch with the fighting along the third line while trying to rally the Second Maryland. Had he been aware that Howard and the First Maryland checked the Guards and stabilized the line, he might have decided to postpone his retreat, possibly throwing back the exhausted British troops and holding the field. Nevertheless such a stand would have risked the loss of his entire force, so Greene was probably wise not to make the gamble.

Greene had also lost touch with some of his units during the battle through no fault of his own. In his initial deployment, Greene had posted Lieutenant Colonel Henry Lee and his legion of cavalry and light infantry, along with Colonel William Campbell's Virginia riflemen, to guard the American left flank and fall back to the second line of defense when the first gave way. Lee, however, did not withdraw parallel to the rest of the army. Instead he inexplicably retreated at an angle to the southeast, away from the main American force. Lee's movement drew the First Battalion of Guards and the Hessian Regiment von Bose with him, depriving Cornwallis of these units but at the same time exposing the American left flank and similarly depriving Greene of the legion and Campbell's troops. Greene had already begun his retreat when Lee abandoned his "private war" and set off with his legion to find the rest of the army. Lee's departure left Campbell isolated, and shortly afterward the Virginians were charged and overrun by Lieutenant Colonel Banastre Tarleton's British dragoons. Campbell was furious with Lee and, ignoring Greene's mollifying letter, resigned his commission.[10] There is no evidence that Greene ever raised the issue of Lee's actions with the flamboyant legion commander. The tendency Lee displayed at Guilford Courthouse to rove about the battlefield without regard for orders or the situation of other units caused problems for Greene later.

The American commander followed the British army toward Wilmington as he considered a new plan, which he explained to George Washington on March 29. "If the Enemy falls down towards Wilmington they will be in a position where it will be impossible for us to injure them," Greene noted. "In this critical and distressing situation I am determined to carry the War immediately into South Carolina. The Enemy will be obliged to follow us or give up their posts in that State." Greene broke off his pursuit of Cornwallis and directed his march toward Camden, the most important British inland post in South Carolina.[11]

Greene arrived at Camden on April 19. He had hoped that the sudden appearance of his army might surprise the British garrison and that he could capitalize on the situation by quickly seizing the town. To his consternation Greene found that the strength of the British force there was "much greater than I expected." Furthermore the British commander had expected Greene's arrival. Lieutenant Colonel Francis, Lord Rawdon, had received a report of Greene's movements from an escaped Loyalist prisoner on April 12. The capable Rawdon immediately surmised that "Camden is Greens object" and prepared to defend the town.[12]

For nearly a week Greene tried to lure the British out of their fortifications to attack the American army. He occupied Hobkirk's Hill north of Camden and sent detachments to attack some of the town's outer defensive works, but Rawdon refused to take the bait. On April 22 Greene began marching his army in a circuitous route around Camden, finally returning to Hobkirk's Hill the next day without having enticed the British to attack. Greene deployed his troops in defensive positions, with the Second Maryland to the east on his left flank, followed by the First Maryland, Second Virginia, and First Virginia on the right. These Continentals numbered about twelve hundred men; the artillery, cavalry, and a small contingent of North Carolina militia raised Greene's strength to about fifteen hundred soldiers.[13]

Despite being outnumbered, Rawdon wanted to attack the Americans and was simply awaiting an opportune moment. It came on the night of April 24, when an American deserter entered Camden and reported that Greene had sent his artillery to the rear. The information was out of date, as Greene had brought the guns back to Hobkirk's Hill, but Rawdon believed that, if the Americans lacked artillery, it would to some extent even the odds against the British. He set about preparing his attack. "By arming our Musicians, our Drummers & in short everything that could carry a Firelock, I mustered above Nine Hundred," he wrote. With this force, supported by two six-pounder cannon, Rawdon marched from Camden on the morning of April 25. To deceive Greene, he marched south, away from the American position. Once the British were in dense woods, they turned "& taking an extensive circuit, came down upon the Enemy's left flank."[14]

Greene, who had been hoping for just such a move by the British, was taken by surprise. Although he had posted pickets in front of his position, he had neglected to assign anyone to watch the British in Camden. His first inkling that a battle was imminent came when American pickets opened fire on Rawdon's advance guard. The British drove back the pickets, whose resistance gave Greene time to form his troops in line of battle and meet the charge of two British regiments. Quickly assessing the situation, Greene realized that, with most of the British troops still in column behind the attacking units, the American army overlapped both of the enemy flanks. He immediately ordered all four Continental regiments to counterattack. "The Enemy were staggered in all quarters," Greene observed. An American victory appeared to be unfolding.[15]

Within minutes the circumstances reversed. A Loyalist sharpshooter killed Captain William Beatty, commander of the rightmost company of the First Maryland, throwing the troops into confusion, which spread to the adjacent company. Colonel Gunby, the regimental commander, ordered the two companies to halt and reform and sent orders to John Eager Howard, who was advancing with the rest of the regiment alongside the Second Maryland, to fall back and rejoin the other two companies. Meanwhile Rawdon had brought up additional units to extend his flanks and renewed his assault. The now isolated Second Maryland was driven back and the First Virginia "got into some disorder," leaving the Second Virginia in an exposed position. Greene, deciding that it was impossible "to recover the fortune of the Day, which once promised us a compleat victory," ordered a retreat. Rawdon pursued the Americans for three miles before returning to Camden. American casualties totaled 269 with British losses nearly equal at 258.[16]

Greene's tactical performance had been solid. He had not been shaken by the unexpected attack, had seen the advantage afforded by the initial narrow front of the British advance, and had taken advantage of it by counterattacking. Apparently dismissing the effects of Rawdon's equally swift and masterful response to his actions, Greene believed that he had done everything in his power to achieve victory, which made the defeat more than painful. It enraged him. Four months later he was still seething, telling Daniel Morgan, "I was content at the floging at Guilford, but I lost all patience at first with that of Lord Rawdons. In the one I considerd victory as doubtful, in the other certain. Under these impressions you may well think the disappointment was not pleasing."[17]

In the immediate aftermath of the battle, Greene focused his anger on John Gunby. He blamed Gunby for the defeat repeatedly and publicly. Gunby demanded a court-martial to clear his name; however, the court found that Gunby's order to withdraw had been improper and "in all probability, the only cause why we did not obtain a complete victory." Humiliated, Gunby asked to return to Maryland on recruiting duty, but Greene, perhaps out of pique, sent him to Charlotte to gather supplies for the army.[18]

Greene's harsh treatment of Gunby contrasted sharply with his response to the disobedience of another subordinate at the Battle of Hobkirk's Hill. When Greene ordered the Continental infantry to counterattack, he also dispatched Lieutenant Colonel William Washington and his cavalry to ride past the British right flank and strike their line from the rear. Had Washington done so, the British infantry would have found themselves caught between two forces and in all probability have been overwhelmed. Instead Washington found a more enticing target: a cluster of British stragglers, wounded men, doctors, and other noncombat troops in the British rear. Ignoring his instructions, Washington captured them, paroling some and mounting others behind his dragoons. By the time this task was completed, the infantry was retreating, and Washington also withdrew. Rawdon dismissed Washington's foray, remarking that "a part of the Enemy's Cavalry got into our rear, exacted paroles from several Officers who lay wounded on the ground from which we had first driven the Enemy, & carried off several Wounded Men." Greene, on the other hand, heaped praise upon his errant subordinate, asserting that Washington "took upwards of 200 prisoners and ten or fifteen Officers," a vast exaggeration, and adding that "the Colonels behaviour and that of his Regiment . . . did them the highest honor."[19]

Washington had taken it upon himself to act independently at the battles of Cowpens and Guilford Courthouse and achieved much success. By the time of the engagement at Hobkirk's Hill, he had evidently concluded that he could exercise as much leeway with his orders as he saw fit. Greene's ignorance of, or refusal to address, Washington's disobedience at Hobkirk's Hill further encouraged the cavalry leader to continue to disregard commands, an ominous portent for the future.

Fortunately for the Americans, their defeat outside Camden was rendered moot because two days before the battle, Lee's Legion and Francis Marion's partisans had captured British Fort Watson on the Santee River, severing the supply line between Charleston and Camden. Rawdon evacuated Camden on May 10, leaving Greene to focus his attention on the now isolated British post at Ninety Six in the South Carolina backcountry.[20]

With his army reduced by detachments and casualties to about 850 Continentals and 200 militia, Greene reached Ninety Six on May 22. He found the town "much better fortified and garrison much stronger in regular troops than was expected." The defenders consisted of 350 provincial regulars from New York and New Jersey augmented by 200 South Carolina Loyalist militiamen. Their commander, Lieutenant Colonel John Harris Cruger, was a former New York politician who had since proven himself a resolute and skillful officer. On May 14 Rawdon had sent him orders to evacuate Ninety Six, but American partisans intercepted the messages, so when Greene's army appeared, Cruger resolved to defend the post as long as possible.[21]

Having ruled out an assault on the town, Greene decided to besiege it. Since he had no training or experience in siege operations, he entrusted those matters to his Polish-born and European-trained engineer officer, Colonel Tadeusz Kościuszko. After studying the palisaded town and its two outworks, Kościuszko concluded that the earthen Star Fort east of the town was the key to the British position. He ordered the troops to begin digging a trench seventy yards from the earthwork, a serious error. Cruger bombarded the work party with artillery and then sent out a detachment that killed or drove off the Americans, captured their tools, and filled the trench.[22] It was an inauspicious start to the siege, although the disaster was Kościuszko's fault, not Greene's.

Kościuszko restarted construction of his siege trenches outside the range of British artillery. By June 3 the lines had reached the point where Kościuszko had tried to dig the first trench two weeks earlier. On Greene's instructions his adjutant, Colonel Otho Holland Williams, sent Cruger a demand for surrender, declaring that the defenders had "no hope but in the generosity of the American Army." Cruger refused to capitulate.[23]

Greene and Kościuszko tried every method they could to force Ninety Six to surrender, including a belated effort to interdict the garrison's water supply that came from a spring that ran between the town and a small stockade fort to the west. Yet even the arrival of reinforcements—Lee's Legion and Andrew Pickens's South Carolina militia fresh from their victory at Augusta, Georgia—failed to shake the defenders' resolve.[24]

As the siege wore on, Greene began to receive ominous reports that British reinforcements had landed in Charleston. By June 12, he had confirmed that Rawdon was marching to the relief of Ninety Six. Three British regiments had indeed arrived on June 3, giving Rawdon enough troops to keep Charleston secure while he took two thousand men to aid Cruger. The British began their march on June 7 and five days later, the same day Greene learned of their approach, a Loyalist messenger rode through the American lines into Ninety Six, bringing word that Rawdon was on the way.[25]

Greene still believed that he could force Cruger to surrender if Thomas Sumter's militia delayed Rawdon's march. Sumter incorrectly guessed the route Rawdon would take, and the British bypassed the militia, brushing off the single regiment that managed to attack their rear. On June 18, unwilling to lift the siege of Ninety Six without a final effort to take the post, Greene ordered picked parties of troops to make a desperate attack, appropriately called a "forlorn hope." His targets were the small stockade fort east of the town and the Star Fort to the west. One American storming party captured the stockade, but the assault on the Star Fort was repulsed. Greene's casualties amounted to 147 while Cruger lost 85 men. With Rawdon only two days' march away, Greene gave up the siege and withdrew. After pursuing Greene some distance in an effort to force a battle, Rawdon gave up the chase, returned to Ninety Six, and evacuated the post, which was too isolated to retain.[26]

The operations against Ninety Six offered Greene few opportunities to display his tactical skills. He wisely chose to besiege the fortified town rather than commit his army to a risky assault. Lacking experience in that kind of warfare, he relied on Kościuszko to manage the siege, and the Polish engineer performed well after correcting his mistake of beginning the trenches too close to the defensive lines. Perhaps Greene should not have ordered the June 18 attack or employed more troops in the assault. Nevertheless the attempt to take Ninety Six before relief arrived was a gamble worth taking, and a larger assault force might not have achieved any greater success while incurring higher losses. Against a foe less resolute than Cruger, Greene might well have captured Ninety Six long before Rawdon was able to march to its rescue.

Following their decision to evacuate Ninety Six, Rawdon and Cruger marched by separate routes to the vicinity of Charleston, the latter accompanied by a large number of Loyalist refugees. Greene led his army after them, but after realizing that he could not bring the British army to battle and with all the British posts in the interior of South Carolina having been abandoned or captured, he retired to the High Hills of Santee. There he established a "camp of repose," where his soldiers could recover from their recent exertions. While his troops rested, Greene worked to gather reinforcements and planned the next phase of his campaign.[27]

Greene would not be facing his nemesis Lord Rawdon the next time he met the British in battle. The young Irish nobleman, who had defeated Greene at Hobkirk's Hill and then thwarted the American commander's siege of Ninety Six, had been suffering from illness, and on his doctor's advice he sailed for England to recuperate. His replacement was the untested Lieutenant Colonel Alexander Stewart, who was held in rather low esteem by his colleagues. Rawdon remarked that Stewart "has too high an opinion of himself" while Major James Wemyss described Stewart as "a brave officer, rather of indolent habits, and a little too fond of the bottle." Greene did not offer an opinion of his new opponent, but he must not have been disappointed by the change.[28]

Stewart had posted his army at the Loyalist stronghold of Orangeburg, where he remained until July 29. The next day Stewart set out on a march that by August 4 took him to McCord's Ferry on the Congaree River, some forty miles south of Camden and half that distance from Greene's camp. Neither commander appeared concerned about the nearness of the opposing army, as they were separated by the Santee River.[29]

Henry Lee, who was with his legion at Howell's Ferry on the Congaree, fewer than ten miles from Stewart's force, suspected that Stewart would march farther upriver. Lee estimated with great accuracy that the British army numbered fewer than fifteen hundred men and suggested that, if Greene fell back to Camden, "it would induce them to venture farther into the country."[30] The implication of this advice was that, if Greene could draw Stewart farther into the interior of South Carolina, the British army might be cut off and destroyed.

Greene disagreed with Lee's assessment. "I am not of opinion that a retrogade [*sic*] movement will induce the enemy to cross the River in force; nor do I believe they will fight us if we cross," he replied. Undeterred by Greene's response, Lee repeated his suggestion on August 10. "Oh that you could move over the Congaree; no army will ever again commit itself so fully, could you but collect tolerable force," Lee asserted. Beginning to see the opportunity Lee had described, Greene agreed that "the position of the enemy puts them much in our power" and expressed regret that he did not have enough troops to risk crossing the Congaree. Greene asked Lee to keep him aware of Stewart's numbers and location, an indication that he might move against the British if he found a favorable opportunity to do so.[31]

Over the next several days Lee continued to urge Greene to take action, and Greene's view of a move against Stewart became more favorable. He agreed that Lee's estimate of Stewart's strength was accurate and was supported by accounts from British deserters. "I have a good mind to put all to the hazard with the regular troops," Greene informed Lee on August 14. "I believe our force if we commit the Cavalry would be compentent [*sic*] to the attack; but the loss must fall heavy on the regular force, and should we meet with a check, or defeat, the consequences would be very disagreeable." The commander added that, if he had six to eight hundred militia to support the Continentals, it "would make the business easy and success certain."[32]

Greene began taking steps to assemble a larger force. On August 15 he instructed Colonel François Lellorquis, Marquis de Malmedy, a French officer commanding the North Carolina militia from Salisbury district, to bring his men to Camden and await further orders. Four days later, in response to further prodding from Lee, Greene suggested that Francis Marion and his militia might also join in an operation against Stewart. Now fully committed to taking action against the British force, Greene assured Lee that "I consider no attempt so easy & so ready as the ruining of Stuarts army." Defeating Stewart, Greene declared, "will put all right & will be more important if possible than the glory of Saratoga." Greene wrote Lee again on August 21, stating that he would also try to get assistance from Andrew Pickens's militia and Colonel William Henderson's South Carolina state troops. "The Army marches to morrow by the way of Camden for the Congaree," Greene announced. "You know the object; therefore be prepard." Greene had made up his mind to attack the British.[33]

For unknown reasons Greene's army did not march until August 23, a day later than he had originally planned. The troops reached Camden the next day and were supposed to cross the Wateree River on the twenty-fifth, but a delay in ferrying the army's baggage over the river forced Greene to postpone the move. While chafing at the delay, Greene took steps to unite his army with Pickens's and Henderson's units. He complained to Lee that he still had heard nothing from Pickens, and "the tardiness with which every body moves who were expected to join us almost makes me repent that I have put the troops in motion."[34]

Henderson reported on August 25 that he had not gotten any messages from Pickens either, but he had heard reports indicating that Pickens was en route to join Greene and was only a few days' march away. The colonel added that his own force numbered 370 men of all ranks, one-third of whom lacked arms. This report must have disappointed Greene, who on reaching Camden had been dismayed to find that Malmedy had brought only 400 North Carolina militiamen.[35]

The American army eventually crossed the Wateree and resumed its march. On August 30 Greene reached the Congaree at Howell's Ferry, but by that time the British had left McCord's Ferry. Stewart had learned that Greene was moving with the intention of crossing the Congaree, and that information, along with his army "being much in want of necessaries," caused Stewart to fall back to Eutaw Springs near the Santee River. Undeterred by Stewart's withdrawal, Greene sent his army southeastward in pursuit. Francis Marion sent Greene welcome news on September 3; he was near Eutaw Springs with his militia. Major Edmund Hyrne, one of Greene's aides, promptly informed Marion that the army was on the way to attack Stewart. Two days later, Greene received a letter from Pickens and replied with orders for the militia leader to unite his force with the rest of the army.[36]

By the evening of September 7, Greene was at Burdell's Tavern, the various units of Continentals and militia assembled at last. Although the American army was only seven miles from Stewart's position, the British commander had no idea of their presence.[37] Greene had done an outstanding job of gathering forces while on the march, adjusting to Stewart's change of position and placing his army within striking range of the British with the opportunity to achieve tactical surprise.

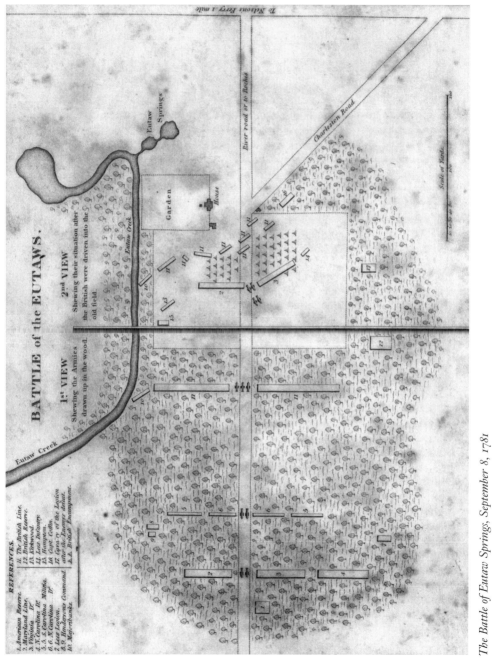

The Battle of Eutaw Springs, September 8, 1781

Greene had also managed to obtain a substantial numerical superiority over Stewart. Historians have estimated the strength of the two armies as about equal, with the Americans having at most an advantage of a few hundred men. In one of the earliest figures given for the numbers of troops, Henry Lee stated that "the effective force of the hostile armies may be fairly estimated as nearly equal, each about two thousand three hundred." William Johnson gave a figure of 2,300 men for the British army and put Greene's force at 2,000. According to John S. Pancake, the Americans numbered 2,400 men and the British 2,000. Terry Golway gives Greene's strength as slightly more than 2,000, the same as the British, while Gerald M. Carbone puts British numbers at 1,800–2,000 with Greene's army a fraction larger. Dennis Conrad, editor of *The Papers of General Nathanael Greene*, stated that "the two armies at Eutaw Springs were roughly equal in size."[38]

The strength of the British army is actually easy to determine, since Stewart prepared a field return on the morning of September 8, just before the battle. It lists a total of 2,720 men of all ranks in the infantry and artillery units. Of these, 255 were on detached duty and 566 sick in hospitals, reducing the British strength to 1,999 infantry and artillerists and 52 cavalry. An additional 106 soldiers were listed as "Sick in Camp" and did not participate in the battle. Nor did the Loyalist militia accompanying the army, who were not counted in the return; Stewart noted that they "did not fire a Shot the whole day." These adjustments give the British a total of 1,945 men of all ranks fit for duty, a figure remarkably close to Henry Lee's August 20 estimate that Stewart commanded 1,700 "effective infantry" and 100 "effective cavalry." Some British soldiers were assigned as "Bat Men and Baggage Guard" on September 8 and did not fight, while the foragers Stewart sent out in the morning took no part in the main action. Stewart in a separate return listed the number of troops who fought in the main battle as 1,396.[39]

American numbers are more difficult to calculate. An August 5 return of the Maryland Continentals lists 454 men of all ranks "Present fit for duty," a figure that is unlikely to have changed significantly by the time of the battle. The number had increased from 426 only eleven days before. The earlier return showed 409 Virginia Continental soldiers of all ranks fit for duty, 411 North Carolina Continentals, 96 Delaware Continentals, and 90 infantry from Lee's Legion. Other returns of July 26 showed the Continental artillery with a strength of 95 men of all ranks fit for duty, 120 cavalry in Lee's Legion, and an estimated 70 effective soldiers in William Washington's Continental cavalry, which had not submitted an official tally. By the time of the battle, Washington's force had been strengthened by the addition of an unknown number of South Carolina mounted militia. If this reinforcement gave Washington 100 effective men, Greene would have had 1,775 men in his Continental infantry, artillery, and cavalry units.[40]

Militia numbers are notoriously difficult to calculate. Malmedy's North Carolina militia mustered 204 men of all ranks fit for duty on August 25. Since Greene reported that 400 North Carolinians joined him at Camden and William Johnson estimated that Greene left 200 men behind as a "camp-guard," it is likely that these 200 troops were North Carolinians who did not accompany the army. William Henderson told Greene that he had 370 South Carolina state troops, one-third of them unarmed, which would have left 247 men available to fight at Eutaw Springs. Johnson provides the only figures for the South Carolina militia, giving the strength of Pickens's brigade as 307 and of Marion's as 240. Since his figures for Malmedy's and Henderson's forces are lower than the known totals, those for Pickens and Marion can be considered low as well. Therefore the total number of militia and state troops with Greene was at least 998, and the aggregate strength of the American army was, at a minimum, 2,773 of all ranks. In the actual battle, Greene outnumbered Stewart approximately two-to-one.[41] Greene had skillfully collected the superior force he wanted to meet the enemy.

Prepared at last to strike the British, Greene got his army under way at four o'clock on the morning of September 8. To speed deployment when the army encountered the British, Greene arranged for the units to march "in order of Battle." Greene intended to employ Daniel Morgan's tactics of multiple battle lines once again, with the militia in front, but this time he adapted these tactics for attack rather than defense. This deployment dictated that the militia head Greene's column; however—given the uncertainty of how they might react when they encountered the British—the American commander did not want to risk entrusting his advance to the militia alone. Thus he assigned the cavalry and infantry of Lee's Legion and Henderson's state troops to accompany the militia in the van. Behind the North and South Carolina militia came the North Carolina Continentals, followed by two three-pounder artillery pieces, the Virginia Continentals, two six-pounder cannon, the Marylanders, and in the rear Washington's cavalry and the Delaware Continentals.[42]

On the morning of September 8, Stewart still had no idea that Greene was nearby or that the American army was marching to attack him. The British commander had made "every exertion . . . to gain intelligence of the enemy's situation," but the Americans "rendered it impossible by waylaying the bypaths and passes." Greene's ability to achieve surprise resulted in Stewart's weakening his army. Because the British were still suffering from a shortage of provisions, early in the morning Stewart dispatched a large foraging party to gather sweet potatoes from the plantations along the Santee River. The party consisted of

310 officers and men, the soldiers carrying only four rounds of ammunition each.[43]

At six o'clock, two hours after Greene's army had begun its march, two American deserters arrived in the British camp. They informed Stewart that Greene was only seven miles away with almost 4,000 men and four pieces of artillery. Stewart ordered his cavalry commander, Major John Coffin, to take 50 cavalrymen and 140 infantry and investigate the deserters' report.[44]

Coffin had advanced about four miles down the road to Burdell's Tavern when at approximately eight o'clock he encountered the head of the American column, which had covered only three miles. The British immediately charged, only to come under heavy fire from Lee's Legion infantry and South Carolina state troops on their front and both flanks. Lee sent the legion cavalry to encircle the British, who fled back down the road. The gunfire attracted the attention of the British foragers, who had split into smaller parties and were in the fields between the road and the Santee River. Hurrying to the road, they stumbled into the American column. Some brief fighting ensued. A few of the foragers were killed or wounded, and most of the remainder captured.[45]

When Coffin returned to confirm the Americans' approach, Stewart formed his army in line of battle. On the right, in thick scrub along the banks of Eutaw Creek, Stewart posted his flank battalion, made up of the grenadier and light-infantry companies of the British and Loyalist regiments. Major John Marjoribanks commanded the unit. Its position along the creek placed it at nearly a right angle to the rest of Stewart's line. Next to Marjoribanks were the "Buffs" of the Third Regiment, followed by the Sixty-Third Regiment, the Sixty-Fourth, Lieutenant Colonel John Harris Cruger's Loyalist battalion, and the Provincial Light Infantry, another Loyalist unit. Stewart held Lieutenant Colonel Isaac Allen's New Jersey Volunteers, Major Henry Sheridan's New York Volunteers, a detachment of the British Eighty-Fourth Regiment, and Coffin's cavalry in reserve.[46]

Greene responded to the encounter with Coffin by ordering his troops to hasten their march. Lee's Legion and Henderson's state troops were the first to engage the British pickets, driving them back to the main line and coming under fire from British cannon. Lee asked Greene for artillery support, and he immediately dispatched Colonel Otho Williams with Captain Gaines's three-pounders to assist Lee. While Lee and Henderson battled the British on the American left flank, Greene brought up the rest of his troops, deployed them for battle, and forced the rest of the British pickets back to Stewart's main line.[47]

When the American troops had finished forming for battle, the South Carolina state troops covered the left (northern) flank of Greene's line. To their right were Pickens's South Carolina militiamen, followed by Malmedy's North

Carolinians and Marion's South Carolinians, with Lee's Legion guarding the right flank. The veteran Maryland Continentals held the left of the American second line, with the Virginia Continentals alongside them and the North Carolina Continentals on the right. Greene held the Delaware Continentals and Washington's cavalry in reserve.[48]

Seeing that Greene's line overlapped the British left flank, Stewart ordered his reserve forward to extend his line, withholding only Coffin's cavalry. Stewart had also taken an unusual step for a British officer by putting Cruger in command of the front line. With all the reserve infantry committed, Cruger had charge of the entire British army except for the cavalry and baggage guards. Most British officers tended to distrust their American counterparts and avoided giving them important assignments. Perhaps Stewart believed that Cruger's experience made him the best choice for the role. Whatever Stewart's reasoning may have been, Greene was about to go into battle against another old nemesis, the officer who had withstood the siege of Ninety Six.[49]

Greene ordered the militia to open the attack. Pressing forward into a storm of British musket fire, the militia held their ground and answered with volleys of their own. The contest lasted for an extended period, prompting Greene to remark that "the Militia fought with a degree of spirit and firmness that reflects the highest honor upon this class of Soldiers." Eventually, however, Malmedy's North Carolinians began to give way. Observing the situation, Greene ordered General Jethro Sumner to bring his North Carolina Continentals forward and fill the gap in the American center. The move was complicated because the Virginia Continentals, rather than Sumner's troops, were behind Malmedy's militia. The North Carolina Continentals, all of them new recruits, had to execute a difficult maneuver to get into position, but they did so successfully.[50] The most likely explanation for Greene's decision was that he wanted to withhold his experienced regulars, the Virginians and Marylanders, until the time came to strike a critical blow.

Neither side appeared able to gain an advantage, except on the British right, where the flank battalion delivered a "galling fire" into the state troops. Henderson asked Greene for permission to charge the British, but the general refused because such a move might leave the left flank of the front line exposed. Shortly afterward Henderson was seriously wounded, and his troops were thrown into disorder for a brief period.[51]

Unexpectedly the tactical situation underwent a dramatic change. Sumner's North Carolina Continentals began to waver under the British fire and then fell back. Their movement exposed the flanks of Pickens's and Marion's South Carolinians, who commenced their own withdrawal. Seeing the American line breaking, the British and Loyalist troops surged forward without orders, and the troops who had composed Greene's first line fled.[52]

Amid the unraveling of his line, Greene remained calm. The British advance had disordered their own ranks. It was the moment Greene had been waiting for. He sent instructions for the Virginia and Maryland Continentals to counter-attack. "The Virginians advanced with impetuosity & beat their foes where'er they found them," Otho Williams, commander of the Maryland brigade, wrote. "The Maryland Line Advancd in good order with trail'd Arms and without regarding or returning the Enemys fire, charg'd and broke their best Troops." Greene praised the Virginians and Marylanders effusively, reporting that they "pressed on with such unshaken resolution that they bore down all before them. The Enemy were routed in all quarters." Henry Lee, seeing the British line collapse, led his legion infantry in an attack on the British left flank and then swept across the battlefield from south to north.[53]

The Americans were on the verge of destroying Stewart's army, the result of the troops' hard fighting and Greene's deft handling of the battle and the moves preliminary to it. He had achieved partial surprise despite the deserters who warned Stewart, had planned his approach march well, and had not let the encounter with Coffin alter his plans. His deployment and troop movements had been wisely calculated, and he had taken advantage of an unforeseen British charge to launch a counterattack that had routed the enemy. All that remained was to eliminate the British remnants still opposing him, and Greene would have the battlefield victory he had sought for so long.

The last pockets of British resistance proved formidable. Before the battle, Stewart had instructed Major Sheridan of the New York Volunteers that, in the event of disaster, the major should take position in a brick house behind the British right flank and "check the enemy should they attempt to pass it." Sheridan did so, and Marjoribanks withdrew along the creek to take a new post in the palisaded garden between the house and the creek and in the creek bed, where his battalion could enfilade the American left flank. Greene brought up his two six-pounders and two British six-pounders abandoned in the enemy's flight to bombard the house—without effect. The gunners pushed their pieces so far forward that they were easy targets for the Loyalists in the brick house, and most of the artillerymen were killed or wounded.[54]

Greene ordered his reserve, Washington's cavalry and Captain Robert Kirkwood's Delaware Continentals along with Colonel Wade Hampton's state cavalry, to dislodge Marjoribanks. Unwilling to wait for Hampton or the infantry, Washington charged the British but could not penetrate the thick brush. After futilely discharging their pistols, the dragoons rode back and forth along the front of the British flank battalion, vainly seeking an opening they could penetrate while British muskets emptied one saddle after another. The fighting ended when Washington's horse was shot; he was pinned beneath the animal and captured.[55] Once again, Washington had chosen to disregard his orders, costing Greene any possibility of dislocating the British right flank.

Greene next tried to push troops through the British camp, bypassing the house. Kirkwood was redirected there and was soon joined by some Virginia Continentals. The tents concealed the Americans from the heavy, "destructive" fire emanating from the house. However, the American troops did not push past the rows of tents, a failure attributed to the camp "presenting many objects to tempt a thirsty, naked and fatigued soldiery to acts of insubordination." Such an explanation is almost certainly inaccurate. The British camp could scarcely have abounded in foodstuffs, given that Stewart had been forced to feed his men by foraging for sweet potatoes. Nor could there have been a plentiful supply of "liquors and refreshments." The British rum supply was in the wagon train and American scouts had seen the British destroy it on the evening of September 9. In fact it was the camp—with its tents, ropes, and stakes—that blocked the American advance. Any unit entering the camp would immediately lose its formation as the troops threaded their way among these obstacles; emerging in a trickle at the other end, they were easy targets for Loyalist marksmen in the brick house.[56] Greene failed to understand the nature of the obstruction that the camp presented; yet he can not be faulted too severely. The other American officers on the field, as well as subsequent historians, made the same error.

One chance remained to drive the British from the field, and Greene seized it. He ordered Lee's Legion cavalry on his right to advance through the clear terrain south of the camp, attack Coffin's troops, and push into the British rear. Greene's aide, Captain Nathaniel Pendleton, discovered on delivering the order that Lee was not with his cavalry. Pendleton gave Greene's instructions to Major Joseph Eggleston, Lee's second in command. When Pendleton rejoined Greene, the commander was upset to find that Lee was not where he expected to find him. Eggleston attacked as ordered and was repulsed. Samuel Hammond, a South Carolina militia officer, later insisted that at the time Greene issued his order to the legion, Lee was engaged in an argument with the officers of the Virginia Continental regiments, apparently trying to take command after the senior officer, Lieutenant Colonel Richard Campbell, had been mortally wounded.[57] Like William Washington, Lee appears to have put his thirst for personal glory ahead of the good of the army and cost Greene his last opportunity to win the battle.

Having committed his last reserves, Greene had run out of tactical options. While he had cast about for a way to end British resistance, Stewart and Cruger had rallied their troops east of the camp. After defeating Eggleston, Coffin led his dragoons forward against the scattered American infantry. Seeing his opportunity, Stewart joined in the attack with his soldiers. Sheridan followed suit, sallying from the brick house while Marjoribanks charged from the garden and creek bed. Attacked in front and on both flanks, the Americans withdrew. Greene described his retreat as orderly and the result of his decision to break off the action once success seemed unlikely. Stewart, on the other hand, declared that "we totally routed them." Otho Williams asserted that the British charged and captured the four cannon outside the brick house, whereupon Greene ordered the army "to retire which was done gradually, the Enemy not presuming to follow."[58]

For the fourth and last time, Greene had battled the British and suffered a tactical defeat. He reported his losses as 138 killed, 378 wounded, and 41 missing. British casualties in the main battle were 84 killed, 351 wounded, and 257 missing, plus an additional 147 foragers from the flank battalion and Third Regiment missing and believed captured. No mention was made of the foragers detached from five other regiments. Stewart's army had been mauled. On the night of September 9 he withdrew toward Charleston. Never again did British forces venture far from that city.[59]

At Eutaw Springs and throughout the campaign leading up to the battle, Nathanael Greene had demonstrated a great deal of tactical ability. Had it not been for the failures of Lee and William Washington, Greene might have destroyed the British army, winning a crucial victory a month before George Washington's success at Yorktown. Yet Greene bears some responsibility for his two subordinates' shortcomings because he never called them to account for their earlier disobedience and thus left them with the impression that they could obey orders at their own discretion. If his subordinates sometimes failed him and if he showed a tendency to break off battles rather than gamble his army on a chance at victory, Greene nonetheless demonstrated a solid grasp of tactics, which evolved over time. He adopted Morgan's defensive technique of deploying his forces in multiple lines with the militia in front and at Eutaw Springs adapted the method for attack. He astutely managed to maneuver his army into position to mount a surprise attack and skillfully arranged his line of march to facilitate the troops' deployment. Greene also showed that he could remain calm and respond to unexpected crises, such as Coffin's attack on the head of his column and the British counterattack that drove off the militia and North Carolina Continentals. These are all hallmarks of a capable tactician.

One other factor must be considered: the battles were not Greene's alone to win or lose. In Cornwallis, Rawdon, and Cruger, Greene faced highly capable adversaries leading veteran British and Loyalist troops. Certainly the skills of the opposing commanders and their soldiers had as much or more to do with the American commander's battlefield failures as did any tactical shortcomings on Greene's part.

NOTES

1. On Greene as a strategist, see Lawrence E. Babits and Joshua B. Howard, *Long, Obstinate, and Bloody: The Battle of Guilford Courthouse* (Chapel Hill: University of North Carolina Press, 2009); Gerald M. Carbone, *Nathanael Greene: A Biography of the American Revolution* (New York: Palgrave Macmillan, 2008); Terry Golway, *Washington's General: Nathanael Greene and the Triumph of the American Revolution* (New York: Holt, 2006); Dan L. Morrill, *Southern Campaigns of the American Revolution* (Baltimore, Md.: Nautical & Aviation Publishing, 1992); Elswyth Thane, *The Fighting Quaker: Nathanael Greene* (New York: Hawthorn, 1972); Theodore Thayer, *Nathanael Greene: Strategist of the American Revolution* (New York: Twayne, 1960); M. F. Treacy, *Prelude to Yorktown: The Southern Campaign of Nathanael Greene, 1780–1781* (Chapel Hill: University of North Carolina Press, 1963); Spencer C. Tucker, *Rise and Fight Again: The Life of Nathanael Greene* (Wilmington, Del.: Intercollegiate Studies Institute, 2009); and Dennis Conrad's essay in this volume.

2. Treacy, *Prelude to Yorktown*, 197. Other observations on Greene's tactical abilities, or lack thereof, appear in Charles Bracelen Flood, *Rise and Fight Again: Perilous Times along the Road to Independence* (New York: Dodd, Mead, 1976), 400; Morrill, *Southern Campaigns*, 151, 160; Golway, *Washington's General*, 302–3.

3. Babits and Howard, *Long, Obstinate, and Bloody*, 56–59; John Buchanan, *The Road to Guilford Courthouse: The American Revolution in the Carolinas* (New York: Wiley, 1997), 372.

4. Babits and Howard, *Long, Obstinate, and Bloody*, 94, 102–13, 216; Buchanan, *The Road to Guilford Courthouse*, 374–76; Nathanael Greene to Samuel Huntington, March 16, 1781, in *The Papers of General Nathanael Greene*, edited by Richard K. Showman, Dennis M. Conrad, and Roger N. Parks, 13 vols. (Chapel Hill: University of North Carolina Press, 1994), 7:434–35 (quotation).

5. Babits and Howard, *Long, Obstinate, and Bloody*, 117–28; Buchanan, *The Road to Guilford Courthouse*, 377; Greene to Huntington, March 16, 1781, *The Papers of General Nathanael Greene*, 7:435 (quotation).

6. Babits and Howard, *Long, Obstinate, and Bloody*, 144.

7. Ibid., 144–58, 162–63; Buchanan, *The Road to Guilford Courthouse*, 378–79; Jim Piecuch and John Beakes, *"Cool Deliberate Courage": John Eager Howard in the American Revolution* (Charleston: Nautical & Aviation Publishing, 2009), 90–91.

8. Babits and Howard, *Long, Obstinate, and Bloody* 164–65, 174–75; Buchanan, 379–80; Greene to Huntington, March 16, 1781, *The Papers of General Nathanael Greene*, 7:435.

9. Babits and Howard, *Long, Obstinate, and Bloody*, 180.

10. Ibid., 129–39; Buchanan, *The Road to Guilford Courthouse*, 374, 376–77, 380 (quotation); Greene to William Campbell, March 18, 1781, *The Papers of General Nathanael Greene*, 7:445.

11. Greene to George Washington, March 29, 1781, *The Papers of General Nathanael Greene*, 7:481.

12. Greene to John Butler, April 19, 1781, ibid., 8:117–18 (quotation); Francis, Lord Rawdon, to Nisbet Balfour, April 12, 1781, Papers of Charles, Earl Cornwallis, National

Archives, Kew, U.K. (cited hereafter as Cornwallis Papers), PRO 30/11/5, 236 (quotation); Rawdon to Balfour, April 13, 1781, ibid., PRO 30/11/5, 239.

13. Piecuch and Beakes, *"Cool Deliberate Courage,"* 100–101, 102; John S. Pancake, *This Destructive War: The British Campaign in the Carolinas, 1780–1782* (University: University of Alabama Press, 1985), 193.

14. Rawdon to Cornwallis, April 26, 1781, Cornwallis Papers, PRO 30/11/5, 262; Pancake, *This Destructive War,* 195.

15. Rawdon to Cornwallis, April 26, 1781, Cornwallis Papers, PRO 30/11/5, 262; Greene to Huntington, April 27, 1781, *The Papers of General Nathanael Greene,* 8:155–56 (quotation).

16. Greene to Huntington, April 27, 1781, *The Papers of General Nathanael Greene,* 8:156–57 (quotations); Rawdon to Cornwallis, April 26, 1781, Cornwallis Papers, PRO 30/11/5, 262; Pancake, *This Destructive War,* 196, 198; Piecuch and Beakes, *"Cool Deliberate Courage,"* 104–5.

17. Greene to Daniel Morgan, August 26, 1781, *The Papers of General Nathanael Greene,* 9:256–57.

18. Piecuch and Beakes, *"Cool Deliberate Courage,"* 105–6.

19. Ibid., 103–4; Pancake, *This Destructive War,* 199; Rawdon to Cornwallis, April 26, 1781, Cornwallis Papers, PRO 30/11/5, 262 (quotation); Greene to Huntington, April 27, 1781, *The Papers of General Nathanael Greene,* 8:156–57 (quotation).

20. Piecuch and Beakes, *"Cool Deliberate Courage,"* 108–9.

21. Greene to Henry Lee, May 22, 1781, *The Papers of General Nathanael Greene,* 8:291–92 (quotation); Pancake, *This Destructive War,* 209–10; Piecuch and Beakes, *"Cool Deliberate Courage,"* 114–15.

22. Pancake, *This Destructive War,* 210; Piecuch and Beakes, *"Cool Deliberate Courage,"* 115; Robert D. Bass, *Ninety Six: The Struggle for the South Carolina Back Country* (Lexington, S.C.: Sandlapper, 1978), 389.

23. Pancake, *This Destructive War,* 210; Otho Holland Williams to John Harris Cruger, June 3, 1781, *The Papers of General Nathanael Greene,* 8:339 (quotation); Cruger to Williams, June 3, 1781, ibid., 8:340.

24. Pancake, *This Destructive War,* 210, 212; Piecuch and Beakes, *"Cool Deliberate Courage,"* 116–17.

25. Greene to Elijah Clarke, June 12, 1781, *The Papers of General Nathanael Greene,* 8:379; Rawdon to Cornwallis, June 5, 1781, Cornwallis Papers, PRO 30/11/6, 174; Pancake, *This Destructive War,* 212; Piecuch and Beakes, *"Cool Deliberate Courage,"* 117.

26. Greene to Thomas Sumter, June 17, 1781, *The Papers of General Nathanael Greene,* 8:405; Greene to Huntington, June 20, 1781, ibid., 8:419, 421 (quotation); Rawdon to Cornwallis, August 2, 1781, Cornwallis Papers, PRO 30/11/6, 347; Pancake, *This Destructive War,* 212–14; Piecuch and Beakes, *"Cool Deliberate Courage,"* 117–18.

27. Greene to Thomas McKean, July 17, 1781, *The Papers of General Nathanael Greene,* 9:27–29; Henry Lee, *Memoirs of the War in the Southern Department of the United States,* edited by Robert E. Lee (1869); republished as *The Revolutionary War Memoirs of General Henry Lee* (New York: Da Capo Press, 1998), 387 (quotation).

28. Rawdon to Cornwallis, June 7, 1781, Cornwallis Papers, PRO 30/11/6, 194 (quotation); James Wemyss, "Sketches of the characters of the General Staff officers and

Heads of Departments of the British Army that served in America during the revolutionary war, (the Northern army excepted) with some remarks connected therewith. By a Field officer who served the whole of that war," in Thomas Sumter Papers, Lyman C. Draper Manuscripts Collection, 17 VV, microfilm (quotation), Wisconsin Historical Society, Madison; Pancake, *This Destructive War*, 215–16.

29. William Washington to Greene, July 30, 1781, *The Papers of General Nathanael Greene*, 9:118; Charles Myddelton to Greene, August 4, 1781, ibid., 9:130–31; Greene to George Washington, August 6, 1781, ibid., 9:141; Pancake, *This Destructive War*, 217.

30. Henry Lee to Greene, August 8, 1781, *The Papers of General Nathanael Greene*, 9:151.

31. Greene to Henry Lee, August 9, 1781, ibid., 9:153 (quotation); Lee to Greene, August 10, 1781, ibid., 9:162 (quotation); Greene to Lee, August 12, 1781, ibid., 9:170–71, (quotation).

32. Henry Lee to Greene, August 13, 1781, ibid., 9:177; Greene to Lee, August 14, 1781, ibid., 9:181 (quotations).

33. Greene to François Lellorquis, Marquis de Malmedy, August 15, 1781, ibid., 9:185; Greene to Henry Lee, August 20, 1781, ibid., 9:214–15 (quotation); Greene to Lee, August 21, 1781, ibid., 9:218 (quotation).

34. General Greene's orders, August 22, 1781, ibid., 9:222; Greene's orders, August 25, 1781, ibid., 9:236; Greene to William Henderson, August 24, 1781, ibid., 9:234; Greene to Lee, August 25, 1781, ibid., 9:239 (quotation).

35. William Henderson to Greene, August 25, 1781, ibid., 9:245; Greene to Henry Lee, August 25, 1781, ibid., 9:239.

36. Greene's orders, August 30, 1781, ibid., 9:271; Henry Lee to Greene, September 1, 1781, ibid., 9:278; Greene's orders, September 2, 1781, ibid., 9:278; Alexander Stewart to Cornwallis, September 9, 1781, in K. G. Davies, ed. *Documents of the American Revolution, 1770–1783: Colonial Office Series*, 21 vols. (Shannon: Irish University Press, 1972–81), 20:227 (quotation); Francis Marion to Greene, September 3, 1781, *The Papers of General Nathanael Greene*, 9:290; Edmund Pendleton to Francis Marion, September 4, 1781, ibid., 9:293; Nathaniel Pendleton to Andrew Pickens, September 5, 1781, ibid., 9:299.

37. Greene's orders, September 7, 1781, ibid., 9:305; Thomas Anderson, "Journal of Lt. Thomas Anderson," September 7, 1781, Microfilm MSS A55, Historical Society of Delaware, Wilmington; Stewart to Cornwallis, September 9, 1781, in Davies, ed. *Documents of the American Revolution*, 20:227.

38. Lee, *Memoirs*, 666 (quotation); William Johnson, *Sketches of the Life and Correspondence of Nathanael Greene*, 2 vols. (Charleston, S.C.: A. E. Miller, 1822), 2:219; Pancake, *This Destructive War*, 216–17; Golway, *Washington's General*, 279–80; Carbone, *Nathanael Greene*, 203, 204. Carbone does not give a figure for American strength but states that Greene's casualties of 522 men amounted to one-fourth of the army; *The Papers of General Nathanael Greene*, 9:333n.

39. "Return of the Army under the Command of Lieutenant Colonel Alexander Stewart, taken on the Morning before the Action at Eutaws," September 8, 1781, Colonial Office Transcripts, Library of Congress, Washington, D.C.; Stewart to Cornwallis, September 26, 1781, Cornwallis Papers, PRO 30/11/6, 399 (quotation); Lee to Greene, August 20, 1781, *The Papers of General Nathanael Greene*, 9:214; "Return of the Number

of Commissioned Non Commissioned Officers, Rank & File in the Action at Eutaws,"
September 8, 1781, Colonial Office Transcripts.

40. "Abstract of a General Muster & Inspection of Colonel Williams' Maryland
Brigade," August 5, 1781, Nathanael Greene Papers, William L. Clements Library, Ann
Arbor, Michigan; "Return of the Infantry Serving in the Southern Army," July 26, 1781,
George Washington Papers, Library of Congress; "Return of the Artillery Commanded
by Colonel Harrison," July 26, 1781, Washington Papers; "Return of the Cavalry Serv-
ing in the Southern Army," July 26, 1781, Washington Papers. On the assignment of
South Carolina mounted militia to Washington's regiment, see John Chaney, Pension
Application S32177, March 29, 1833, National Archives, Washington, D.C.

41. "Field Return of the No. Carolina Militia Commanded by Colonel Malmady,"
August 25, 1781, Greene Papers, Clements Library; Johnson, *Sketches*, 2:219; Henderson
to Greene, August 25, 1781, *The Papers of General Nathanael Greene*, 9:245.

42. Greene to McKean, September 11, 1781, *The Papers of General Nathanael Greene*,
9:328–29; Robert Kirkwood, *The Journal and Order Book of Captain Robert Kirkwood of the
Continental Line*, edited by Joseph Brown Turner (Wilmington: Historical Society of
Delaware, 1910), 22 (quotation).

43. Stewart to Cornwallis, September 9, 1781, in Davies, ed., *Documents of the American Revolution*, 20:227 (quotation), 228; Stewart to Cornwallis, September 26, 1781, Cornwallis Papers, PRO 30/11/6, 399; "Return of Officers Non Commissioned Officers, Rank
& File sent out on a Rooting Party," September 8, 1781, Colonial Office Transcripts,
Library of Congress.

44. Stewart to Cornwallis, September 9, 1781, in Davies, ed., *Documents of the American Revolution*, 20:227.

45. Lee, *Memoirs*, 466; Anderson, "Journal," September 8, 1781; Kirkwood, *Journal
and Order Book*, 23; "Battle of Eutaw. Account furnished by Colonel Otho Williams, with
additions by Colonels W. Hampton, Polk, Howard and Watt," in Robert W. Gibbes, ed.,
*Documentary History of the American Revolution, Consisting of Letters and Papers Relating to
the Contest for Liberty Chiefly in South Carolina*, 3 vols. (New York: Appleton, 1857), 3:145.

46. Stewart to Cornwallis, September 26, 1781, Cornwallis Papers, PRO 30/11/6, 399.

47. Greene to Thomas McKean, September 11, 1781, *The Papers of General Nathanael
Greene*, 20:329; Lee, *Memoirs*, 466–67.

48. "Battle of Eutaw," in Gibbes, ed., *Documentary History*, 3:146.

49. Stewart to Cornwallis, September 9, 1781, in Davies, ed., *Documents of the American Revolution*, 20:228.

50. Greene to Thomas McKean, September 11, 1781, *The Papers of General Nathanael
Greene*, 9:329 (quotation); "Battle of Eutaw," in Gibbes, ed., *Documentary History*, 3:148;
Lee, *Memoirs*, 468.

51. "Battle of Eutaw," in Gibbes, ed., *Documentary History*, 3:149.

52. Ibid.; Stewart to Cornwallis, September 9, 1781, in Davies, ed., *Documents of the
American Revolution*, 20:228; Stewart to Cornwallis, September 26, 1781, Cornwallis
Papers, PRO 30/11/6, 399.

53. Otho Holland Williams to Edward Giles, September 23, 1781, Otho Holland
Williams Papers, Maryland Historical Society, Baltimore (quotation); Greene to Mc-
Kean, September 11, 1781, *The Papers of General Nathanael Greene*, 9:331 (quotation).

54. Stewart to Cornwallis, September 9, 1781, in Davies, ed., *Documents of the American Revolution*, 20:228 (quotation); Greene to Thomas McKean, September 11, 1781, *The Papers of General Nathanael Greene*, 9:331; "Battle of Eutaw," in Gibbes, ed., *Documentary History*, 3:151. Marjoribanks's movement along the creek is a conclusion reached by the author after an examination of the battlefield.

55. Greene to Thomas McKean, September 11, 1781, *The Papers of General Nathanael Greene*, 9:331; "Battle of Eutaw," in Gibbes, ed., *Documentary History*, 3:152.

56. Kirkwood, *Journal and Order Book*, 23; "Battle of Eutaw," in Gibbes, ed., *Documentary History*, 3:153–54 (quotations); Greene to McKean, September 11, 1781, *The Papers of General Nathanael Greene*, 9:332; Piecuch and Beakes, *"Cool Deliberate Courage,"* 125–26.

57. "Battle of Eutaw," in Gibbes, ed., *Documentary History*, 3:154–55; Samuel Hammond, "Notes on the Battle of Eutaw," n.d., Draper Collection, 1 DD, microfilm.

58. "Battle of Eutaw," in Gibbes, ed., *Documentary History*, 3:155; Stewart to Cornwallis, September 26, 1781, Cornwallis Papers, PRO 30/11/6, 399 (quotation); Greene to McKean, September 11, 1781, *The Papers of General Nathanael Greene*, 9:332; Williams to Giles, September 23, 1781, Williams Papers (quotation).

59. "Return of the Killed, Wounded and Missing of the Southern Army," September 25, 1781, in *The State Records of North Carolina*, edited by Walter Clark, 16 vols., numbered 11–26 (Winston & Goldsboro, N.C.: State of North Carolina, 1895–1905), 15:637; "Return of the Killed, Wounded, and Missing . . . in the Action at Eutaws," September 8, 1781, and "Return of . . . a Rooting Party," September 8, 1781, Colonial Office Transcripts.

Independence and Slavery

The Transformation of
Nathanael Greene, 1781–1786

Gregory D. Massey

*A*merican independence was not a reality until it was won by force of arms, until the British relinquished their claim of sovereignty over the rebellious colonies. By December 1781, independence lay within the grasp of the United States, thanks in no small part to the performance of Nathanael Greene and the men under his command in the Southern Department. Aided by able subordinates and the combined efforts of Continental regulars and state militiamen, Greene blocked British efforts to subjugate the South and regained territory that the redcoats had once conquered. In addition to the past summer's battles, sieges, and skirmishes in South Carolina, Greene's army affected events elsewhere, particularly in Yorktown, Virginia. Greene was not present at the Franco-American siege that defeated the British army under Charles, Earl Cornwallis, but the wily Rhode Islander's strategic and tactical decisions initiated the chain of events that led to the great victory at Yorktown. Greene could look back on these accomplishments with pardonable pride, but he had limited time for self-absorbed reflection. He still faced pressing concerns. The British maintained their hold on Charleston, South Carolina, and Savannah, Georgia; and Greene's army was too weak to go on the offensive. Having shown a penchant for thinking outside the box, he conceived a way to end this stalemate. He knew it was a controversial proposal and a bitter pill for civilian leaders to swallow. On December 9 Greene wrote a letter to Governor John Rutledge of South Carolina and—in an argument that was both passionate and reasoned—proposed that slaves be enlisted in the Continental army. Winning independence in the South, Greene argued, required arming slaves and eventually freeing them in return for their military service.

This proposal proved ironic. Less than a year later, when Greene again faced a military quandary, one involving the need to clothe and provision his army, he made financial arrangements that left him deeply in debt and dependent on the mercy of his creditors. The only way to regain his financial independence, he decided, was to rely on plantations granted him by the grateful states of South Carolina and Georgia, plantations worked by slaves. Greene's transformation from a successful general advocating that slaves be armed to a struggling planter dependent on slave labor illustrates the paradoxical relationship between independence and slavery during the American Revolution.

A native of Rhode Island, the New England state with the highest proportion of slaves, Nathanael Greene knew slavery firsthand. He had grown up near Warwick, where one-tenth of the residents were black and enslaved. But that experience could not have prepared him for the plantation culture of low-country South Carolina. The differences in scale between South Carolina and Rhode Island were striking. In lowcountry South Carolina, slavery existed on a large scale; in the rural parishes dotted by rice and indigo plantations, black people comprised upward of 70 percent of the population. By contrast slave ownership in Rhode Island was decidedly small-scale; for example Greene and his wife, Caty, owned three or four slaves who functioned as household servants.[1]

The differences in scale accounted for different perspectives on arming and freeing slaves. In 1778, facing a manpower shortage in its Continental battalions, the Rhode Island legislature temporarily authorized the enlistment of slaves. Eventually the First Rhode Island Regiment enlisted free black men, Narragansett Indians, and slaves, who were to receive freedom for their service while their masters received monetary compensation for relinquishing their property. In this regiment, black men served well, distinguishing themselves for bravery when they held the American right flank at the Battle of Rhode Island in July 1778.[2] Greene probably thought of their example, which showed what was possible. But did he also think of the differences in scale between slave ownership in Rhode Island and in South Carolina? In South Carolina arming slaves meant putting muskets in the hands of large numbers of black men. As he wrote his letter to John Rutledge, Greene was proposing a stark change in the social order of a plantation society—and in the way southern Whigs had been fighting the war.

Since Greene arrived in the South a year earlier to assume command of the Southern Department, the war—brutal as it was—had pitted free white men against each other. Both sides were content to use black manpower behind the scenes. Greene for example had authorized the employment of slaves to dig approach trenches at the siege of Ninety Six, and he used slaves to carry provisions and maintain ferries.[3] His British counterparts had been slightly less conventional in their use of black men. Sir Henry Clinton's 1779 Phillipsburg

Proclamation had welcomed fugitive slaves within British lines at New York, where eventually thousands of bondsmen took refuge. Although the British did not issue a similar proclamation in the South, thousands more slaves joined them there. Despite the availability of this manpower resource, the British used former slaves as soldiers only in small groups and on an ad hoc basis, always stopping short of a systematic policy of arming large numbers of black men.[4]

Now, Greene informed Governor Rutledge, the British appeared to have shifted their policy and planned to send more black soldiers into the field. Based on those reports, coupled with intelligence that the British also were organizing Loyalists and agitating Indians, Greene believed the redcoats were contemplating offensive operations. If he were wrong and the enemy merely planned to hold Charleston, Greene doubted they would do so if it required a large, expensive force, much larger than their present garrison. Thus he thought it was imperative that the Americans move immediately to raise an army large enough to force a British evacuation. After all Charleston was vital to South Carolina's economy; it was in the interest of the state that the city be recovered and quickly.

The state could not raise an army to counter a British offensive or to regain Charleston without enlisting black men. "The natural strength of this country in point of numbers," Greene asserted, "appears to me to consist much more of the blacks than the whites." There were not enough white men in South Carolina to augment the army's numbers, nor did the state have the financial resources to attract soldiers. Greene was certain that slaves would make good soldiers. Contrary to some arguments, he did not believe enlisting a large number of slaves would create discontent and rebelliousness among other slaves. He did not recognize that arming large numbers of slaves in a plantation society such as South Carolina was more threatening to masters and their property interests than arming small numbers of slaves in a small-scale setting such as Rhode Island. Having dismissed possible social consequences, he proposed to Rutledge that South Carolina raise two Continental regiments and two state regiments. The slaves "should have their freedom, and be cloathed, and treated in all respects as other soldiers; without which, they will be unfit for the duty expected of them."[5]

Rutledge's council voted to refer Greene's proposal to the state legislature, which was scheduled to meet in early January at Jacksonborough, a sleepy town about thirty miles from Charleston.[6] A few days after Greene received notification of this vote, he heard a decidedly different viewpoint from John Laurens, a Carolina native and Continental officer who had earlier failed to convince the state government to form a black regiment. Probably unaware that Rutledge and the council had decided to pass on the decision to the assembly, Laurens wrote, "It appears to me that the Governor & Council should not lose a moment in carrying the black levy plan into execution, but I know that unless they are goaded upon the subject, their deliberations and delays will lose the opportunity which now offers." Implicit in the letter was Laurens's hope that Greene would be the one who "goaded" Rutledge and the council.[7]

Greene waited until an opportune moment, when the assembly finally met at Jacksonborough, to goad Rutledge and his council. On January 21, 1782, he wrote Rutledge another, more forceful letter. This time Greene raised the possibility that the British might negotiate peace on the basis of *uti possidetis*, which would allow them to retain territories they held when hostilities ceased. In such a scenario, both South Carolina and Georgia would remain in British hands. As evidence that this alarming possibility was not far-fetched, Greene reported that the British themselves were arming black men in Charleston and hoped to augment the city's defenses with three thousand slaves. In reality the British never armed significant numbers of black men, but Greene relied on recent, faulty intelligence that maximized this particular threat.

In addition to citing, or overstating, present threats, Greene gave Rutledge a history lesson, lacing the lecture with more sarcasm. The general acknowledged that his proposal was tough for South Carolina's political leaders—all of them slave masters—to swallow. "The remedy may be disagreeable," Greene wrote, "but who among you could they have foreseen what has happened would not have adopted this measure . . . to have prevented so great an evil?" Before Charleston fell to the British in May 1780, the state legislature twice rejected Laurens's plan to form a black regiment. Had the legislators and Governor Rutledge acted differently, they could have protected their state "against all the miseries it has undergone and possibly by removing the hopes from the ministry of Great Britain and increasing the difficulty of conquest of the Southern States might have given peace long since to all America."[8]

Such stinging words and logically convincing argument might have afflicted some readers with guilt because of paths not taken—but not John Rutledge. In May 1779, angered that Congress failed to send Continental reinforcements to South Carolina and instead endorsed Laurens's proposal that Carolinians arm slaves, Rutledge and his privy council had offered to surrender their state if the British guaranteed its neutrality. A governor who had once been willing to surrender rather than arm slaves, Rutledge was hardly disposed to change his mind when the British were bottled up in Charleston and momentum seemed to rest with the Americans.[9]

When the assembly met in Jacksonborough from January to late February 1782, most legislators shared Rutledge's mood. Elected to the House of Representatives, John Laurens again proposed arming slaves, who would come from confiscated Loyalist estates, a politically adroit idea that threatened the property interests of no revolutionaries. Despite a heated debate, the plan won few adherents, but it struck a deep chord in the minds of opponents. "I was very much alarmed on the Occasion," confessed Edward Rutledge, brother of John. "I was repeatedly told that a large party was made & I believe it was; but upon a fair full Argument, people in general returned to their Senses." Another delegate, Aedanus Burke, noted a sinister outside influence that had temporarily deprived some legislators of their senses. In a letter to Arthur Middleton, a South Carolina delegate to Congress, Burke mentioned that Greene had championed the proposal to arm slaves. Burke then discussed his belief that most northerners, presumably including Greene, "secretly wish for a general Emancipation, if the present struggle was over." One northern friend had even suggested that "our Country would be a fine one, if our whites & blacks intermarried—the breed would be a hardy excellent race . . . fit to bear our climate."[10]

It is not difficult to see in Burke's words fear of men such as Greene, northerners bent on subverting the social and economic order of the lower South. It did not matter that Greene, a general grasping for ways to augment his army, was motivated by military expediency and had no thoughts of social and biological engineering. Intermarriage between white people and black people was the furthest thing from his mind, but image, not reality, mattered most. Burke expressed a fear other white Carolinians undoubtedly shared, even if they did not write it on paper. This frightening image of radical social change implemented by northerners served as a reminder that Greene, for all his military success, was an outsider whom South Carolinians could not fully trust. Greene at least partially recognized and understood the fears of men such as Rutledge and Burke. When Greene learned that the Jacksonborough assembly had rejected the proposal to arm slaves, he wrote that they did so "not because they objected to the expence (for they give a most enormous bounty for white men, and pay in Slaves) but from an apprehension of the consequences."[11] Greene felt no need to spell out those consequences to the recipient of the letter, Virginia planter and slave owner George Washington.

During the legislative sessions at Jacksonborough, John Rutledge's tenure as governor ended. The new governor, John Mathews, informed Greene that the assembly had rejected the proposal to arm slaves. Mathews thought the legislature was amenable, however, to enlisting slaves as officers' servants and as laborers. He asked Greene to furnish an estimate of the numbers he needed. Greene responded that the army could use more than four hundred waggoners, pioneers, and artificers, and between twenty and thirty servants. To ensure that the slaves had "an interest in their servitude," he recommended that they be clothed at public expense and "allowed the same wages granted by Congress to the Soldiers of the Continental army." Greene astutely realized that slaves, as human beings, were governed by self-interest. They would not work well in the army if they sensed they were exchanging one form of servitude for another, perhaps more dangerous. If freedom were not in the offing, financial compensation and good treatment might attract willing workers and servants.[12]

Ultimately the Jacksonborough assembly followed Greene's advice in this matter. The legislature resolved to recruit slaves from confiscated Loyalist plantations to serve as laborers and servants for Greene's army. In addition legislators demonstrated their willingness to use slaves to resurrect the state's dormant Continental battalions, but their plan went in the opposite direction from Greene's proposal that black men be enlisted as soldiers. Under the assembly's plan, white soldiers who enlisted in the state's Continental line would receive one slave for each year of military service. Using slaves as bonuses to stimulate white enlistments followed a precedent set the previous spring by partisan commander Thomas Sumter and his nominal commanding officer, Nathanael Greene. In an expedient known as "Sumter's Law," Greene had authorized Sumter's plan to take slaves owned by Loyalists and offer them as bonuses to soldiers under his command.[13] As the war wound down, Carolinians looked to the future: an independent United States of America, where slaveholding would be the foundation of white men's pursuits of happiness. Common soldiers and officers alike wanted a piece of the action. Soon Nathanael Greene claimed his piece too.

Obviously slaves were a tool to Greene, to be used expediently depending on the circumstances at hand. In April 1781, in the middle of hard fighting in the South Carolina backcountry, he could endorse Sumter's plan to use slaves as enlistment bonuses so long as they were "not claimed by good Whiggs."[14] Eight months later, with the backcountry secured but the British in control of Charleston, he could endorse a decidedly different plan, John Laurens's proposal to arm slaves. Despite the Jacksonborough legislature's overwhelming rejection of that plan, Greene did not give up. The British, after all, still maintained a stronghold in Savannah, Georgia, where their strategy to reconquer the South had begun in December 1778. After the British seizure of Savannah, Congress's recommendation that slaves be armed had applied to both South Carolina and Georgia. With that in mind, Greene decided to press the issue in Georgia.

While he awaited the outcome of debates in Jacksonborough, Greene had written to Governor John Martin of Georgia. Martin received copies of the letters Greene had written to Rutledge, as well as the general's recommendation that Georgia also arm slaves. "One common evil threatens you both," Greene insisted. As for South Carolina, he believed, "it is much to be feared, that private interest and imagenary evils, will frighten the Legislature out of a measure that cannot fail if adopted to fix their liberties upon a secure and certain footing."[15] Greene doubtless did not recognize the irony in his own words. Under his proposal, planter-legislators would win their collective independence by freeing slaves whose labor was the cornerstone of the wealth and individual independence these white masters enjoyed. Rather than "fix their liberties upon a secure and certain footing," arming slaves potentially made the slaveholders' liberty quite insecure, resting on an uncertain footing more akin to quicksand than to bedrock. Would Georgia planter-legislators, men who modeled themselves after their wealthier and more established South Carolina counterparts, view the matter any differently? In mid-March, Governor Martin informed Greene that he planned to convene Georgia's legislature and present the proposal to arm slaves. Martin was less than sanguine about his chances for success: "A body of blacks I am sure would answer every purpose intended; but, am afraid it will not go down with the people here, however, it shall not want my exertions to carry it into effect."[16]

Despite assurances that he would forward the proposal to arm slaves, there is no evidence that Martin submitted Greene's letters to the assembly when it convened in late April. The Georgia assembly, like its counterpart in South Carolina, focused attention on confiscating the property of Loyalists. The legislature also devised an inducement to attract militia to serve under General Anthony Wayne, the ranking Continental commander in the state. Here too the Georgians imitated their South Carolina counterparts. They voted to offer a bounty of twenty guineas, "to be paid in Negro's," to militiamen who enlisted for three months of service.[17]

Greene wrote Martin again in early June. Richard Howley, former Georgia governor and delegate to Congress, had discussed the issue with Greene. Their conversation convinced Howley to endorse the proposal to arm slaves, which in turn convinced Greene to try again. He urged Martin not to be deceived by the appearances of peace. Only strong military preparations by the Americans, including the formation of black regiments, would convince the British to relinquish their claims in the South.[18] Martin again stonewalled and did not submit Greene's letters to the Georgia assembly until its summer session was nearly completed. On August 4 the assembly referred the letters to a committee. The assembly adjourned the next day, apparently without ever acting on Greene's proposal.[19]

With a decisive "no" vote in South Carolina and executive-legislative runaround in Georgia, the matter of arming slaves, as Edward Rutledge put it, rested "for ever & a day."[20] So also rested Greene's hopes of renewing offensive operations against the British in Charleston. The military campaign in 1782, such as it was, consisted of British raids to obtain supplies and capture slaves while the Americans responded with futile efforts to attack these foraging expeditions. For example, in late March, Major Thomas Fraser led about two hundred British cavalry and Loyalist mounted militia in a raid on plantations along the Santee River. Greene received intelligence that the raid was an effort to distract part of the American force so the British could attack the main army. He ordered John Laurens, then in command of the army's light troops, to coordinate his movements with Francis Marion and attack Fraser's detachment. Laurens and Marion were unable to nab Fraser, but they did learn that Greene's intelligence was inaccurate. Fraser's raid was not a decoy, an adjunct of a larger British operation; rather his force was the main operation, and its objective was quite limited and focused. "Their object," reported Laurens, "was the capture of Negroes." Fraser in fact returned to Charleston with about 150 slaves seized from plantations owned by prominent Whigs. Fraser's expedition was retaliatory, a British response to the Jacksonborough assembly's confiscation of Loyalist property.[21]

The hit-and-run British foraging expeditions and hit-and-miss American counterattacks continued into the summer, even after it was clear that peace was near and that the redcoats intended to leave Charleston. On August 1, Alexander Leslie, the commanding British general in Charleston, received orders to prepare an evacuation. Leslie requested a cessation of hostilities and rice provisions for his garrison and for the Loyalist refugees in Charleston. Governor John Mathews and his council, with Greene's concurrence, rejected Leslie's request. For his part Greene worried that the British were buying time until they could renew offensive operations, or at least that was what he wrote in his official dispatch to John Hanson, president of Congress. For their part Mathews and his advisers worried that providing rice to sustain the garrison in Charleston would allow the British to postpone their departure indefinitely. A better policy, Mathews and Greene reasoned, was to risk British foraging raids in return for forcing an earlier evacuation.[22]

Greene, who spoke publicly of his concern that the British were playing a duplicitous waiting game, privately conveyed other concerns that made him reject cooperation. In early August, prior to Leslie's request for trade and a ceasefire, Greene received intelligence that the British garrison needed rice "and unless they can procure some they cannot subsist the Negroes in their Garrison." This information influenced Greene's remarks to Francis Marion, which contradicted what the general later told his civilian superiors in Congress. Despite his expressed distrust of British intentions, Greene's real concern was that they leave sooner rather than later, with as few slaves as possible. "Great preparations are making in Charles Town for the evacuation of the place," he told Marion. "I am persuaded it will take place soon and the more scanty we can render their supplies of provisions the sooner it will take place and the fewer Negroes they will have it in their power to take with them."[23]

Greene undoubtedly expressed the wishes of Mathews and the Privy Council. As leaders of South Carolina's master class, they desperately wanted to prevent the British from taking large numbers of slaves. But Greene also had private motives that he left unspoken. He had become a plantation owner himself, an owner of rice plantations that needed slave labor. The Jacksonborough assembly that overwhelmingly rejected the proposal that slaves be armed had awarded him Boone's Barony, a plantation confiscated from former royal lieutenant governor William Bull. In the same summer legislative session that tabled the issue of arming slaves, the Georgia House of Assembly had voted to reward Greene with Mulberry Grove plantation on the Savannah River. Both properties, especially the Georgia plantation with "its very elegant house," promised to bring Greene profits. He was definitely interested in profits. During the war, he had been a partner in two merchant firms, one of them a family business with his brother Jacob and cousin Griffin, that strived to profit from the war. He once told Jacob, "Money becomes more and more the Americans' object. You must get rich, or you will be of no consequence." After the war he intended to focus on getting rich and establishing a legacy of financial independence for his children. The plantations were his latest and best hope to achieve that goal.[24]

The plantations would earn profits for Greene only if he found slaves to work the land. Current prospects for purchasing slaves were bleak. Joseph Clay, former paymaster for the Continental army's Southern Department and a member of the Georgia assembly, tersely informed Greene, "As to the purchasing of Negros 'tis not practicable, there being none to be disposed of." One group that might have liquidated its slave property, exiled Georgia Loyalists, had instead departed Savannah with their slaves. Greene wanted to avoid the reenactment of that scenario when the British and Carolina Loyalist refuges evacuated Charleston.[25]

Amid concerns that the British would depart with Carolina slaves, the redcoats were finally employing armed black men, though in a limited fashion. A small unit labeled the "Black Dragoons" foraged for supplies and patrolled between the two armies, occasionally engaging American soldiers in skirmishes, more often striving to prevent British and Hessian troops from deserting. Their presence, armed and menacing, fulfilled the worst nightmares of white Carolinians such as Edmund Petrie, who warned that the dragoons cared "not for Sex or Life of any they meet with." When American units successfully engaged the feared Black Dragoons, retribution was swift. In early November, an advance unit commanded by Colonel Tadeusz Kościuszko engaged about ten of these dragoons. Kościuszko reported that two of the dragoons were captured "in life" according to Greene's wishes and would be sent to the main army's camp. The Polish officer's mysterious phrase raises a question: why did Greene desire the capture of Black Dragoons? It seems likely he acted in accordance with the wishes of South Carolina civilian authorities. A month earlier John Mathews had insisted that Black Dragoons "taken in arms must be tried by the negro law; and if found guilty, executed." Summary justice served notice that the old order of white mastery and black servitude had returned. Less than a year after Greene raised the prospect of arming and freeing slaves, a proposal that undercut that social order, he was now enforcing it, and was even part of it, as he anticipated a postwar career as a planter and master of slaves.[26]

As Greene awaited the British evacuation of Charleston, he attended to private needs, securing labor for his recently received plantations, and to public needs, securing clothes and provisions for his army. The American army needed clothing, for winter was approaching. Greene's predecessor as commander of the Southern Department, Benjamin Lincoln, was serving as secretary of war. From his office in Philadelphia, Lincoln informed Greene that it would be better to obtain clothing in Charleston, regardless of the price, than to expect shipments from the North. Greene needed to find someone willing and able to relieve the army's needs. In November he found that someone, the merchant John Banks.

In Charleston on a flag of truce, Banks had access to surplus clothing held by British merchants. Banks made Greene an attractive offer. If Banks received specie to make the payments, he could save 30 percent on the purchases. Greene procured specie from George Abbot Hall, an agent in the employ of Robert Morris, superintendent of finance, Banks purchased the clothing, and the army, for the first time since Greene took command, was adequately clothed.[27]

The long-awaited British evacuation finally occurred on December 14. The British took with them more than five thousand slaves. The contributions African Americans made to the British war effort did not go unrecorded in Greene's official report to Congress. "The struggle and conflict has been long and severe," he reflected, "but when it is considered that the Enemy had upwards of 18,000 regular Troops, besides several thousands Militia and Negroes employed for the reduction of the Southern States, I hope that the progress of the Southern Army, has been no less honorable than important." With understandable and justifiable pride, Greene further praised the men under his command: "Perhaps no Army ever exhibited greater proofs of patriotism and public virtue. It has been my constant care to alleviate their distresses as much as possible, but my endeavors have been far short of my wishes, or their merit." To some degree Greene's endorsement of arming slaves had been an attempt to alleviate his army's distress, to augment its numbers and relieve some of the burden placed on white men who had fought so hard to liberate backcountry South Carolina. Only a month before the evacuation he eased the army's distress in a more direct way, procuring clothing for the half-naked troops. Despite the outcome everyone longed for, the army's distresses continued unabated. Until Greene had definite orders from Congress, he needed to keep his army together, and its provisions ran dangerously low.[28]

The soldiers first resorted to impressing provisions from war-weary Carolinians, civilians ready to get on with their lives and reluctant to supply an army whose work was practically done. Always mindful of civilian-military relations, Greene looked for another alternative. On November 23 he advertised for bids from merchants who would agree to provision his troops, but by mid-February 1783 there had been no responses, save one: John Banks again stepped into the vacuum. This time, however, he lacked capital, and his offer was less financially advantageous to Greene than the earlier contract to procure clothing. Seeking advice and political cover, Greene referred the matter to South Carolina's General Assembly. The legislature informed Greene that it too could find no businessmen willing to provision the army. Lacking any alternative, the assembly endorsed the arrangement with Banks. So he received the contract that no one else wanted.

Twice Banks had stepped up when Greene's army needed supplies. In April, a little more than a month after signing the contract to provision the army, Banks himself needed help. In debt to the British merchants, he asked Greene to bolster his credit and guarantee the purchases of provisions. Greene signed notes making himself liable if Banks failed to pay his debts. Given the circumstances, the general thought he could do little else. As he later explained to Congress, he had two choices: either to "turn the Army loose upon the Country or take the risque upon me of supporting the contractors. I chose the latter as the least evil." Greene's future financial security now rested on faith that Banks would honor his debts.[29]

Greene did not know it at the time, but when he guaranteed Banks's debts, he signed away his own independence. What Greene did know at the time was that his rice plantations, given him for his vital role in winning the independence of the southern states, promised to restore his financial standing, which had become shaky during the war. The plantations, however, would yield dividends only if he could obtain slaves. In South Carolina, the General Assembly allowed him to purchase on credit the slaves already on Boone's Barony plantation; he also purchased slaves from confiscated Loyalist estates. His representatives in Georgia, however, still struggled to find slaves for the Mulberry Grove plantation. The need for slaves probably explains Greene's advice to Governor Lyman Hall of Georgia. He advised Hall to invite Loyalist refugees from Florida to resettle in Georgia, a move he called "a most capital stroke in politics." Now that peace negotiations had resulted in the transfer of Florida to Spain, many of the Loyalists would be "unwilling to live under Spanish government." Their settlement in Georgia, Greene predicted, would "be the means of enriching the Country with a large number of negroes." Greene's economic self-interest and the interests of the planter elite of Georgia had become one and the same.[30]

By June, Greene had received orders to dismiss the remaining remnants of his army. Aside from taking care of paperwork, his public service in the South was at an end. He pondered his future financial prospects, which rested so heavily on his plantations. To his cousin Griffin Greene he wrote, "My landed property in this Country I am endeavoring to put in the way of improvement; which if I can effect, it will afford me a genteel Independence." These twin goals, maintaining gentility, his status as one of the American elite, and independence, his ownership of property and freedom from debt, were achievable only if he made the plantations profitable. More prophetically than he knew, Greene added, "To put this in the power of fortune may leave me in the decline of life, with a shattered constitution to struggle with difficulties painful to contemplate. But if hazarding something would give the concern any great advantages, I should be willing to run some risque." To increase his capital, he was indeed willing to take risks. He considered dabbling in the slave trade, albeit by proxy. The Greene family mercantile firm was part owner of the frigate *Flora*. If South Carolina reopened the slave trade, Greene suggested to Griffin, their business could earn profits by bringing to Charleston a cargo of slaves.[31]

Greene was willing to risk the vagaries of the slave trade because he had put his financial independence greatly at risk when he became surety for John Banks's debts. Already there were signs that Banks was not on the up-and-up, as his expenses exceeded his capital. Greene put aside any suspicions he should have formed. Instead he took comfort that one of his former aides, Ichabod Burnet, had formed a partnership with Banks. "Banks is a sanguine young fellow and of an adventerous make," Greene observed, "but Burnets caution will limit his enterprise." He attributed their business mistakes to inexperience not to any want of honor. As he put the best face on one financial arrangement, he received reality checks about his business interests to the northward. His investments, including the family business, had lost considerable money during the war. His need to invest in his plantations meant incurring more debt—at least in the short term.[32]

With these concerns in mind, he rebuked his wife, Caty, for purchasing an expensive chariot and horses. Under ordinary circumstances, her conspicuous display of consumption marked the Greenes as members of elite society. Under present circumstances, she endangered their ability to maintain the precarious foundation on which their gentility rested. "As fortune is necessary to continue us upon a respectable footing in life as well as to educate our children properly," he lectured her, "it is our duty and our interest to limit our expences to our income." What bothered him most was his loss of independence; he knew his

growing indebtedness made him subject to the will of other men. "The mortification of being in another mans power, or called upon for what one cannot
pay," he wrote Caty, "is not a little distressing to ones feelings."[33]

In mid-August 1783 Greene departed Charleston and returned north after
an absence of nearly three years. He reached Newport, Caty, and their five children in late November. Never far from his mind were the estates he had left
behind in Georgia and South Carolina. He desperately needed capital to make
the plantations profit-earning enterprises. Using Robert Morris as an interme-
diary, he tried but failed to obtain a loan from a Dutch merchant firm.[34]

Friends saw the plantations as sirens luring Greene to an alien land polluted
with the stain of slavery. William Gordon, a Congregationalist minister who
was collecting materials for a history of the Revolution, corresponded with
Greene, seeking information on the southern campaigns. Gordon offered unsolicited advice: Greene belonged in his native Rhode Island, not in the hot and
humid South, "where slaves are more numerous than Freeman." "By that means
you may live the longer & enjoy life the more fully," Gordon predicted, with
more prescience than he knew. Former Continental army adjutant general
Joseph Reed saw the issue in material terms. He believed Greene was seduced
by the opulence of the planter lifestyle. Indeed South Carolina rice planters had
been the wealthiest Americans prior to the Revolution. That wealth, however,
came with a price. Was Greene willing to pay that price? Reed posed two stark
questions: "Will you be a Planter with a Retinue of Slaves? Or will you come
Northward to enjoy more Ease, but less Splendor?"[35] Greene did not see the
clear choice that Gordon and Reed saw. The southern plantations, Greene believed, promised a more secure economic foundation for his children's future
and a quicker escape from the financial labyrinth of his present. He and his family would go to the South once his affairs were in order.

He also received a letter from a man who mistakenly considered him a pro-
gressive thinker on slavery. Warner Mifflin, a Delaware Quaker who had freed
his slaves, wrote to former Quaker Nathanael Greene of Rhode Island. Mifflin
reminded Greene of his earlier stated goal to establish liberty on a lasting foundation. He encouraged the general-turned-planter to strike a blow against slavery and not operate his plantations with slave labor. If Greene opted to profit
by the enslavement of other men, he would "encourage the Petty Tyrants of
America to hold on their Oppression . . . and so to draw down renew'd displeasure from Heaven." Greene's response made clear his intention. "On the subject of slavery, nothing can be said in its defense," he wrote. "But you are much
mistaken respecting my influence in the business." He perhaps thought of an
earlier letter he had received from the prominent political figure, physician, and
author Benjamin Rush. With an exaggerated sense of Greene's influence, Rush
had encouraged the general to convince South Carolinians not to reopen the

slave trade. "The citizens of South Carolina view you already as a member of their state," Rush had written, an assertion belied by Aedanus Burke's reaction to Greene's proposal that Carolinians arm and free a few of their slaves.[36]

One did not join the planter elite by challenging the labor and social system that was the foundation on which the master class's wealth and independence rested. One could, however, strive to mitigate the inherent brutality of slavery. Greene took that course as he tried to rationalize his choice and make it more palatable to a man of antislavery sentiments such as Mifflin. The southern states had placed slaves in his hands, Greene informed Mifflin, "and I trust their condition will not be worse but better. They are, generally, as much attached to a plantation as a man is to his family; and to remove them from one to another is their great punishment."[37] Left unstated by Greene was the possibility that slaves were attached to a plantation not because of ties to the land but because of ties to kith and kin who lived there. Also left unstated was Greene's own avid pursuit of slaves to operate his plantations. His rationalization showed how much he already resembled other planters. They tended to blame the British for operating the slave trade, not themselves for owning slaves; in a similar vein Greene laid responsibility for his ownership of slaves at the foot of the grateful states of Georgia and South Carolina.[38]

To Greene's credit, from afar he did practice what he preached. He gave orders that his slaves be treated humanely. To Roger Parker Saunders and William Gibbons Jr., who oversaw the properties in South Carolina and Georgia respectively, Greene wrote similar directives: "Don't fail to find & cloth the Negroes well," he told Saunders. "You will take care to have the Negroes well clothed and properly fed," he told Gibbons. "I don't wish to have my Negroes worked too hard," he further instructed Gibbons, "but cannot they get out considerable lumber . . . without injury to other business in the course of the Winter?" While attempting to purchase slaves at St. Augustine, Florida, Saunders wrote that "we will not lay violent hands on them when I bring them here," implying that Greene had issued a specific injunction against physical coercion. Greene, it also seems, strived to keep husbands and wives together.[39]

Greene recognized a shared humanity that bound him to his slaves, even as he also saw them as inferiors. His ambivalence toward slavery is perhaps explained by his sensibility and by his religious beliefs. Greene's letters, particularly those addressed to his friend Samuel Ward Jr., and his allusions to his favorite book, Laurence Sterne's *Tristram Shandy*, illustrate that he was a man of sensibility, part of the Anglo-American cultural movement that promoted "mutual sympathy" with fellow beings. Influenced by the tenets of sensibility, some slave owners in South Carolina and Georgia had begun to treat their slaves more humanely. Though no longer a member of the Society of Friends, Greene admired many Quaker principles. Rhode Island Quakers had condemned the slave trade, an admonition he ignored, but Quakers also urged slave-owning brethren to treat their chattel "with tenderness," an injunction that comported with his own actions. Sensibility and religion merged in his friendship with the minister John Murray, former chaplain of Greene's Rhode Island brigade and a proponent of universal salvation, an idea Greene apparently found appealing. Sensibility and Universalism recognized a common humanity and spirit that connected people of different cultural and ethnic backgrounds. Greene neither defended slavery nor rejected the opportunity to profit from the labor of slaves. But something pricked his conscience enough that he insisted that his slaves be fed, clothed, and not overworked.[40]

In the meantime financial concerns pressed on Greene and consumed his time, energies, and emotions. John Banks was evading rather than paying his creditors. No longer could Greene depend on his former aide, Ichabod Burnet, to be a brake on Banks, as Burnet had become ill and died suddenly the previous autumn during a business trip to Havana, Cuba. Banks's creditors, particularly the British merchant E. John Collett, were pressuring Greene, the guarantor of the debts. "I have made use of every argument in my power to induce Mr. Banks to settle & pay you," Greene wrote Collett, "& have told him that he & I would not live long in the same World if he brought me into difficulties in the matter, and I will follow him to the Ends of the Earth for Satisfaction." In mid-July, Greene sailed from Newport to Charleston, the beginning of his journey in search of John Banks and a resolution to his growing financial crisis.[41]

While in South Carolina, Greene learned the enormity of his situation. Banks had fled the state, leaving behind angry creditors who had nowhere to turn for satisfaction but to Greene. "Mr. Banks is a great vilian and deserves nothing short of hanging," he said. Gone were the rosy pronouncements that Banks was overly confident and inexperienced. To Collett, who was in Virginia attempting to acquire assets belonging to Banks's merchant firm, Greene wrote with desperation: "I am reduced to worse than beggary unless you can get hold of property to cover your demands." Needing to buy time, he assured Collett that "this difficulty may be got over with Negotiation."[42]

The loss of independence bothered Greene most. A proud man—proud of his status as a successful man of property before the Revolution and proud of his military fame won during the war—he could not abide being subject to the whims of other men. That had been a driving force behind the war for independence, the desire for liberty, the freedom to chart one's own destiny and pursue one's own happiness. "Here is the Labyrinth in which we are placed," he wrote Caty. "I am not anxious to be rich, but wish to be independant. . . . To have a decent income is much to be wished; but to be free from debt more so. I never owned so much property as now, and yet never felt so poor and unhappy." It was indeed an ironic situation. He was a man of property yet a dependent; in Anglo-American political culture, ownership of property was supposedly the basis of a man's independence. There was further irony. In his public role as commander of the Southern Department, Greene made the decision that placed him in his current predicament. Indeed that was the only consolation he found, that his travails came from a public rather than a private act.[43]

The bitter ironies continued. From Charleston, Greene set out in pursuit of Banks. Three years earlier, in his greatest tactical triumph, Greene had eluded Cornwallis in their race to the Dan River. Now in a different part of North Carolina, the coastal region of sand and pine, Greene was the pursuer and Banks the elusive quarry. The outcome was similar, the quarry again eluded capture, yet different, as Banks escaped through death. He died in Washington, North Carolina, and was buried two days before Greene arrived. From there Greene traveled to Virginia to consult with Banks's brother, Henry, and achieve some satisfaction from the deceased merchant's remaining business partners, Robert Forsyth and James Hunter. "I trust you will not oblige me to go to Gaol or sell my property until you have parted with yours," he told Forsyth. "I leave this place with a heavy heart," Greene said, "the business which brought me here hangs still over my head like a threatning Cloud which embitters every moment of my life."[44]

In November, Greene rejoined his family in Newport, but his stay was brief. He returned to Charleston two months later. This visit focused less on his tangle of debts and more on the properties that he hoped would bring back the independence he had lost. Greene was perplexed with the productivity of his plantations. He learned what other rice planters had learned before him: weather and rice prices were forces that lay out of his control. The previous August he had predicted, barring any "misfortune unforeseen," that his rice would earn him a profit of fifteen hundred pounds. Instead heavy rains proved the "misfortune unforeseen," leading to disappointing crop yields in South Carolina and Georgia. Rice from Mulberry Grove, low in quantity and poor in quality, netted him a mere two hundred pounds. He also faced the quandaries of an absentee landlord who relied on the diligence and honesty of the overseer. The overseer at Mulberry Grove, a Mr. Roberts, claimed that the slaves stole rice. To the manager of his Georgia affairs, William Gibbons Jr., Greene complained, "If Mr Roberts has sufferd the Rice to be stolen away or wasted it in any improper manner he ought to be accountable. He certainly cannot be intitled to his wages unless he performs the duty expected from him. To say the Negroes stole the Rice only proves inattention in him."[45]

The poor crops further hampered Greene's efforts to climb out of debt. In desperation he clung to the one bright spot in the tangled web created by his agreements with John Banks. From Banks he had acquired title to one-half of

Cumberland Island, Georgia, which was rich in timber reserves. Convinced that the island's live oak was ideal for shipbuilding, he contacted Charles Eugène Gabriel de La Croix, Marquis de Castries, the French minister of the marine, and enlisted his old friend Marie Joseph Gilbert du Motier, Marquis de Lafayette, as an unofficial lobbyist in France. The French were interested in the island as a source of naval stores, and the preliminary negotiations gave Greene some cause for hope.[46]

He hoped to settle his family on Cumberland Island. "I find it a very valuable property," he told Caty, "and had I funds to improve it to advantage it might be made one of the first commercial objects on the Continent." He hoped also to settle other white families on the island. Lacking funds, he contacted David Hillhouse, a Connecticut native interested in relocating in Georgia. Hillhouse tried without success to secure skilled laborers from Philadelphia to cut the island's timber.[47]

The newly independent United States was a land of unlimited potential and blasted dreams. Greene could envision the potential of Cumberland Island, but he lacked the capital to make his dreams a reality. The war's end had contracted the economy, causing financial reverses and making investors and lenders more cautious than usual. "Merchants are breaking in every part of America," Greene informed Caty. He thought again of the daunting task that lay ahead. "I tremble at my own situation when I think of the enormous sums I owe and the great difficulty of obtaining Money," he said. "I seem to be doomed to a life of slavery and anxiety."[48]

There it was. An admission that he saw himself as a slave, implying an uncommon commonality with his own slaves. In the political parlance of the day, slavery stood as an abstraction, the opposite state of liberty. In the first of his letters to Caty that has survived, written in the early days of the war, he explained his decision to take up arms by asserting that the alternative was to lose his rights and be enslaved.[49] Now enslavement was less an abstraction of natural-rights language than a personal reality that consumed his waking thoughts and actions. His decisions were no longer his own. He made each choice under the influence of indebtedness, subject to men who continued to press for payment of debts owed them. Would this move or this investment pave his way from dependence to independence? Unlike the slaves he owned, however, Greene could hope for liberty, that one day he would reclaim the independence he had lost. Yet even if he were to regain his financial independence, he would always remain a dependent, subject to weather and prices beyond his control and dependent also on the labor of his slaves. For their performance of their tasks was crucial to the success of his rice crops; and they in turn would remain dependent on him, for in his path to independence lay their futures, whether or not they remained his property, owned by a master who recognized their humanity.

The next time Greene sailed south, in October 1785, he took his family with him. The previous months had been professionally and personally difficult. In August, Greene wrote to Congress requesting relief from the debts he had incurred obtaining provisions for the army. Despite its civilian authority over that army, Congress did not act on his request. It took a different Congress, after the ratification of the U.S. Constitution, to settle Greene's affairs, and the process was not completed until a decade after his death. Less than a week after he appealed to Congress, personal tragedy struck. The Greenes' sixth child, Catherine, who had been born earlier that month, died from "the throat distemper."[50] With heavy hearts and an uncertain future, the Greenes left their native Rhode Island. Without the intervention of Congress, Greene's efforts to regain his independence and prepare a legacy for his children rested, more than ever, on the productivity of his southern properties.

The Greenes reached Savannah on October 30 after a voyage plagued by bad weather. Worried over the family's finances and in mourning for her infant daughter, Caty was pregnant again and suffered from extreme emotional and physical stress during the journey. The Greenes found Mulberry Grove in disarray, but they immediately began working on repairing their "Magnificient but very dirty" house. Greene hoped the large poultry house and garden would keep Caty busy and mitigate her depression.[51]

Unforeseen misfortunes continued unabated. The day after the family's arrival, a slave built a fire too near the rice fields, resulting in the destruction of rice Greene deemed worth at least two hundred pounds. He lost another forty-five barrels in Savannah, where the rice apparently fell into the water while being unloaded at the docks. From his Boone's Barony plantation came predictions of another bad crop, owing to wet weather and late planting. "My family is in distress and I am overwhelmed with difficulties and God knows when or where they will end," he wrote candidly to a friend. "I work hard and live poor but I fear all this will not extricate me." To a merchant firm seeking payment for a debt, he tempered the bad news with optimism, expressing the hope that his presence on the scene would lead to more productive crops.[52]

Greene's final months, spent as a planter and slave owner, are shrouded in some mystery. His surviving correspondence largely concerns his continued efforts to extricate himself from debt. Evidence of his on-the-spot attention to the details of running a plantation is sketchy at best. He hired a new overseer at Mulberry Grove, but the contract did not spell out how he wanted his slaves treated. In one tantalizing letter, William Gordon, whose historical research continued to rely on Greene's memory of past battles and campaigns, referred to the novice planter's plans for his future operations. "I shall rejoice to hear," Gordon wrote, "that you have tried and succeeded in the plan of admitting the Negroes to the rights of copyholders, which if it could be once effected might possibly tend to their increasing so as to render further importations of them needless. Could you, by your example, prove instrumental in demolishing slavery and the importation of Negroes, I should think you rendered the human species nearly as much service, as when you was fighting successfully against British attempts to reduce the white inhabitants of America to the hard condition of slaves."[53] Did Greene really intend to achieve an innovative transformation in labor relations, from master-slave to owner-tenant? Or did he merely write words he knew the antislavery Gordon wanted to see?

Whatever the answer to those questions, the surviving evidence points less to Greene's innovating and more to his fitting in, becoming a conventional if humane master, with the concerns and complaints attendant to a member of the plantation elite. Shortly after his arrival, he received a letter from Aedanus Burke, formerly the vocal opponent of Greene's plan to arm and free slaves. Burke had seen in the plan a sinister effort to foster emancipation and miscegenation; now the two men were allies against a common enemy, British merchants permitted by the state government to remain in Charleston to sell their merchandise and collect debts. In the letter Burke announced his authorship of a pamphlet, *A Few Salutary Hints, Pointing Out the Policy and Consequences of Admitting British Subjects to Engross Our Trade and Become Citizens. Addressed to Those Who Either Risqued or Lost Their All in Bringing about the Revolution.*

Burke's pamphlet warned its readers of the insidious British merchants, more menacing than Cornwallis because of the stealth with which they deprived Carolinians of their independence. Burke included in the pamphlet excerpts from a letter written by Greene, in which the former general poured out invective against British merchants such as E. John Collett, who pressed him to pay the debts incurred by John Banks. The military analogies in the pamphlet probably came from Greene, including the politically laden reference to the merchants as a "standing army." Americans knew of the inherent dangers of standing armies, which inevitably threatened liberty. Merchants threatened liberty, as Greene knew firsthand. Indeed the pamphlet's subtitle poignantly illustrated his plight—he saw himself as one who risked or lost all in the cause of independence.[54]

The collaboration with Burke highlighted Greene's transformation from military outsider to planter insider. His transformation was further highlighted in the last recorded acts of his life. On Tuesday, June 13, 1786, after a one-day visit, he and Caty rode in their carriage from Savannah to Mulberry Grove. She came to Savannah for a much-needed change of scenery. Her husband knew she needed a diversion, as she was recovering emotionally and physically from a pregnancy that ended a month earlier with the loss of a boy, who would have been the couple's sixth child. For his part Greene met with his principal creditor, Collett. Greene signed new bonds to cover the amount he owed Collett; their arrangement bought Greene time, something he needed more than anything else. Time might bring some positive turn in his fortunes, better crops perhaps or payment from an impoverished Congress. He had reason to be more positive than he had been for months. In addition to the agreement with Collett, the Greene family looked forward to moving to Cumberland Island the next month.

On the way to Mulberry Grove the Greenes stopped at the plantation of William Gibbons Jr. While Caty rested, Greene toured the rice fields with Gibbons. Visual tours of rice fields were a part of plantation culture. Gibbons could inspect his property and impress his visitor, and Greene could benefit from any insights gained from a man he considered an experienced and enterprising planter. Soon after Greene departed he began complaining of a headache, the first symptom of the illness that led to his death on Monday morning, June 19. In effect, touring the plantation was Greene's last act outside his own household.[55]

It serves as final testimony to the transformation that marked Greene's life after he came to command the Southern Department. He went from commanding armies and influencing public policy to chasing an elusive shyster and holding off pushy creditors. No longer the confident general who dared recommend that rice planters arm and free their slaves, he had become one of those planters, subject to the whims of weather and prices, as dependent on his slaves as they were on him. He won fame as the military leader most responsible for winning independence in the South, but in the process he lost something precious that he never regained, his own independence.

NOTES

1. Lorenzo Johnston Greene, *The Negro in Colonial New England* (New York: Columbia University Press, 1942; reprint, New York: Atheneum, 1971), 85–88, 344; Sydney V. James, *Colonial Rhode Island: A History* (New York: Scribners, 1975), 250–51; Theodore Thayer, *Nathanael Greene: Strategist of the American Revolution* (New York: Twayne, 1960), 16, 17–18, 21; Philip D. Morgan, *Slave Counterpoint: Black Culture in the Eighteenth-Century Chesapeake & Lowcountry* (Chapel Hill & London: University of North Carolina Press, 1998), 95–97. For the Greenes' ownership of slaves, see Jacob Greene to Nathanael Greene, July 13, 1780, *The Papers of General Nathanael Greene*, edited by Richard K. Showman, Dennis R. Conrad, and Roger N. Parks, 13 vols. (Chapel Hill: University of North Carolina Press, 1976–2005), 6:93, 96n; and Nathanael Greene to Catherine Littlefield Greene, March 18, 1781, ibid., 7:446–47.

2. John Russell Bartlett, ed., *Records of the State of Rhode Island and Providence Plantations in New England*, 10 vols. (Providence: Printed by A. C. Green, 1856–1865; reprint,

New York: AMS Press, 1968), 8:359–60, 640–41; Lorenzo J. Greene, "Some Thoughts on the Black Regiment of Rhode Island in the American Revolution," *Journal of Negro History* 37 (April 1942): 142–72, especially 162, which details the temporary nature of the enlistments; and Paul F. Dearden, *The Rhode Island Campaign of 1778: Inauspicious Dawn of Alliance* (Providence: Rhode Island Historical Society, 1980), xiii, 23–24, 120–27.

3. For the employment of slave labor, see Greene to Francis Marion, January 16, 1781, Marion to Greene, January 20, 1781, *The Papers of General Nathanael Greene*, 7: 130–32, 164–65; and Greene to John Marshel, May 11, 1781; James Mayson to William Pierce, May 23, 1781; Ichabod Burnet to Andrew Pickens, June 7, 1781; Greene to Joseph Clay, June 9, 1781; ibid., 8:238, 304, 304n, 357–58, 361–62.

4. See Benjamin Quarles, *The Negro in the American Revolution* (Chapel Hill: University of North Carolina Press, 1961), 113–15, 134–51; Sylvia R. Frey, *Water from the Rock: Black Resistance in a Revolutionary Age* (Princeton: Princeton University Press, 1991), 113–42; Philip D. Morgan and Andrew Jackson O'Shaughnessy, "Arming Slaves in the American Revolution," in *Arming Slaves from Classical Times to the Modern Age*, edited by Christopher Leslie Brown and Philip D. Morgan (New Haven & London: Yale University Press, 2006), 190–92.

5. The preceding two paragraphs were drawn from Greene to John Rutledge, December 9, 1781, *The Papers of General Nathanael Greene*, 10:20–23.

6. John Rutledge to Greene, December 24, 1781, Nathanael Greene Papers, Clements Library, University of Michigan.

7. John Laurens to Greene, December 28, 1781, *The Papers of General Nathanael Greene*, 10:130–31.

8. The preceding two paragraphs were drawn from Greene to John Rutledge, January 21, 1782, *The Papers of General Nathanael Greene*, 10:228–30. For Laurens's efforts to convince his fellow Carolinians to arm and free slaves, see Gregory D. Massey, *John Laurens and the American Revolution* (Columbia: University of South Carolina Press, 2000), 140–43, 155–56.

9. On the brief British threat to Charleston in May 1779 and Rutledge's surrender proposal, see Massey, *John Laurens*, 136–39.

10. Ibid., 207–9; Edward Rutledge to Arthur Middleton, February 8, 1782, in Joseph W. Barnwell, ed., "Correspondence of Hon. Arthur Middleton, Signer of the Declaration of Independence" [part 2], *South Carolina Historical Magazine* 27 (January 1926): 4; Aedanus Burke to Middleton, January 25–February 5, 1782, in Barnwell, ed., "Correspondence of Hon. Arthur Middleton, Signer of the Declaration of Independence" [part 1], *South Carolina Historical Magazine* 26 (October 1925): 194.

11. Greene to George Washington, March 9, 1782, *The Papers of General Nathanael Greene*, 10:472.

12. John Mathews to Greene, February 6, 1782, Greene Papers, Clements Library; Greene to John Mathews, February 11, 1782, *The Papers of General Nathanael Greene*, 10:355–56.

13. Massey, *John Laurens*, 207, 209; Thomas Cooper and David J. McCord, eds., *The Statutes at Large of South Carolina*, 10 vols. (Columbia, S.C.: A. S. Johnston, 1836–41), 4:520; Greene to Thomas Sumter, May 17, 1781, *The Papers of General Nathanael Greene*, 8:278–79; Greene to Thomas McKean, August 25, 1781, ibid., 9:242; Rachel N. Klein,

Unification of a Slave State: The Rise of the Planter Class in the South Carolina Backcountry, 1760–1808 (Chapel Hill & London: University of North Carolina Press, 1990), 106–7.

14. Greene to Thomas Sumter, May 17, 1781, *The Papers of General Nathanael Greene,* 8:278–79.

15. Greene to John Martin, February 2, 1782, ibid., 10:304.

16. John Martin to Greene, March 15, 1782, ibid., 10:506–7.

17. Joseph Clay to Greene, May 13, 1782, ibid., 11:189–90, 191n.

18. Greene to Richard Howley, June 8, 1782, and Greene to John Martin, June 8, 1782, ibid., 11:307–8.

19. John Martin to Greene, August 8, 1782, ibid., 11:504. On the Georgia assembly's inaction see ibid., 11:309n, and Allen D. Candler, ed., *The Revolutionary Records of the State of Georgia,* 3 vols. (Atlanta: Franklin-Turner, 1908), 3:118–88, especially 179 and 188.

20. Edward Rutledge to Arthur Middleton, February 8, 1782, in Barnwell, ed.," Correspondence of Hon. Arthur Middleton" [part 2], 4.

21. Francis Marion to Greene, March 29, 1782; Ichabod Burnet to John Laurens, April 2, 1782; John Laurens to Greene, April 2, 1782; *The Papers of General Nathanael Greene,* 10:561, 565n, 575, 576. Massey, *John Laurens,* 215–16.

22. Alexander Leslie to Guy Carleton, August 2, 1782 (EM 15623), and August 10, 1782 (EM 15628), Alexander Leslie Letterbook, Thomas Addis Emmet Collection, New York Public Library. Leslie to Greene, August 13, 1782; John Mathews to Greene, August 14, 1782; Greene to Leslie, August 15, 1782; Greene to John Hanson, August 28, 1782, *The Papers of General Nathanael Greene,* 11:338 39, 346 48, 383 84.

23. Richard Lushington to Greene, August 4, 1782, and Greene to Francis Marion, [August 9, 1782], *The Papers of General Nathanael Greene,* 11:487–88, 510.

24. For the state's award of the plantations, see Hugh Rutledge to Greene, February 26, 1782, ibid., 10:411, and Richard Howly to Greene, July 30, 1782, ibid., 11:473. For Greene's wartime business investments, see Terry Golway, *Washington's General: Nathanael Greene and the Triumph of the American Revolution* (New York: Holt, 2005), 167 (Greene quotation), 171–73, 202–4.

25. Joseph Clay to Greene, August 6, 1782, *The Papers of General Nathanael Greene,* 11:494–95.

26. Jim Piecuch, *Three Peoples, One King: Loyalists, Indians, and Slaves in the Revolutionary South, 1775–1782* (Columbia: University of South Carolina Press, 2008), 316–18 (John Mathews quoted on 318); E[dmund] P[etrie] to John Laurens, August 12, 1782, Greene Papers, Clements Library; Tadeusz Kościuszko to Greene, November 5, 1782, *The Papers of General Nathanael Greene,* 12:150 (quotation); William Seymour, "A Journal of the Southern Expedition, 1780–1783," *Pennsylvania Magazine of History and Biography* 7, no. 3 (1883): 393.

27. Greene's financial arrangements with the merchant John Banks plagued him for the remainder of his life. This account of their initial deal relies on Thayer, *Nathanael Greene,* 413–20, and Dennis Conrad's introduction to *The Papers of General Nathanael Greene,* 12:xv, as well as Greene to George Abbott Hall, November 9, 1782, and Greene to Benjamin Lincoln, November 11, 1782, ibid., 12:162, 168.

28. Piecuch, *Three Peoples, One King,* 323; Greene to Elias Boudinot, December 19, 1782, *The Papers of General Nathanael Greene,* 12:303; introduction to ibid., 12:xvii.

29. The previous two paragraphs draw on Conrad's introduction to *The Papers of General Nathanael Greene*, 12:xv–xvi; Greene to Benjamin Lincoln, February 2, 1783, and Greene to Robert Morris, February 2, 1783, ibid., 12:401–5; Greene to Richard Henry Lee, August 22, 1785, ibid., 13:564–68 (quotation on 566).

30. For Greene's purchases of slaves in South Carolina, see ibid., 12:341n. For the South Carolina General Assembly's actions on Greene's behalf, see John F. Grimké to Greene, November 13, 1782, and Greene to Hugh Rutledge, February 26, 1783, ibid., 12:178–79, 478, 478n, 479n. On Greene's efforts in Georgia, see William Gibbons to Greene, February 25, 1783; Greene to Joseph Clay, [before March 15, 1783]; Greene to Charles Pettit, April 3, 1783; and Greene to Lyman Hall, April 17, 1783, ibid., 12:475, 476n, 520, 564, 616 (quotation).

31. Greene to Griffin Greene, June 10, and June 14, 1783, and Greene to James Hunter, June 14, 1783, ibid., 13:26–28 (quotation on 26), 32–33.

32. Greene to Catherine Littlefield Greene, August 4, 1783, and Greene to Charles Pettit, August 4, 1783, ibid., 13:83, 84 (quotation).

33. Greene to Catherine Littlefield Greene, August 4, 1783, and August 7, 1783, ibid., 13:83, 92 (quotations).

34. Estimate of Nathanael Greene's estate, [before January 9, 1784]; Greene to Robert Morris, January 9, 1784; Morris to Greene, May 19, 1784, July 12, 1784, and June 28, 1785; Greene to Wilhem and Jan Willink, January 7, 1786, ibid., 13:219–21, 221–24, 315–18, 352–53, 545, 642–43.

35. William Gordon to Greene, February 26–[March 3], 1783, and Joseph Reed to Greene, March 14, 1783, ibid., 12:489–90, 518.

36. Warner Mifflin to Greene, October 21, 1783, and Greene to Mifflin, [November 1783], ibid., 13:157–58, 192; Benjamin Rush to Greene, September 16, 1782, ibid., 11:667.

37. Warner Mifflin to Greene, October 21, 1783, and Greene to Mifflin, [November 1783], ibid., 13:157–58, 192.

38. On the rationalizations of other slave owners, see generally Duncan MacLeod, *Slavery, Race and the American Revolution* (London & New York: Cambridge University Press, 1974), 31–47, 136–39; and specifically Henry Laurens to John Laurens, August 14, 1776, in David R. Chesnutt and C. James Taylor, eds., *The Papers of Henry Laurens*, vol. 11 (Columbia: University of South Carolina Press, 1988), 223–25.

39. Greene to Roger Parker Saunders, January 4, 1784; Greene to William Gibbons Jr., August 29, 1784; Saunders to Greene, November 25, 1783; Samuel Clegg to Greene, March 9, 1784; *The Papers of General Nathanael Greene*, 13:182 (fourth quotation), 217 (first quotation), 260, 381–82 (second and third quotations).

40. On Greene as a man of sensibility, see Greene to Samuel Ward Jr., March 5, 1771; July 20, 1772; August 29, 772; [after August 29, 1772?]; January 25, 1773; ibid., 1:20–21, 31–32, 38–43, 44–46, 51–54. For examples of Greene's references to *Tristram Shandy*, see Greene to Henry Lee, October 7, 1782, and Greene to George Weedon, December 21, 1782, ibid., 12:40, 329, and 329n. On sensibility in general and references to Greene in particular, see Sarah Knott, *Sensibility and the American Revolution* (Chapel Hill: University of North Carolina Press, 2009), 153–93, 194 (Greene and "mutual sympathy"). On slave owners and humanity, see Joyce E. Chaplin, *An Anxious Pursuit: Agricultural Innovation and Modernity in the Lower South, 1730–1815* (Chapel Hill & London: University of

North Carolina Press, 1993), 53–60. For Rhode Island Quakers and slavery, see Lorenzo Johnston Greene, *The Negro in Colonial New England*, 239; and James, *Colonial Rhode Island*, 219. On Greene and the Society of Friends, see Thayer, *Nathanael Greene*, 40–41, and Greene to Warner Mifflin, [November 1783], *The Papers of General Nathanael Greene*, 13:192. For Greene's friendship with John Murray and their mutual expressions of sensibility, see ibid., 1:81n; Greene to Catherine Littlefield Greene, September 10, 1775, ibid., 1:116; Greene to Whom It May Concern, May 27, 1777; Greene to John Murray, [January 1778?], and after September 1, 1778; ibid., 2:96, 262, 506; and Murray to Greene, January 3, 1779, ibid., 3:135–39; Murray to Greene, January 21, 1780, ibid., 5: 298–300.

41. Greene to William Pierce Jr., October 15, 1783; Greene to E. John Collett, June 23, 1784; Greene to Charles Pettit, June 23, 1784; Greene to Robert Morris, July 3, 1784; ibid., 13:144, 145n, 333 (quotation), 334–35, 343, 344n.

42. Greene to E. John Collett, August 8, 1784, and Greene to Charles Pettit, August 15, 1784, ibid., 13:366 (second quotation), 371 (first quotation).

43. Greene to Catherine Littlefield Greene, September 8, 1784, and September 10, 1784, ibid., 13:387 (quotation), 391.

44. Greene to Hugh Rutledge, [after September 30, 1784], and Greene to Robert Forsyth, October 25, 1784, ibid., 13:401, 402n, 411 (quotation).

45. Greene to Welcome Arnold, August 17, 1784; Greene to George Gibbs, August 17, 1784, and February 3, 1785; Greene to William Gibbons Jr., April 26, 1785; William Pierce Jr. to Greene, May 13, 1785; ibid., 13:371–73, 446, 515–16 (quotation), 521.

46. Greene to Dennis De Berdt, March 9, 1785, ibid., 13:471–72; Mary R. Bullard, *Cumberland Island: A History* (Athens & London: University of Georgia Press, 2003), 88. On Greene's contacts with the French, see Greene to the Marquis de Barbe-Marbois, April 15, 1785, Greene to the Marquis de Castries, June 1, 1785, December 1785?; the Marquis de Barbe-Marbois to Greene, May 18, 1785; Nathaniel Pendleton to Greene, September 23, 1785; the Marquis de Lafayette to Greene, December 3, 1785, and December 29, 1785; the Chevalier de la Foreste to Greene, December 16, 1785; the Marquis de Castries to Greene, January 22, 1786; *The Papers of General Nathanael Greene*, 13:496–500, 524–25, 532–33, 594–95, 626–27, 633–34, 639, 640–41, 655.

47. Greene to Catherine Littlefield Greene, April 14, 1785; Daniel McLane to Greene, July 3, 1785; David Hillhouse to Greene, July 19, 1785, and October 4, 1785; ibid., 13:490 (quotation), 547, 555, 607–8.

48. Greene to Catherine Littlefield Greene, April 14, 1785, ibid., 13:492–93.

49. Greene to Catherine Littlefield Greene, June 2, 1775, ibid., 1:83.

50. Greene to Richard Henry Lee, August 22, 1785, ibid., 13:564–68. For a thorough account of the final settlement of Greene's debts, consult ibid., 13:367–69n. On the death of the Greenes' infant daughter, see Greene to Jeremiah Wadsworth, August 30, 1785, ibid., 13:576, 577n.

51. Greene to Ethan Clarke, November 23, 1785, ibid., 13:621–23. On Caty's emotional state, see also John F. Stegeman and Janet A. Stegeman, *Caty: A Biography of Catherine Littlefield Greene* (Athens: University of Georgia Press, 1985), 115–17.

52. Greene to Ethan Clarke, November 23, 1785; Greene to Henry Knox, March 12, 1786; Greene to Randall Son & Stewarts, March 12, 1786; John Croskeys to Greene,

February 16, 1786; *The Papers of General Nathanael Greene,* 13:622, 664–65, 668–69 (quotation), 671.

53. William Gordon to Greene, September 26, 1785, and agreement between Greene and William Williams, January 5, 1786, ibid., 13:599 (quotation), 600n, 641–42.

54. The preceding two paragraphs are drawn from Aedanus Burke to Greene, November 27, 1785, ibid., 13:623–25; and George C. Rogers Jr., "Aedanus Burke, Nathanael Greene, Anthony Wayne, and the British Merchants of Charleston," *South Carolina Historical Magazine* 67 (April 1976): 75–81.

55. On Greene's final days, see the epilogue to *The Papers of General Nathanael Greene,* 13:697. On the proposed move to Cumberland Island, see Greene to Samuel Ward Jr., April 4, 1786, ibid., 13:675. On planters' tours of their rice fields, see S. Max Edelson, *Plantation Enterprise in Colonial South Carolina* (Cambridge, Mass.: Harvard University Press, 2006), 172.

Contributors

GREG BROOKING is a Ph.D. candidate in history at Georgia State University. He has published articles in the *Georgia Historical Quarterly* and the *Encyclopedia of the War of 1812*.

JOHN BUCHANAN is an independent historian living in New York City. He was chief registrar in charge of worldwide art movements at the Metropolitan Museum of Art. Since retiring he has published *The Road to Guilford Courthouse: The American Revolution in the Carolinas* (1997), *Jackson's Way: Andrew Jackson and the People of the Western Waters* (2001), and *The Road to Valley Forge: How Washington Built the Army That Won the Revolution* (2004).

ROBERT M. CALHOON is professor of history at the University of North Carolina at Greensboro. Among his many publications are *The Loyalists in Revolutionary America, 1760–1781* (1973), *Evangelicals and Conservatives in the Early South, 1740–1861* (1988), *The Loyalist Perception and Other Essays* (1989), and *Dominion and Liberty: Ideology in the Anglo-American World, 1660–1801* (1994).

DENNIS M. CONRAD is a historian with the Early History Branch of the Naval Historical Center in Washington, D.C., where he edits *Naval Documents of the American Revolution*. A recognized authority on Nathanael Greene, he edited volumes 7–12 of *The Papers of General Nathanael Greene*.

JOHN R. MAASS is a historian at the U.S. Army Center of Military History in Washington, D.C. The author of *"That Unhappy Affair": Horatio Gates and the Battle of Camden* (2001), he has also published articles in the *Journal of Military History*, the *North Carolina Historical Review*, and the *Virginia Cavalcade*.

GREGORY D. MASSEY is professor of history at Freed-Hardeman University in Tennessee. He is the author of *John Laurens and the American Revolution* (2000).

JAMES R. MC INTYRE is assistant professor of history at Moraine Valley Community College in Illinois. His primary research focus is the American War of

Independence. In addition he has written articles and lectured on topics as diverse as the Chicago home front in World War II and the Korean War.

Curtis F. Morgan Jr. is professor of history at Lord Fairfax Community College in Virginia. He is the author of *James F. Byrnes, Lucius Clay, and American Policy in Germany, 1945–1947* (2002) and is currently working on a military biography of Nathanael Greene.

John M. Moseley is an independent scholar who lives in Wilmington, North Carolina.

Jim Piecuch is an associate professor of history at Kennesaw State University in Georgia. He is the author of many articles on colonial and Revolutionary history as well as several books, including *The Battle of Camden: A Documentary History* (2006), *Three Peoples, One King: Loyalists, Indians, and Slaves in the Revolutionary South* (2008), *"Cool Deliberate Courage": John Eager Howard in the American Revolution* (coauthored with John Beakes, 2009), and *"The Blood Be upon Your Head": Tarleton and the Myth of Buford's Massacre* (2010).

David K. Wilson is an independent scholar who lives in Plano, Texas, and works in the advertising industry. He holds an M.A. degree in history from the University of Texas at Arlington and is the author of *The Southern Strategy: Britain's Conquest of South Carolina and Georgia, 1775–1780* (2005).

Index